THIS PRESENT DARKNESS

STEPHEN ELLIS

This Present Darkness

A History of Nigerian Organised Crime

HURST & COMPANY, LONDON

First published in the United Kingdom in 2016 by
C. Hurst & Co. (Publishers) Ltd.,
41 Great Russell Street, London, WC1B 3PL
This paperback edition published 2018
© Stephen Ellis, 2016
All rights reserved.
Printed in England

A Cataloguing-in-Publication data record for this book
is available from the British Library.

ISBN: 9781787380271

This book is printed using paper from registered sustainable
and managed sources.

www.hurstpublishers.com

For we do not wrestle against flesh and blood, but against the rulers, against the authorities, against the cosmic powers over this present darkness, against the spiritual forces of evil in the heavenly places.

St Paul's Letter to the Ephesians

For Gerrie

Professor Stephen Ellis, 1953–2015

CONTENTS

Acknowledgements	xi
Foreword	xiii
List of Abbreviations	xv
Introduction	1
How to Read This Book	3
A Note on Sources	5
1. Rules of Law	7
The Civilising Mission	9
Indirect Rule and Law	12
A School for Deception	18
2. Wonder-Workers	23
The Professor of Wonders	25
Wealth, Risk, Destiny	31
A Hollow System	38
3. Enter the Politicians	43
The Impact of the Second World War	44
Nationalism and Corruption	50
Political Parties and Corruption	57
4. The National Cake	61
Independence	62
The Foreign Contribution	68
Corruption Spreads to Daily Life	74
5. The Men in Uniform	79
Coup and Counter-coup	80

CONTENTS

The Oil Issue   85
The New Criminality   89

6. Boom Time   95
   Nigeria Rampant   96
   Corruption, Crime, Cults   106
   The Second Republic   114

7. Crime Goes Global   119
   The Drug Trade   121
   Four One Nine   124
   The Rise and Fall of Anti-corruption   128
   Ethnic Issues   133

8. Godfathers   137
   Babangida…And Another Criminal Arrives   138
   Oil as Loot   147
   Democrats / Kleptocrats   153

9. The Business of Crime   157
   Crime as a Career   158
   The Kings of Four One Nine   165
   Drugs   170
   Sex Work   180
   Organisation   187

10. Cosmic Powers   193
    Cults and Shrines   194
    The Okija Shrine   198
    Law versus Reality   206
    Religion and Self-Fashioning   211

11. Nigerian Organised Crime   215
    State Crime   217
    Why Nigeria?   223
    Nigerian Crime in Globalisation   229

Appendix   231

Notes   233
Bibliography   279
Index   299

ACKNOWLEDGEMENTS

It is a pleasant duty for an author to write an acknowledgements page, listing the people who have helped in the preparation and research of a book that has at last been completed.

In this case, it will be my last book. Accordingly, I would like to mention some of the people who have helped and inspired me in my work on Africa since I first set foot on African soil in 1971.

My first job in Africa was as an English teacher at the excellent Collège Libermann in Douala, where my boss was Father Eric de Rosny. He always showed great kindness to a young Englishman far away from home. Some weekends he took me with him to the Douala townships where he had many friends. I used to sit and listen while they talked about the old days. Looking back, this was the start of my interest in African history. Only gradually did it occur to me what a remarkable man Eric de Rosny was—a Jesuit priest and an initiated healer as well as a successful author.

At university, I followed a course on African history taught by Tony Kirk-Greene, who I must thank for introducing me to the formal study of the subject that became my career.

When I was aiming to do research in Madagascar in the late 1970s, at a time when it was hard to get a visa, I was given valuable help by Simon Ayache. Again, it's a story of appreciating more with the passage of time—it was only after learning the ways of bureaucracies that it dawned on me what efforts Simon Ayache had made on my behalf. I am glad that I was able to resume contact with him quite recently, and to thank him formally.

ACKNOWLEDGEMENTS

During and after my doctoral studies I came to know two people in Paris who became close friends, but who I have always considered as mentors in their respective disciplines. These were Françoise Raison and Jean-François Bayart. Both of them have been an inspiration for decades.

Among my contemporaries, I have enjoyed close friendships with Oyama Mabandla, Solofo Randrianja and Tiébilé Dramé, and I have learned an enormous amount from them, more than they can realise.

I must also thank Michael Dwyer, who has published many of my books and has become more than a publisher, a friend.

I have learned most of all from Gerrie, my partner for close to three decades and herself an expert in the study of religion. Our endless conversations about the spirit world have fascinated me and have helped me not only better to understand Africa, but to understand the world.

Stephen Ellis   *Amsterdam, July 2015*

FOREWORD

Stephen Ellis's rigour as a researcher and writer was matched by an unflinching search to understand Africa and its historical vicissitudes and to explain these to the reader. In pursuit of these goals he worked the archive, spent years tramping the continent, from South Africa to Liberia to Madagascar, and interviewed hundreds of informants, from apartheid-era spooks and humble rural pastors to notorious faction fighters and men now wealthy from the profits of crime.

Aside from the information he gleaned from such encounters, Stephen was fascinated by his interlocutors, above all by the dilemmas they were presented with in their lives and how they dealt with them. What mattered to him as an historian and analyst was the profound impact on people's lives of the social and political factors that shaped Africa leading up to, during and after colonialism.

Another constant theme in Stephen's writing on and engagement with Africa was the metaphysical. In this he was regarded by some as unorthodox, but his fascination with spirituality and the ethics of living—above all how the temporal world was perceived and responded to—informed his intellectual trajectory, his private life and bolstered his determination never to succumb to the vagaries of academic fashion.

After having had the pleasure and honour of working with Stephen Ellis on five books, one of which, on Charles Taylor's murderous regime in Liberia, precipitated a lengthy legal case, it is with great sadness that I know that this, his scrupulously researched history of Nigerian organised crime, will be his last.

I will miss learning from him, I already miss his friendship.

FOREWORD

Stephen Ellis had been ill for several years before finishing the manuscript of *This Present Darkness*, in July 2015, shortly before his death on the 29th of that month. At that point some sources and other aspects of the book's scholarly framework remained incomplete, hence the publisher sought the advice of his widow, Professor Gerrie ter Haar, of Professors Christopher Clapham and Richard Fardon, and of Elvire Eijkman, of the African Studies Centre Library in Leiden, all of whom gave generously of their time and expertise in helping bring the project to fruition.

Michael Dwyer   *London, March 2016*

LIST OF ABBREVIATIONS

ACB	African Continental Bank
ANC	African National Congress
BCCI	Bank of Credit and Commerce International
CID	Criminal Investigation Department
DEA	Drug Enforcement Administration
ECGD	Export Credit Guarantee Department
ECOWAS	Economic Community of West African States
EFCC	Economic and Financial Crimes Commission
GDP	Gross Domestic Product
IBB	Ibrahim Badamasi Babangida
MEND	Movement for the Emancipation of the Niger Delta
NAPTIP	National Agency for the Prohibition of Trafficking in Persons
NCNC	National Council of Nigeria and the Cameroons
NDLEA	Nigerian Drug Law Enforcement Agency
NITEL	Nigerian Telecommunications Limited
NNDP	Nigerian National Democratic Party
NNPC	Nigerian National Petroleum Corporation
NPC	Northern People's Congress
NRG	Northern Regional Government
NUNS	National Union of Nigerian Students
OPEC	Organisation of the Petroleum Exporting Countries
PDP	People's Democratic Party
UNODC	United Nations Office on Drugs and Crime
WAI	War Against Indiscipline

INTRODUCTION

You have probably received an email like this one that arrived in my inbox some time ago:

> We are pleased to inform you of the result of the STAATSLOTERIJ NL Email Winners International programs held on 7th day of September .... Your email address have [sic] been selected as one of the lucky winners in the 3rd category, therefore you have been approved for a lump sum payout of 920,000.00 Euro (Nine Hundred and Twenty Thousand Euro).

It seems that, without even buying a ticket, I had been randomly selected by the Dutch state lottery to receive almost a million euros.

> To file and claim your winning, please contact our claim-processing department for the processing of your winning particulars with the contact information's [sic] below.

The contact person is one Gert Gilbertson. His phone number is listed, but it's a mobile, not a fixed phone line. Gilbertson's email address is contactgertgilbertson@gmail.com, which doesn't look like that of a state lottery company. Then there are the small grammatical errors that draw attention to the fact that this message may not be quite as official as it purports to be. Something is definitely wrong here.

If I were to respond to Mr Gilbertson's communication, he would no doubt inform me that several fees are required for bureaucratic or legal purposes before the transfer of €920,000 to my account can take place. It's quite likely he will ask for my bank account details also. He might invite me to meet him in person in order to discuss my amazing lottery win. The meeting will probably be held in a public place, perhaps the lobby of a smart hotel or of a leading bank in Amsterdam. In any event, were I to pursue this matter I could end up paying out hundreds or even thousands of euros without getting a cent in return.

Ever since money was invented, there have probably been dishonest people perpetrating advance-fee frauds—requesting payment upfront for goods or services that do not exist or that they have no intention actually to deliver. However, this particular hoax has some of the hallmarks of a Nigerian scam. Nigerian scammers are generally regarded as pioneers in the sending of mass letters, messages and emails seeking to defraud any recipient foolish and greedy enough to fall for their tricks, although all the signs are that the practice has now spread worldwide. Nigerians call scams like these "Four One Nine", so called by reference to Article 419 of the country's criminal code, which concerns fraud. Four One Nines are not the only field in which Nigeria and Nigerians have established an unfortunate reputation for fraud or crime more generally.

If I were to fall for this trick, I would be joining the five or six Dutch people who, every week in the early years of this century, responded to a message like the one above and ended up parting with substantial sums of money to Nigerian fraudsters. At that time scams like these regularly featured on a true-life crime show called *Opgelicht* ("Conned") broadcast on Dutch television. Journalists have filmed interviews with Four One Nine victims or even, wired for sound, have themselves met the conmen and have recorded fleeting conversations with them. The gangs seem to consist of Nigerians and Dutch fraudsters working together.[1] The Nigerian embassy in the Netherlands has repeatedly issued warnings to the public to be on guard against these frauds which, it says, began in the 1980s.

According to the Dutch police, Amsterdam was at one point a favourite European operations centre for Nigerian fraudsters. After a police clampdown many of the fraudsters moved to Madrid, where they set up a gigantic scam aimed at fooling victims into believing that they had won the Spanish state lottery. It was said to be the biggest fraud in the world at that time.[2] In 2005, the Spanish police arrested over 300 Nigerians in connection with the fake lottery scam, by which some 20,000 people were said to have been swindled by means of some six million missives per year, bringing in an estimated €100 million per year to the organisers. During this wave of arrests the police seized €218,000 in cash, nearly 2,000 mobile phones, 327 computers and 165 fax machines.[3] Three years later the Spanish police again made a mass arrest, this time holding 87 Nigerians suspected of defrauding at least 1,000 people to the tune of some €20 million.[4] Yet, despite the move of some major Nigerian fraudsters to Spain, by 2012 the Dutch police were still estimating that 90 per cent of advance-fee fraud perpetrated in the Netherlands was the work of Nigerian criminals.[5]

Colin Powell, the urbane former United States' Secretary of State, once told an interviewer that "Nigerians as a group, frankly, are marvellous scammers", adding by way of explanation "I mean, it is in their natural culture".[6] I have often met police officers outside Nigeria who have expressed more or less the same idea.

Can culture be an explanation for such behaviour? In any case, how does a specific culture come into being? Didn't the experience of colonial rule play some part? These and many other questions concerning Nigerian crime are discussed later in the chapters that follow.

How to read this book

Nigerian crime gangs, like all human organisations, have a history. To continue with the case of Nigerian Four One Nine scams, this practice has a longer pedigree than many people realise. The first properly documented Four One Nine letter in the history of Nigeria dates from 1920 and was written by one P. Crentsil, who called himself a Professor of Wonders. He was duly prosecuted under section 419 of Nigeria's criminal code. "Professor" Crentsil's story is told in Chapter Two. But it was only in the 1980s that Four One Nine fraud became the vast international activity that it has now become. In those days, most scam letters emanating from Nigeria were written on headed notepaper belonging to a government office, or possibly a firm of lawyers or accountants, and purported to offer the possibility of sharing in funds embezzled from a government account. In the 1990s, more and more messages of the same sort began to arrive by email rather than letter or fax, and increasingly often purported to be on behalf of firms or individuals situated outside Nigeria. Where Four One Nines were originally the speciality of Nigerian conmen, these days there is no knowing who writes them, or from what location.

Thirty years before the emergence of mass advance-fee fraud, Nigeria had the misfortune to acquire a political elite and a political system that were shot through with practices of fraud and embezzlement, not to mention illicit violence. So pervasive and systematic were these practices that they led a group of soldiers to launch the country's first military coup in 1966, which the putschists justified by saying they were going to root out official corruption. Most Nigerian practices of organised crime, including document fraud, embezzlement and large-scale smuggling, originate in politics and the state itself, or at least have important and durable connections to the state. This is not the place to examine different definitions of organised crime[7] other than to say that most of them imply that to qualify for this label criminal activity has to be associated with an identifiable group of people existing for a substantial period of time. This description actually fits the Nigerian state better than any other group.

It is in order to trace the political origins of organised crime in Nigeria that this book starts with a description of the country's government during colonial times, that is to say from the early twentieth century until Independence in 1960. A British official in 1944 found that "the number of persistent and professional criminals is not great….Crime as a career has so far made little appeal to the young Nigerian".[8] I nevertheless believe that we need to study the colonial experience of Indirect Rule if we are to understand the origin of later practices of organised crime and corruption. So, to those readers who finish Chapter One without finding any mention of organised crime, I say: carry on reading, and you will see what I mean.

Oddly enough, one of the prerequisites for analysing crime in Nigeria is an understanding of the spirit world. Nigerians have thought, and generally still believe today, that wealth and prosperity have their ultimate origins in the spirit world and that no one can succeed in their career, whether in crime or in some legitimate profession, without securing blessings from the spirit world. That is why I begin this book with an epigram quoting St Paul on the spiritual nature of evil.

Here too I advise readers who see crime as a series of purely material activities to persist with reading. It is only by delving into the spirit world that we can hope to understand what causes people to act the way they do—in this case, to investigate some of the psychology of Nigerian organised crime.

INTRODUCTION

A note on sources

In reconstructing the early history of Nigerian organised crime, that is to say from Nigeria's creation in 1914 until Independence in 1960, I have relied on the usual sources used by historians writing on that period, namely state archives and contemporary publications as well as the substantial secondary literature concerning Nigeria under colonial rule. In particular, I made several visits to the National Archives of Nigeria at Ibadan. The organisation of Nigeria's state archives reflects the colonial division of the country into three administrative regions, with headquarters at Enugu, Ibadan and Kaduna. However, the Ibadan archives are particularly rich inasmuch as they contain not only material relating to the former Western Region, but also documents from the central administration, making this the most important of the three main national repositories for present purposes.[9] Unfortunately I have been prevented by ill health from visiting branches of the national archives elsewhere, most particularly at Enugu and Kaduna, and from looking for other depositories of either state or private papers.

The key reality concerning historical research on the post-Independence period, however, is that none of the state archives contains any substantial collection of records generated by government ministries and departments. In many cases it is quite unclear what has happened to such papers. In any event, it has obliged me to turn to other sources of information. In this regard the US national archives held at College Park, Maryland,[10] and the National Archives of the United Kingdom held at Kew, Surrey,[11] have been invaluable. Their holdings of diplomatic and consular material have been especially useful. These records tend to concern elite politics rather than analyses of social developments, but this gap can to some extent be rectified by access to Nigerian newspapers that I was able to view at the excellent press clippings library at the Nigerian Institute for International Affairs in Lagos. Moreover, Nigeria is home to a number of publishing companies that have produced a stream of essays, memoirs and other works that provide insight into contemporary social realities. Many Nigerian publications do not find their way into foreign libraries, but I am fortunate to have worked for twenty-five years at the Afrika Studiecentrum, Leiden, that is home to one of the world's best Africana libraries. Regarding the most recent historical period, the Internet has become an endless mine of material that has helped me compile documentation on my subject, including not only online versions of newspapers but also a great variety of reports, blogs, conference papers, home pages and other material.

In regard to interviews, it is obvious that few criminals are willing to speak openly about their activities—and even if they were to do so, it would be hard for an interviewer to know whether the information being provided was accurate. To be sure, this applies to interviews of all descriptions, as all interviewees, no matter how honest, convey information that reflects their particular experience and personal insights rather than any corpus of "objective" knowledge. Nevertheless, over more than a decade I have sought out people who can claim to have some expert knowledge of Nigerian organised crime, including law enforcement officers both in Nigeria and abroad. I have attended some invitation-only conferences that were most helpful in this regard, notably one held in Bangkok on 16–19 May 2005 at which law enforcement officers from many countries in Asia and elsewhere presented papers on Nigerian organised crime. I should also acknowledge that there are many organisations that publish regularly on this subject, most notably the United Nations Office on Drugs and Crime (UNODC) but also official bodies with more specific terms of reference, such as the Drug Enforcement Administration of the United States.

1

RULES OF LAW

Zungeru in Niger State—one of the thirty-six states that today compose the Federal Republic of Nigeria—is a neglected town, hot and dusty. Far away from Nigeria's most vibrant city, Lagos, and from its modern capital, Abuja, Zungeru is not often visited by foreigners. Yet this is where Nigeria began.

When Nigerians were gearing up to celebrate their country's centenary in 2014, a newspaper printed a photo of the very house where the document was signed that brought Nigeria into existence, revealing it to be no more than a sad ruin.[1] It was in this building that the British official Frederick Lugard, better known as Lord Lugard, put his signature to an order that various British-ruled territories were to be merged into a single unit called Nigeria. At that time, Zungeru was the headquarters of colonial administration in the Northern Protectorate, and it briefly served as the capital of the new country overseen by Lugard in the office of governor-general. It was Lugard's wife, the former journalist Flora Shaw, who actually invented the name of the new colony, using it in a newspaper article in 1897.[2]

Lugard signed the document amalgamating the British-ruled territories of the Northern and Southern Protectorates into a single colony and protectorate of Nigeria on 1 January 1914. A military parade was held to mark the occasion. The small population of Zungeru, mostly railwaymen and civil servants working for the colonial administration and their families, turned out to watch. It is very likely that one of them was a nine-year old boy called Nnamdi Azikiwe. Although Azikiwe was from the Igbo people[3] whose homeland is southeast Nigeria, he was born at Zungeru in the North after his father had moved there to work as a clerk for the colonial government. "Zik", as the boy was to become nationally known, was eventually to become Nigeria's first president.

There is a recording of Lugard's speech declaring the amalgamation of the former protectorates into the single new entity of Nigeria. This record reveals him to have had a rather high-pitched voice and to have spoken with the clipped accent and strangled vowels characteristic of the British upper classes in the age of empire. "His Majesty the King has decided that…all the country…shall be one single country", he told the small crowd in Zungeru.[4] He made it sound as though Britain's King George V had personally made the decision to merge the various British possessions clustered around the Niger valley, whereas the King, being the ceremonial figurehead of a parliamentary system of government, actually had little to do with it.

Technically speaking, the creation of Nigeria was the result of an order-in-council made by the British government. It was a measure that Lugard had lobbied for with the invaluable existence of Lady Lugard, the former colonial editor of the London *Times*, the newspaper of Britain's top people. Her network of connections was impressive. The key person who had to be convinced about the creation of a new colony was the Secretary of State for the Colonies, Lewis Vernon Harcourt, today little remembered although his name is carried by Nigeria's leading oil town, Port Harcourt. The main argument in favour of amalgamation was based on administrative convenience, as it would allow the governor-general to create a single budget for all the territories acquired by the British Crown in bits and pieces since 1861, when it had annexed Lagos as a base for the Royal Navy's activities against the slave trade. If all the British possessions were treated as a single unit for fiscal purposes, customs and excise duties from the South of the country, where there was a lively import-export trade, including in spirits that could be heavily taxed, could be used to subsidise spending in the landlocked North, where raising revenue was proving more difficult.

Nigerians generally look back at Lugard's 1914 announcement with mixed feelings. Amalgamation marked the inauguration of a country that at Independence in 1960 seemed destined to become an African superpower, not least because it has the biggest population of any African country, today somewhere around 175 million people. But many Nigerians, reflecting on their country's chronic inability to fulfil its promise, see the amalgamation decree as a fatal design error because it enforced cohabitation between populations that had little in common or were even enemies. Years later, the British colonial expert Lord Hailey called Nigeria "perhaps the most artificial of the many administrative units created in the course of the European occupation of Africa".[5] A leading colonial theorist, the Oxford academic Margery Perham, referred to it as an "arbitrary block" carved out of Africa.[6]

One thing that nearly all Nigerians can probably agree on is that the foundation of their country was the result of a decision carried out solely in the British interest. "God did not create Nigeria", a later politician quipped. "The British did".[7]

The civilising mission

Lord Lugard, GCMG, CB, DSO, was an imperialist of the old school. With his handlebar moustache, he looked the part. Born in India, educated at public school and at the Sandhurst military academy, he began his career as an army officer serving in campaigns in Afghanistan, Sudan and Burma. He worked for more than one of the commercial chartered companies that in Victorian times administered various bits of the world in the British interest before being appointed High Commissioner of the Protectorate of Northern Nigeria in 1900 at a time when the independent emirates of Hausaland still posed a military threat to British control of the region. Lugard was responsible for subduing them in a series of short military campaigns. He fell in love with Northern Nigeria and stayed in Nigeria throughout his subsequent career, except for a brief interlude as governor of Hong Kong.

Underlying all Lugard's work was his belief in the colonising genius of Britain in the hands of its great imperial administrators. It was this that gave to Britain "a kind of divine right" to rule, as a later colonial official described Britain's self-evident authority to take control of various parts of the globe.[8] The assumed right to colonise is as difficult to understand today as the claim made by European kings four centuries ago that they had a divine right to rule their countries. Like other British imperialists of his time, Lugard believed that his country possessed a moral superiority that, combined with the organisational skills of public servants like himself, would introduce law and justice where none had existed previously. And, like other European colonisers too, the British thought most highly of themselves when they were suppressing customs that they found morally repugnant, such as the slave trade, the use of ordeal by poison to detect guilt in criminal cases, the infliction of cruel punishments, the killing of twins, and the slaughter of servants to accompany a dead master to the other world as well as other killings perpetrated in the name of religious duty or custom.

Prior to the assertion of British control, southern districts of Nigeria were—in Lugard's own words—"populated by tribes in the lowest stage of primitive savagery".[9] The only real exception was the western region of Yorubaland, where complex hierarchies and a long history of self-governing city-states suggested a higher degree of sophistication, although here too rulers had been addicted to what Lugard described as "many barbarous rites".[10] The North was more promising for someone intent on introducing a colonial bureaucracy, as the area was governed by a string of Hausa-Fulani emirates and the Bornu kingdom, all of which had "an elaborate administrative machinery, though it had become corrupt and degraded".[11]

Lugard and other officials of his generation thought that the superiority of the new colonial order would be perceived by any Nigerians not themselves corrupted by their own vested interests. Victorians often believed that chiefs in Africa were intent on exploiting their people by selling them into slavery and that a coloniser with a higher moral conception had a duty to protect the people from their own leaders. It was on account of this perception that British officials had chosen to govern their original colony at Lagos directly, in the years when it was little more than a collection of fishing villages grouped around a lagoon. The system of justice was "the principal organ of local government"[12] in Lagos colony in the late nineteenth century, before Nigeria itself was willed into existence. But once British authority had spread beyond Lagos, incorporating the valley of the mighty Niger River, the main artery for trade from the interior to the coast, the idea of establishing British courts in such a vast area became unappealing, as apart from anything else, it would be hugely expensive.

It was at this juncture that Lugard arrived in the region. Having overseen the conquest of the Northern emirates, he needed to take stock of the existing systems of justice in the territory for which he was now responsible. In Northern Nigeria the system of government before colonial times was the consequence of the jihad led by Usman dan Fodio at the beginning of the nineteenth century. Zealous Islamic reformers, intent on imposing a purer form of religion on the Hausa emirs of the Sahel, had taken control of the area by force and established a caliphate at Sokoto. Since that time, a century before the British takeover, central authority in the emirates had been transmitted through fief-holders, with justice being administered by judges trained in the Maliki school of Islamic law. However, there were many parts of the North where Muslim law codes were hardly used and communities continued to draw on their own traditions for settling disputes. The Sokoto caliphate and its affiliates were one of the world's last great slaving states,[13] making regular raids for human plunder into the territories further south into the region that the British dubbed the Middle Belt. Stamping out slave-raiding was one of Lugard's most urgent tasks.

As for the Southern Protectorate, where the jihad had not reached and there were relatively few Muslims, Lugard wrote that the entire region was "deprived of the instruments on which the ultimate enforcement of all law...depends".[14] The city-states of Yorubaland had elements of a rational bureaucracy but Lugard found the administration of justice there to be rife with "corruption and bribery".[15] All the institutions of public administration were liable to subversion by members of the Ogboni secret society that was very influential in Yorubaland and were affected by what Lugard regarded as native superstition.[16] Lugard didn't make explicit exactly what he meant by corruption, which is generally defined as the abuse of entrusted power for personal benefit. Presumably he was referring to the habit of supplicants bringing gifts to bearers of public office, applying a distinction between the public and private realms that did not exist in Nigeria in the way that it did in his own country, Britain.

The circumstances in which colonial power had been established seemed to many British officials to have an effect on the subsequent success of their administration. Lugard, who had personally supervised the military campaigns that overcame the emirates of what was soon to become Northern Nigeria, knew that colonial rule in the North reposed on conquest. It was clear who was in ultimate control. In the South, this was not quite so obvious. British rule there had been inaugurated in hundreds of individual agreements signed with local authorities, and Lugard found that there was consequently some lack of clarity about precisely what executive powers were vested in the colonial government.[17] Beyond Yorubaland, vast tracts of Southern Nigeria lacked even a semblance of central authority and seemed to the British to be the most backward of all the territories in Nigeria. Here, British penetration had been "reluctant, uncertain, and rather haphazard", according to Margery Perham, whereas in the North it had been "confident and rapid".[18]

One of the most common forms of authority in Southern Nigeria was what British officials referred to as a "secret society", a group of initiates usually classed by age, whose activities and deliberations were not communicated to those outside the group. In the south and southeast of Nigeria there were communities without any centralised state structure at all, not even a chief. These are sometimes called "stateless societies". The anthropologist Robin Horton, who has lived in Southern Nigeria for forty years, lists four features shared by stateless societies such as those that British colonisers found in Igboland and in the Niger delta:[19]

1. There is little concentration of authority. It is difficult to point to any individual or limited group of people as the ruler or rulers of the society.
2. Such authority roles as exist affect a rather limited sector of the lives of those subject to them.
3. The wielding of authority as a specialised, full-time occupation is virtually unknown.
4. The unit within which people feel an obligation to settle their disputes according to agreed rules and without resort to force tends to be relatively small.

Indirect rule and law

Lugard's solution to the problem of governing a vast country composed of such a great variety of communities and polities as Nigeria was a system he called Indirect Rule. This was something he had encountered in India, where it was a key technique of British control. The core idea of Indirect Rule was that the colonial authority should confirm the tenure of indigenous rulers where they existed, subject to direction from a British official who would ensure that the native rulers would govern justly and without recourse to methods the British considered barbarous, such as enslavement and cruel forms of execution. Native rulers were forbidden to sign agreements with representatives of foreign powers. In places where there were no such rulers, the government would appoint them.

Indirect Rule was well suited to British needs in the North, which was ruled by a Muslim aristocracy whose sense of conservatism and hierarchy was appreciated by Lugard and other British officials. The British found the system in the North so useful that they went as far as to keep Northern Nigeria administratively separate from the South in many respects, even after the amalgamation of 1914, and to restrict the work of Christian missionaries in the interests of retaining the rule of the Muslim establishment. While this seemed an ideal solution in the short term, in the longer term it created a major problem. The lack of a corpus of mission-school graduates literate in English meant that the colonial administration in the North had to import English-speakers from other parts of Nigeria, which was exactly how Nnamdi Azikiwe's father came to be living in Zungeru. Small Yoruba and Igbo communities sprang up in the main Northern cities, notably in the ancient trading hubs of Kano and Kaduna. Indirect Rule was less easily implemented in the South of Nigeria, which had fewer centralised institutions and was considered by the British to be at a lower stage of historical evolution. However, Christian missionaries had been at work in parts of the South for decades already and had produced a small number of school graduates literate in English and attuned to the ideas they had picked up from their teachers.

Thus, the precise effects of Indirect Rule differed widely from place to place. In the Northern emirates, still governed by the descendants of conquering jihadists, but now accompanied by a British Resident on the model developed by the British in India, old patterns of rule were preserved in a rather artificial isolation. In the South, British administrators at first tried to create chieftaincies out of nothing, but later tried to make the doctrine of Indirect Rule work through existing institutions that lacked the clear hierarchy of the emirates.

North or South, under Indirect Rule every individual Native Administration was responsible for raising taxes with which it would pay its officials, replacing "the unlimited exactions on which they had previously lived".[20] The British in Nigeria, like colonial governments elsewhere in Africa, claimed legitimacy not only on the basis of laws that they had written but above all on the grounds that they were bringing progress, as defined by their own notions of order, justice and knowledge.

Lugard thought he had created a system that would preserve indigenous culture and would as far as possible prevent Nigerians from acquiring pernicious foreign ideas that were liable to lead to political problems. Nigeria would to a large extent be run by Nigerians, with British officials being needed only at strategic points. Indirect Rule was inexpensive, since it was locally financed, and by 1939 the cost of administering Nigeria was lower than in any British colony in Africa except Nyasaland.[21] However the whole edifice depended on native rulers who knew their place. Lugard had a deep dislike of educated Nigerians, especially lawyers who could use arguments from English law and Western philosophy to argue against colonial rule and who even had the gall to criticise their own natural leaders, the chiefs.

Lugard wrote extensively about some of the more theoretical aspects of Indirect Rule,[22] and such was his prestige within the colonial service that his version of it was to become the foundation stone of colonial government not only in Nigeria but also in British colonies further afield. Most British officials were sure that their system, designed to preserve indigenous systems as far as possible, was better than that in French colonies, based on a desire to instill French culture and methods into the natives.[23] When African colonies became independent in the 1960s, former colonial officials were still arguing about whether Lugard's method or the French method was better.[24]

Law in the protectorate territories—all of Nigeria except for the original colony of Lagos—was based on powers derived from the Foreign Jurisdiction Act passed by the British parliament in 1890.[25] This gave the British Crown the authority to create a legislative body or to authorise the governor to issue ordinances. Colonial rule instituted the rule of law in the sense that the executive was assumed to have no powers entitling it to take action against individual liberty or property, other than such as were covered by statute or common law.[26] As in other European traditions, British officials were powerfully influenced by their own country's history, which they took to be the norm of historical development, and above all by the convention that law is derived ultimately from a written authority.

In Britain, as in the rest of Europe, the idea that law emerged from divine revelation[27] had evolved over centuries into a secular convention whereby law is seen as the rules of a political community that governs itself (or, in the case of a colony, is governed by a foreign power). Law in the colonial system was an expression of power in that it resulted from a command; it was not based on any perception of truth held by the indigenous population. For the vast majority of Britain's new colonial subjects in Nigeria, the colonial law code, when people were aware of its existence at all, did not represent a body of rules that had to be followed because of their inherent legitimacy, but only because they were enunciated by an authority able to impose punishment. If people respected the colonial law, or even just pretended they did, it was because they were in awe of the people who proclaimed the law rather than for any other reason. White people in general enjoyed great prestige. Obafemi Awolowo, later to be a leading nationalist politician, recalled how, as a child in the 1910s, he had thought of the white man as "a superman". The mere glimpse of a white person filled him with wonder.[28]

With the exception of the Muslim emirates of the Sahel, which made limited use of law based on the scriptural authority of the Qur'an, in most of Nigeria the introduction of written law was a revolutionary innovation. In contrast to the European tradition of law-making introduced by colonial officials, the customary law previously existing in hundreds of communities all over Nigeria was based on principles of natural law in the sense that indigenous lawmakers enacted rules that they thought conformed to the principles of cosmology applying in the invisible world,[29] the home of spiritual beings with effective powers over the material world. They perceived the spiritual and material worlds as two distinct but related spheres. Religious experts were expected to have a refined knowledge of the properties of things, animal, vegetable or mineral, each of which was thought to have "its own natural law, as well as its own essence".[30] Justice was usually the prerogative of a ruler or of a committee or an assembly acting in accordance with whatever could be represented as tradition, based on precedent. It was generally inseparable from the spiritual knowledge articulated by ritual experts or priests, who in effect constituted checks and balances and legitimised political rule.

Most importantly, law before colonial times was generally unwritten. "Prior to colonialism", a Nigerian criminologist has observed, "Africans primarily saw crime as a threat to religious morality and responded with rituals for the purification of the community for the benefit of all".[31] This may sound naively benign to a modern sensibility, but legal regimes of this sort were more ruthless than they appear, since a threat to religiously based morality could arise from the breaking of a taboo, such as the birth of twins. The punishment for an offence of an essentially ritual nature could be enslavement or death, in keeping with the gravity of breaking rules that were considered to reflect the cosmic order. Punishments this severe could take place on a large scale, as Lugard recorded when he wrote to his wife in 1912 that he had just dealt with a file concerning 744 "murders by ordeal".[32]

Other than in Muslim communities, religious knowledge was itself based not on written dogma but on the assumed efficacy of communication with an invisible world. Attainable through ritual, the spirit world could be shaped to the requirements of an individual religious actor. The extraordinary intimacy and closeness of the spirit world in the societies that were incorporated into Nigeria is something quite difficult for modern Europeans or Americans to grasp, as their own ideas about what constitutes religion are so different. For people living in the communities that became part of Nigeria in 1914, and even for their descendants today, religion was neither a corpus of dogma nor a search for meaning in life. Rather, it consisted of a belief in the existence of an invisible world, distinct but not separate from the visible one, that is home to spiritual beings with effective powers over the material world.[33] Nigerians then and now maintain a dialogue with the invisible realm, in effect trying to shape their own well-being through a process of negotiation with the spirit world. This is not as strange as may seem: after all, even convinced atheists believe in invisible entities or forces, such as social structure or capital (not to be confused with money, which is visible), that they try to manipulate in order to achieve particular outcomes. The invisible world that most Nigerians believe in is one populated by specific spirits with their own names. Divination, which has always played an important part in religious communication in West Africa, is perhaps closer to the modern practice of psychiatry than anything else, as it involves an individual shaping her or his own destiny in a dialogue with the spirit world via a skilled intermediary. In other circumstances consultation might be via a shrine or an oracle, often involving a physical object that is thought able to transmit mystical powers. Nigerians often refer to an object of this sort as a juju.

In considering the nature of religion in West Africa, it is helpful to bear in mind some of the particularities of the history of Christianity in Europe that have done so much to shape Western ideas about the world. As the French philosopher Marcel Gauchet has pointed out, all monotheisms tend to consider the divine as an otherworldly realm. Christianity in particular, by locating the promise of personal fulfilment in the inner recesses of the human soul, emphasises divine authority as something exterior to creation. Gauchet has shown the effect this has had on Europe's history, as the kings who founded absolutist states in early modern times inadvertently presided over a transition in which political authority ceased to be regarded as an incarnation of the divine (since Jesus alone could be that) but rather as emanating from the will of individuals. When authority in politics changed to coming from below, from the people, rather than streaming downwards from heaven to earth, the notion of a social contract emerged.[34]

Some of this ideology was transmitted via colonial administration to Nigerians during the earlier twentieth century, and subsequently by the free flow of ideas associated with an international legal order, but it has met resistance from other ideas deeply entrenched in local societies. The dual religious heritage resulting from the encounter between Europe and Africa has shaped Nigerians' ideas about law and morality. Whereas in the European tradition law is derived from a written authority, and individuals are expected to adhere to a fixed moral code, in the older African tradition a morally correct course of action is not deduced from a written source, but is formed in the process of consulting the invisible world. As we shall see, this affects people's ideas of right and wrong to the present day.

A school for deception

Generally speaking, the most important effect of Indirect Rule in Nigeria was to make local rulers less accountable to their subjects, since whatever traditional means existed to remove an overbearing chief had become less effective.[35] The fact that there were twin sources of authority in the form of the colonial government on the one hand, and local custom on the other, gave astute chiefs room to play the two against each other. When it suited them, they claimed to be acting in conformity with colonial law, and also when it suited them, they could act in contravention of the law on the grounds that they were upholding the real traditions of their people. They could continue using traditional mechanisms of rule informally, even when these were technically outlawed. In the early years of colonial rule, there were even cases of people masquerading as local officials of the colonial government in order to enrich themselves, setting up pseudo-courts that purported to have the backing of the colonial authorities but that were no more than personal creations. One such entrepreneur issued false summonses demanding heavy fines from his victims. A former shrine priest, "he was got up to represent a District Commissioner, giving out that he was opening a new District for the Government. He had his own police, court messengers and prison warders; all sufficiently like the real thing to deceive the ignorant population with whom he had to deal".[36] A benevolent way of interpreting this incident was that a shrine priest was simply trying to continue his traditional authority in a new guise, which required a claim that he represented the colonial government along with all its accoutrements of police and messengers. But one could also consider such a person to be a charlatan or a confidence trickster, a breed that could flourish in Nigeria as people learned to manipulate the symbols of colonial authority.

The nationalist leader Obafemi Awolowo was one of those educated Nigerians whom Lugard so despised, whose legal training equipped him to identify some of the key defects of Indirect Rule. Awolowo was not impressed with the argument that an administration run by traditional leaders was always best for the people. He thought that corruption was "the greatest defect of the Native Court system", although, he claimed, "Government Officials and Administrative Officers always pretend it does not exist".[37] Corruption, he wrote, most commonly took the form of bribes, but it could also involve the use of social connections or political office for personal benefit.[38] In private, British officials also found Native Administration authorities in many parts of the country to have a distressing tendency towards corruption, although they were so determined to make Indirect Rule a success that they did not like admitting its shortcomings to a politician like Awolowo—precisely because arguing politics outside the sphere of the traditional rulers could only undermine Indirect Rule.

In debates like these, corruption was rarely defined, but the practices to which Awolowo and others referred were to some extent the continuance of older habits in a new context. Thus, in the North there had long existed a "spoils system" whereby "an incoming Emir turned all the relatives and supporters of his predecessor out of office and replaced them with his own".[39] In Igboland, honour required that a wealthy person would make gifts to shrines and distribute money among village elders in order to obtain titles that bestowed prestige. In Yorubaland, officials were accustomed to keeping a proportion of the tax revenue collected on its way from the taxpayer to the central government. To the British all of this represented "corruption, waste, inefficiency, and extortion".[40] A more sympathetic analysis emphasises the degree to which ex-gratia payments articulated conceptions of honour. "Africans and their leaders were concerned with honour in its older forms", a leading historian tells us, "practising gift-exchange and rarely distinguishing between public and private wealth, at a time when rulers had lost many sources of revenue, numerous activities were for the first time monetised, and bureaucratisation multiplied opportunities for impersonal extortion".[41]

British colonial officials generally showed a high level of probity despite occasional incidents of theft or fraud.[42] If colonial rule could be considered as corrupting, it was not because of the misdeeds of individual officials but because it was based on extracting wealth from Nigeria and transferring it to foreigners. The entire system of colonial rule was aimed to raising enough tax revenue to pay for itself at the same time as it worked to create commercial opportunities for British companies and to provide raw materials for British industries.

All over Nigeria, when people had disputes in need of regulation, they continued to use tried and tested techniques rather than going to the colonial courts. In the North this could mean attending the Sharia courts, which had British approval. In the South, where secret societies, shrines and oracles were in theory made irrelevant or even illegal by colonial laws banning the administration of oaths and ordeals on the grounds that they were "repugnant practices",[43] these institutions often continued in existence unofficially.[44] "It is difficult for the average European to understand the significance of an 'oath by blood' to an African", one group of petitioners explained. "It is the highest form of oath in African Social Institutions and an African bound by oath of blood to carry out any principle scheme is prepared to sacrifice his life for the maintenance of the said principle for tradition has it that a breach of an oath by blood meant instant death and damnation in the spirit world; also all initiated men both living and dead will war against the descendants of such victims who breaks an oath by blood."[45] However, when oaths were manipulated by local rulers who were able to use both local tradition and colonial law in their own interest, oath-taking became "a parody of traditional practice".[46]

It was in southeastern Nigeria that British officials were most concerned by the conduct of people appointed as local agents of the administration. The main reason for this was the lack of centralised authority in many local societies in that area. At first, the British tried to rule Nigeria's southeast via local officials selected by themselves, known as Warrant Chiefs, but they found these government-appointed chiefs to lack legitimacy and often to be dishonest and self-serving. Interpreters, messengers, clerks and other categories of native official gained an odious reputation among the population.[47] After serious disturbances caused by dissatisfaction with local government had spread throughout the region in 1929, the British tried to apply Indirect Rule using "mass collections of family heads gathered in unwieldy councils."[48] This too was never very satisfactory.

In the south of Nigeria especially, the traditional religious authorities and practices that were such an important part of political power were changing in ways that were not always conducive to honesty in government. Moreover, the South continued as a field of action for Christian missionaries, as it had been since the mid-nineteenth century, and missionaries continued to offer to Nigerians not only new cosmological and religious insights, but also education. Many students perceived mission schools as though they were a new version of the societies into which youths were traditionally initiated, and mission schools represented an intrusion on "the familiar political space of the secret societies".[49] Despite the small number of colonial officials, in parts of Southern Nigeria the system of Indirect Rule was the unwitting cause of a genuine social revolution.

Conversely, in the North, where the Native Authorities had been much stronger to start with, being based on the conquest states that had emerged from Usman dan Fodio's jihad, Christian missionaries were highly restricted. This resulted in a lack of Western education. The outcome was a lack of social movement most obvious in the fact that mission-school graduates from the South had to be recruited to fill various clerical posts, creating islands of Southerners in the sea of Hausa-Fulani authority.

The differing experience of Indirect Rule in North and South was to mark the future Federal Republic of Nigeria in many ways, not least in the patterns of criminality that emerged. It is hard to identify much in the colonial period that could reasonably be called "organised crime" in Nigeria, although older ideas in regard to slavery could be said to constitute a historical reality from which contemporary people-trafficking emerged at a later stage. More generally, however, the actual experience of Indirect Rule in Southern Nigeria especially involved such a high degree of deceit and manipulation as to amount to a training in subterfuge for anyone who had close experience of it. As we will see in the next chapter, this stimulated specific practices of self-representation and deception, sometimes deliberately targeting foreigners, that we could see as early contributions to a culture of corruption.

2

WONDER-WORKERS

Colonial officials spent much of their time on run-of-the-mill administrative tasks aimed at getting Native Authorities—the local units of Indirect Rule—to function in line with the regulations set down by the government. The ambition to spread new ideas about the world and about the nature of the cosmos was not the routine task of government officials but of missionaries and of the teachers working at mission schools. These included not only people from Europe or America who felt a calling to spread the gospel in Africa, but also the Nigerian evangelists working for one or other mission church or for one of the independent churches set up by Africans themselves. As we have seen, Northern Nigeria was an exception inasmuch as Christian missionaries were restricted in their activities there by order of the government.

Since they gave instruction in both technical and religious fields, mission schools provided students with plenty of material that might cause them to question their whole outlook on the world. British officials quite often met Nigerian school graduates who, in their opinion, had misunderstood elements of the Western-style education they had received. One such case concerned "an educated Native" who claimed that he had learned how to "read" fingerprints, since he had seen police officers doing this as a means of acquiring forensic evidence, but in this case the man was studying fingerprints as one might examine tea-leaves or the entrails of an animal, as a means of divination.[1] This was actually a prime example of a general principle applicable both in technical education and in religious conversion, namely that new information may be assimilated into an older matrix of cultural knowledge.[2]

The same British police officer who recorded the case of the finger-print-diviner in 1922 also noted that some Nigerians were ordering patent medicines by post from India,[3] a country that even a century ago had a reputation among West Africans as a centre of mystical power and knowledge. Some literate Nigerians were using the postal service to buy literature on mysticism and on homeopathic medicine not only from India, but from addresses in Britain and the United States as well.[4]

One British resident of Nigeria who was disturbed by this trend was J.K. Macgregor, who for thirty-six years was the headmaster of the Hope Waddell Institute, a famous missionary school in Calabar founded by Scottish Presbyterians with a view to instilling a high standard of "integrity and justice" into the sons of chiefs.[5] Among the stream of distinguished alumni produced by the Hope Waddell Institute was Nnamdi Azikiwe, the boy from Zungeru who was to become Nigeria's first president. He was a student at the school at precisely the time when Macgregor discovered that some of his pupils were in possession of letters sent from abroad "dealing with quack medicines and quack methods of treating disease, catalogues of all kinds of magical works and letters from various societies that professed to give an esoteric teaching that was sure to bring success and happiness".[6] Macgregor found over a hundred such missives in one mail delivery alone. He was so disturbed by this that in 1925 he wrote to the governor-general, specifying that "a great deal of this literature emanates from America. Some of it from England and from India."[7] Macgregor gave the example of one Hope Waddell boy, a twelve-year, who had bought through the post an object advertised as a "Mystic Charm" from an address in India. "It arrived, a piece of valueless metal containing some wax, enclosed in the heart of a newspaper", Macgregor wrote.[8] With this package was a set of instructions that included a requirement to send more money in order to receive blessings from the Hindu deity Siddheswari, the sign of which would be discerned "by watching the flow of his nasal mucus", according to Macgregor's scathing report.[9] So many cases of this sort arose that the Colonial Secretary in London—at that time, Winston Churchill—wrote to the governor-general of

Nigeria suggesting the introduction of a law making such correspondence illegal.[10]

One may, like Headmaster Macgregor, lament the ignorance of the schoolboys who spent their pocket money on stuff like this. There is a deeper point to consider, however, which is that the consumption of such material reflected a deep belief in the possibility of achieving material success through harnessing mystical powers that might be channelled through a material object, called a juju in pidgin English. Any Nigerian able to read English could wonder whether juju-type objects from abroad might not have exceptional powers in light of the prestige attached in colonial times to imported goods.

The Professor of Wonders

On 18 December 1920, a certain Mr Crentsil, a former employee of the Marine Department of the colonial government in Lagos, wrote an extraordinary letter to a contact in the British colony of the Gold Coast, today's Ghana.[11] Crentsil, who almost certainly originally came from the Gold Coast himself although he had been living for many years in Nigeria, launched into a long description of the magical powers that were in his possession and that could, on payment of a fee, be used to the benefit of his correspondent. Crentsil signed himself "P. Crentsil, Prof. of Wonders".

According to the evidence at hand, "Professor" Crentsil has to be regarded as the first[12] known exponent of the modern Four One Nine fraud, for which Nigeria has become notorious throughout the world. It is ironic that the first known Four One Nine fraudster known to history was not a Nigerian at all, but rather a Ghanaian!

Crentsil seems to have written a number of similar letters, each time offering to provide magical services on payment of a fee. In December 1921, he was charged by the police with three counts under various sections of the criminal code including section 419, the one to which Nigerians make reference when they speak of "Four One Nine". But Crentsil was in luck: the magistrate presiding over his case discharged him with a caution on the first count and acquitted him on the two others for lack of corroborating evidence, as a result of which "he (Crentsil) is now boasting that he got off owing to his 'juju' powers", reported the Chief of Police in Onitsha Province. The same officer stated that he had known Crentsil for some years, during which time the "Professor" "had slipped through the hands of the police so often that I shall soon, myself, begin to believe in his magic powers".[13]

There is no way of knowing how many similar cases may have occurred, but the colonial authorities became sufficiently concerned by the number of letters addressed to Nigerians from outside the country soliciting money for what the British regarded as fraudulent purposes that they started to intercept items of what was called "charlatanic correspondence". The Director of Posts and Telegraphs made clear that this term embraced adverts concerning "medicines of potency, and unfailing healing power, lucky charms, love philtres, magic pens with which examinations can be passed, powders and potions to inspire personal magnetism, remove kinks from hair—or insert them—counter-act sterility and ensure football prowess".[14] The Posts and Telegraphs department recorded 2,855 such items in the years 1935–8, 355 in 1945, 5,630 in 1946 and 9,570 in 1947, by which time the amount of money returned to senders was some £1,205.[15] In the mid-1940s there was a spate of financial scams perpetrated by people known as "Wayo tricksters".[16] In 1946 some of these Wayo tricksters were operating a trick that involved posing as agents of a "New York Currency Note Firm", selling to a gullible victim boxes of blank paper with a promise that this could be turned into banknotes by application of a special chemical.[17]

The claims to possess mystical wealth-creating powers articulated by "Professor" Crentsil and others belonged recognisably to an existing repertoire of behaviour. A sharp-eyed visitor to just about any large market in Southern Nigeria could see that such markets often contained "money-doublers",[18] people claiming to have a mystical power by which they could increase a client's money. The money-doublers usually occupied a place in the market next to healers claiming extraordinary powers over the human person, and near the herbalists, who used a pharmacopoeia of plants and animal body parts to effect cures, and also close to the diviners who could discern a client's destiny in the course of a consultation. Itinerant "native doctors" with connections to one or another shrine offered access to local oracles that they claimed could produce wealth through intervention in the spirit world.[19] A mid-twentieth century writer recorded that itinerant medicine sellers were known as "Ajasco Boys", and money-doublers as "Black Boys",[20] whom he described as among the legions of poor people scrabbling to make money.[21] There were occasional cases of money-doublers being prosecuted under the colonial law code,[22] which indicates how they were viewed by the colonial authorities.

Whether those Nigerians who offered mystical services for a price were vulgar charlatans, as the colonial police thought, or people who really believed themselves to have gifts of prophecy, is hard to know. What we can say, though, is that the activities of people who offered magical charms via mail order can be understood within an established repertoire of techniques for communication with the invisible world by "making" good fortune. The only true proof of such powers is their effectiveness. If a man buys an amulet and wins a football match, or a woman buys a fertility charm and becomes pregnant, they may think that the medicine worked. The person who produced it gains in reputation.

Behaviour of a sort that British officials probably would have classified as charlatanic was sometimes recorded on the part of the relatively small number of Nigerians who travelled overseas in the first half of the twentieth century. One of these was one Prince Modupe, also known as Modupe Paris and David Modupe, who spent years in the United States under a variety of fantastical guises. In 1935 he was in Los Angeles presenting himself as a graduate of Jesus College, Oxford, although Oxford University had no record of him. In March 1947 he appeared on the bill at the San Francisco Opera House under the name His Royal Highness Prince Modupe of Dubrica. Seven months later he was still in San Francisco, now claiming to be the "Crown Prince of Nigeria" and representing himself as a successful businessman who had obtained a variety of commercial contracts. Modupe seems to have been in effect a professional confidence trickster.[23] Nor was he the only Nigerian operating in this field in the United States. Another was Prince Peter Eket Inyang Udo, a businessman who lived in America and Britain for some seventeen years. Eket Inyang Udo attracted the attention of the colonial authorities not only on account of his dubious commercial practices but also because of his political ideas and connections.[24]

Another controversial case, in which fraud and nationalist politics seem to have been mixed, concerned an Igbo man who became a minor celebrity in America under the name Prince Orizu. He was so well known that an Australian official working in New York for the United Nations, who had a special interest in Nigeria as he had previously worked for the colonial administration there, wondered in his memoirs: "What happened to the Ibo adventurer who called himself Prince Orizu?" Noting that "there are no hereditary chiefs let alone princes in Ibo-land", the Australian wrote that Orizu "seemed to have no difficulty in getting a write-up in the *New Yorker* or the *New York Times* every now and then".[25] The person he was describing also went under the name Dr Abyssinia Akweke Nwafor Orizu, and it was under this name that he was convicted by a magistrate in Nigeria in September 1953 on seven counts of fraud and theft of funds ostensibly intended to fund scholarships in the United States. Himself US-educated, Orizu had collected over £32,000 in the three years prior to his conviction. What makes the case all the more interesting is that Orizu was a stalwart of the National Council of Nigeria and the Cameroons (NCNC), the leading political party founded in 1944, and was also a member of the Regional Government established under Nigeria's 1951 constitution.[26] He went on to have a distinguished political career, becoming president of the Senate after Nigeria's Independence. Although it has been alleged[27] that Orizu's conviction for fraud was a miscarriage of justice, it seems fair to observe that modern politics, which emerged in Nigeria only in the 1940s, offered opportunities for a type of self-fashioning comparable in many respects to that practised by fabulists and fraudsters like Crentsil, Modupe and others we have met on these pages.

Some of a new breed of chancers began at a young age. In 1949, the US consul-general in Lagos reported the existence of one "Prince Bil Morrison", who turned out to be a fourteen-year old boy who specialised in writing to correspondents in America to solicit funds. Clearly Morrison was one of many, as the police remarked that this case was just "one more in which generous, but possibly gullible, American citizens have allowed themselves to be taken in by African schoolboys."[28] The consul-general wrote: "These young Nigerians are stated by the Police to be excellent psychologists", noting that their practice of writing to people in the United States and Canada for money was "widespread".[29] Frauds by Nigerian students in the United States and Canada in the late 1940s were said to include the offer for sale of diamonds, ivory and other exotic luxuries.[30]

Comparable cases were also recorded in the religious field, such as the activities of the Reverend R.N.Y. Bassey, who in 1948 was claiming to be the local superintendent in Nigeria of the Federated Full Gospel Assemblies of the USA. According to the colonial authorities, he "appeared to specialise in making contact with religious groups in Canada and the U.S.A., adopting their name and representing himself as the leader of an African branch".[31] An editorial in the *Nigerian Catholic Herald* of 22 February 1952 reported "false appeals for help by a number of Nigerians under pseudo-titles such as 'Reverend Father', 'Reverend Brother' and 'Superior-General'." There were said to be "hundreds of Nigerian appeals addressed to charitable institutions and private individuals".[32]

In some cases, the element of fraud was particularly blatant, such as the Lagos firm that published adverts offering to provide training in the United States for £114 per year and simply keeping the money.[33] Another example concerned Henry Nwafor, a trader who paid thirty guineas to a self-proclaimed "spiritual leader", one Christopher White, in the hope that the latter could heal his sick brother. White took Nwafor to a house where he heard a voice telling him to bring a sacrifice to a spirit known as Jupiter. This scene was repeated several times during the 1950s, during the course of which Nwafor paid White a total of £65 and 15 shillings as well as giving him a cock, brandy, gin and palm wine, traditional requirements for an animal sacrifice. Only later did he discover that the mysterious voice was projected by means of a secret pipe into the room where White had left him, allowing a person outside to project their own voice. Nwafor took the case to court.[34]

To modern eyes, all of these cases may seem to be examples of barefaced deceit and fraud. Perhaps that is indeed what they were. However, to dismiss such behaviour without further comment risks missing some factors important for understanding the context in which this kind of trickery emerged. For example, it is striking that no known reports of such misrepresentation on an international scale concern people from Northern Nigeria. All come from or relate to Southern Nigeria, concerning people socialised in communities characterised by a relative lack of central authority and codified religion but, under colonial rule, influenced by new structures of political authority, Christian religion and missionary education. The combination created new possibilities for self-advancement that were without limits beyond those defined by the colonial law code—itself poorly known, and not generally seen as legitimate. New realms of risk, destiny and self-fashioning existed for people adventurous enough to explore them. Sometimes new forms of wealth were attainable by straightforward means, such as among the artisans in one particular division of Yorubaland who specialised in forging the new colonial currency, producing very credible copies. Since coins had value, it made sense to make them from scratch.[35]

Much of this may seem frankly bizarre to modern readers, yet something roughly similar has occurred in the history of many countries in times when attitudes to wealth and destiny are changing fast. In Europe, a revolution in attitudes to money in the seventeenth century was closely related to changes in theology and new notions about the place of humankind in the cosmos. Japanese society too was transformed by money in the same period.[36] The Greek *polis* of the sixth century BCE is said to have been one of the first societies in history to be pervaded by money, and the effects of this financial revolution preoccupied the philosophers and tragedians of antiquity.[37] Like Africans to this day, the Greeks had a vibrant oral culture in which the invisible world was represented as the home of identifiable beings with which humans could enter into dialogue. In both cases religious communication was a means for people to shape their own destiny, by means of divination and oracles.

Today, when money has become central to just about every single area of life in advanced capitalist countries, it requires a real intellectual effort to appreciate just how extraordinary is the imputation of value to pieces of paper—banknotes—that have no inherent worth. Policy-makers often see money as just a commodity for market transactions. In rich countries today, money has become an expression of obligations that has lost any connection to particular social relationships. Still more extraordinary is the attribution of value to pure abstractions, such as financial value. "Being transcendent to material and social reality", yet also being the pivot around which material and social reality is continually reconstructed", one study concludes, "financial value is essentially religious".[38]

Wealth, risk, destiny

As in the rest of Africa, people living before colonial times in the area later to become Nigeria set great store by wealth-in-people—the children, wives, junior kin, slaves or dependents maintained by a Big Man. Money, which existed in a wide variety of forms including cowrie shells and iron bars, was generally less important than people as a register of wealth. Even so, money could play a vital role in the accumulation of dependents by attracting support or through the purchase of a slave. Scholars have taught us that money does not need to be physically exchanged for goods in order for it to play a role in exchange, and that it has been often an expression of debt rather than a means of making definitive payment.[39] Like a traditional "medicine"—an object endowed with natural power that, in the hands of a person with expert knowledge, could be used to effect change in a human life—money was seen as morally ambivalent, neither good nor bad in itself.

Until the age of Christian evangelisation and colonial rule, Africans generally ascribed to the spiritual powers of the invisible world a morally neutral character, rather than considering them intrinsically good or evil, as Christianity does. Rather, they thought that the moral nature of spirits depends on the nature of the relationship between human beings and the spirit world with which they interact. They needed a good relationship with the spirit world in order to maintain stability in their lives. This requires regular attention, just like all social relations. If the relationship is well maintained, the spirit will be content and placid. If not, a troubled spirit will attract attention by causing trouble. People could seek good offices from a spirit, such as to protect themselves or advance their own prosperity, or malevolent services, in order to harm others.

As a result of both Christian and Muslim teaching, over time people have come to see traditional spirits as harmful by nature. The spirit world as a whole has become radically simplified, with the chief Christian and Islamic spirits being regarded as good but opposed by others—namely Satan and his agents—that are implacably evil.[40] Traditional techniques for dealing with spirits have become less effective. The reason for this is that orthodox Christianity and Islam both insist on monotheism, and both have core doctrines that are recorded in sacred texts that believers consider to be the product of divine revelation. These books and their associated doctrines are regarded as having binding authority. Moreover, both Christianity and Islam have a tendency towards exclusiveness in the sense that those who do not adhere to the doctrine recorded in the sacred texts are beyond the pale, at least by implication.

In older times, the moral ambiguity of the spirit world was connected to the realities of making a living in the territories that now compose Nigeria. Since there was no mechanised production in precolonial times, a person could become richer than his neighbours in only a limited number of ways. Perhaps the most obvious paths to rapid self-enrichment were by a successful trading expedition or through war, with its rewards of slaves and plunder. During the chronic wars between rival towns that afflicted Yorubaland throughout the nineteenth century, organised gangs of armed robbers were formed, and brigandage became a source of livelihood for the warrior class.[41] A farmer who produced more than his neighbours would normally be one with more land and labourers, making the source of his or her wealth obvious. Those who acquired money without visible work or effort were generally supposed to have used theft or some powerful form of magic,[42] but every method of accumulation was thought to involve some kind of intervention in the invisible world. People attributed mystical powers to money, presuming that a rich person was one who had effective knowledge of the true "source" of wealth.[43] The most extreme form of intervention in the invisible world that could be undertaken in order to obtain wealth involved the killing of a victim, considered as the offer of a human life in exchange for money made available by a spirit.[44] This has often been described by Europeans as a "ritual murder".

The accumulation of wealth in olden days generally required the maintenance of an extensive network of social relationships,[45] and the maintenance of those relationships was a key factor in determining the moral value of enrichment. Social obligations were maintained through gifts (of things, money, services or even people) that generated a sense of indebtedness, probably leading sooner or later to a reciprocal gesture. These relationships extended into the invisible world, with gifts and debts also existing between people and spirits. "Big Men" were close to gods not least in their power over life and death. Powerful allies and protectors could turn into captors and masters. Working the relationships between people, material enrichment and the invisible world could involve very radical social operations. The anthropologist John Peel has noted how, among the Yoruba of southwestern Nigeria, strangers could become the means for preserving the life of a community by various methods including their slaying at the funerals of important people.[46] Sacrifices and mortuary killings could take place on quite a large scale, such as the seventy people reportedly killed on the death of Basorun Oluyole in 1847.[47]

One quite common way to acquire wealth before colonial times was by obtaining a slave. Both the Northern and Southern regions of Nigeria were implicated in systems of long-distance slave-trading for centuries. In the north, this had traditionally been oriented towards North Africa, with the trade-routes also being corridors for the transmission of Islam. In the south, the import-export trade in slaves was with Europeans arriving by sea. The slave trade was of particular importance not only because of its size, but because of its effect on relationships in which personal contact, money and debt were all at issue, extending from the material into the invisible world. A slave represented a store of value whereby wealth-in-people could be turned into wealth-in-money.

At the time of slavery's abolition by the British, a quarter of the population of the Sokoto caliphate was enslaved—about two and a half million people out of a total ten million.[48] But the most developed system of slave-trading (as distinct from slave-raiding) was in the south-east of Nigeria. There, slave-holding and slave-dealing were described as "part of the life of the Ibo people" before colonial times.[49] Slave-trading was often the business of specialist merchants. According to one of Nigeria's leading historians, it was up to the time of colonisation "more or less synonymous with the Aro",[50] an Igbo group that had developed a widespread trading diaspora, with every Igbo town "of any size" containing an Aro community. "These settlers acted as agents and were kept in constant touch with the central authority", wrote an early ethnographer.[51] This central authority was formed by a shrine known as Arochukwu ("the Arrow of God"), called by the British the Long Juju, located on the Cross River. In precolonial times the Chukwu shrine "had emissaries all over eastern Nigeria", who would hear cases of suspected witchcraft and other ritual offences that they then sent to the shrine for judgement.[52] Those convicted were often sentenced by the shrine priests to enslavement.[53] The Chukwu shrine exercised a judicial function all over eastern Nigeria, and was known even as far away as Sierra Leone and Congo.[54] In the heyday of the Chukwu shrine, "the whole of the criminal judicial system was built up on the possibility of being able to sell the accused. If his own family would not redeem him then the Aros would always be willing to offer a price".[55] The integration of a judicial and a slave-dealing function brought great wealth to the Aro shrine and those associated with it. In the early twentieth century it had an income of some £16,000 per year.[56] "If these figures are current", a colonial officer noted, "the revenue of the Juju in its palmy days, especially before energetic steps had been taken for the suppression of the slave trade, must have been stupendous".[57] (For purposes of comparison, a Yoruba farmer at the time this calculation was made was reckoned to earn about £12 per year). So powerful were the shrines in Igboland generally, and so weak the chiefs, that a colonial ethnographer described the whole southeast region as living under "a theocratic administration"[58] whose backbone was the Aro network.

One of the first acts of the British after they took control of Nigeria was to outlaw slavery and the slave trade—it was, after all, the original reason for establishing a colony on Lagos Island in 1861, to serve as a basis for the Royal Navy's anti-slavery squadron. The colonial administration in southeastern Nigeria is said to have launched some forty expeditions against slave-trading and ritual killings in this region alone in 1900–1914, with a smaller number in the years up to 1926.[59] However, the abolition of slavery had consequences that were not foreseen. In eastern Nigeria, after the legal abolition of slavery former slaves were often required to pay rent to their ex-owners,[60] turning them into a source of cash. The increasing circulation of money was also causing a decline in the practice of pawning people in return for cash loans, as people were tending to use land or other property as collateral rather than people.[61] Most importantly, the suppression of slave-raiding under colonial rule put an end to the main way for young men to amass enough resources to pay bride-wealth, the name used for the compensation given to a family for the loss of their daughter when she moved to the household of a suitor.

The system of payments that permitted young men to marry and become family heads and by which fathers were able to control the fertility of their female dependents, has been described by the historian John Iliffe as "the core of patriarchy".[62] Under colonial rule, the greater circulation of coinage and the possibilities of wage employment pushed up the bride-price of an unmarried girl to the point where a male suitor found it difficult to save enough money to get married at all. Husbands who had already paid bride-price might be so attracted by the rising value of dowries that there were even cases of them making their spouse available to a new suitor, in effect divorcing their wives if they received an offer higher than the dowry they themselves had paid. This made young women an object of financial speculation.[63]

The need to acquire dependents continued, even when the means to be used were illegal. An official report on slavery in the south of Nigeria in 1934 confirmed that slave-trading was continuing underground with a central role being played by Aro men, just as it had been during the days of the Atlantic slave trade. Slaves were in demand for a variety of purposes, including because they indicated social standing, conferring prestige on their owners. In the Ikom and Obubra areas, for example, possession of slaves was reported to be necessary for any person aspiring to membership of two initiation societies known as Oboribori and Ekpoti.[64] In the Bende Division Aro-Chuku men were said to be involved "in almost all cases of this description which were investigated".[65] The great Chukwu shrine at Ibini Ukpabi had been destroyed by British military action in 1902 but the shrine-keepers had simply recreated it, and it was to continue in activity until the 1940s[66] and, indeed, up to the present century.

In some areas of the country "there appear to be gangs who carry on a steady trade in stolen children", one official reported,[67] many of them destined for adoption by childless couples.[68] The trade was sufficiently well organised for there to be identifiable hubs, such as the large Uburu market in the Afikpo divison of Igboland, described in 1933 as "the chief clearing centre" for a trade in children.[69] A particular centre of demand seemed to be in the Cross River area, where a chronically low birth rate resulted in a high number of childless couples buying children very young and then raising them as their own.[70] Colonial administrators came to realise that the trade in slaves had not so much ceased as it had gone underground. It changed from being largely oriented towards the sale of men for export, as in the days of the Atlantic trade, to a trade particularly in children.[71]

A detailed inquiry by the administration of the Southern Provinces included investigations by a senior police officer, Assistant Commissioner of Police Major J.W. Garden. He came to the conclusion that slave dealing was still "a recognised part of the economic life of the Owerri Province," in spite of its illegality.[72] Garden wrote a detailed report on the routes used by professional slave-traders and on their modus operandi, noting that the children concerned were often escorted by women posing as mothers or sisters, "and armed men have been known to act as scouts".[73] Generally speaking, there seemed to be two different types of slave-trader. The first was "parents who sell their children to the highest bidder, often under the guise of marriage, for the purpose of obtaining ready money".[74] The second type was professional slave-dealers who kidnapped victims or acquired them directly from parents. The main sources of supply were in Owerri Province, but slaves were also sourced as far away as Northern Nigeria and the Cameroons. However, despite the regularity of the trade and the leading role of Aro men, officials could find little evidence "that there exists any organised traffic of this description carried on by definite gangs of persons",[75] although at other times in the 1930s the police suspected that trafficking of people might be organised by secret societies.[76] What is most clear is that people continued to be kept as slaves and to be sold.

One particular incident caused colonial officials to make an in-depth study of the trafficking of girls and young women outside Nigeria. This arose as a result of a complaint by one Prince Eikineh, a Nigerian man who had studied at Fourah Bay College in Sierra Leone, West Africa's oldest university, and had moved to the Gold Coast to set up a business as a store-manager and bar-owner. The fact that Eikineh was one of Nigeria's early political activists in a modern idiom, being president of the Gold Coast branch of the Nigerian Youth Movement,[77] may have caused officials to take his complaint particularly seriously. Founded in 1934 as the Lagos Youth Movement, this is often regarded as Nigeria's first genuine nationalist organisation.[78]

In 1939 Eikineh wrote to the government complaining about the numbers of Nigerian girls and women who were coming to the Gold

Coast to work in the sex business. His inquiries led him to believe that the trade was organised by older women who were taking money from the young women under their authority. Fees paid by clients were of the order of two shillings for sex or six shillings to spend the whole night with a prostitute. Eikineh reckoned that there were some 150 Nigerian women and 56 girls working in this trade in the two port towns of Sekondi and Takoradi alone,[79] including girls "kidnapped and brought here as a Training Ground".[80] He maintained that this traffic was dominated by a "ring-leader" named Alice, a native of Nigeria's Warri Province.[81] The girls and women concerned did not seem to look on the work as shameful, but saw it rather as "ordinary work undertaken with a view to earning money which they intended to take back to Nigeria as savings or in finery".[82]

A police investigation found that the women concerned in this business were emigrating from Nigeria of their own free will, and that there was no kidnapping taking place as Eikineh had at one point alleged.[83] An official in Calabar Province thought that there was some trade in women being organised in the Arochuku Division,[84] the historic centre of slave-dealing in the southeast of the country. Further investigation among Nigerian sex workers in the Gold Coast suggested that the women concerned considered their business to be no different from any other type of work. Some of them had even organised a trade union, with a recognised leadership.[85] However, as Eikineh had alleged, the business was indeed largely run by older women who had themselves worked as prostitutes before graduating to becoming an organiser. It was found that women with experience of the sex business in the Gold Coast were returning to their home areas in Nigeria where they would "obtain young girls on the pretext of marriage or in order to teach them trading and domestic work", but then requiring them to work in the sex trade for a couple of years.[86] A girl wishing to enter this line of trade "first of all approaches one of the retired members of which there are many. From this woman she obtains details as to route, transport costs to the [Gold] Coast, and routine, also usually the name of the man from whom she can borrow the necessary funds".[87] An inquiry in the Cross River area from which so many of these sex workers came suggested there had been a breakdown in the institution of marriage, largely due to the attitude taken by the area's men. Fathers were found to have "connived at the break up of the old dowry system either because they stand to gain more by taking a rake off from their daughters' immoral earnings or because they have not the influence and energy to control their daughters and are afraid to refund dowry if they run away."[88] In some parts of southeastern Nigeria, the bride-price had risen vertiginously to over £100.[89] In some cases women working in the sex trade in the Gold Coast were actually receiving their initial start-up capital from husbands back home in Nigeria, who would advance the money for their travel to Sekondi. Before leaving home they would visit a herbalist or healer who gave them medicine said to make them immune to venereal disease.[90]

The overall conclusion to the investigation sparked by Prince Eikineh's complaint was that prostitution was "a profitable and very well organised trade", in which many families in the Cross River area had an interest.[91] This regional specialisation was largely because the trade was dominated by women who had experience of the trade and who passed on information on the business to others whom they knew, resulting in tight networks of patrons and clients that in some parts of the Cross River area involved almost every single family.[92] This description is in many respects similar to later accounts of the trade in sex workers to Europe, which flourishes up to the present day, as will be discussed further in due course.

A hollow system

The discovery that a trade in people, including for sex work, was so well organised is exceptional insofar as there was otherwise very little sign of organised crime in Nigeria, according to informed colonial officials. Before the mid-twentieth century the British authorities did not perceive Nigeria as generally a lawless society. A Commissioner of Prisons reported in 1944 that there was no need for "alarm or despondency" in this regard. He pointed out that the murder rate was lower than that of either the Gold Coast or the United States and that "the number of persistent and professional criminals is not great....".[93]

During the Second World War, however, there was a perceptible rise in crime in some areas, especially the Eastern Region. This took the form of "a tangled mess of petty offences". It was doubtless motivated by hunger and the prevailing conditions of austerity, but the perception of a crime wave caused officials to consider other possible explanations as well. There was clearly an underlying problem in that the penal code "is still alien to the ethics and instincts of many [of Nigeria's] constituent peoples".[94]

In fact, a whole way of life continued underground despite having been declared illegal by the colonial government, and this included not only slavery but a host of other practices including mortuary slayings during burial rites and the requirement that a candidate for membership of certain secret societies be in possession of slaves as a mark of status.[95] Among other practices or institutions the colonial administration moved to suppress were those oracles that British officials considered barbarous or that they thought might compete with official courts of law.[96] "The government was paranoid about oracles", one later analyst has noted.[97]

Just as officials continued to receive occasional reports of continued slave-trading, so did they hear about other outlawed practices, for example at Ikorodu, where a local man wrote to a senior British official in 1945 about "the dreadful practice of stealing human beings for either secret immolation or juju making".[98] The man, Amos Oshinowo Shopitan, claimed that his own two-year old son had been kidnapped for this nefarious purpose.[99] The following year the government recorded 161 persons as having been killed as a result of secret society business in the Ibibio area alone. Seventy-five people were subsequently charged with murder.[100] The United States consul in Lagos recorded figures for murders committed by secret societies in 1947, noting 88 proven cases and 96 suspected ones, many of them relating to just one single division of the Ibibio area.[101] British officials often maintained that the number of children reported missing, with suspicions of sinister motives lurking in the background, was greatly exaggerated. They claimed that those reported missing quite often returned home without the authorities being informed.

Reports of clandestine economic activity and ritual killings were often connected to the secret societies that played such an important role in the traditional governance of Southern areas especially. Some deaths that had apparently been caused by wild animals could possibly have been caused by initiates of human leopards, powerful sodalities whose members were thought to be possessed by the spirit of a leopard and who carried out murderous attacks with knives that inflicted cuts similar to the wounds from a leopard's claws. Rumours about human leopards led to a debate among colonial officials on the causes of the disturbances and the possible role of the secret societies that continued to exist under the surface of the formal system of Indirect Rule.[102] An example of what some societies had become is the Odozi Obodo cult in Abakaliki. Originally committed to bringing cases of theft and adultery to the attention of chiefs, it is reported to have "degenerated into a killing squad" specialised in eliminating suspected criminals by strangulation.[103] By 1958 it was reported to have committed no fewer than 200 murders at the behest of a local chief.[104]

Some commentators maintain that officials attached excessive importance to the secret societies. Officials in Calabar Province attributed almost everything to "the workings of shadowy sodalities of initiates".[105] Those officials who regarded secret societies as no more than bands of thugs who committed murders for personal gain were overlooking "the intentions behind the executions they witnessed or heard about",[106] which were often political in nature. It required subtlety to recognise the importance of secret societies in upholding the social order. In this regard, the British Resident in Calabar, for example, noted that "Like all other Ibibio and Annang societies its general purpose is the formation of a social structure to uphold the authority of the elders".[107] Accusations of murder by human leopards—members of certain secret societies—and accusations of witchcraft, whether grounded or not, could be interpreted as "a way of making sense of a world riven with social tensions and ambiguous relationships and served to 'personalize the universe'."[108] The ranks of colonial officialdom included some talented ethnographers, who recognised that the changing practices of various Nigerian communities reflected wider influences associated with economic pressures, for example. Consequently, many British officials believed that secret societies, like other key institutions of Nigerian society, were becoming more mercenary and even criminal in nature as a result of social changes that had taken place under colonial rule.

Colonial officials had to navigate between their need to maintain Indirect Rule, which depended on indigenous institutions, and their need to enforce the colonial law code. At least in private, they quite often recognised the hollowness of the system of justice they had created. One official, describing the decline of the redoubtable Chukwu shrine after its banning, noted how in its place "an artificial judicial body came into being, a body having behind it, in native eyes, no sanction but forces as represented by the District Officer, and the Police".[109] The widespread protests led by women in southeastern Nigeria in 1929 and subsequently dubbed the Women's War indicated the utter failure of the system of warrant chiefs in Igboland, which had so little tradition of centralised government.[110] Being essentially weak, some of the British-appointed chiefs secretly connived with the restoration of traditional shrines that could help provide them with the legitimacy they otherwise lacked. Often associated with these shrines were the same secret societies that officials despised as repositories of barbarism and primitivism and suspected of being associated with various forms of crime.

Margery Perham more or less summed up the British dilemma when she described how, "the Europeans, in penetrating a country, come into collision with a native institution which has certain obviously barbarian features. It is only after it is destroyed or driven underground that it is realised, in the task of reconstruction, that it supplied a social nexus".[111]

3

ENTER THE POLITICIANS

The main argument used by Nigeria's colonial masters to justify their rule was that they were laying the foundations for a modern state and society that would one day emerge under British guidance. Margery Perham, who travelled widely in Nigeria in the 1930s, recalled that "There was an atmosphere of almost unlimited time in which to carry on the task, regarded then as hardly begun, of building a new Nigeria from the bottom up."[1]

Only towards the end of the 1930s did officials really begin to discuss the possible role of Nigerians in the higher levels of government, and even then hesitantly. In 1939 Governor-General Bernard Bourdillon wrote a report on future political development that was classified as "confidential" but circulated to a small number of people. Bourdillon was himself a child of empire just as Lugard had been, born in Australia and serving in India, Ceylon and Uganda before taking up the top job in Nigeria. In his report on Nigeria's future he quoted approvingly Perham's view that the country had the potential to build "a sound united state" because, thanks to Indirect Rule, it had experienced "the least possible breach with the past" and there had been a minimum "dislocation of tradition and familiar methods of administration".[2]

By this time Lugard's vision of Indirect Rule had become a doctrine that no official would publicly reject without risking damage to his career. Bourdillon's vision was a classic case of a complacent authority becoming convinced by its own high opinion of itself. It underestimated the depth of the social revolution initiated by colonisation and Christian evangelism, especially in the south of Nigeria.

Moreover, Nigeria was acquiring a growingly sophisticated national elite. The Nigerian Youth Movement, the very same that we have encountered protesting to the colonial government about the activities of Nigerian sex workers abroad, attracted a modest following among educated people in the 1930s, recruiting members from all parts of the country.

The Impact of the Second World War

During the Second World War, Nigerians joined the armed forces and fought overseas, notably in Southeast Asia. The country's few newspapers became filled with stories about foreign countries and world affairs. Some readers were able to grasp at least dimly the enormous geo-political issues at stake in the great struggle in which their own country too was involved, for while Nigeria was spared military operations, Britain needed its colonies more than ever to supply raw materials. The colonial government intervened directly in the economy by imposing rationing. Those who noted the ringing statements on freedom produced by the British government wondered how these might apply to their own country. In London, imperial strategists and planners realised that Britain no longer had the strength to defend all of its empire and, noting the anti-colonial attitude of US President Franklin D. Roosevelt, began to discern that their African territories might cease to be colonies sooner than they had anticipated.

Wartime conditions sent up the price of basic goods and, we have seen, may also have caused exceptional criminal activity in the Eastern Region. Some villagers took to organising their own systems of night-guards to protect themselves against robbers.[3] In 1946 "cowboy" gangs made an appearance, young hooligans who dressed in imitation of the heroes of the cowboy films they loved to watch.[4]

Small numbers of Nigerians who had spent long periods in Britain and the United States, often for study, were returning home, some of them brimming with nationalist and pan-Africanist ideas. Among these was Nnamdi "Zik" Azikiwe, a former pupil at the Hope Waddell

Training Institute. After leaving school, Azikiwe moved to the USA, where he studied at Lincoln University, Pennsylvania, obtaining a Master's degree in 1932 and a second Master's (in anthropology) from the University of Pennsylvania in 1934. He briefly worked as an instructor at Lincoln before returning to West Africa. His first stop in the old continent was in the Gold Coast, where he edited a newspaper before finally returning to Nigeria in 1937. Back home, he founded a new paper, the *West African Pilot*, going on to create a stable of newspapers and becoming a successful businessman. In 1944 he was one of the co-founders of the National Council of Nigeria and the Cameroons (NCNC), which within years had become a major political party. In 1947 he set up his own bank, the African Continental Bank, with a view to financing his own group of companies.[5] Azikiwe was an ardent nationalist with the resources to gain a national following and even to command some international attention.

The Second World War made obsolete the earlier lack of urgency concerning Nigeria's future. Development became the guiding principle of colonial policy. In 1946 Nigeria got its first development plan and soon the British government in Westminster was pressing the colonial administration in Lagos to offer loans to African entrepreneurs in a bid to stimulate local business.[6] Development was intended to increase Nigeria's production of export commodities—palm oil, cocoa and groundnuts were the staples—and to stimulate local consumer markets. In 1947 the government established marketing boards to buy crops from local producers at fixed prices before selling them on international markets.[7] One of the most attractive aspects of the marketing boards from a government point of view was that they could stimulate the production of export commodities that could earn hard currency at a time when Britain was suffering from a chronic shortage of US dollars.

Nationalist agitators like Azikiwe presented the government with a new type of challenge. After the War's end, the Governor-General, Sir Arthur Richards, introduced a constitution providing for a legislative assembly in each of the country's three Regions and increased African participation in the Legislative Council that provided advice to the government on a national level, but this arrangement attracted little support from the country's aspiring political and intellectual class, which criticised Richards for his failure to consult more widely before introducing these measures. Azikiwe denounced the new arrangement in his newspaper. Even within the small political class there was little sense of national unity. None of the major politicians was much in favour of developing a strong central authority. As Zik's rival, the Yoruba lawyer, businessman and politician Obafemi Awolowo later wrote in his autobiography, at this point "the question as to what type of constitution Nigeria should have was not at all an issue in the country's politics".[8]

A new governor, Sir John Macpherson, promulgated a revised version of the constitution in 1951, based on the same vision of giving Nigerians limited powers at regional level while the British continued to retain control at the centre. After Independence it became fashionable for young nationalists to claim that federalism was imposed on Nigeria by the British in order to keep it weak and divided,[9] but this is to ignore the gusto with which the main political leaders took up the game of regional politics and the lack of a national constituency. As Awolowo famously noted, in a book against colonial rule that he published in 1947, "Nigeria is not a nation. It is a mere geographical expression."[10]

Almost every subsequent commentator has noted how flawed was the British concept of developing regional government, since it encouraged future political leaders to develop a provincial power-base above all else. Nigeria's apprentice politicians formed parties using the material available, especially the ethnic and cultural organisations that had proliferated in recent years. The leading nationalist party, the NCNC, gained a stronger Igbo identity as it became intertwined with the Ibo Federal Union, renamed the Igbo State Union in 1948. In 1949, three of the few Northerners to have received a substantial education in the British tradition at the Region's leading secondary school founded the Northern People's Congress (NPC). In 1951, Awolowo founded the Action Group on the basis of a Yoruba ethnic association, Egbe Omo Oduduwa, named after the deity considered to be the founding father of the Yoruba. Awolowo and a group of like-minded activists purposefully designed Egbe Omo Oduduwa along the lines of a secret society.[11] When the 1951 constitution came into effect, politics fell into a regional pattern, with one major party dominating each of Nigeria's constituent regions: the NCNC in the East, the NPC in the North and the Action Group in the West.

The foundation of these political parties has generally been seen by historians and political scientists as a step towards political modernity, but it is at least as important to note just how much the new nationalist political parties continued to use the repertoire of traditional secret societies and of religion. The NCNC, led by Azikiwe, trailed in its wake a body called the National Church of Nigeria and the Cameroons, with an official primate and a chief priest named Egbutche.[12] There is a record from 1948 of this institution staging an event that was a parody of a Church of England service, with the singing of nationalist hymns such as "Alien Rule Must Go", and readings from the book *Renascent Africa*, published by Azikiwe in America in 1937. The sermon was on "The God of Africa".[13] When one of Azikiwe's political opponents, Alvan Ikoku, reconciled with the NCNC leader, the *West African Pilot* newspaper of 20 July 1951 represented the event in the form of a cartoon showing the Apostle Zik baptizing "Paul" Ikoku by the "Holy Niger River". Zik is shown saying: "I baptise thee into the holy order of Nigerian Nationalism".[14]

The situation in Benin City provides an instructive example of the intricacies surrounding the creation of modern political parties amid a tradition of secret society activity. Benin was a historically important town with its own ruler, known as the Oba. The people of Benin have a historic relationship with the Yoruba but are considered to form a separate ethnic group. After the promulgation of the 1951 constitution that provided an elected government for Nigeria's three Regions, Benin City politicians tended to resent the fact that the whole of the Western Region, in which their own city was situated, was dominated by the Yoruba, especially Awolowo's Action Group.

In struggles of this nature, an important role was played by the Ogboni society, which before colonial times had wielded power all over Western Nigeria. The Ogboni society was an institution of long standing in each of the city-states that were common throughout the region. Many of the most senior men in each community joined the Society locally, providing a counterweight to the power of kings and chiefs. After 1914 there were in fact two rival Ogboni societies in Western Nigeria, as some Christian members, disturbed by elements of Ogboni ritual that they thought unchristian, founded an offshoot known as the Reformed Ogboni Fraternity in an attempt to reconcile the Ogboni tradition with Christianity.[15] Being outside the control of the colonial administration, Ogboni, like other secret societies, was viewed with suspicion by British officials.

By the mid-twentieth century, the Ogboni society in Benin City "dominated the life of the province", according to the British Resident there. He noted how the membership of so many influential individuals in the area around Benin City made it difficult to operate an impartial system of justice. "So many people had committed one crime or another that it was a simple matter for the Fraternity to take up the crime committed by somebody who did not belong and to ignore the crime committed by a member", he wrote.[16] The leader of the town-chiefs of Benin City, Gaius Obaseki, was also the leader of the local branch of the Reformed Ogboni Fraternity. Furthermore, there were still other secret societies in Benin City. The City's traditional ruler, the Oba, had founded his own society, called the Aruosa church, with a view to propagating the traditional religion of the area,[17] and in 1944 an ambitious politician, Humphrey Omo-Osagie, founded yet another secret society, called Owegbe, after he had gathered a number of healers to supply him with medicine to help him win a libel case in the courts, although it is also said that Omo-Osagie may have developed from an existing cult. The Owegbe society had its headquarters in Benin City and was run by a Divisional Executive Committee headed by Omo-Osagie himself. Below this were individual branches, each associated with a shrine, mimicking the traditional hierarchy of the Benin kingship. Owegbe leaders made use of shrine initiations, oaths, and juju medicine.[18]

In other words, at the very time when nationalist political parties were appearing in Nigeria, Benin City contained at least four powerful secret societies vying for influence. All four of them claimed to represent tradition in some sense. According to a local informant, 90 per cent of members of the Benin Native Administration were members of one or other Ogboni society alone.[19]

Further complexity arose from the fact that after the election of 1951, the government of the Western Region was dominated by the Action Group, the political party run by Obafemi Awolowo and his associates. As the Action Group sought local allies in Benin City to boost its authority throughout the Western Region, it recruited among members of the various secret societies in the City. The situation was well summarised by Richard Sklar, the American author of a book on Nigerian political parties. He wrote:[20]

> By 1950 *Ogbonism* had become synonymous with oppression. Moreover the people of Benin identified it with the bugbear of Yoruba domination and their anxieties mounted in 1951 when the principal Ogboni leaders affiliated with the Action Group, a new political party under Yoruba control. Meanwhile, non-Ogbonis formed a popular party, known as the *Otu Edo* (Benin Community), dedicated to defend tradition and the sacred institution of *Oba*-ship (kingship) against the alleged encroachment of usurpers. In 1951 the popular party swept the Ogbonis from office in local government elections, and defeated them soundly in contests for the Regional House of Assembly.

Translated into English, Otu Edu meant simply "Citizens of Edo" (an alternative name for Benin). The leading figure in Otu Edu was Humphrey Omo-Osagie, who thus dominated not just one, but two secret societies. Members of Otu Edo claimed that their organisation represented all the indigenous tax-payers of Benin City, together with women and children. Members of other ethnic groups or of any secret cult deemed to be "against national progress", or "their satellites", as well as Europeans, were forbidden from joining. "The Otu Edu is therefore not a Union but the Benin body politic", its leaders claimed.[21] During the 1951 elections, in its effort to escape the Regional hegemony of the Yoruba-controlled Action Group, Otu Edu allied with Nnamdi Azikiwe's NCNC. The subsequent Otu Edu/NCNC electoral victory sparked a wave of anti-Ogboni violence in the area.[22] In 1959, the Action Group was to take revenge on the Owegbe society in Benin City by officially banning it.

The creation of neo-traditional initiation societies occurred not only in the political realm, but also at Nigeria's premier seat of learning, University College in Ibadan, which conferred University of London degrees. In 1952[23] (or, in some accounts, 1953), a group of seven students led by the future Nobel laureate Wole Soyinka established their own mock-secret society, known as the Pyrates Confraternity. It was partly a student jape, requiring members to dress up as pirates, Long John Silver-style. But there was also a more serious purpose, as the students saw themselves as advocates of the Nigerianisation of their institution, which tended to ape Oxford and Cambridge rituals.[24] They aimed to galvanise the fusty, Oxbridge-style atmosphere of what remained for some twelve years Nigeria's only university and to lobby for a more radical university politics generally. According to a later analyst, they aspired to "a social liberating role", and represented "an attempt to create a better society".[25]

Historians have largely neglected the role of secret societies, whether traditional, quasi-traditional or recent inventions, in modern times. There are several reasons for this. No doubt the very secrecy of these institutions causes them to make scant appearance in official archives, but that is probably not the main reason. More important is that many of the most influential academic writers on Nigerian nationalist politics in the mid-twentieth century simply assumed that secret societies were an archaic feature of Nigerian life that would disappear as the country developed. Nigerian intellectuals and politicians themselves were very sensitive to any suggestion of involvement in practices that could be considered primitive or uncivilised and preferred to remain discreet on the subject.

Nationalism and corruption

In 1944, a US consular official who toured Nigeria in company with a new governor making his introductory round was impressed above all with the immense size of the country and its lack of development. The American estimated that perhaps one million people were literate out of a total population of twenty million. Of the still smaller number of educated people, he made an interesting observation. "Several thousands of these think that early self-government is desirable", Consul Lynch wrote, but he continued: "I have formed the opinion that not twenty of the Africans I have met holding these views are sincere, and that to the majority self-government offers simply an unparalled [sic] opportunity for self-advancement. Personal gain seems to be the controlling motive and they have not developed that sense of responsibility towards their own people which, after all, must be the first qualification for self-government."[26]

This perception was compatible with the evidence of growing corruption in the administration of government.[27] On the whole the

British administration was remarkably free of individual corruption despite occasional cases of dishonesty. "In its early days the Civil Service was almost immune from *awuf*", wrote a later Nigerian, using a local word for bribery. "British officials…who manned the key posts saw to it that *awuf* was reduced to the barest minimum. As the British officials were gradually replaced by Nigerians, the incidence of *awuf* increased."[28] The issue attracted increasing comment as Nigerian officials began to occupy more senior positions in the federal civil service. In 1946, a senior British official wrote in a circular letter that the government was "appalled" at the extent of corruption and bribery "throughout the African Civil Service.…It appears to permeate practically every branch and seems to be rapidly undermining the activities of Government".[29] Another circular letter distributed to all government departments five years later referred to "the disturbing increase in the number of cases of fraud and irregularity", which the writer attributed to the fact that senior staff were preoccupied with new duties associated with "the accelerated pace of development", so that they were unable to exercise their supervisory role fully.[30]

It may be thought that such accusations stemmed from a sense of superiority on the part of British officials, or even from crude racism, but similar statements were often made by Nigerians themselves. In 1950, the Northern politician Abubakar Tafawa Balewa caused a sensation by referring to "the twin curses of bribery and corruption which pervade every rank and department"[31] of government. A later Nigerian writer noted: "When the British colonialists brought the public service apparatus, it did not take much time before Nigerians successfully prostituted these agencies and negated the ideal of service for its own sake into service for what I can get for myself".[32] As a new generation of politicians emerged in control of the governments of Nigeria's three Regions, commentators both Nigerian and foreign noted how deeply ingrained corruption and bribery were. These became favourite themes of the novelists and writers that Nigeria began to produce in abundance, perhaps because bribery and corruption were rooted in social networks and moral conventions familiar to everyone.

Formal punishment by means of the justice system and prison sentences was ineffective in combatting corruption since it lacked legitimacy. The Commissioner of Prisons who reported on crime and punishment in 1944, Alexander Patterson, reported that the stigma of having been in prison depended largely on the offence concerned. Dishonour was attached to those who had stolen food or cattle, especially in their own village,[33] indicating that Nigerians regarded theft as a serious crime. However, if an offender "has cheated the Government, or swindled some business concern, he will probably be accorded the approbation and welcome due to a David who has dealt faithfully with Goliath", Patterson wrote.[34] Respect for the system of criminal justice was not helped by the social composition of the police force, as in southwestern Nigeria the British had made a habit during the early years of colonial rule of recruiting ex-slaves to both the police and the military. Constables from such a background were of low status and, perhaps by way of compensation, were seen to behave with conspicuous arrogance.[35] Policing in the north of the country was perhaps more straightforward, as Indirect Rule there simply reinforced existing traditions of justice. Sir Ahmadu Bello, a towering figure in Northern politics, recalled how in his youth law was enforced not by any police force but by village and district heads. When he was himself a district head in the 1930s, he recalled, "his boys" used to catch suspected wrongdoers. They would pass the offender to the police and report the matter to their superiors only later. Even after Independence there was only one federal police officer in the whole of Katsina Province, and just 127 in Sokoto Province.[36] Many Nigerians, believing in the legitimacy of traditional ways of delivering justice, continued discreetly with familiar practices that were illegal under colonial law. This could involve serious offence. Customary acts that appeared to local elders as duties "under our rule have become serious and even capital crimes", Margery Perham noted.[37]

When professional politicians made their appearance in Nigeria, it was often hard to distinguish their personal financial ambitions from their political goals. This was certainly the case with "Zik" Azikiwe, who famously swore an oath to become rich on New Year's Eve in 1937, more or less at the start of his political career. He repeated the oath in a letter he wrote on 21 November 1943.[38] An astute critic discerned in the autobiographies of both Zik and his great rival, Awolowo, a complete identification of their own personal prosperity with that of the nation.[39] The foremost political leader in the North of the country was of a different stamp but equally given to personal enrichment. This was Sir Ahmadu Bello, Sardauna of Sokoto and great-great-grandson of Usman dan Fodio, the man who had proclaimed a holy war in the Sahel at the beginning of the nineteenth century and who had established the Sokoto caliphate. His political aim was to maintain the Fulani aristocracy founded by his ancestor. So conscious was Bello of his pedigree that even Britain's Queen Elizabeth was said to consider him a prima donna. "When he was touring villages", it was noted, "he used to have his flowing robes stuffed with banknotes which he then distributed among those whom he judged be deserving a special reward". This munificence "in his mind, took the place of political campaigning".[40] One interpretation was that in terms of morality Bello "was no doubt better than the completely unprincipled kleptocrats of the South".[41] Bello saw himself as the true leader of Nigeria, whose unity would help him achieve a position of influence in the Muslim world, the main focus of his attention in international affairs. In his distribution of patrimonial wealth he was in accordance with an established tradition whereby the rulers of Northern Nigeria were expected to distribute largesse to their subjects. Many Southern politicians could not claim to come from any such aristocratic tradition. They were simply men on the make.

The aspiration to become rich was not just a personal trait of Nigeria's three most prominent politicians, Bello, Awolowo and Azikiwe, nor even of the political class as a whole, but a general tendency throughout society. As we have seen, colonial rule and mission education had created new social space, although more in Southern Nigeria than in the conservative, hierarchical and tightly controlled societies of the North. Among the novel arrangements introduced by the British were the Native Administrations, run according to fixed rules, British-style schools and Christian missions. These were all associated with new economic possibilities, and some people thought that it was precisely these new opportunities for acquiring wealth and consumer goods that were the cause of the corruption that was so apparent. A Nigerian university lecturer wrote that "it was neither the science, philosophy nor even religion of the West which most impressed the natives: it was the material wealth, together with the power that was associated with it, which caught the imagination".[42]

Writers both Nigerian and British identified a range of social changes that encouraged the extraordinary cupidity that was the hallmark of

Nigerian politicians from the outset but that also permeated those parts of society that were in touch with the new opportunities. Education is said to have reduced the fear of divine punishment underpinning traditional moral beliefs. Other significant social changes were said to be the creation of a class of *nouveaux riches* holders of public office without any ethos of public responsibility; the separation of traditions of gift-giving from their original context; the growth of cities; and new ways of articulating concepts of honour that were deeply ingrained.[43] The general colonial tendency to denigrate or undermine African customs also stimulated corruption in society at large.[44] It was in ways like these that colonial rule opened up vast new spaces beyond the lineage or extended family,[45] sometimes by design but more often inadvertently.

All of these trends, and others, tended to make the young less respectful of their elders, in societies where respect for age was deeply rooted, and this tendency was increased by the rapid population growth in evidence from the mid-twentieth century, disturbing the balance between generations. Igboland, always a densely populated area dependent on intensive farming to support itself, saw its population density rise from some 236 people per square mile in 1929 to as many as a thousand per square mile in parts of Igboland in the 1940s.[46] From perhaps 24 million people in 1945,[47] Nigeria's population has grown to over 180 million today—an astonishing 750 per cent in just seventy years. The influx of youth to the cities was related to the overpopulation of certain rural areas, notably in Igboland, where people without access to land could not easily migrate to other parts of the country. Here Indirect Rule played a crucial role, as Native Authorities that were deemed to represent an authentic local population under its natural leaders, with the support of the central government, were loath to admit immigrants from other parts of the country, thus limiting the choices of Igbo migrants desperate to leave their own home area. Similar situations existed within other major ethnic groups that were now emerging as political blocs, for example in the Yoruba city of Ibadan, where the Native Administration was ill disposed to incomers from the Ijebu sub-group of the Yoruba.[48]

In the south of the country especially, where modern education was most widespread, the cities were seeing the emergence of a stratum of partially educated but unemployed youth who were often said to be responsible for a rising incidence of crime. The reasons invoked included the effects of school education, which in Southern Nigeria produced a nationalist constituency in the form of the "Standard VI boys", for whom there was no equivalent in the North.[49] They were joined by families or individuals moving from rural areas. There was an issue of vagrancy in all the main urban areas of Nigeria by the middle of the twentieth century. At the same time, the towns exerted a strong cultural attraction, since for young people especially "anything seems better than the tight discipline of the family and the dreary monotony of village life in the bush".[50] Traditional social life, suffused with "an elaborate and steady equilibration of rights, duties and loyalties, sanctified by usage and religion"[51] was giving way to a new climate in the towns and cities especially. These were home to young men who were disposed to violence, not in the form of the gangsterism that was producing the very concept of organised crime in the United States, but in "a kind of diffuse, unregulated scramble stemming from the fluidity of the social structures and the absence of efficient organisation".[52]

The problem of unemployed youth was compounded by the radical expansion of education in the Western Region during the very last days of colonial rule, which in December 1960 delivered a first cohort of school graduates consisting of some 200,000 boys and girls, compared to 60,000 in the previous year.[53] Within three years, according to the Regional Minister of Finance, universal primary education was producing 180,000 school graduates per year in the Western Region alone, of whom 100,000 were unemployed.[54]

Literacy in English opened up a means to debate a prosperity that was without precedent, modest though it was by later standards, and the spread of a new spirit of acquisitiveness. The town of Onitsha, the largest market-place in West Africa, was the home of a thriving publishing industry that specialised in producing pamphlets that were sold at affordable prices, some of which discussed the emerging issue of corruption. A Nigerian pamphleteer and anti-corruption campaigner named Eyo A. Akak was prophetic in denouncing the dangers of the materialism brought about by development as early as 1952. "Only serious thinking men of the community can realise the great disaster ahead of us", he warned.[55] Akak was the honorary secretary of the

Ibadan branch of the Nigerian League of Bribe Scorners, an anti-corruption organisation that began at an elite school in Lagos in 1952, the same year that Akak published his pamphlet on bribery and corruption. Even at this relatively early date, Akak believed that "bribery with its allied corruption is deeply planted in this country."[56] He related in a series of personal experiences and anecdotes that Europeans were certainly not innocent of this practice. In fact, he placed the prime responsibility for the growth of bribery in his country on expatriates not only from Britain but also from India and elsewhere, on the grounds that they had brought their bad habits with them to Africa. He compared Nigeria to the biblical Israel, originally uncorrupt, in Akak's reading, but debauched by the commercial system introduced by King Ahab. He maintained that the story of Israel was replicated in his own time by the abolition of the slave trade, the rise of "legitimate" trade and the monetisation of the economy. These developments were causing Nigerians to abandon farming in favour of trade because this gave easier access to money, just as the Israelites were said to have done. The result was the stimulation of people's material ambitions. He distinguished this new materialism from the older tradition of gift-giving to the wealthy, which, he thought, was "no bribery at all", because "it is the natural culture of the Africans to be generous and respectful".[57] Gift exchange had been replaced by a crass desire to consume. "Every ex-serviceman," he noted *à propos* of the considerable number of World War Two veterans, "wants to own a Raleigh bicycle before he returns to his village".[58] Senior civil servants aspired to own a car. Interestingly, Akak thought that women were making a specific contribution to the rise of materialism and the corruption of society because they were more inclined to seek out wealthy men as marriage partners or boyfriends.

Clear discrepancies of wealth, as some people gained access to newly available consumer goods through receipt of bureaucratic salaries or through forms of commerce made possible by the colonial economy, were creating new perceptions of relative poverty that were not rooted in traditional cosmologies. The growing influence of Christianity and Islam tended to dissolve traditional morality, the former by teaching that God forgives all, the latter by creating an impression that ritual correctness is the highest goal in religious practice.[59]

Political parties and corruption

The Regional elections of 1951 that marked a breakthrough of Nigerian politicians into higher levels of government were reported to be "marked by great corruption".[60] Once they were installed in government, elected politicians were almost entirely consumed with "the control over men and resources"[61] rather than any more ideological projects. Tenure of public office brought them influence over trade and production at a time when many of the big British companies that before the War had traded in commodities, where the big profits were, were leaving the local trade in cocoa, palm oil and groundnuts to Nigerians and to the Lebanese who had established themselves as shop-keepers and petty traders during the earlier colonial period. The big companies instead began to concentrate on importing more expensive products, semi-manufactures, machines and raw materials.[62]

Public office also put politicians in a position where they could use government resources for their own private or party purposes. Among the main cash-cows were the produce marketing boards that were officially intended to stabilise the prices of agricultural commodities. In 1954, the produce marketing boards were reorganised on a Regional basis, which meant that the politicians who ran government at that level could use the boards' resources to pay for schools or other government programmes but also to fund their own political parties, or simply for private interests.[63] "A Nigerian oligarchy is thus placed in a position to run the boards and to appoint as buying agents the major British firms and African-owned companies, in which politicians have an interest", noted one Nigerian commentator.[64] This situation existed in all parts of the country. The most blatant government corruption was in the Eastern and Western Regions. At the start of 1956 two Eastern Region ministers and one federal minister from Azikiwe's NCNC party were forced to resign on that account.[65] According to a top secret memorandum written by a British official, corruption in the Eastern Region was "rife". While life in the North often seemed to the British to be marked by greater decorum and restraint than in the South, the Northern Region too had its share of corruption within the public administration, especially "in Government service, in the Railway administration and in the Department of Post and Telegraphs", where it was "closely organised".[66]

The abuse of government funds in the Eastern Region was so flagrant that, in 1955, the government in Lagos felt obliged to take action, setting up an official tribunal that began work the following year. Headed by Sir Stafford Foster-Sutton, Chief Justice of Nigeria, the main target of its inquiries was "Zik" Azikiwe, then Premier of the Eastern Region, on account of his involvement in the affairs of African Continental Bank, an institution that he had created and continued to dominate. Under the code of conduct for ministers, a government officer was required to relinquish his holdings in private business on assuming public office. But, according to the Secretary for the Colonies in Westminster, during 1955 £877,000 of public money was invested in the Bank, and other large sums deposited with it, out of Marketing Board funds made available to the Finance Corporation established by the Eastern Region government.[67] The African Continental Bank, of which Azikiwe was the main shareholder, had also made low-interest loans to the Zik Group of Companies. In other words Azikiwe was using his control of the Regional government to prop up his own bank and his own businesses.

The Foster-Sutton tribunal found that Zik did not sever his connections to the African Continental Bank when he became a minister but continued to use his influence to further the interests of ACB while he was in government. However, at least one serious analyst has argued that Azikiwe did no more than to follow "normal acceptable procedures for European-owned banks" and found plausible Zik's claim that he was the victim of an effort by British banks to stymie the emergence of Nigerian competitors.[68] Faced with the prospect of giving testimony to Foster-Sutton, Zik was said to have sworn an oath at a traditional shrine with a key member of his cabinet, Eastern Region Finance Minister Mbonu Ojike, to protect one another. The fact that Zik lied under oath at the official enquiry indicates the greater importance he attached to an oath sworn at a shrine than one sworn on the Bible before a judicial hearing.

There can be no doubt that the combination of public office and private interest of the type laid bare by the Foster-Sutton tribunal was widespread in Nigeria's new political parties. Nigeria's indigenous banking sector was weak and open to abuse. Of the couple of dozen Nigerian banks operating by the 1950s, many suffered from poor management and under-capitalisation and there were many allegations of fraud. Many were excessively reliant on political connections. One "even had a full set of forged books" alongside the ones it showed to inspectors.[69] No fewer than sixteen indigenous banks failed in 1954 while the government took no action to assist them.[70] In the Western Region also similar practices were in operation. In 1953, the police received information from a whistleblower that confirmed their suspicions of abuses inside the National Bank of Nigeria, an institution in which the Western Regional Production Development Board and the Cocoa Marketing Board had deposited large amounts. The Bank's directors were leading members of the Action Group, and they acted in collusion with its leader, Chief Awolowo. Awolowo and his colleagues were alleged to have obliged senior staff members to swear an oath of political allegiance.[71] After Independence, a proper commission of inquiry was launched into the administration of the Western Region and confirmed the situation remained unchanged, as the Action Group used its control of the Region and of the National Bank of Nigeria to use government funds for the benefit of itself and its own directors.[72]

By the time of Independence, politics in general and tenure of public office most specifically had become the key site for self-advancement insofar as "the fortunes of businesses, communities and households in Nigeria hinged on governmental favour and political influence".[73] One academic noted that "Nearly all businessmen were necessarily in politics, because the state had become the main source of both finance and contracts; and nearly all politicians were in business."[74] Nigeria's economic life became politicised not so much through the imposition of colonial rule as the manner of its withdrawal.

4

THE NATIONAL CAKE

Nigeria's last election of colonial times took place at the end of 1959, for members of the federal parliament. The NPC, the party of the emirs, emerged with the greatest number of seats. The people who ran the North now had the loudest voice at the federal centre as well.

An American academic who wrote on Nigeria in the early years of Independence described the construction of the Northern Region as "one of the greatest acts of gerrymandering in history".[1] There are rumours that British officials rigged the pre-Independence elections so as to ensure that the federal government was under safe management. In recent years the most direct allegations of ballot-rigging have come from a former British official, Harold Smith (1927–2011), who served from 1955 to 1960 in the labour department of Nigeria's federal government. In the last years of his life, Smith made an extraordinary series of allegations about official malpractice. "I was chosen by his Excellency the Governor General, Sir James Robertson, to spearhead a covert operation to interfere with the elections," he claimed,[2] actually in reference not to the 1959 elections but to an earlier election in the Western Region. These allegations were widely broadcast and caused a sensation in the Nigerian press. They are, though, incoherent and unproven. Given Smith's quite lowly status in the colonial government, they are also highly unlikely. They have been expertly demolished by the Nigerian academics Alkasum Abba[3] and Peregrino Brimah.[4]

British officials were certainly pleased with the Northern influence on the new state of Nigeria.[5] The NPC did not have the type of argumentative lawyers and demagogues that were found in the NCNC and the Action Group. The Northern elite was aristocratic, conservative and Anglophile, and could be relied upon not to allow an independent Nigeria to make alliances with Communist powers or to indulge in a mindless populism. Over decades, British officials, themselves coming from a country in which a hierarchy of social classes was topped by a monarchy, had developed a romantic attachment to a region where they had privileged access to an aristocracy with which they could discuss the finer points of history and Islamic theology.[6]

British officials in the North, horse-riding and Hausa-speaking, liked to think of themselves as a finer breed than their colleagues in the South, whom they despised as desk-bound functionaries who took their first gin-and-tonic of the evening a good thirty minutes too early. Many British expatriates felt no such sympathy for the people of the Niger Delta region especially. Rather, in the words of Margery Perham, they felt a "sense of revulsion more extreme here than in any other part of British Africa".[7] The reason for this dislike seems to have stemmed from a combination of customs deemed by the British to be barbaric, a lack of stable political hierarchies, and a hot and unhealthy climate.

This is ironic because it was at Oloibiri in the Niger Delta that oil was discovered in 1956 by a consortium of the Shell and BP companies following half a century of exploration. The first oil was pumped two years later. At that time, Shell-BP was the only oil company licenced to work in Nigeria. After Independence in 1960, exploration rights in areas adjoining the Niger Delta were sold to other foreign companies. By 1963 it was being said that Nigeria's oil reserves were "greater than Kuwait".[8] Oil was soon to become the mainstay of the Nigerian economy and the main source of income of the Nigerian state.

Independence

The new federal government was formed by a coalition of the NPC and Azikiwe's NCNC, the first dominant in the Northern Region, the other controlling the Eastern Region. The Action Group, which governed the West, formed the main opposition. The existence of three Regional governments created the logic of an eternal triangle at the national level, with two of the three parties being required to form a coalition to govern at the centre. Each of the three major parties continued to dominate its home Region, as during the last years of colonial rule.

Politicians paid no more than lip-service to the ideal of national unity, devoting their real energies to cultivating ethnic constituencies within each of the three Regions. "Ruling Nigeria became, for them, not nation-building but the control of Federal power and therefore the resources of the nation. Armed with that power, the incumbents could then seize a disproportionate share of the nation's resources for the benefit of their Regions or ethnic groups", wrote Ken Saro-Wiwa,[9] later to become famous when he was executed after incurring the displeasure of a military government. This pattern has recurred throughout Nigeria's subsequent history. Using a metaphor that was already in wide use, Saro-Wiwa remarked that "the nation was seen as a 'cake' that had already been baked", and that the politicians were concerned to cut into slices.[10] A US academic similarly observed a short time after Independence that "[a] pattern is already discernible. Unscrupulous but skilled politicians, having been lifted into positions of influence through the electoral processes, seek to exploit the newly gained positions of strength for personal advantage".[11] The federal Prime Minister, Abubakar Tafawa Balewa, was one of the few politicians widely regarded as honest. The British High Commissioner to Nigeria thought that Prime Minister Balewa had had "some very naive illusions about politics at the time of Independence".[12] However, Balewa was evidently aware of the situation, as he told the same British diplomat in 1963 that "he was deeply disillusioned by the venality and self-seeking of most of his Ministers and by the fact that most of their activity, actions and decisions were based not on what was best for Nigeria but on what was best for them".[13]

An American diplomat described the nature of corruption among politicians with more nuance by comparing it to what sometimes took place in the United States itself. "A Nigerian politician", the American wrote, "is expected to support worthy causes in his district, to help his constituents with jobs and finance, and to be always good for a touch. He is likely to hold an influential position in his clan union, and to contribute to its treasury. He needs a force of organisers, ward heelers, and thugs to perform his political errands. In short, he operates in much the same fashion as the old-fashioned American political boss".[14]

The heart of power was situated in the three Regional governments whose capitals were at Ibadan, Enugu and Kaduna rather than in Lagos. Political corruption was rife in all three Regions. In regard to the North, Mallam Liman Ciroma, described by a US consul as "one of the abler and more articulate of the Northern career civil servants", stated that "the Northern Nigeria's Marketing Board's loans to the Licensed Buying Agents was a source of great corruption".[15] The Region was described by one of Nigeria's leading economists as having "a highly complex system of exactions," which were "quite often a lure to corruption and speculation".[16] In the Western Region, an official commission of enquiry in 1962 found overwhelming evidence of financial misconduct by the Action Group to rival that exposed earlier in regard to the East.[17] This finding facilitated a political rebellion against Action Group rule of the Western Region led by a senior politician, Chief S.L. Akintola, who set up his own splinter-party known as the Nigerian National Democratic Party (NNDP) and took over the government of the Region. As part of the reaction against the former Action Group government, a British official named McCall and a commissioner from the NCNC party were tasked with forming a caretaker administration in one part of the Western Region, the Mid-West division, based in Benin City. On taking up their task, "both the Commissioner and McCall were astonished at the extent of the corruption in the mid-West, which pervades every level of society.... The customary Court judges, who are all Action Group members, have put politics before legality in their judgements. As a result the people are sick of politicians, whatever their party affiliations".[18] However, the new administration in the Western Region led by Chief Akintola was no better in this regard than Awolowo's Action Group. There was a corrupt relationship between Akintola and a prominent British company, the Leventis Group. Akintola was said to have "a close personal friendship" with C.P. Leventis. The Premier's daughter, Omodele, was employed by the Leventis company as a public relations officer. The Leventis brothers who ran the group were "becoming more and more deeply involved in the finances of Western Nigeria, as they have elsewhere in English-speaking West Africa",[19] noted a US official. Similar reports came from the East, where the Governor of the Region (by the 1960s, a Nigerian) complained of corruption on the part of the Regional government and the wasting of money on "frivolities", such as new official residences.[20]

In their 1963 discussion on corruption in government, both the British High Commissioner and Prime Minister Balewa agreed that party-funding was at the heart of the issue.[21] In similar vein, the Western Region Minister of Finance told the US Ambassador in 1963 that the cost of political parties was too high, and he said that Prime Minister Balewa was interested in negotiating some form of voluntary capping of costs. Ambassador Palmer was sceptical, as the new generation of politicians was very extravagant. He referred to the "wild-eyed irresponsibility of approach" of some of them.[22]

Prime Minister Balewa was not strong enough to disrupt the system that was emerging even before Independence. Since the federal government was weak, and beholden to the great Regional barons, it became a pump for redistributing money to those same political barons. A British civil servant who chaired an enquiry—which went unpublished on grounds of sensitivity—into the Kano Native Authority referred to an "unholy (i.e. corrupt) trio" of federal ministers who were key to the system. He named them as Festus Okotie-Eboh, the Minister of Finance, Defence Minister Muhammadu Ribadu and the Minister of Works, Inua Wada, the latter being the son-in-law of the Emir of Kano who was forced to resign in March 1963 on account of corruption.[23] All three were politicians with their own local power-base but were beholden to the great political barons who ran the Regions. Ribadu and Wada ran ministries with large budgets, making it relatively easy for them to divert monies into other accounts.

The most important of the "unholy trio" of corrupt federal ministers was surely Finance Minister Okotie-Eboh, who emerged as the key figure in the vast system of political corruption that became apparent. Originally one of Zik's protégés, Okotie-Eboh was appointed as National Treasurer of the NCNC party in 1954 and three years later became the Minister of Finance of the federal government that served Nigeria's colonial administration. From then on, Okotie-Eboh combined the two posts of party treasurer and national finance chief. An American diplomat described Okotie-Eboh as "an inveterate ten-percenter...a super-salesman who attracted much foreign investment to his country and was spurred to do so because he operated on a straight commission basis," adding that the NCNC "also received a substantial portion of his 'take'."[24] However, the most revealing information concerning Okotie-Eboh's corruption was that he was "widely believed to be a 'bagman for the Sardauna', who profitted from his deals."[25] A Swedish businessman based in the North confirmed that Okotie-Eboh sent a monthly sum to the Sardauna,[26] Sir Ahmadu Bello, the grand Muslim aristocrat who regarded himself as the true leader of Nigeria. In other words, in his key role as finance minister Okotie-Eboh was embezzling funds that subsequently went to both the parties that composed the federal government, his own NCNC and also the NPC. Okotie-Eboh himself enjoyed living the high life. David Williams, the veteran editor of *West Africa* magazine, recalled seeing this legendary bag-man in his pomp "drinking liqueur brandy by the tumblerfull" with dozens of guests in attendance.[27]

The Polish-British sociologist Stanislav Andreski, who was working in Ibadan in the early 1960s, invented the term "kleptocracy" to describe the system of government he found in Nigeria. "The essence of kleptocracy", Andreski wrote, "is that the functioning of the organs of authority is determined by the mechanisms of supply and demand rather than the laws and regulations."[28] Even at this relatively early date, he believed, Nigeria was "the most perfect example of kleptocracy", since "power itself rested upon the ability to bribe".[29]

Andreski described Festus Okotie-Eboh as an "arch kleptocrat".[30] Indeed, Okotie-Eboh was perhaps the single most prominent individual involved in creating the system of government corruption in the years immediately before and after Nigerian Independence. Now half-forgotten, he deserves to be remembered as the master-builder of what in time was to become one of the world's most astonishing examples of state corruption.

A glimpse into the implications of this system for individual candidates for election to public office is provided by the example of one politician whose sights were set on becoming deputy speaker of the Eastern Region House of Representatives. He was unsuccessful despite spending the then large sum of £7,800 on his election campaign.[31] Thwarted at the first attempt, the same person then went on to spend a further £12,000 to get a post on the Regional electoral commission,[32] meaning that he had now invested some £20,000 that he would need to claw back by using his new position. Bribery, noted the US consul who reported this case, "has played a significant—and even controlling—role" in many appointments in the Eastern Region.[33]

The expenditure of such large sums in order to obtain an official post turned public office into a type of prebend, a term borrowed from church history that was applied by a later political scientist[34] to designate public offices that, having been purchased, were then exploited in order to recoup the initial investment as well as to make further profits. Senior civil servants pressured their juniors for money in various ways, as a result of which those lower down the chain were obliged to do the same to others. Few of Nigeria's new politicians were much concerned with ideology or even with policy matters unless they could see a personal advantage in them. Politicians of this stamp were largely uninterested in the nature of the state they were conspiring to run. One of the Onitsha pamphleteers whose publications provide a window into popular opinions in Southern Nigeria at least thought that moral and intellectual qualities had ceased to exercise much appeal to Nigerians. What mattered instead, he thought, "is the number of persons they know and the number of persons who know them. This, they believe, is the passport to success".[35] "What emerges from this is a politics that does not know legitimacy or legality, only expediency",[36] one intellectual later explained.

According to the pamphleteer Eyo Akak, who showed great insight into the growing problem of corruption in the years before Independence, Native Administration was "the den from which I trace the origin of this evil".[37] The reason, he thought, was because the time-honoured custom of gift-giving had turned into the compulsory payment of bribes. One might add that the 1951 constitution had encouraged politicians to form rival ethnic and regional blocs as their political base. Mallam Liman Ciroma, a senior official of the Northern Region, the area in which Indirect Rule had had the most cogent logic, agreed with Akak's analysis on the fatal defects of Indirect Rule. Referring to his home Region, he told the US consul in Kaduna that "the British Colonial Government began it all when they intrenched [sic] the traditional rule in the Native Authorities".[38] It was from this system that parliamentarians and other senior office-holders had emerged. Ciroma was clear in stating that "politicians of all tribes had created and exacerbated tribal differences for political purposes".[39] In his experience, ordinary people were far more inclined to tolerance.

The fish rots from the head, as West Africans say.

The foreign contribution

According to that fine observer Stanislas Andreski, "The West African business class was developing well until independence", as might be expected in view of the region's long commercial tradition.[40] Thereafter, "illegal or semi-legal squeeze has caused the ruin of many small businessmen without political connections and too poor to afford adequate bribes; and [there is] a concentration of ownership of capital in the hands of the ruling cliques."[41]

However, it was not only the indigenous political class and newly-empowered Nigerian bureaucrats that were responsible for penalising business people without political connections and for introducing official corruption into the private sector. The first British High Commissioner to Nigeria wrote that he had "no doubt that foreign firms are largely to blame in this respect."[42] This situation too had roots in the last decade of colonial rule. As soon as Nigerian politicians began to acquire substantial power at Regional level, in the 1950s, foreign companies began courting them in the search for contracts. An early example was the Eastern Region's Minister of Finance, Mbonu Ojike, who in 1955 took a kickback for awarding contracts to an Italian firm, Borini Prono, for a construction project.[43] The connections between politicians and foreign businesses were made and nurtured in this environment. The atmosphere was rather frenetic, as many foreign businesses had little confidence in the long-term stability of the business climate, while "corruption and omnipresent politics"[44] could hardly be avoided. Yet there was so much money to be made in a young country with a growing population that "many new foreign firms [were] coming into Nigeria" regardless.[45]

The solution adopted by many companies to the problem of doing business in a market that was lucrative although marked by corruption and political instability was to find unofficial or even illegal ways to get their money out of the country while they could. Resident Lebanese and Indian traders who were uncomfortably aware that their foreign status could easily make them victims of such a politicised system did the same. A young American businessman who began working in Nigeria in 1962 discovered that foreign companies were systematically writing inflated invoices for goods that they were importing in order to justify exporting excessive sums abroad, thus expatriating their profits. "Most foreign-owned companies", he wrote, "were doing largely the same thing".[46] During the colonial period, the big trading companies as well as statutory corporations and government agencies had been used to separating their balances of international payments from those of their domestic economy, so for companies that had been doing business in Nigeria for many years already, it was not too difficult to adjust to the country's new sovereignty "as their earnings, payments and reserves were individually recorded outside Nigeria".[47] Apart from paying bribes and falsifying their paperwork, some foreign companies were also capable simply of cheating their Nigerian partners, such as a US company that secured a contract to build a textile plant in Sokoto Province, and then supplied equipment so sub-standard as to provoke a court action in New York.[48] This "unethical American promotor took the NRG [Northern Regional Government] to the cleaners for several hundred thousand pounds", a US official recorded.[49] However, such blatant dishonesty was not only on the part of foreigners, as there were also occasional accounts of simple fraud by Nigerian companies, such as a Lagos firm that in 1963 published advertisements offering to provide training in the USA in weaving, in return for payment of £114 per year. The training programme was simply non-existent.[50]

Other than the examples of Italian and US firms quoted in the preceding paragraphs, the archives contain documented cases of bribery in the securing of contracts by firms from other industrialised countries, including Britain, Germany, Israel and Sweden. Thus, in 1964 a British company offered a 10 per cent discount on a bulk sale of 600 motor-scooters to the NNDP (Nigerian National Democratic Party), the party that had split from the Action Group and that was now ruling the Western Region. One onlooker noted that "On NNDP purchases, however, the practice is to give a 10 per cent discount but to show only 7.5 per cent on the invoice. The remaining 2.5 per cent is kicked back, in cash, directly to the individual politician concerned".[51] This was actually a very modest percentage, as a leading civil servant later recalled that there were "people taking 5 per cent, 10 per cent".[52] Another senior official referred in a published article to a normal level of corruption on a contract of 10 per cent, which was said to be a "widely-held view".[53]

One of the most illuminating accounts of corruption in government contracting was given by a Swedish businessman, one A.A. Aklint, in an interview with an American diplomat who was doing research on what was known as the "dash" system—"dash" is a word used in pidgin English all along the West African coast to designate a small gift or tip given in the course of a business transaction. It derives from the Dutch word *dasje*, meaning a small strip of cloth, which indicates its origins in the far-off days when trade was often done by barter, typically with consumer goods and firearms being offered in return for slaves, when honour required a whole sequence of gift-giving between seller and buyer. Aklint freely admitted that he habitually bribed officials in the Northern Region, where he was based, in order to obtain contracts. He claimed that it was impossible to obtain contracts with either the Regional or federal government without bribing the appropriate minister. He said that kickbacks were usually between 3 and 6 per cent of a contract, but that one West German company—interestingly, one that has had remarkable success in obtaining government civil engineering contracts up to the present day—was prepared to go up to 10 per cent.[54] Another German company went as high as 11.5 per cent.[55] Aklint went on to describe how his company headquarters back home in Sweden regarded bribery "as a normal transaction in the firm's accounting system". He added that many of his business friends "felt that Nigeria was one of the most corrupt countries in Africa along with Liberia and Morocco".[56] The scale of kickbacks seems to have risen fast in the early years after Independence, as a senior engineer claimed in 1964 that a project in the Western Region that should have been priced at a mere £700,000 ended up costing £1.25 million. The extra £550,000 was described as "pure dash".[57] For most of the colonial period, bidding for government contracts in Nigeria had been dominated by British firms subject to British legal and ethical codes of conduct. As nationalist politicians took hold of the keys to the political kingdom, "all of these safeguards evaporated in some instances", while in other cases "only some" did.[58]

While politicians were the most obvious hubs of corruption, many ministers were reported to "derive their positions from association with individuals and groups not part of the formal structure",[59] who demanded their own cut of the bribes and kickbacks on offer. Even federal government ministers were beholden to unofficial power brokers who put them under pressure to embezzle the funds entrusted to them. One location of these hidden power brokers who were able to blackmail ministers was within the political parties themselves, as a result of which ministers who failed to provide money to the political parties to which they owed allegiance could be removed from office by the party, as various examples showed. One very senior civil servant, looking back many years later, claimed that the practice of skimming percentages off the top of contracts was the work of "two or three ministers in each political party, as fundraisers, mostly not putting their hands in the till."[60] This seems to be a very complacent view that reflects the tendency of old people to feel nostalgia when they think about the days of their youth. The contemporary evidence suggests that corruption was more widespread than this, and that party fundraisers normally managed to keep some of the booty for themselves.

The logic of corrupt payments came to determine who occupied which position, who was removed from office, and even what laws got passed. A senior judge respected for his integrity commented "that he had been close to Nigerian politics for enough years to know that when certain events occurred for which there was no other explanation, the answer would be found by determining 'whose pockets are being lined'".[61] Generally speaking, individuals of the greatest talent did not rise to the top in Nigeria's political system, with the result that "fortunes are being made by individuals commanding no more intelligence and no more skills than some modestly compensated civil servants nailed to a position of inferior rank and low responsibility."[62]

Traditional rulers also exerted pressure from behind the scenes. They and their supporters often regarded state politics as the arena of "social-revolutionary forces to be resisted and, if possible, destroyed—or at, least, subverted to forms more in keeping with traditional thoughts and practices".[63] Even more than in colonial times, traditional rulers, one analyst wrote, "regard as customary and entirely permissible what the modern legal system regards as criminal".[64] They could blithely use their influence to demand bribes from a government offi-cial or even from a minister whose family came from their area of authority on the grounds that this was the customary gift or tribute due to a chief. Sometimes traditional leaders stole money directly by means of a non-governmental organisation. A leading chief in the south of the country, the Olu of Warri, was accused of stealing £4,000 belonging to the Itsekiri Communal Lands Trust. The money was a rental payment by the National Bank of Nigeria to a body called the Socio-Cultural Corporation. The latter body was described by a US diplomat as "a type of funnel through which the funds of the Land Trust were piped to the pockets of its officers".[65]

The corruption of Nigeria's politics in the mid-twentieth century occurred at the very time when most of Africa was embarked on the process of decolonisation. The two processes of corruption and decolo-nisation were intimately related. As we have seen, business people from developed countries were looking for new markets and new commer-cial opportunities and were not slow to see Nigeria's potential. Many were quick to offer bribes to ministers who could sign government purchase orders. As a US academic wrote, "foreigners find [in bribery] the keys to the political kingdom that independence was to have granted to the Africans".[66] Ministers did not hesitate to demand kick-backs and bribes and proved themselves to be enthusiastic takers, mak-ing corruption a meeting of minds and a conjoining of interests.

The world's biggest companies reorganised themselves and revised their operating techniques in order to adjust to a world of sovereign states, creating in the process the multinationals of today. Inasmuch as this process was a reflection of a wider strategy, then a large part of the responsibility has to be attributed to the City of London. This is per-haps not what many people may think—London has a local govern-ment, like any other large city, but the City of London Corporation is something distinct from this, a strange mixture of mediaeval privilege and financial wizardry, "an ancient, semi-alien entity lodged inside the British nation state", often better known as the Square Mile by refer-ence to its small size.[67] This has been for over three centuries the physical location of many leading institutions of global finance.

City bankers and lawyers were quick to see that decolonisation would soon destroy a vital institution of the space in which they were accustomed to operate, namely the British empire. In 1950 the City of London acquired the status of an offshore centre, following a decision taken by Harold Wilson, president of the Board of Trade between 1947 and 1951, and later to be twice Britain's prime minister.[68] So important did the City's work with other offshore banking centres become that one may even argue that it was the most important single decision that Harold Wilson made in his entire political career, even though one of the least known. It meant that, even as the British Empire was disappearing from the political map, it was nonetheless able to perpetuate its existence in the financial world. London was even able to attract American banks that could avoid some domestic regulation by setting up branches in London, which became the centre of dollar loans made outside the United States in the so-called Eurodollar market.[69]

The bankers and lawyers who developed the City's new role discovered the legal possibilities offered by dependencies of the British Crown with archaic jurisdictions, such as the Channel Islands and the Isle of Man, and by colonies such as the Cayman Islands and Hong Kong. US business interests were already making similar use of the Republic of Liberia, whose sovereign status could be used to avoid various laws and regulations notably through the flag of convenience system for shipping, but also in the field of finance. For, whereas economic transactions take place in a specific place and at a specific time, they also take place in a legal sphere that is purely conceptual and that may be separated from these.[70] By exploiting the disconnection between the physical location of a transaction and the legal space where it is recorded, companies were able to exploit the gap between law and reality—just as Nigerian politicians were doing in their own way in their own country. The idea that a legal space exists, although it is immaterial, is strikingly similar to the widespread African view concerning the existence of a world of spirits. Both are equally immaterial, but both can become useful for the organisation of daily life when institutions are created for the management of these abstractions.

Although the offshore system has its origins in the nineteenth century, the period of decolonisation of the British empire was crucial to its rapid evolution. In just a couple of decades, the offshore world developed as a set of spatial enclaves that enable a rent or profit to be harvested from the world economy. By the early twenty-first century,

80 per cent of international financial transactions by value were taking place offshore and 20 per cent of private wealth was located in tax havens.[71] The offshore system had become the means for grand corruption to operate worldwide.

Within a few years of Independence, wealthy Nigerians were moving their money offshore to banks in secure destinations, in continental Europe, the UK and the USA especially. Politicians who took bribes from foreign firms became vulnerable to blackmail. As a result, "corruption, foreign influence, and domestic politics became hopelessly entangled".[72]

Pursuing this line of thought, Harold Smith, the colonial civil servant who claimed that Britain had rigged pre-Independence elections, also maintained that Britain encouraged corruption among Nigerians "the better to control or blackmail them".[73] There is little evidence to support such a claim. Actually, no such conspiracy theory is necessary to appreciate the role of foreign businesses in producing the distinctive brand of political corruption that emerged in Nigeria between 1951 and the early 1960s.

Corruption spreads to daily life

By the early 1960s, knowledge of the corruption that regularly occurred in relation to government contracts was "no longer confined to a few top civil servants and European advisors in Lagos and regional capitals. Instead, this information has begun seeping downwards to the small towns and villages of Nigeria", an American consul wrote.[74] A prominent clergyman thought that corruption had "eaten deep into the fabric of the society".[75] In regard to education, for example, the finance minister in the Western Region said that he was "searching for some method of cracking down on school principals who are illegally collecting fees for a variety of services to students", such as by requiring parents to pay for their children's school-books.[76] He reckoned that this racket was worth a million pounds sterling annually in the Western Region alone.[77] In Port Harcourt, students who had dropped out of rural schools claimed that they had been left with no other choice, as to get secondary schooling required paying not only the school fee but also a dash of £60 to the relevant local government councillor, "and only government officials, traders and landlords can afford these sums".[78] Regional governments were creating excessive numbers of local councils in order to satisfy local interests and opportunities for graft and to build a constituency for parliamentary candidates, who at election time could go to the local government councillors they had helped into office and call on their votes. Local councils gathered very little in the way of tax that made its way to the revenue authority. As a result, local government hardly functioned. What did emerge, however, was what one civil servant referred to as a sub-sub-sub-sub-tribalism as small people aspiring to election to local councils competed with one another.[79] This, plus the lack of an effective land register, caused local land disputes to become bitter. Asked what could be done, a senior judge responded that "any hoped-for change in Nigerian politics will depend less on constitutional reform than upon reform in the minds of men".[80]

In ways like these, political corruption spread from the official sphere into wider circles of daily life, making law-breaking a routine practice detached from any particular moral opprobrium for substantial numbers of people. The general public came to perceive politics as "a source of miraculous benefits".[81] Ministers' houses were often full of people who regarded them as public places.[82] After Obafemi Awolowo had been humiliated by the 1962 Coker tribunal that inquired into corruption in the Region over which he presided, he was arrested in the presence of a huge crowd of his supporters who, it was recalled, "wanted Awo to take a lot more of public funds for himself as he was their son and his money was their money".[83] Awolowo was a nationalist hero, and today he is a semi-divinity in Yorubaland.

Yet the public attitude was deeply ambivalent, since ministers known for corruption were also widely reviled. By 1963, the NCNC had become unpopular in the very Eastern Region that it governed, its heartland. Although the Regional government frequently condemned bribery and nepotism, it always did so "in very general terms". Meanwhile, it was "far from popular", particularly in the towns, "and a major reason is unquestionably the growing realisation that most of the members of the ruling clique are enriching themselves".[84] Voters all over Nigeria were torn between their wish to benefit from the largesse distributed by politicians by joining their patronage systems, and revulsion at the bribery concerned and the consequent inefficiencies in providing state services. Citizens who failed to play the political game according to the rules set by the dominant political party in each Region of Nigeria were liable to be punished. For example, a water distribution system was completed in Ondo in July 1965 but not put into operation in order to remind the people of Ondo of the consequences of supporting an opposition party.[85] In ways like this, political allegiance determined whether or not people were able to access public services.

Politicians had a second option more radical than cutting people off from public goods—violence. This was most clear in the Western Region, where the dissident faction led by Chief Akintola that broke away from the Action Group and called itself the NNDP took power in 1962. With the support of the NCNC party that dominated the Eastern Region and was seeking to gain a foothold in the West as well, the NNDP succeeded in deposing Awolowo and his Action Group. The immediate cause of the split between them was a squabble over control over the National Investment Properties Company Ltd., which, with £10 million in assets, was an important vehicle for party funding.[86] Akintola's NNDP Regional government relied steadily more on coercion to keep its grip. Within four years of its emergence it was said that it "had ceased to be a government and became simply a clique of politicians without support manipulating whatever security forces it could control, or create, in order to maintain itself in power".[87] NNDP leaders bribed the chiefs of the Regional police force to ensure their support. In October 1964, in preparation for Western Region elections the following year, the Regional Premier, Samuel Akintola, had the Alafin of Oyo install him in the regalia of a traditional war leader. During the ensuing election campaign his NNDP party hired thugs in the market-place for 10 shillings per day, plus bonuses. Some of the leading party thugs acquired a great sense of their own importance, and were described as living "like a semi-Minister".[88] The most active wing of the NNDP was the youth movement led by the deputy premier of the Western Region, Remilekun Fani-Kayode, known as "Fani Power". His goon squad became known as the Fani-Power Youth Movement.[89] Probably some 200–500 people were killed in politically related violence during the election campaign prior to the ballot in which the NNDP faced voters for the first time, in 1965.[90] The NNDP won.

It was not only the NNDP—there was election rigging and organised violence in every one of Nigeria's Regions, which numbered four after the creation in 1963 of a new Mid-West Region. The Action Group had its own thugs, as did the NCNC in the East,[91] whose party goons were controlled by Dr Mbanugo, chair of the NCNC's Eastern Working Committee.[92] In the North, there was said to be massive fraud in the December 1963 elections, with a confusion of relationships between district heads and candidates of the governing party.[93]

In fact, if anything, the scale of violence was greatest in the North, not in election campaigns but in rural struggles that generally had little impact on national politics. The deeper history of these struggles lay in the history of slave-raiding by the armies of the Northern emirs into the non-Muslim lands to their south, known to colonial officials as the Middle Belt to distinguish them from both the North proper and the South. Local opponents of the NPC, the vehicle by which the emirs continued to dominate the Northern Region, were harassed and attacked by the government "under the pretext of punishment for tax evasion".[94] There were at least two revolts among the Tiv people in 1960 and 1964, and the restoration of order in 1965 led to no less than 2,000 deaths.[95] But this was not a strategy free of risk, as the national army included a large number of soldiers from the Tiv and other peoples of the Middle Belt.

5

THE MEN IN UNIFORM

Festus Okotie-Eboh, Minister of Finance, national treasurer of the NCNC party and arch-kleptocrat,[1] had a premonition of his own death. During a casual chat with a British hotelier, the manager of one of his favourite Lagos watering-holes, he mentioned that his Indian astrologer had warned that his enemies were exceptionally active.[2]

His enemies were indeed plotting against him. Shortly after midnight on 16 January 1966, a group of soldiers raided Okotie-Eboh's Lagos home, took him from his bed, bundled him into a military vehicle and took him to the outskirts of the city. His abductors subjected him to a crude interrogation in which Okotie-Eboh is said to have confessed to "holding £15 million in Geneva, [and] to loaning 5 million of it to the government of Nigeria at 15 per cent interest".[3] Then they shot him dead.

Okotie-Eboh's murderers were young army officers who were executing a planned coup d'état. Although their move took everyone by surprise, rumours of an impending military putsch had been circulating for years, but the prime minister had never taken them seriously.[4] The mostly Igbo officers who took part in the coup were intent on killing those they held responsible for corruption in Nigeria. Okotie-Eboh was a prime target as he "typified...the epitome of greed of which Nigerian politicians were capable".[5] Among others the putschists murdered when they struck on the night of 15–16 January

79

1966 were Prime Minister Tafawa Balewa, the Northern Region Premier, Ahmadu Bello, and the Western Region Premier, Samuel Akintola. They spared the Eastern Region's Michael Okpara and the President of the Republic, Nnamdi Azikiwe, both Igbos. Since so many of the coup-plotters were Igbos, with family roots in the East, their lack of even-handedness immediately became a source of popular speculation and, very soon, of deep problems.

Coup and counter-coup

When a spokesman for the coup-makers made a public radio broadcast to announce the overthrow of the elected government, he informed Nigerians that the military had taken power "to bring to an end gangsterism and disorder, corruption and despotism". "You will no longer need to be ashamed to be Nigerians", he told his listeners.[6] He denounced "the political profiteers, the swindlers, the men in the high and low places that seek bribes and demand ten per cent".[7]

The young soldiers' spokesman was Major Patrick Nzeogwu, born in 1937 to an Igbo family living in Kaduna in Northern Nigeria. Growing up in the North, Nzeogwu had learned as a boy to speak Hausa as well as English and his Igbo mother-tongue. Joining the army after school, he made a successful career in the infantry, where he specialised in intelligence work. Like many Igbos, the Nzeogwu family was Roman Catholic. In his case, his Catholicism had instilled a puritan streak in him that caused him to admire General Franco, the ruthless dictator of Spain, another Catholic who had intervened in national politics.[8]

A Nigerian diplomat who was not one of the conspirators but who broadly supported the coup told a US diplomat that it had been years in the making. He said that "university graduates who had dedicated themselves 'in a secret society' to bring down the regime had been quietly entering the armed forces at the rank of colonel, major, etc". The man who made this claim, Alhaji Sani Kontagora, referred to the coup-plotters as "technicians" and "ideologists". He said that they were admirers of Kwame Nkrumah,[9] the Ghanaian president who had pioneered the cause of African freedom and had made such a name for himself as an apostle of pan-African unity. The fact that many of the coup-plotters were Igbo was largely a reflection of the fact that the

Igbo, having been exposed to Western education for longer than many other groups, had been recruited to the officer corps in disproportionate numbers.

A further reason for the coup given by Nzeogwu himself was the brutality of the regime they were targeting and especially the repression in the Middle Belt that had caused resentment among the many Tiv soldiers serving in the federal army. According to Nzeogwu, 10,000 Tiv had been killed since Independence, and a further 3,000 people in the Western Region when the NNDP party was campaigning for elections in 1965.[10] Both figures seem exaggerated, but there is no reason to doubt that the coup-makers were genuine in the indignation they felt about the violence casually perpetrated on the orders of politicians.

On 16 January, supreme power passed into the hands of a Supreme Military Council led by Major-General Johnson Aguiyi-Ironsi. As a senior officer Ironsi had been targetted for assassination by some of the coup-makers, but he had used his superior rank to wrest control of the Lagos area, apparently taking the initiative from the younger officers who were the real coup-plotters. Ironsi soon imposed himself on the situation. He located the most senior ranking state official who could be found, the president of the Senate, and made him formally surrender power to him, thus preserving both the continuity of rule and the army's hierarchy of ranks. Ironically, the Senate president who formally transmitted power from the civilian government to the military was none other than Nwafor Orizu, an early exponent of Four One Nine-style fraud.[11] Orizu was described by a US diplomat as "an ex-convict who did time for selling fraudulent scholarships to US schools".[12]

The junta's commitment to eliminate corruption threw foreign businesses into a panic. "Everybody is burning their little black books", it was reported,[13] as they tried to destroy incriminating files linking them to the corruption of the defunct regime. A source within the NCNC, the ruling party in the Eastern Region, revealed that party leaders were concerned about what the new military government might do when it discovered that the party owed £3.2 million to the African Continental Bank, itself owned by the Regional government. This was money that had been used to fund elections campaigns.[14] The new junta set up three committees of inquiry into corruption in parastatal companies that identified as culprits some Nigerians and also some British expatriates, whose names were known to diplomats.[15] Eventually twelve Regional ministers and seven other officials were found guilty of the theft of over £62,000, but so entrenched was the system of state corruption that this hardly even made a dent.[16] On the other hand, the installation of a new and inexperienced government offered an opportunity of sorts to astute business operators, such as the Shell-BP oil company, which used the occasion of the military coup in January 1966 to offer new terms to the incoming Ironsi regime.[17]

The American ambassador commented that corruption was "not a major cause for the underpaid, poorly-housed, insecure condition of the average Nigerian citizen", yet "the man on the street believes otherwise, and in any case does not want any former official to enjoy the fruits of his dishonesty".[18] While politicians were the most obvious targets of popular anger, Nigeria's civil servants had also drawn extraordinary benefits from the politics of the First Republic.[19] There were officially 54,989 civil servants working for the federal government in 1966[20] and a further 90,000 working for provincial governments.[21] The civil service was one of the main nurseries of politicians, as a partial analysis of the 312 people elected to the federal parliament in 1965 showed when it discovered that 44 per cent were government employees. The average age of the whole sample was forty-two years.[22]

Another act of the military government in 1966 was to launch an inquiry into the Owegbe cult in the Mid-West Region, which was reckoned to have tens of thousands of members subject to physical discipline and which aspired to control the Regional government.[23] "Partly out of necessity and partly out of appeal to the superstitious nature of many villagers, the 'Owegbe Cult' has reportedly devised an elaborate system of oaths and 'juju' shrines," a foreign diplomat reported.[24] Owegbe had continued to flourish despite having been banned by the Action Group government in 1959.

In his analysis of the situation immediately after the coup, the American ambassador cynically, but accurately, remarked that "investigations can only be permitted to go so far. A too-thorough delving into the affairs of too many people would uncover too many unpleasant facts. Key persons [in the National Military Government] could be implicated....Any investigation in Nigeria into corruption in public life must be limited by the very pervasiveness of the corruption."[25] This was certainly the case in regard to the Northern Region. "Corruption in some quarters in the North was comparable in degree to that which existed in other parts of Nigeria", the US consul in the Region noted, but he thought that the various committees of inquiry did not want to deal harshly with people belonging to the traditional ruling class that wielded such power in the Region.[26] Thus, when on 13 July 1966 the ruling junta issued a decree on corruption among public officials who had held office since 1960 that contained draconian provisions, including placing the onus of proof on the accused, this caused as much disquiet in the North as anywhere.

The fact that Ironsi was an Igbo, like so many of the coup-plotters, and that he failed to punish any of those who had overthrown the constitutional order, strengthened perceptions that this was an ethnic government. However, Ironsi's major blunder was Decree No. 34, announced in May 1966, by which he abolished Nigeria's Regions and announced the creation of a unitary state.[27] Some leading members of the Northern elite, perturbed by the murder of Ahmadu Bello and by the investigations into corruption,[28] organised a second coup on 28–29 July 1966. This resulted in Ironsi's murder and the replacement of his governing military council with a new military junta. Among the main organisers of the counter-coup were two senior officers, Murtala Muhammed[29] and the military governor of the North, Lieutenant-Colonel Hassan Katsina, who had been an intelligence officer in the Tiv area during the repression there in 1965. To finance the coup Katsina secured from a Kaduna bank £100,000 in funds belonging to the NPC that had been frozen pending official investigation. He probably used this money to pay the soldiers and thugs who carried out the coup and killed the leading Igbo officers of the Supreme Military Council.[30] This event was followed by a massive pogrom of Igbos living in the North, in which thousands were killed, with financing from what were described as Northern "feudalists".

Observers both Nigerian and foreign tended to emphasise that the deadly attacks on Igbos that took place in Northern cities in the middle of 1966 were motivated less by politics than by economic and cultural factors. "What they covet", said the British managing director of a regional newspaper, describing the rioters' motives, "is the primary perquisite of power in the Nth., viz., money".[31] Another foreign resident agreed that the violence "proceeds more from economic and cultural factors than political", noting that most Igbos living in the North actually voted for the ruling NPC.[32] The Igbo had their own tribal union and were felt to be too clannish. Many of the Igbos living in the North had been brought in to staff government offices, since the local supply of clerks and administrators literate in English was limited as a result of the restrictions maintained for so many years on missionary activity and Western education. As a result of their prominence in government bureaucracies, Igbos were said to have control of the railways and other parastatals. Yet while many Igbo families in the North were flourishing, they were not implicated in local circuits of reciprocity, preferring to send money to relatives in their home villages rather than spending it locally. By the same token, when they had business opportunities, they would summon family members from the East rather than fill the vacancy with local staff. The Igbo, a US diplomat was told, "does not bargain like a Northerner. Instead he arranges a fixed price with his fellow Ibo tradesmen." One Northern luminary thought that the Igbo communities in the North had angered the local population by their disrespect to traditional authority. He thought that Yorubas living in the Northern Region were more acceptable because they had a tradition of chieftaincy themselves, "which produces a similar attitude of respect toward traditional authority".[33] Another Northerner summed it up by saying: "it is not the number of Ibos who live among us that bothers us; it is the way they live among us".

The successful coup makers organised a new military junta, this time under the chairmanship of the army chief of staff, Lieutenant-Colonel Yakubu Gowon, a Christian from the Middle Belt. Gowon's first major decision was to rescind his predecessor's creation of a unitary state and to restore the federal system, now consisting of four Regions in place of the original three. But the legacy of two coups in six months, followed by a wave of ethnic killings in which thousands of Igbos lost their lives and hundreds of thousands fled from their Northern homes, had soured relations between the federal government and the Eastern Region. In May 1967 the Eastern Regional government under Colonel Chukwuemeka Odumegwu Ojukwu announced its secession as the Republic of Biafra. It took three years of civil war and hundreds of thousands of deaths before federal forces were able to defeat Biafra and forcibly re-incorporate the region into the Republic.

The oil issue

Before the War, officials in the Eastern Region, where Nigeria's oil was located, were concerned that taxes on oil profits would be kept by the federal government and would replace the practice whereby operating companies were obliged to pay various rents and royalties of which half were retained by the region of origin.[34] The land that the Republic of Biafra claimed in the east and south of Nigeria included the oil wells in the Niger Delta. In the early 1960s, before oil had started to flow in really large quantities, throughout the region there was "a pervading air of poverty, hopelessness, gloom, and long neglect".[35] The villages were described by a foreign observer as "pathetic rural slums", many of them accessible only by boat.[36] This was an area in which expatriate firms had been doing business for centuries, dealing first in slaves and later in palm products. Yet this long tradition of foreign commerce, rather than stimulating the growth of domestic business, had resulted in a surly and resentful acquisitiveness that one US diplomat called "a 'gimme' attitude".[37] The foreign slave-traders were long gone and the palm-oil business was in decline, which was soon to leave oil as the only show in town.

The civil war breakaway by Biafra, dominated by the Igbos, created fears among the many minor ethnic groups of the Niger Delta that incorporation into this putative new state would, if anything, further reduce their control over the oil wealth underneath their land. In December 1966, when trouble was clearly brewing but Colonel Ojukwu had not yet declared his secession, a chief from the oil town of Port Harcourt presented Nigeria's military head of state, General Gowon, with a well-written memorandum arguing for the establishment of a separate Rivers State and a host of other measures calculated to ensure that this depressed region would benefit from its oil wealth. Some US oil companies were interested in making contact with local activists to see if there was a way of leveraging their work in order to lobby for an improved tax regime.[38] There were already signs of the emergence of a class of "professional minority leader" that traded in ethnic politics, that is to say people from the many dozens of smaller ethnic groups within each of Nigeria's four Regions that could make a case for saying that they were oppressed by the major groups, the Hausa-Fulani, the Yoruba and the Igbos. It was cynically observed that many such purported leaders of minority groups lived in Lagos, but this did not prevent them from articulating minority grievances in order to improve their own political standing.[39] An indication of just how unpleasant the atmosphere was in Nigeria's oil-producing region was the situation in Port Harcourt itself, where smuggling was rife even before the war, as were armed robbery and burglary. There were cases of piracy in which merchant vessels were attacked while they were in the Bonny River.[40]

Already in February 1966, before the outbreak of civil war, there had been a minor uprising by a group calling itself the Niger Delta Volunteer Service, led by one Isaac Adaka Boro, which decades later was to assume a quasi-legendary status. Boro was a former student activist who was reported by the US Embassy to have a history of mental instability.[41] He and his followers claimed to be a vanguard acting on behalf of the Ijaws of the Eastern Region, Nigeria's fourth biggest ethnic group, but one without a Region of its own. The Niger Delta Volunteer Service consisted of about 100 militants who wore military uniforms and were quite well armed. Working in small groups, they launched a campaign of sabotage "with the express aim of carving out a separate 'Delta Republic'."[42] They cut the trans-Niger oil pipeline at two points, reducing flows of crude oil to the oil terminal at Bonny by about one-fifth. The government responded by arresting Boro's relatives.[43] This was soon followed by the arrest of Boro himself and some of his lieutenants. They were tried, convicted and sentenced to death,[44] although the sentences were never carried out.

Oil production, which should have been about 600,000 barrels per day, was reduced by about a quarter to 450,000 barrels.[45] Since Nigeria's only oil refinery was at Port Harcourt, in Biafran territory, the outbreak of civil war in 1967 meant that oil companies had to make a political decision as which of the two rival authorities they should recognise, Biafra or Nigeria, and to whom they should pay taxes and royalties. All eventually chose the federal side, although they attempted to keep channels of communication with Biafra open. Unable to use the Port

Harcourt refinery, the oil companies temporarily imported petroleum products from abroad via the port in Lagos, the federal capital. According to the permanent secretary at the Ministry of Finance, A.A. Atta, the war may have cost the Nigerian state some £2.5–3 million per month in foreign exchange and £12 million per month in local currency.[46]

Like most wars, the Biafra conflict created great opportunities for profiteering and corruption, "sweeping from arms procurement into all aspects of government activity", according to a senior officer of the federal army.[47] Numbers of foreign adventurers arrived in the country, such as a public relations man from California who admitted taking journalists to Biafra originally "to make a dollar" but later claimed to have become "emotionally involved", or a counterfeiter of dollar bills from St Louis, Missouri, who took to printing fake Nigerian pounds.[48] When the police collared him he claimed that he had received a commission for the Nigerian forgeries from a Ghanaian named Raymond Okudzeto. A man of this name was later to be well known to British law enforcement officials, being acquitted on a charge of heroin trafficking in the UK in 1993.[49] The Biafran Students' Association in the Americas publicly collected funds for its cause from the general public in the USA, claiming that these were tax-deductible, although it never filed for status as a tax-exempt organisation.[50] One Sylvester Okereke, apparently a former intelligence operative for Biafra, died mysteriously in London in November 1974 after seemingly falling foul of a group of shady businessmen; he was confirmed as having been an acquaintance of a disgraced minister of the British government, John Stonehouse, who had been implicated in a variety of frauds.[51]

With its battery of emergency restrictions on trade, the war also became a great stimulus to smuggling of all sorts. Before 1967 there had been rather few prohibited imports, and therefore little incentive to smuggle. At war's end, the national currency, which was still the Nigerian version of sterling, was so overvalued as a result of its oil-backed status that it had the effect of sucking in imports. Import-export traders more than ever padded their import invoices, probably by about 10 per cent in most cases,[52] as a way of repatriating their profits. Another effect of the high value of the Nigerian currency was to penalise producers of goods for export, which since colonial times mainly meant farmers. Since Nigeria was surrounded by French-speaking countries using the CFA franc, farmers had every incentive to export their produce illegally, while importers could flourish by importing goods to a neighbouring country legally and then smuggling them over the border into Nigeria. The small Republic of Dahomey (renamed the Republic of Benin in 1975, not to be confused with Benin City in Nigeria) played a key role as a trade intermediary. In 1970, Dahomey, which hardly produced cocoa, was able to offer a producer price of up to £360 per ton, based almost entirely on the smuggling of produce from Nigeria. The Nigerian government was said to be losing some £1 million per month in lost revenue from this trade alone. In Nigeria's North there was substantial smuggling of the Region's traditional cash-crop, groundnuts, which could be sold at an official price of £86 per ton in neighbouring Niger as opposed to only £36 in Nigeria. This particular smuggling trade led to occasional fire-fights between smugglers and law enforcement officers.[53] Some currency dealers specialised in taking Nigerian banknotes over one or other border and exchanging them for CFA francs.

Many currency traders were said to be Lebanese or Syrian residents of the country, who were particularly unsure of their future in such an unstable environment as Nigeria had become, and who wanted to keep their local assets liquid and to take their profits out of the country whenever they could.[54] Some Levantine traders confirmed to a newspaper reporter that the main reason they were involved in smuggling was actually not to make extra money so much as to get their profits out of Nigeria. When the Uganda dictator Idi Amin seized expatriate properties and expelled foreign businessmen from his country in 1972, Lebanese businessmen in Nigeria said that "Uganda has taught us a lesson. We will not let it happen to us".[55] At the same time, CFA francs were being imported illegally into Nigeria to provide foreign exchange, for which the demand exceeded the legal supply. The governor of Nigeria's Central Bank publicly condemned "organised syndicates for the evasion of exchange control regulations".[56] It seems that many of the Levantine and Indian currency traffickers secretly collaborated with senior officials, who were able to use their position to obtain foreign exchange and who could then sell it on the black market, and who were well placed to manipulate the regulations in force or information in their possession more generally. Senior officials usually avoided getting involved directly in smuggling rackets, preferring to offer protection to others in return for cash or other services. Women were said to be particularly adept on account of their negotiating skills and what was known as their "bottom power (B.P.)"—a coded reference to sexual favours.[57] Many senior officials had girlfriends and mistresses who doubled as partners in smuggling. State officials were crucial to the business of contraband as the gatekeepers who could facilitate access to markets.[58]

The new criminality

According to the later Nobel Prize winner Wole Soyinka, the success of the federal army in its war against Biafra resulted in "a consolidation of crime, an acceptance of the scale of values that created the conflict".[59] Victory had resulted in the values of Nigeria's ruling group becoming "intimately bound to the sense of national identity".[60] In effect, government corruption came to be seen as something close to patriotism, a feature of the national system that was under threat. This entrenched the very kleptocracy that had earlier come into being and that Major Nzeogwu and his colleagues had pledged to destroy. The 1966 putschists had failed in this ambition, as the US ambassador predicted they would, by underestimating the scale, complexity and embeddedness of the corruption they wanted to root out. As a later military leader correctly pointed out, the Nigerian political parties that were banned under military government had been "'in fact little more than armies organised for fighting elections", for whom winning elections was "a life and death struggle".[61] Victory at the ballot gave access to the true locus of power, the state.

Once Nigeria had become subject to a military government that forbade open contestation, state corruption became more entrenched than ever, especially in the fevered atmosphere of a civil war. The entire security apparatus was affected. Even before the Biafran War, travellers in the Mid-West Region were reported to meet with frequent police roadblocks where officers asked for bribes on the pretext that a person's papers were not in order.[62] By the end of the war, a journalist who travelled the 581 kilometres from Lagos to Enugu by bus crossed many such police checkpoints but never actually had anyone look at his papers. At each roadblock, the driver would each time discreetly give a bribe to the police officers. Within a few years no such discretion was necessary—police officers and military personnel simply took bribes openly at roadblocks.

An eminent American criminologist who stayed in Ibadan during the war years of 1967–68 found that "the acceptance of bribes by government officials is blatantly public and virtually universal".[63] He discovered that his colleagues, fellow-professors, were often keen to propose black-market deals of various sorts, sometimes on behalf of the military governors to whom they were connected. Thieves had connections to the police. The American, who conducted a small survey in Ibadan, found that one in eight people in his sample had been victims of burglary.[64] He concluded that in these circumstances, the concepts of "crime" and "criminal" were ceasing to have much meaning. Crime was not something one either did or didn't do: it had become a matter of "who can pin the label on whom", underlying which was a person's social standing and the strength or otherwise of their social relations.[65]

One clear consequence of military rule and the accompanying ban on political parties was a flourishing of closed organisations, some of them secret and even cult-like, and others more open and social in nature. The military were constantly subject to special demands, in spite of their condemnation of corruption. Gowon being a low-profile leader, "there was little except force and the selective distribution of largesse" to sustain political order "in the absence of a supreme patrimonial leader and an appropriate state ideology."[66] Individual military strongmen, such as the military governors who ran each state or who headed parastatal bodies, could more or less do as they pleased.

Broadly speaking, the first coup of January 1966 had had at least three unanticipated consequences. First, it led to the military, having now taken control of the state, remaining in that position for much of the twentieth century, becoming deeply politicised in the process. One might add to this that even in the democracy that Nigeria has become since 1999, ex-generals have continued to prosper by turning themselves into politicians. Second, what one prominent political scientist calls a pre-modern form of state organisation became entrenched in modern form in a distinctive type of prebendalism.[67] Third, the coup-makers instituted a discourse of anti-corruption that was to be used by every military government that followed. Every subsequent military leader was to claim that only military discipline and the ruthless elimination of individuals identified as guilty could address the problem of corruption that was holding Nigeria back. In reality, successive military governments soon learned that the rhetoric of anti-corruption, like the law itself, was less a rule to be applied than a set of measures that could be invoked selectively, according to the political needs of those in power.[68]

A Nigerian professor, speaking just before the outbreak of the civil war, maintained that there had been a subtle shift in the ethos associated with corruption. People were intent on making money to put into their own pockets, he maintained, "but when caught with their hand in the till, they claim it was for the tribe, or the person catching them is practicing tribalism". Interestingly, he added that "faculty and students in universities are the most bigoted" in the latter regard,[69] implying that the discourse of tribalism and the corruption associated with it were not the residue of some ancient system embedded deep in popular mentalities, as was sometimes said, but emanated from the most educated part of the population. And education had indelibly marked the population, particularly in the Western Region, as it was the main form in which Regional governments had chosen to deliver mass welfare. The initial results were "to some extent, disastrous", since the more widely available education became, "the less effective it was in unlocking access to power and wealth".[70] Towards the end of the civil war, Nigeria was estimated to be seeking to absorb some 100,000 school-leavers per year. At the same time the armed forces had increased from some 9,000 to over 200,000.

The contours of a distinctive Nigerian pattern of criminality had been clearly established by the time of the two coups of 1966. There does not seem to have been much organised crime in the modern meaning of the term. One of Stanislav Andreski's many brilliant insights was to distinguish between organised crime in the American sense, which was not really present, and a ruthless competitiveness that was based on fluid relationships and little in the way of corporate organisation.[71] It is interesting to note, however, that Nigeria was being used as a staging-post for heroin smuggling as early as 1952, when US officials noted that parcels of the drug were being transported by a Lebanese syndicate from Beirut to New York via Kano and

Accra, using couriers on commercial airlines.[72] The US consul-general in Lagos was told by a Lebanese source, described as "a competent narcotics and diamond smuggler",[73] that the existing "heavy dope traffic" from the Near East to the USA via Europe was being diverted to Nigeria "to an increasing extent" to avoid the attention of law enforcement officers on the European route. One of those implicated at the Nigerian stage of the pipeline was one O. Chagoury.[74] A few decades later, a Lebanese family with the same name had become very influential in both business and in political finance: Gilbert Chagoury, born in 1946, describes himself as an "industrialist, ambassador, advisor and philanthropist".[75] He was very close to the military dictator of the 1990s, Sani Abacha. He is reported to be a major donor to the Clinton Foundation. It seems that he is a descendant of a heroin trader who arrived in Nigeria in 1952, which is no reflection on his own character but does tell us something about the possibility that the heroin trade may provide start-up capital for other forms of business. It appears that a commercial dynasty of the late twentieth century actually acquired its initial capital in the drug trade. By 1966, Nigeria's first military government took the issue of drug smuggling seriously enough to decree ten-year jail terms for persons found guilty of exporting cannabis, although it is not clear that anyone was actually convicted under the terms of this legislation.

Foreigners of various nationalities became involved in currency frauds during the civil war years and afterwards, such as one Colin S. Gold, a British citizen representing a US financial company with headquarters in the Bahamas who visited Nigeria in early 1969 to drum up business. The aptly-named Mr Gold was taking deposits in Nigerian currency that would be accepted by a Swiss bank that had on its books other Nigerian customers requiring Nigerian pounds. Gold had not informed the Nigerian authorities of this arrangement. In other words, he was offering a service to avoid official exchange controls. Similar discounting of Nigerian foreign currency, in contravention of Nigerian law, was "common practice".[76] A US diplomat reported that Gold was the first representative of an international fund that he had met in Nigeria since the days of Investors Overseas Services Ltd.,[77] the notorious mutual fund sales company that became one of the biggest financial scandals of the 1960s.

Other than minor traces of organised crime like this, what certainly existed on a large scale was a voracious and pervasive system of state corruption that was led by politicians. Those in office had established practices of collusion with the foreign businesses that were prominent in importing consumer goods and that were needed to implement contracts in civil engineering and other fields. Much of the pressure on public officials to embezzle money came from the political parties that had helped them into office, which required money for campaigning, but it also came from family, friends, clients and others who saw public officials as sources of money, jobs and other opportunities for enrichment. The use of public office for personal gain had spread to the lower level of public servants, such as schoolteachers and school principals who demanded money from the parents of their pupils. A widespread culture of gift-giving and exchange had turned into a generalised practice of blackmail and embezzlement that, rather than lubricating social relations, was dedicated to the amassing of money by individuals. There were also old-established practices, notably in regard to trafficking in people, that had been criminalised by a law code that, in this respect at least, had hardly been assimilated in popular mentalities. Criminality thus had a very marked political character. Politicians also led the way in the murder of political opponents, most obviously in the Western Region, and of entire populations in some rural areas, notably in the Middle Belt within the Northern Region. A population that had been judged generally law-abiding just twenty years earlier acquired habits of fraud in this environment.

Before the civil war, the systematic abuse of public office that was the most striking form of serious crime in Nigeria was of little concern outside the country other than among business people or others with direct interests there. There were relatively few Nigerians living abroad, and most of those Nigerians who did live overseas, often in Europe and North America, were students or professionals without any particular connection to crime of any description. The Biafran emergency, however, resulted in the exodus of as many as 100,000 Igbos according to Professor Kenneth Dike, one of the first of a generation of outstanding Nigerian historians and a senior official of the Biafran government.[78] This would help to establish the basis for the globalisation of Nigerian criminal networks explored in Chapter Seven.

6

BOOM TIME

Not just within the military itself but among a wider public, there was a sense that the Nigerian nation had come through an ordeal by fire. It was widely believed that the country had taken a further step towards liberating itself from foreign influence, perhaps on account of the success that the federal government had in fending off international recognition of Biafra. "However", an American diplomat reported in 1971, in reference to corruption, "there is an enormous skepticism within the country that much can be done about what many Nigerians call a national way of life".[1]

A new US envoy, Ambassador John E. Reinhardt, one of the first African-Americans to serve the Department of State at a senior level, arrived after the War. He coined a new word to describe the distinctive type of patriotism that he found during his term of office in the 1970s. He labelled it "Nigerianism". The existence of oil in God-given abundance added to the sense of national destiny to turn Nigerianism into what Reinhardt called a "near-ideology". Nigerians had a belief in manifest destiny that could be compared to that of Americans themselves.[2] Oddly enough, at the same time that Nigerians celebrated their country's unique identity and its status as an African superpower, there was a widespread feeling "that anything indigenous is inferior to its foreign counterpart".[3] A culture of conspicuous consumption made the latest imported fashion a must-have for every aspiring Nigerian.

At the core of this reigning near-ideology was the idea that Nigeria had a distinctive place in the world. While this was often mistaken for simple arrogance, Reinhardt thought that such a view was not quite accurate. The roots of Nigerianism he believed to lie in the country's precolonial societies.

Nigeria rampant

Nigerianism was associated with grandiose expectations of development and international power that caused Nigeria's rulers, the Federal Military Government headed by General Gowon, to embark on an ambitious series of prestige projects. Many of Nigeria's military leaders were veterans of the July 1966 counter-coup that had put them at the heart of networks of power. Actual policy-making was the realm of senior civil servants known as "superpermsecs" after their official title of Permanent Secretary at one ministry or another. The superpermsecs were seasoned administrators, but some of them had also been seized with the exuberance of Nigerianism.

The key maker of government oil policy was just such a civil servant. He was M.O. Feyide, the director of Petroleum Resources at the Ministry of Mines and Power. Around him was a very small team with just a handful of engineers, indicating how thin was the country's expertise even in the vital field of oil.[4] In July 1971, Nigeria joined the Organisation of the Petroleum Exporting Countries (OPEC), then moving towards the height of its influence. Like other OPEC countries, the Lagos government renegotiated the terms of its agreements with oil companies, creating the Nigerian National Petroleum Corporation (NNPC) in 1973 as the vehicle for its business dealings in the oil sector. Starting with a claim for a 35 per cent stake in the new company, within a year the government had increased its participation to 55 per cent.[5] Would-be traders and intermediaries swarmed around the oil business. Foreign oil firms found themselves more or less required to hire local middlemen who could cultivate the political links necessary to secure contracts. Many Nigerians with contacts in the oil business actually preferred to become middlemen rather than managers, since mediation required no capital, did not compete with foreign companies, and offered easy profits.[6] All manner of irregular payments and trade-offs took place as a result of the activities of middlemen inserting themselves between sellers and buyers of Nigerian oil. By way of example, the US Embassy in Paris in 1973 was visited by a US national, a former stock exchange trader, who claimed to be in possession of a two-year contract for two million long tons of Nigerian crude. He told the Embassy "that a great deal of under-the-table payments were taking place in Nigeria to obtain crude there".[7] By the late 1970s an illegal oil trade was flourishing, often through foreign intermediaries such as the Greek and Lebanese traders resident in Nigeria or by way of their international connections. This sort of complex influence-peddling was a perfect breeding-ground for fraud. A Nigerian-Canadian professor who wrote a book on Four One Nine fraud believes that it was news reports about corrupt politicians funnelling oil proceeds to foreign bank accounts that inspired unemployed Nigerians to offer non-existent oil for sale, a practice that seems to have begun at this time.[8]

At the end of the civil war, Nigeria was still using sterling as its currency and its currency transactions were largely settled in UK sterling.[9] Such a hangover from colonial times could not be tolerated for long, especially since Britain was an economic power in decline. On 1 January 1973 Nigeria abandoned sterling and created its own currency, the naira, introduced at a rate of two naira to one pound. In late 1973 and early 1974, a worldwide oil crisis resulted in a four-fold increase in the price of crude oil in just six months, producing a windfall for the Nigerian government. British banks remained well-placed in Nigeria, but were uninterested in financing development projects or conventional enterprises, since these involved risk. "Where they are interested is in financing British companies supplying agricultural equipment etc (with ECGD guarantees of course)...", wrote a British official,[10] referring to his country's Export Credits Guarantee Department, which offered state funds to insure British exporters against potential losses.

Nigeria had shifted from the economic slow lane to the fast lane. Money flooded in—and left almost as quickly, in search of security. In ten years from 1967, federal government revenues increased by a massive 2,200 per cent, managed by a military government unaccountable to anyone at all.[11] Everyone who could claim some sort of official connection was qualified for a piece of the national cake, as Nigerians were used to terming the wealth associated with government activity. Nigeria's military government and many members of the political class and the intelligentsia saw the country as on the verge of superpower status.[12]

Nigeria's entire economy came to repose on a vastly overvalued exchange rate, kept high by the fact that the naira was backed by oil, and an unquenchable thirst for imported goods. So overvalued was the official exchange rate of the naira against the US dollar that anyone with the right connections to senior officials could make a 10 per cent profit simply by using their nairas to buy dollars from the Nigerian Central Bank and selling them in London.[13] Profiting from the spread between official and black-market rates for the naira was big business. Owning a company was sometimes just another means of smuggling currency. There were over 25 registered shipping companies owned by Nigerians, which entered into over-priced contracts in order to kick back a part of the official costs to the charterer's foreign bank account, in defiance of foreign exchange regulations.[14] Those Nigerians who had grown rich in just a few years, as well as foreign business people and the Lebanese, Syrian and Indian traders and entrepreneurs who were prominent at the lower levels of the import sector, all knew that their money was not guaranteed to remain safe in such a febrile environment. People with money smuggled it out of the country any way they could, with over-invoicing for imported goods being a favourite. It is said that some customs officials set up a consultancy service to advise new entrants into the smuggling business.[15]

Professional smugglers developed business models adapted to their particular branch of illegality. The countries neighbouring Nigeria are all French-speaking, and all were using versions of the CFA franc, which in the 1970s was considered as hard currency by virtue of its convertibility into French francs. Smugglers taking Nigerian goods abroad to neighbouring countries sold them for payment in CFA francs and would generally use these hard currency profits to buy consumer goods for import into Nigeria. Cars both new and second-hand were a favourite for smuggling from Dahomey into Nigeria, especially Mercedes, but also leading French makes. By the late 1970s a further twist to this business was the sale in the Republic of Benin—Dahomey's new name—of cars stolen in Nigeria.[16] "Smuggling operations in Nigeria are fast becoming an organised crime in view of the efficiency and the amount of banned goods being brazenly displayed in the country", one newspaper opined. The writer added rather breathlessly: "Indeed, smuggling activities in the country now is [sic] comparable to the Mafia organisation in the violation of criminal laws in the United States of America".[17] In 1977 the Federal Military Government acted belatedly against the haemorrhaging of Nigeria's wealth by introducing an Exchange Control decree that laid out strong measures against the evasion of exchange controls, especially by means of false invoicing.[18] It was ineffective. By 1980, it was estimated that Nigeria was still losing 10 billion naira or 25 per cent of its GDP in smuggling and that the amount of currency leaving the country through illegal trade were more than through legal trade.[19]

Despite the existence of Nigeria's oil industry, the country's refinery at Port Harcourt was unable to produce enough petroleum products to supply the domestic market, including in fuel for motor vehicles. This provided an opportunity for middlemen with the necessary connections to smuggle petroleum products from refineries abroad. By 1976, fuel shortages were evidence that the import of petroleum products was in the hands of smugglers with excellent political connections, "men who own the means of transportation of the liquid gold and have good connections both within the country and across its borders".[20] By 1973, imports of petroleum products were running at 1.6 million barrels per year, or 10 per cent of consumption,[21] at the same time as petroleum products were being smuggled to neighbouring countries such as Niger and Chad.[22] The large-scale smuggling of petroleum products was the work of people wealthy enough to own the necessary trucks or other vehicles but, above all, with the right political connections. Corrupt, distrusting the major oil companies but not always having the means to implement its own policy, the Nigerian government was a perfect target for a new generation of international commodity traders, among whom Marc Rich was the star. He was able to induce Nigeria and other producer countries to sell to him directly, cutting out the oil majors, while he offered services in financing, insurance and a host of other technicalities. Rich signed long-term contracts with the state-owned Nigerian National Petroleum Corporation in November 1976 and September 1978.[23]

In the mania created by such sudden wealth as Nigeria acquired in the 1970s, incredible displays of extravagance became almost normal among the elite. The military head of state from 1966 to 1975, Yakubu Gowon, himself lived rather frugally, but he was probably the only senior member of his administration who did.[24] Many of the military officers who governed each of the twelve federal states—increased to nineteen in 1976—were constantly going on foreign junkets. Some assumed the style due to princes, such as the military governor of Kano, Alhaji Audu Bako, who kept a party of trumpeters at his residence to herald the comings and goings of his official car with its military outriders. Disdaining routine business, he often failed to show up at official ceremonies.[25] At social occasions the practice of "spraying" made its appearance, the spreading of banknotes—the higher the denomination, the better—among those present. Especially fashionable was to invite prominent musicians to play at a party and then shower them with high-value notes. The sweatier the musician, the more banknotes would stick. Meanwhile, the most famous musician of all, Fela Anikulapo Kuti, spurned this style but instead cultivated a sort of alternative consumerism—of women and marijuana. His most famous songs denounced corruption and military rule.

The Federal Military Government and the military governors who ruled the provinces—now divided into twelve States to replace the former four Regions—began manically to embark on infrastructure and prestige projects, most of them doubtless calculated to raise money through the kickbacks attached to government contracts. By 1975 the government had placed accumulated orders for a mind-boggling 20 million tonnes of cement to fulfil these projects, all of it coming from abroad and to be paid for with the buoyant petro-naira. A measure of just how fantastic this building mania was is that 20 million tonnes of cement exceeded the exporting capacity of Europe and the USSR combined. Half the merchant ships in the world adapted for carrying cement were supplying Nigeria.[26] The main port at Apapa in Lagos was overwhelmed.[27] Dozens of new companies were formed with the sole aim of supplying Nigeria with cement, "with the connivance of civil servants in a position to lay down the terms of delivery".[28] The main beneficiaries of the cement boom were officials at the ministries of defence and housing, army officers, Central Bank officials, top diplomats and Nigeria's biggest cement distributors, ship-owners and ship-charterers, as well as foreign suppliers. The probable cost of this folly was $2 billion, or one quarter of Nigeria's oil revenue in 1975.[29] The manic spending of those years did nothing for Nigeria's economic production, which stagnated in most sectors. Official development policy was based on the three pillars of oil, steel and agriculture, but the only one of these three that showed real progress was oil production. Not coincidentally, it was the only major sector of economic activity that was still substantially under the control of expatriates who did not share the unrestrained urge for growth of those in control of government policy.

Given the lucrative contracts on offer, foreign firms were prepared to offer key officials very large bribes. The US aircraft manufacturer Lockheed, for example, paid out $3.6 million in bribes on a deal worth $45 million.[30] Its key local lobbyist was a Lagos company chaired by Alhaji Waziri Ibrahim, a senior member of the Northern elite.[31] In another scandal, a Federal Commissioner was identified as having played a similar mediating role in obtaining a contract for the import of buses from Britain.[32] The real number of major procurement scandals was far higher than those "forced into the open by circumstances beyond the Government's control",[33] a British official noted. One of his colleagues pointed out that "there is no prospect of substantial business in Nigeria without the granting of special commissions".[34]

"The signs of development", an anthropologist noted, "were equated with its substance".[35] The country became an enormous and grotesque carnival of consumption. Many people wondered where wealth on the scale they were now seeing really came from, and what its precise relationship was to the spirit world. Given the deeply rooted assumption of a connection between prosperity and the invisible world, many people assumed that somewhere behind the most outrageous displays of wealth lay hidden networks and cults.[36] There was a rise in ritual killings. Rumours circulated that penis-thieves were active, people who were thought to collect male organs for obscure ritual purposes.[37]

The mania for consumption included human life itself. A military decree in 1970 made the death penalty mandatory for armed robbery. Public executions made their reappearance with the public execution of a convicted armed robber at Bar Beach, Lagos, on 26 April 1971, after which these became popular events. Armed robbers and oil saboteurs were represented "as the modern witch of Nigerian society",[38] since they were considered to have obtained money by causing death and undermining the normal flow of wealth. They themselves had to be killed.[39] By 1976, there had been over 400 public executions since the end of the civil war.[40] The highest incidence of executions seems to have been in the South, with some 338 executions there—most of them not public—in 1984 alone.[41] According to Amnesty International[42] altogether 1,200 prisoners were executed between 1983 and 1996, most of them sentenced by Robbery and Firearms tribunals, but about 90 after political trials.

The military government's tendency to deflect blame by displacing it onto certain categories of criminals, especially armed robbers, actually helped to politicise even this form of crime. There were deep historical precedents for armed robbery and organised thuggery. Even in colonial times, there had been criminal gangs who boasted of complicity with the police.[43] In the North, many organised gangs began when nationalist political parties started to use them as party thugs in the 1950s. There was always a tendency for them to escape the control of their political masters.[44] However, armed robbery does not appear to have posed a particular problem until shortly before the civil war, when government broke down in some parts of the Western Region and there was a blurred line between political violence, crime and organised insurgency.[45] In April 1970, Kano saw its first-ever daytime armed bank robbery, in which three robbers escaped with some £27,750.[46] The culprits were held at an army road block, but over £5,000 of their haul mysteriously went missing.[47] Crime statistics exist, but are very unreliable. Some sources refer to 270,000 robberies being reported to police in 1982, rising to 364,000 by 1984.[48] By 1986, some armed robbers were daring enough to launch attacks on moving aircraft at Lagos airport. According to the police, there was even a training school for armed robbers in the Ajegunle area of Lagos, with applicants being formally interviewed for places.[49]

Immediately after the civil war, both US and British diplomats thought quite highly of the Nigerian police, but the police's performance seems to have gone down as a result of military rule. A police superintendent in Ogun State was reported as saying that 70 per cent of armed robbers were former members of the armed forces or the police.[50] Some armed robbers were described by a senior police officer as operating with complicity from the police or from bank staff, and "often highly placed persons in the society, are patrons or confidents of these criminals".[51] By the end of the decade, armed forces uniforms and weapons were described as "easily rented for an operation by the poorly-paid rank and file of the forces".[52]

The most notorious armed robber in Nigeria's history was Lawrence Anini. Gaining the status of a national legend, he encapsulated many of these features of crime and policing. Born around the time of Independence in what was later to become Benin State, he was alleged to have mystical powers. In his prime, he published letters describing himself as a crusader against state corruption, which made him appear to some people as a Robin Hood figure.[53] In reality, he was protected by a deputy superintendent of police who fulfilled the role of *amala*, the big man who organises or protects an armed gang.[54]

Elite crimes and criminals were "hardly ever" recorded by the police, although they "appear to have been predominating the country's crime scene since 1971", an academic noted.[55] Senior military officers were well placed to tap into the oil boom, but those with a mind to do so could also establish private networks dedicated to fraud. It is said that it was customary for a junior officer engaged in this kind of operation to pay a percentage of his profits to his military superior for the right to continue unpunished.[56] Some military officers are said to have had their own staff dealing in parallel banking networks or even engaged in common crime.[57] In some cases, this included drug trafficking. It should be said that the use of marijuana had been identified by the police as early as 1954 as a "growing problem", and that there was some smuggling of the drug with Congo and South Africa in the 1950s.[58] One of the first reports of substantial amounts of marijuana being smuggled abroad relates to a leading army officer, in fact no less than the civil war hero Brigadier Benjamin Adekunle, known to the press as the Black Scorpion on account of his military prowess. He was suspected of association with a Nigerian high-society woman convicted in London of smuggling some 78 kilograms of marijuana.[59] The woman named as accomplices Adekunle and another senior officer of the Nigerian army.[60] Adekunle was suspended from duty on account of the case, although his alleged role was not proved.[61] He never resumed his military career.

Despite the prominence of Brigadier Adekunle, early West African marijuana-traffickers seem to have been mostly individuals travelling by air to the United Kingdom in particular, carrying relatively small quantities of the drug hidden in their personal baggage or in cargo. A Nigerian government information leaflet concerning trade in cannabis "across the border and overseas" claimed that some smugglers made use of unwitting couriers by persuading innocent passengers to carry parcels on their behalf, not revealing the true contents of the packages.[62] In the early 1970s there were reports of amphetamines being smuggled from Nigeria to neighbouring countries.[63] In 1971, Nigeria's Federal Commissioner for Health, Dr J.O.J. Okezie, described marijuana-smuggling from Nigeria and other African countries as "rampant".[64] By the end of the decade, a Nigerian Federal Ministry of Information official claimed that drug smuggling had become so common that "Nigerian travellers are often subjected to rigorous search each time they travel abroad".[65]

Significantly, among Nigerians arrested for smuggling cannabis in 1972 were pilgrims travelling to Saudi Arabia for the hajj.[66] This is important for the light it throws on an aspect of Nigerian drug trafficking that appears to be almost completely unresearched, that is the trade with the Middle East. Most reports on West African drug traders over the last forty years, whether by law enforcement agencies or emanating from other sources, have concerned the supply of consumer markets in North America and Western Europe. In fact, the smuggling of drugs to Saudi Arabia by Nigerians travelling under cover of the hajj seems to have been quite extensive. Nigerians were very prominent among those undertaking the annual pilgrimage, rising from a figure of 12,181 in 1965 to some 44,061 by 1972.[67] Presumably most of those arrested were Muslims, more likely to be from Northern Nigeria than from the South.

In such a corrupt environment, enterprising people who did not have the official connections necessary to get an official contract could still hope to tap into the vast amounts of money that were to be made as long as they left their scruples behind them. A new generation of the money-doublers that, as we have seen, had traditionally been a regular fixture in local markets made its appearance in a more modern setting, as did new versions of the type of confidence trickster that had been recorded in the colonial period.[68] One journalist described the "many so-called business directors and managers who have no offices but who parade the streets with big portfolios and expensive business cards. Such business cards always say a thing or two about them that they are importers and exporters of none [sic] existing goods…"[69] Their victims were especially market-women "because they too want to make quick money".[70] Fraudsters would arrange to send goods to the market-sellers, taking payment upfront, and then simply abscond with the money. Another commentator declared that "chaos, corruption and coups" had been joined by "forgery, a twin-sister of racketeering". Quite a common trick in the port city of Lagos was for a fraudster to pose as a foreign sailor with cut-price goods to offer to local traders.[71] Moreover domestic fraud, such as in forged cheques, was spreading. Forgers of bank accounts and other white-collar criminals were described as "gentlemen robbers", in other words having the manners of educated people. Such people were alleged to have "invaded all the indigenous banks of Nigeria almost without exception", while others were to be found at seaports and airports where they made use of false bills of lading.[72] "Just as Pele has made Brazil famous through football, our port racketeers have made Nigeria 'famous' as a tropical homeland of rogues, robbers and racketeers", one journalist observed.[73] So notorious did Nigeria's corruption become that an enterprising American journalist decided to test the system by entering Nigeria without any papers at all. He even succeeded in obtaining a Nigerian birth certificate, simply by bribery.[74]

During the anything-goes years of the 1970s, many a personal fortune was made through frauds and evasions that were always much easier for those who were themselves in government or who knew the right people. Wealthy dynasties were founded in the 1970s that, today vaunting their respectability, had their origins in the fraud and trafficking of those crazy times. The biggest Nigerian fishing company in the 1970s, for example, was also used as a cover for smuggling and became the nursery of a political and business dynasty. While many Nigerians believed that their country was on the verge of superpower status, and there was even talk of acquiring a nuclear weapon, Nigeria had become above all a superpower of corruption.

Corruption became rife throughout the armed forces. A spot check by the commander of the Second Infantry Division based in Benin City in 1971 revealed 11,000 phantom names on the army payroll, and a further 15,000 ghosts were identified subsequently.[75] In the same year Obafemi Awolowo, who was serving the military government as federal finance minister, resigned in frustration at Gowon's steady refusal to inquire into the army's organisation and finances.[76] Even when Gowon was supplied with full details of a bribe taken by one of his Commissioners, including bank details and cheque numbers, he took no action.[77] His failure to act against even the most blatant corruption culminated in an attempt by the head of state to prevent the swearing of affidavits containing allegations of corruption against leading members of his government.[78]

Some of the government's top civilian administrators were frank in acknowledging that the grand policy of development was contributing rapidly to the growth of a yawning gap between rich and poor. A US diplomat quoted a conversation that he had had with Nigeria's top financial civil servant in December 1973, coincidentally the very month of the first OPEC price rise. The American reported that the Permanent Secretary at the Finance ministry, Alison Ayida, had told him "with disarming frankness" that the government "knows perfectly well that its development policies are contributing to an exacerbation of income disparities in Nigeria, but accepts this as part of the price of rapid development. The next generation, he added, will have to deal with the consequences".[79]

The novelist Chinua Achebe, addressing an audience at Lagos University in 1977, had a dark foreboding. "God forbid", he told his audience, "that we should be the generation that had the opportunity to create Africa's first truly modern state but frittered away the chance in parochialism, inefficiency, corruption and cynicism".[80]

Corruption, crime, cults

The official justification for military rule was still the necessity of clamping down on civilian corruption, as it had been ever since the first coup in January 1966. Grand corruption made the pretence ever more hollow, undermining whatever legitimacy the military government enjoyed. In 1975, some senior veterans of the civil war, knowing that Gowon would never act on corruption, turned to General Murtala

Muhammed, one of the chief plotters of the July 1966 counter-coup. When Gowon was out of the country, Murtala simply displaced him to become head of the ruling council. The change was publicly announced by the army Chief of Staff, General Theophilus Danjuma, another veteran of the July 1966 counter-coup. He told the nation on air in 1976 that the army had become corrupt and that it was permeated by secret societies and protection rackets.[81] He described cults as "a cancer which has eaten deep into all ranks of the Nigerian army and which, if not checked, will destroy the army in the long run". They were also said to have penetrated the ranks of high court judges, the police, and even church leaders. He called them "nothing but a protection racket invariably with the sole motive of avoiding and neutralising justice".[82] In August 1977 the military government banned public servants from joining any secret society.[83] One of the superpermsecs who ran Nigeria's civil service later recalled that the Murtala coup was actually precipitated by the appointment at the head of the national oil company of a person whom Murtala opposed, suggesting intrigues surrounding the control of oil wealth as a further motive for Gowon's removal.[84]

Murtala immediately launched a hyperactive flurry of reforms, firing senior federal and state officials and dismissing more than 10,000 civil servants, officially described as "dead wood". One of Murtala's chief motives in ridding the government of so many "deadwoods", as those laid off in his purge were dubbed, was probably a conviction that their ranks included many bureaucrats who were members of secret societies and cults that posed a threat to military control. The problem of secret societies continued.[85] However, firing so many civil servants in one swoop destroyed morale in the civil service, in the opinion of the same superpermsec.[86]

A World Bank official seemed to confirm this reading when during a routine visit to Nigeria he found the machinery of government to be "near-paralysis".[87] Murtala also began to reduce the size of the armed forces, still swollen from the war years.

Murtala was hailed by many Nigerians as a saviour on account of his dynamism—and when he was assassinated in 1976 in the course of a botched coup attempt he became a martyr. Murtala was succeeded by his deputy, Brigadier-General Olusegun Obasanjo,[88] also a civil war veteran. Murtala is still remembered by many Nigerians as a hero, the leader who was snatched from his people. The country's leading international airport, outside Lagos, is named after him. In truth, though, General Murtala was an unlikely messiah. A US ambassador, perhaps stung by Murtala's open dislike of the USA,[89] described him as "erratic, vainglorious, impetuous, corrupt, vindictive, intelligent, articulate, daring." He was also said to have been "involved in the only documented cases of genocide" during the civil war.[90] Archive documents leave little doubt that Murtala's propensity to embezzlement and corruption differed little from that of other Nigerian oligarchs.[91]

Although secret societies had deep historic roots, some people felt that the proliferation of secret societies was connected with the endless manoeuvring to obtain government contracts.[92] The figures of secret society membership bandied around in the press at that time are impossible to verify, but they suggested that up to 2.5 million Nigerians may have been members of secret cults by that time, including no less than 1.2 million members of the Ogboni society.[93] Some journalists reckoned that there were judges and even bishops who were members of secret societies, while one traditional ruler admitted to being a member of no fewer than thirteen such organisations.[94] The controversy surrounding secret societies offers a glimpse into the spiritual battle taking place in the country, as, alongside the law and a significant section of public opinion, a new generation of pentecostal preachers like Benson Idahosa, later to become the most famous of all Nigerian pentecostalist preachers, and founder of a university that bears his name, held services of cleansing for members of secret societies.[95] After General Obasanjo had become head of state in 1976, he tried to address the issue of corruption by saying that it stemmed from an erosion of traditional values and a failure to replace them with anything more than "individualism, egotism, materialism and the so-called sophistication of European society".[96] Rather than tackle actual cases of corruption, he aimed to stage a nationwide revival of traditional values. In keeping with the ideology of Nigerianism, Obasanjo's revival culminated in the huge carnival of consumption known as FESTAC 77, an international festival dedicated to black arts and culture.[97] Nigeria's growing band of charismatic Christians were later to consider FESTAC an orgy of quasi-satanic proportions, sinister by reason of its celebration of traditional religions that they themselves rejected.

Nigeria's new generation of pentecostal churches became autonomous spaces of religious practice that gained a following among the middle classes and students especially. Sites of new forms of sociability and new ideologies, Nigeria's university campuses became the site of fierce rivalries among religious groups. Pentecostal student groups emerged as perhaps the most powerful youth movement that the country had seen since Independence, to the extent that they soon eclipsed the secular student movement. The universities of Ibadan and Ile-Ife became "hotbeds of Pentecostalism".[98] On college campuses, especially at the leading universities of Ibadan and Ile-Ife, new students were targeted for recruitment by religious zealots, offering not only spiritual security but also practical services such as access to accommodation.[99] On campuses with a significant presence of Muslim students, new Islamic movements also became popular, contesting the Sufi brotherhoods that were closely connected to traditional forms of patronage and that young reformers criticised as inconsistent with correct forms of Islamic practice. The struggle for Nigeria's soul had a deeply spiritual component as well as a material one.

Alongside the emergence of quasi-traditional cults on college campuses there was also a flowering of new social clubs that were open to anyone who could afford the price of entry. "Social clubs may be regarded as open and more practical versions of secret societies", noted a Nigerian writer, comparing them to the initiation societies that have such a long history in the country.[100] Many of the new associations and social clubs that were established in these years, dispensing with most of the ritual or spiritual aspects associated with secret societies, represented people's attempts to address the problems of life in Nigeria's burgeoning cities, comparable to the burial societies and other mutual help societies that, in the absence of affordable commercial insurance, were means of spreading risk.[101] The plethora of new societies that came into existence in the 1970s no doubt owed something to people's general familiarity with the idea of social action through membership of a specific group.

Before 1960, Nigeria had only one university, originally called University College Ibadan and later renamed the University of Ibadan. After Independence, the number of universities grew rapidly. With the advent of the 1970s oil boom, the government founded universities in every part of the country. As new universities were created, the student society known as the Pyrates, established by Wole Soyinka and his friends in 1952, also became popular on many of the new campuses, founding a branch, for example, at the University of Nigeria at Nsukka that was opened immediately after Independence. By 1978, the Pyrates Confraternity claimed some 22,000 members.[102]

Nigerian student politics in those days, as in most other countries in the world, was dominated by a rhetoric of radicalism. The most influential student leaders were stridently anti-colonialist. Marxism, pan-Africanism and opposition to apartheid in South Africa became favoured themes of student activists. As the number of students increased with the opening of new universities, the National Union of Nigerian Students (NUNS) became directly involved in national politics, being invited to join the 1977 Constituent Assembly that was discussing a new constitution that would accompany a return to civilian rule. The military government under General Obasanjo became so annoyed by the students' radicalism that it proscribed NUNS and detained its president. Radical university lecturers in Ibadan, Lagos, Calabar and at Ahmadu Bello University in Zaria were detained or fired.[103] By this time universities were turning out graduates, especially in the South, at a rate far in excess of their chances of employment. Higher education had escaped the control of the government. "The National Universities Commission lacks teeth with which to control this growth, particularly where the State is establishing and financing the institution", the World Bank commented.[104]

On university campuses a sordid and cynical game emerged whereby military rulers gave covert support to student groups that they could use as a means of disrupting official student unions, feared by the military men on account of their political forthrightness at a time when Marxism was *de rigueur* among would-be intellectuals.[105] University administrators, often appointed for their loyalty to the military government rather than in regard to any academic or managerial qualification, played off one faction against another among the students at their institutions. Some university lecturers encouraged their students to join campus cults in order to recruit followers for their struggle with administrative staff who had been installed by the Federal Military Government in order to out its policies on the nation's campuses.

The Pyrates were generally in sympathy with the radical turn taken by student politics and remained an influential force within the student movement. According to a man who had been[106] a Pyrate in the early 1970s, members of the Pyrates at that time wore uniforms for formal ceremonies and followed rules that were enforced by the society's officers, which could even include beatings. Initiation involved signing a pledge in red ink and drinking a Bloody Mary, a cocktail made with tomato juice that some non-members are said to have thought was made with human blood.[107]

The first rival to the Pyrates was the Eiye group, founded in 1965,[108] which in 1969 instituted the Supreme Eiye Confraternity (National Association of Airlords).[109] During the 1970s, there was a multiplication of student confraternities that had a direct genealogical connection to the Pyrates. In 1971[110] or 1972 an internal disagreement led to a dissident group leaving or being expelled from the Pyrates and founding a new confraternity at the University of Ibadan, known as the Buccaneers or the National Association of Sea Lords.[111] The Buccaneers claimed to have ideological differences with the Pyrates, whom they accused of elitism. With student numbers increasing rapidly, there were further splits. Among new cults were the Vikings, Red Beret, Mafia, and dozens of others.[112] Colleges in the Niger Delta region seem to have been particularly fertile ground for new campus groups, such as the Klansmen Confraternity, instituted at the University of Calabar, and the Supreme Vikings Confraternity, formed in 1984 at the University of Port Harcourt.[113] This was to become a factor in the region's politics in later years.[114]

Campus cults seem to have proliferated in Southern universities particularly, no doubt because that area is home to such a strong tradition of initiation societies, rather than in the Northern ones, where the leading activists on campus tended to be Islamist reformers. Wole Soyinka has pointed to the Gamji association, said to have been favoured by senior figures in Northern Nigeria, and later manipulated by the dictator General Sani Abacha in his bid to prolong his tenure of power in the 1990s, as an example of a similar type of organisation with its roots in the North.[115] Nevertheless, it appears that activism on college campuses in Northern Nigeria generally takes a form in keeping with the history of the region—Islamist activism.

Many of the new groups that emerged in the 1970s and 1980s displayed some ideological orientation, like the Neo Black Movement of
Africa formed at the University of Benin in 1977, aligned with the
fashionable philosophy of black consciousness.[116] Its news magazine,
The Black Axe, later became the name of a new confraternity,[117]
although some people believe that the Neo Black Movement and the
Black Axe are the same thing. Most secret societies cultivated an air of
esoteric knowledge, and all aimed to protect their members against
interference by non-members. Like their forebears, they continued to
regard themselves as fighters for justice.[118] A veteran of the period
recalled that the fraternities "were an avenue to express strong feelings
about the happenings in society" in those days, as well as appealing to
youths who wanted "to live out their most exciting fantasies".[119] It was
apparently as a consequence of the 1977 ban on secret societies in
public administration that the old-established student society, the
Pyrates, was banned on some campuses, such as at the University of
Calabar and the Calabar College of Technology, where some fifteen
students were arrested in 1977 for membership of the Pyrates.[120]

Pentecostalists, cultists and, on some campuses, Islamist reformers,
competed not only for the bodies but also the souls of students, the
nation's future elite in its formative years. In pentecostal theology, the
fight with the cultists is a battle with Satan and the forces of darkness
that threaten Nigeria. The various societies were liable to manipulation
by powerful people, including military governments concerned to
defend themselves against student radicalism and to demobilise social
movements of many sorts, and also unscrupulous university administrators and even academic staff concerned to protect their position
within their institutions.

Holding their meetings at night and in secret, some of the new
groups became associated with violent attacks on university campuses.
Their behaviour moved far beyond the rather light-hearted mock-sin-
ister that had been the original style of the Pyrates. One ex-member of
a student group recalled initiation as consisting of three weeks of what
he called "rigorous and heartbreaking activities", whose purpose was
"to toughen the heart of the otherwise innocent looking boy",[121] similar to military basic training or initiation into one of the traditional
secret societies that were so important in many parts of Nigeria since

precolonial times. Many of the new confraternities made use during their induction ceremonies of religious objects, universally referred to in Nigeria as juju, which further strengthened the resemblance with initiation into a traditional power society. So worrying did campus violence become that the leadership of the Pyrates announced its intention to withdraw from university campuses entirely, and to relaunch the group as an adult society called the National Association of Seadogs. Nevertheless, student Pyrates continued to operate on Nigerian campuses in disregard of the national leadership.

Some people had quite positive views of what were now becoming called "campus cults", recalling their origins in the idealism and social activism of an earlier generation. Philip Aghedo, a member of Buccaneers for some fifteen years after being introduced at the University of Benin in 1981 by his uncle, maintained that in his day, candidate members of Buccaneers were vetted for their intelligence and good behaviour before being invited to join. "They train you to be useful to yourself and the society", Aghedo stated in regard to the student confraternities, "because the thinking governing conduct of the cult is that there must be somebody controlling the environment otherwise the environment will be controlling itself and there could be anarchy. If the cults fail to exercise some level of control in University, the lecturers and administrators can do whatever they like and get away with it".[122] He attributed the violent clashes that occurred between rival groups to the fact that they were competing with each other in the unregulated social environment formed by students on campus. Some of the new generation of campus cults were becoming deeply involved in violence and associated forms of crime, such as armed robbery. Cultists had their "godfathers", "just as armed robbers have their 'sponsor'",[123] it was reported.

The degeneration from confraternity to cult was a consequence of the policies adopted by some of the military governments that had dominated Nigeria with only brief interruption from 1966 to 1999. General Obasanjo's banning of the National Union of Nigerian Students during his first period as head of state between 1976 and 1979 was the first of several attempts by the military to assert their control over the universities. Even in secondary schools, there were cases of military governments drafting soldiers to work as teachers in an attempt to impose a military discipline on impressionable young minds. The former Buccaneer Philip Aghedo believed that the military, sent to institutions of learning in various capacities, "unwittingly taught the youngsters the art of weapon handling and management".[124] Professor Ayo Banjo has broadly agreed with this analysis, noting that many cultists "admired the machismo of the tough military men, who ordered things to be done with immediate effect and brutally swept all obstacles out of their way".[125]

Military rulers came to appreciate the force of Stanislav Andreski's insightful remark that "over-production of graduates is the surest means so far discovered for conjuring up subversive movements".[126] Unable to provide jobs for the hundreds of thousands of new graduates emerging every year, Nigeria's rulers regarded the emigration of young Nigerians overseas as a useful safety-valve. So began Nigeria's brain-drain, but also its reputation as the heart of a criminal diaspora.

The Second Republic

Broadly speaking, the favoured strategy for pursuing political hegemony in Northern Nigeria for two centuries has been via the language and organisational structures associated with Islam, and this has served many Northern elites well. The colonial system of Indirect Rule had functioned more successfully in the North than elsewhere because its tradition of centralised government and its well established traditional hierarchies lent themselves to British purposes most easily. There existed what one of Nigeria's most influential powerbrokers, General Theophilus Danjuma, in 1978 called a "military-business complex".[127] A prominent Igbo intellectual commented that "of all the power-blocs in Nigeria, the Northern power-bloc is the most serious, most political and most sophisticated. It knows best what power is, and what to do to retain it. While members of this bloc spend several hours every day and for a life-time plotting how to retain power and extend their hegemony in the country, their opponents elsewhere in the country take politics like any other business, like trading, armed robbery or prostitution."[128]

The same Igbo author went on to assert that "As a way of protecting their group interests, Nigerians now regroup into mafia-like associations: ethnic, religious, and quasi-political". The most notorious such group in national politics was the so-called Kaduna Mafia, a network of influential

Northerner powerbrokers and politicians, many of whom had attended the same secondary school. This group was well placed to exploit a new political opening that emerged after Gowon's fall. General Murtala, sensing that military rule was losing its legitimacy, began the process of returning to civilian rule by establishing a committee charged with drafting a new constitution. This was nursed towards new national elections in July and August 1979 by the two strong men of the military government who took over from Murtala, Generals Olusegun Obasanjo and Shehu Yar'Adua. The military government continued to borrow and spend extravagantly, with the governors of individual states being empowered to borrow on international markets. In 1978 the Federal Military Government, under pressure to reduce capital expenditure, took out a series of huge balance of payment loans, known as jumbo loans, in the cynical knowledge that the generals would no longer be in power when these loans had to be repaid.

So it was that on 1 October 1979 a new civilian government under President Shehu Shagari took power. A new US-style constitution provided for a national House of Representatives and Senate plus nineteen federal states, each with its House of Representatives and Governor. This government too continued to spend as though there were no tomorrow. As the finance Permanent Secretary Philip Asiodu said, "it was so much easier to sign up road and harbour projects, and other infrastructural constructions projects, and run down our reserves in the process."[129] Insiders knew that profligacy on this scale was not sustainable. A rapid fall in the world price of oil led to financial chaos, with government oil revenues falling from $24 billion to $9 billion between 1980 and 1983.[130] The government had difficulty making the investments in oil production required by its joint-ventures with oil majors, notably Shell, the leading operator. Government debt also ballooned, even though it remained small in comparison to other large developing countries such as Brazil and Mexico, and even nearby Côte d'Ivoire. However, the need for debt repayments coincided with a massive build-up of arrears on short-term trade payments. Debt service in 1978 was a mere $104 million[131] but in that same year the schedule for repayment on the first of the "jumbo" loans became due. By 1982, repayments stood at $1.13 billion or 8.7 per cent of export receipts, meaning that the country was forced to pay its debts with a growing

proportion of government receipts at the very time these were suffering from a lower oil price. By 1983 debt servicing burden stood at $1.9
billion, or nearly 20 per cent of export earnings,[132] excluding invisi-
bles like freight, insurance, student fees and the cost of food imports.
Foreign banks and the Nigerian authorities colluded in their handling
of the debt issue. "One trick of recent years has been to finance 100 per
cent of the cost of a particular project from foreign borrowing,
although part of the cost would obviously be spent only in naira", noted
a journalist from Britain's *Financial Times*. "The portion of the loan not
tied to procurement of imported goods really amounted to a disguised
balance of payments' loan, rather than project finance. Yet for quite
some time the banks were prepared to go along with the deceit".[133]

Only in April 1982 did the Shagari government react to the cata-
strophic financial situation, by rationing foreign exchange. However,
since the naira was overvalued by some 80 per cent, this did nothing to
prevent people with access to foreign exchange at the official rate from
making money by exploiting the margin between the official and black-
market rates or by continuing to import goods for sale. The Minister of
Trade, Maitama Yusuf, issued import licences with reckless abandon,
causing importers to open letters of credit with foreign banks as the
foreign exchange earnings of the Central Bank were not sufficient to
finance imports. This added trade arrears to the deficits created by
declining oil sales. Another trick was to inflate management fees, paid
up-front, rather than increase the interest on the total loan. International
banks continued to regard Nigeria as "underborrowed".[134] By 1983, the
financial situation was so desperate that foreign banks were refusing to
issue letters of credit to Nigeria because of uncleared debts.

Among the most scandalous episodes of this period was a collaboration between Johnson Matthey, one of the most venerable banks of the
City of London, and the Nigerian Central Bank. Johnson Matthey
issued false documentation to facilitate the export from Nigeria of
large amounts of cash in contravention of the country's foreign
exchange regulations. Essentially, it was a British-Nigerian collaboration to swindle the Nigerian state treasury. Johnson Matthey's manoeuvre was connected to the financing of the ruling party that implicated
Umaru Dikko, Minister of Transport and campaign manager for the
ruling party in its 1979 campaign, suggesting that this particular scam

was also related to election financing. Johnson Matthey Bank itself became a victim of the affair, as it collapsed under the weight of unsecured loans to Nigeria. It was rescued by the Bank of England in 1984 with a £100 million bail-out, the first such rescue of a private bank in British history. One of those associated with the collapse of Johnson Matthey was convicted in Britain as late as 2011.[135]

Under the Second Republic, the machinery of state corruption attained what one military insider called "a transnational efficiency... maturing from purely local currency deals to exclusively foreign exchange transactions".[136] The Central Bank colluded in transferring naira loans abroad by providing false documentation at the absurdly over-valued exchange rate. By distributing foreign loan funds to the nineteen federal states for political reasons, the government created "an urge and indeed a stampede to spend this money".[137] The government completely lost control of the state budget.

Perhaps the most important collateral damage of the oil boom and the spendthrift 1970s was the collapse of Nigeria's other exports, including notably the old agricultural staples of groundnuts, palm oil and cocoa. Since oil revenue was rigidly centralised, this made obsolete the earlier convention by which Regions had considered themselves largely self-sufficient. Yet in spite of its oil wealth, Nigeria had been a significant importer of petroleum products since 1973, making it particularly vulnerable to movements on world markets. Senior Nigerian officials were able to divert crude oil cargoes on the high seas to take advantage of market movements.[138] Nigerian oil mysteriously appeared on the Rotterdam spot market or even ended up being exported to apartheid South Africa by international oil traders, in disregard of international sanctions. A subsequent oil minister claimed that Nigeria lost $16 billion of oil income, or 20 per cent of its oil revenue, in 1979–83 due to fraud perpetrated by syndicates of foreign traders working with corrupt officials.[139]

7

CRIME GOES GLOBAL

"Let us call a spade a spade", said Nigeria's most famous fighter against corruption, Nuhu Ribadu, when he was reminiscing about the Second Republic of 1979–83. "This is the period when we started hearing about 419,[1] it is the period we started having drug problems. It is a period when Majors (in the army) started buying property in London."[2] It was also perhaps the most critical moment in West Africa's insertion into global patterns of crime, as millions of Nigerians moved abroad in search of work—legal or otherwise. The shock of a financial crash after the spendthrift oil boom of the previous decade punctured the illusions of an entire generation of Nigerians. Prosperity, association with education and familiarity with European ways of managing public affairs appeared to have been offered and snatched away in just a few years.

Even before the end of the 1970s observers were noting the number of people with some education who could not find jobs in the civil service or the formal sector but who nevertheless called themselves "businessmen" or "directors". Graduates, well equipped to understand the techniques of over-invoicing, evading currency controls and manipulating paperwork that had become widespread in official bureaucracies, specialised in the typically white-collar crimes of fraud and embezzlement.[3] Whereas the happy few could invest their money overseas and buy houses in Britain, unemployed graduates were also

119

tempted to go abroad to try their luck but without much capital base to start from.

Contributing to the dramatic shift in the patterns of Nigerian criminality was a simple question of population numbers. At Independence in 1960, there were some 45.2 million Nigerians. Just one generation later, in 1983, there were about 80 million.[4] Mass education had resulted in "the emergence of large numbers of persons qualified by education to claim a place in the civil service, the army, and the professions or, having access to the necessary financial resources, to thrust their way forward in business enterprises",[5] but now without jobs to go to. Nigeria, which had long been a magnet for immigrants from nearby Ghana especially, suddenly became an exporter of people, many of them young and many of them with school diplomas and even university degrees, thanks to the number of universities established in the previous twenty years. According to official statistics, by 1991 there were 47,000 Nigerians living in the United Kingdom, and almost double that number ten years later.[6] The USA was home to some 100,000 Nigerians by 1993, nearly half of them having originally entered with temporary foreign student visas and then finding ways and means of staying on. These figures are likely to be underestimates due to the numbers of people staying without permits. Other people went to other parts of the world, to the extent that by the early twenty-first century there was hardly a country in the world that had not become home to at least some Nigerians.

Many of these emigrants were too young to remember clearly the sins of the First Republic that had inspired the 1966 military coup. They had come to believe that corruption and mismanagement were all the fault of the military, the only government they had really known. When the civilian government of the Second Republic collapsed under financial pressure and was overthrown by another military coup at the end of 1982, many Nigerians refused to believe that a global recession had anything to do with it. They thought that the only reason for the collapse of the civilian government was because the thieves and looters who manned Nigeria's state institutions had overdone things. As the military *éminence grise* General Danjuma said, "it was widely held that the military taught the politicians how to do it. There was a rich, unbroken line of opportunities for corruption that stretched from the wartime army contracts, through the cement scandal, Universal Primary Education contracts, FESTAC, to the Abuja contracts".[7] This last was a reference to the decision to build from scratch a new national capital at Abuja, in the middle of the country.

The Nigerian emigrants of the late twentieth century had grown up in what one Nigerian academic called "a legitimizing culture of thievery".[8] Many of them left home to seek their fortune abroad with little in their luggage except perhaps a diploma from an obscure university or college and the phone number of a college-mate or a relative who was already living outside the country. What they did have was brains and a spirit of enterprise that would not countenance failure. During the oil boom years Nigerian society became more than ever suffused with the idea that "the attainment of material riches is the supreme object of human endeavour", and that "it is this which largely conditions our moral point of view".[9]

The drug trade

"Prior to 1982", the US Embassy in Lagos stated, "Nigerians played an insignificant role in the marketing of narcotics and dangerous drugs in the United States".[10] That changed dramatically with the rapid emigration of Nigerians in response to their country's financial difficulties. In 1982, US authorities arrested twenty-one Nigerians for narcotics offences, and the figures rose rapidly in succeeding years.[11] A similar pattern emerged in Europe, where an official of the West German Interior ministry was reported as stating in 1983 that Hamburg was importing significant quantities of drugs from West Africa including a ship from Nigeria whose cargo included cocaine, heroin and marijuana.[12] A year later, the director of West Germany's customs service stated that Nigeria was one of the top six exporters of cocaine to his country.[13] Also in 1983, Thailand witnessed its first known case of a Nigerian convicted of possessing heroin.[14]

There are various stories, all of them unverifiable, about how the large-scale involvement of Nigerians in the drug trade began. Some say it started when Nigerian students living in Europe and North America failed to receive their government bursaries and in desperation took to trading in drugs.[15] The US Drug Enforcement Administration has claimed that the trade was pioneered by Nigerian naval officers under-going training in India, who bought heroin at source and sent it back to West Africa with couriers whom they had recruited from among Nigerian students there.[16] Whatever the exact circumstances may have been, this early cohort of heroin and cocaine traders was surely unaware that a Lebanese syndicate had been trading narcotics in Nigeria a gen-eration previously.

As we have seen, there had for some years already been a small export trade in marijuana from Nigeria by individual traders, some of whom may have had connections to senior officials. This became the precursor of the narcotics trade that emerged on a much larger scale in the early 1980s as Nigerian traders entered the international narcot-ics market with extraordinary speed. Some travelled to South America or Asia to buy small quantities of cocaine or heroin that they could carry to West Africa in their personal luggage for onward transmission to the consumer markets of the North Atlantic, and others took up residence in producer countries and recruited couriers to carry the packages for them. Nigerian smugglers were sending heroin by air courier from Pakistan to Nigeria, where it was repackaged and re-exported to the United States.[17] One Pakistani heroin dealer was reported in 1985 as saying that he had made regular sales of heroin to a locally-based Nigerian for eight months.[18] There was also a small Nigerian community resident in Thailand. Interestingly, even in the 1980s, Saudi Arabia figured prominently on the list of countries where Nigerians had been arrested for drug offences, in third place behind the USA and the United Kingdom.[19] Whereas the great majority of Nigerians detained for drug trafficking in Europe and North America were of Southern origin, the transport of illegal drugs by Nigerians to the Middle East, including under cover of the hajj, was far more likely to involve people of Northern Nigerian origin, as a consequence of the historic links between that region and the Muslim world.

The great advantage of West African smugglers in the early days of the drug trade was that European and North American law enforce-ment officers were not expecting narcotics to be imported from West Africa, since it was not a producing area. However, the reputation of Nigeria soon changed, to the extent that by 1985, British customs agents were said to be systematically searching Nigerians entering the country.[20] Nigerian drug traffickers pioneered the technique of swallowing cocaine and heroin wrapped in condoms and carrying contraband through customs in their stomachs, for later retrieval. This became a hallmark of the West African carrying trade. With Nigerians so heavily involved in drug smuggling, it was inevitable that a market for cocaine would soon emerge in Nigeria itself. In 1983 a Nigerian newspaper reported the existence of what it called "a tiny cocaine world" in fashionable Lagos society.[21]

When the head of the Ghanaian police anti-drug unit visited Bangkok in 1986, he found "a lot of Ghanaians and Nigerians" in prison for drug offences.[22] By 1988, some 2,000 Nigerians were reported to be serving sentences for drug offences abroad.[23] US authorities reportedly arrested 851 Nigerians for drug offences between 1984 and 1989, by which time they reckoned that just over half of the heroin arriving at New York's John F. Kennedy airport was being carried by Nigerians.[24] In 1991, Nigeria's own Ministry of Justice reported that 15,433 Nigerians had been arrested worldwide for drug offences in the previous seven years.[25] Of these, 4,802 had been convicted.[26] According to a statement attributed to the deputy director-general of the Ministry of External Affairs, Nigerians were the leading nationality arrested for drug offences in India, Pakistan, Saudi Arabia and Thailand.[27]

Nigerian traders showed great ingenuity in switching their smuggling techniques and routes, for example exporting from Thailand overland to Malaysia or by sea to Taiwan or Hong Kong for onward transmission to Europe and North America.[28] Professional drug traders were constantly adapting and improving their methods. The Nigerians' commercial skills were also attracting the attention of fellow-traffickers from other continents. Scrutiny of arrest figures suggests that major Colombian drug-smuggling groups, reacting to the near-saturation of the US market, had begun seeking relationships with West African traders even by the late 1980s,[29] interested in using the West Africans' highly developed marketing channels as a way of penetrating new areas, notably in Europe.

Among Nigerians involved in the drug trade were figures of privilege and influence, as became clear in 1989 when a former member of Nigeria's Senate was arrested in New York for heroin trafficking and subsequently convicted. He had previously offered $20 million of his own money, purportedly as a patriotic gesture, to pay a debt owed by Nigerian Airways that had caused French authorities to impound a Nigerian Airways airbus. Although this scheme did not succeed, his intention had apparently been to use the plane to transport drug cargoes. For some time thereafter Lagos heroin dealers referred to their product as "senator".[30] A later member of the upper house of Nigeria's legislature, who had previously held a senior position in the police, once alleged that the Senate was infested with ex-fraudsters and drug traders.[31] Even the law enforcement agencies were not immune to the lure of drug money. A head of the Nigerian Drug Law Enforcement Agency (NDLEA), a unit established in 1990 largely as a concession to US pressure, reportedly stated in 1994 that "those charged with the responsibility of eliminating drug trafficking are by far more interested in drug trafficking than the professional traffickers".[32] One of his predecessors had acquired a particular notoriety in this regard.[33]

Four One Nine

While some of Nigeria's new emigrants took to trading in drugs to earn a living abroad, others used methods of fraud that they had already acquired in their home environment. Nigerian students in the United States had already developed a reputation for fraud with student loans.[34] In 1984, the US Customs Service reckoned that of 30–50,000 Nigerians then living in the USA, some 75–90 per cent were involved in fraud,[35] although lower estimates were also in circulation. It is sometimes said that US law enforcement agencies began to take the Nigerian scammers seriously only when the investment bank Merrill Lynch discovered that the cleaners who came into their office at night, many of them West African immigrants, were photocopying customer information that was then passed to Nigerian fraudsters for their use.[36]

A Senate sub-committee investigating Nigerian fraud reckoned that most Nigerian fraudsters were not members of major gangs, but were self-employed individuals who had learned the basic techniques from others, sometimes in exchange for a fee. US law enforcement officers had believed for years that Nigerian fraudsters were in possession of training manuals, and eventually they found one, although it turned out to be a pirated copy of an American handbook. This seventeen-page document found by agents in Atlanta, Georgia finishes with a summary checklist of the steps to committing credit card fraud:[37]

1. First go the newspaper office or library
2. Find several good prospects you can use
3. Apply for the birth certificate (wait for its arrival in the mail)
4. Apply for the social security card (wait until it arrives then get drivers license)
5. Apply for drivers license (New Mexico & Kansas—same-day service)
6. Open the bank accounts (3) need $500 total
   ....and so on, up to tip number 16.

Similar reports came from the United Kingdom, where London in particular had been home to a significant Nigerian population since the late colonial period that was now enhanced with thousands of new arrivals. In 1978, British police seized counterfeit hundred-dollar bills of excellent quality that were said to have been printed in South America and exported to Nigeria for worldwide distribution. Notes with a face value of $9 million had found their way to the United Kingdom.[38] Scotland Yard, investigating another network of fraud, discovered a London bank account linked to one of the chief suspects through which $27 million had flowed in 18 months in the mid-1990s. Among those tried in connection with this bank account was a Nigerian former insurance broker who had formed part of a network that included both Nigerian and British nationals. The leader of the group was one Fred Akosa, based in Lagos. According to the police, the fraudsters operated like a terrorist cell, each member being hermetically sealed from others in the network and able to identify only Akosa in Lagos. One of their victims, a businessman named Lawrence Martin, had no doubts that the gang had a much wider network of associates as, in search of what he thought to be a genuine military contract, he had visited Nigeria and been taken in an official limousine to the headquarters of the Ministry of Defence.[39] Cases like this were so damaging to Nigeria's international reputation that Nigerian embassies in Europe bought full-page adverts in national newspapers warning readers against fraudsters offering too-good-to-be-true deals.

The scale of the frauds perpetrated by the new wave of Nigerian scammers was staggering, although figures are unreliable and vary enormously. By 2000, Americans alone are estimated to have lost at least $100 million in advance-fee fraud, much of it Nigerian,[40] although other sources give figures ten times as high.[41] Some scams similar to that involving the Briton Lawrence Martin were sufficiently persuasive to motivate businessmen to fly to Nigeria in pursuit of non-existent deals, as a result of which seventeen Western businessmen, including two Americans, are reported to have been killed in Nigeria between 1992 and 1997. Others were rescued by the US Embassy.[42] The scale of Four One Nine-type frauds grew from year to year, per-petrated by Nigerians abroad or by others at home who had honed their skills. It was reported that between April 1998 and November 1999, staff at the postal centre at New York's JFK airport intercepted more than five million Four One Nine scam letters. While estimates were always inaccurate, it was said that Nigerian Four One Nine scams were worth no less than £8 billion per year worldwide.[43] Citing Nigerian sources, US law enforcement officials estimated that up to 90 per cent of Nigerians in the USA had at some point been involved in fraud.[44] British and American newspapers quite often contained stories about individual victims. One of the most prominent was Edward Mezvinsky, an American politician who had sat in the House of Representatives for Iowa in the 1970s. He was taken for over €760,000 after falling for a Nigerian scam.[45] Mezvinsky's son, Marc, was later to marry Chelsea Clinton, daughter of Bill and Hillary.

Many of the Four One Nine frauds in Europe and North America in the 1980s and early 90s began with letters or faxes offering imaginary profits connected to the oil business. Some analysts claim that the perpe-trators were "mainly dismissed civil servants who worked either at the Central Bank of Nigeria or the Nigerian National Petroleum Corpora-tion".[46] Some of these early scams are also said to have been perpetrated with the collaboration of senior officials from the Nigerian national tele-communications company, NITEL.[47] If so, this was ironic, as in 2002 a mixed Dutch-Nigerian group is said to have cheated NITEL out of $45 million when it was privatised.[48] In Western Europe, some early Nigerian scams in 1989 were initiated by a telex message advertising opportunities to buy a tanker of Nigerian crude oil at rock-bottom prices:[49] given the practice of selling cargoes at sea, this was not such an outlandish proposition in the world of oil-trading. In 1989–90, the Dutch authorities alone recorded 35 maritime frauds within the range of $300,000–$2 million, no doubt targeted at the Netherlands because of the existence of the oil spot market in Rotterdam, where cargoes could be offered for immediate sale. Sometimes false cargoes were sold and resold several times.[50] A Dutch policeman who began to investigate West African fraud in 1989 travelled to Nigeria to investigate some oil frauds in the early 1990s and discovered the involvement of army officers up to the level of colonel.[51]

The very biggest oil frauds concerned Nigeria itself. In 1984 the country's oil minister said that Nigeria had lost $16 billion of oil proceeds, about a fifth of its oil revenue, in 1979–83 because of fraud by what he termed an international mafia. He claimed that crude oil was being diverted at sea by senior officials who received payment in dollars. Oil was also being sold illegally by officials of the government oil company, the NNPC, at its Warri refinery.[52] Product from Nigeria's own refineries was being diverted to foreign ships for sale abroad in a process known as bunkering. The fact that petrol was heavily subsidised for sale in Nigeria meant that it was easy to manipulate price differentials on imports and exports through smuggling.[53]

Nigerian fraudsters were moving to other parts of Africa itself, especially South Africa, which became a key site after the transition from apartheid in 1994. In 1997 the US Embassy in South Africa issued an official warning against the black money scam, an updated version of the old market-place trick whereby a seller offers a quantity of banknotes that have allegedly been adulterated and need only be cleaned to become useable once more. "We know of one case in which a person, persuaded that this was the chance of a lifetime, paid R500,000 [rands] for a suitcase full of dirty paper",[54] the Embassy reported. In those days, half a million rands was worth somewhere over $100,000. Nigerian scammers even managed to defraud the apartheid intelligence service, the National Intelligence Service, to the tune of R1.9 million, as its director sheepishly told his parliament's public accounts committee.[55] A diplomat at the embassy in Nigeria of newly independent Namibia confessed that he was shocked by the scale of fraud in Nigeria, including that perpetrated by Nigerian companies that simply ordered goods from Namibia and did not pay for them. He believed that senior officials of the Nigerian government were participating in rackets of this sort.[56]

With the arrival of the computer age, Four One Niners in Nigeria itself who succeeded in hooking a victim overseas—known as a *mugu*—might sell their lead to a "chairman" who was based in Europe and would be able to follow up on the spot.[57] In Nigeria, there were phoney companies that existed only to reply to credit inquiries and provide bogus references for fraudsters. Some local con artists were said to work in groups of up to fifteen with an identifiable leader, many of them with connections formed on college campuses.[58] Their chairman bought computer time and took the lion's share of any successful scam.

Four One Nine scammers in Nigeria itself created a distinctive culture that was brash and extravagant. Their favourite music was hip-hop. Successful Four One Niners sported the cars, sunglasses and gold chains that came with the territory. They referred to hundred-dollar bills as Benjamins from the portrait of Benjamin Franklin. Their whole ethos was of hot money that, having been gained dishonestly, was to be spent immediately, preferably on consumption. Four One Niners even had their own songs, of which the most notorious was "I Go Chop Your Dollar" by the actor and comedian Nkem Oweh. Videos of Oweh singing his hit song, complete with an idiot dance making fun of his victims, are to be seen on YouTube.[59]

Some Four One Nine scams turned to tragedy, such as in the case of Dutchman Johannes van Damme. Married to a Nigerian woman and living in Nigeria, he was the victim of a kidnap and his daughter was cheated by Four One Niners. He became so desperate that he went into the drug business and was arrested in Singapore carrying 4.2 kilos of heroin.[60] He was hanged in 1994.[61] There were also astonishing stories of success, such as that of Maurice Ibekwe. Moving to Libya in the 1980s, he was said to have perpetrated a series of frauds that set him up as a big player in the Four One Nine business. In 1992–95, he defrauded a German businessman of $390,000. Using his money to make a political career, he moved into politics during the military dictatorship of the late 1990s and eventually became chairman of the House Police Affairs sub-committee.[62]

The rise and fall of anti-corruption

Nigeria is the giant of West Africa, in terms of population and economic weight, but it is not unique in matters of government corruption. And corruption has bred its own politics and rhetoric of anti-corruption.

Perhaps the most significant popular backlash against corrupt politicians and business people was in Ghana in the late 1970s. A junior officer in the Ghanaian air force who was well known for his tirades against senior officers, Flight-Lieutenant Jerry Rawlings, was arrested and put on trial in 1979 for planning a coup d'état against what he saw as a corrupt military establishment. In June 1979, a group of junior officers sprung him from jail and installed him as the chairman of a military junta. The new ruling group had no mercy, executing no fewer than three former military heads of state in a single day at a firing-range by the beach outside Accra on the grounds of their self-evident corruption. The next year a lower-ranks coup shook up Liberia; the new junta took a leaf out of the Ghanaian playbook, executing thirteen former ministers and officials on the beach in Monrovia. In 1983 another anti-corruption radical, army Captain Thomas Sankara, took power in Upper Volta (renamed Burkina Faso), becoming a hero to the young all over West Africa. The fact that he had sophisticated presentational skills, some understanding of Marxism and an alliance with Libya's Colonel Gadaffi caused jitters in several African capitals and in Paris.

The West African tilt against corruption in government reached Nigeria at the end of 1983. At the start of the working day on 31 December, national radio broadcasts were interrupted with an announcement read by one Brigadier Sani Abacha, a name unknown to the general public. Abacha informed his fellow-countrymen that the armed forces had decided to enforce a change of government "in discharge of [their] national role as the promoters and protectors of our national interest."[63] Quite a few Nigerians at that time were prepared to give some credence to the idea that the military could clean things up. The new coup brought to the fore General Muhammadu Buhari, who justified his assumption of power with the claim that he was going to clean up corruption in Nigeria with military rigour. Buhari had a reputation for personal austerity but was a veteran of military politics, having been one of the conspirators in the July 1966 counter-coup and having served as Federal Commissioner for Petroleum Resources in the military government of the late 1970s. The Supreme

Military Council that he chaired was rather top-heavy with Northerners, reflecting the composition of the higher reaches of the officer corps. Although the regime's number two, Major-General Tunde Idiagbon, was a Yoruba, he too had been born and brought up in the North. Both he and Buhari were Muslims, as were many prominent members of the junta. The Buhari/Idiagbon government was the nearest Nigeria has ever known to one single-mindedly intent on tackling corruption. Within three months the new junta had introduced a programme called the War Against Indiscipline, whose unfortunate acronym, WAI, enabled opponents to call it "Why?" The War Against Indiscipline targeted what Idiagbon called "little but important manifestations of indiscipline". This meant slovenly behaviour by individuals, such as failing to queue, littering, jay-walking, creating a public nuisance, but also more major abuses such as cheating, the hoarding of goods, price-rigging, working without commitment and more besides.[64] Punishment was instant, with soldiers meting out on-the-spot punishments by ordering offenders to do press-ups and frog-jumps until the point of exhaustion.

The junta soon established special tribunals staffed by military officers that were supposed to stamp out corruption through martial law.[65] The State Security Detention of Persons Decree No 2 of 1984 was used to detain politicians suspected of corruption. On 28 March 1985 a Special Military Tribunal sentenced one former governor to twenty-one years in jail for bribing no fewer than ninety-six legislators of the State House of Assembly with a gift of N500,000 [naira]. Abba Musa Rimi said he had given the money to the legislators "for keeping law and order in their constituencies."[66] A raft of other ex-governors got equally heavy sentences. In the twenty months of the military government led by the Buhari/Idiagbon duo, about 500 politicians, officials and businessmen were jailed on corruption charges. It is no exaggeration to say that the major part of the political class was in jail. In addition, the new regime's Decree 4 made it a criminal offence to publish any article that brought the government or any public official into disrepute. This was a crude attempt to muzzle Nigeria's dynamic (but often wayward) press. Buhari's many critics alleged that Decree 4 was enacted to prevent the media from digging into a scandal which he was supposed to have known something about: the mysterious disappearance of the huge sum of N2.8 billion from the state oil corporation, the NNPC, while it was under his supervision.[67]

As part of the new get-tough policy, the new military junta introduced a decree making drug trafficking punishable by death. Decree 20, Section 3 (2) (K) stated that "any person who, without lawful authority deals in, sells, smokes or inhales the drug known as cocaine or other similar drugs, shall be ... liable on conviction to suffer death sentence by firing squad." The first victims of Decree 20 were three petty drug smugglers who were executed by firing squad in public at 11am on Wednesday 10 April, 1985. One of the three had committed the offence before it carried the death penalty, which was applied retroactively. All three victims received widespread public sympathy, not least because they were perceived as minor dealers in a product that most Nigerians at that time hardly knew, and which they perceived to be legitimate, while politicians who had committed far worse crimes were not made to face a firing squad. Those few Nigerians who had even heard of cocaine and heroin tended to regard them as luxury products that were consumed in the rich world. They attached little social stigma to people who simply transported drugs from one part of the world to another in an effort to earn a living.

Of all the actions against politicians from the Second Republic, the most spectacular was also the least successful: the attempted abduction from London of the former Minister of Transport, Umaru Dikko, brother-in-law to ex-President Shagari and a key financier of his party. Dikko had taken refuge in London after the 1983 overthrow of the civilian government but the new junta set about organising his kidnapping, enlisting the help of former agents of the Israeli secret service—while Israel had no diplomatic relations with Nigeria at that time, it was a buyer of Nigerian oil and was keen to improve its relationship with such an important oil producer. A team of mixed Nigerian and Israeli ex-Mossad officers led by a former Nigerian army major, Mohammed Yusufu, travelled to London. The Nigerians rented an apartment on Cromwell Road, while the Israelis posed as tourists and stayed in hotel rooms. Yusufu worked out of the Nigerian High Commission on Northumberland Avenue in the heart of London's West End. Staking out the area around Hyde Park, where many wealthy Nigerians had properties, members of the team eventually spotted

Dikko walking down the main artery of the neighbourhood, Queensway. An Israeli agent followed Dikko to a house at 47 Porchester Terrace, which turned out to be his London residence. An Israeli team kept watch on Dikko's house and on 5 July 1984 abducted him from the street as he left home, drugged him and took him away in a van. Having taken him to their own premises they placed Dikko, still drugged, in a large wooden crate together with an Israeli anaesthetist, one Dr Levi-Arie Shapiro.[68] His job was to monitor Dikko's condition and make sure that he remained drugged and unconscious. Two crates—one containing Dikko and Shapiro, the other containing two other Israeli operatives—were then transported by road to Stansted airport, east of London, to be put on board a Nigerian Airways flight to Lagos as diplomatic luggage. Fortunately for Dikko, an alert customs officer saw that the crates were not correctly labelled and demanded to look inside. Dikko was freed. The Israeli secret operatives were arrested and duly convicted and sent to prison. The Nigerian High Commissioner in London was expelled from Britain.

In the economic field too Buhari's Supreme Military Council was active. Its priority was to deal with the accumulated trade arrears that were causing foreign banks to refuse lines of credit for Nigerian customers. Sacking thousands of civil servants in the name of austerity, the military government made a show of contempt for politics and public opinion, on the grounds that corruption could be cured only with tough remedies. Yet Buhari was careful to mend his relations to the so-called Kaduna Mafia, the network of Northern powerbrokers that had gained such widespread influence during the military governments post-1966 as well as under the Second Republic. The Kaduna Mafia is said to have "dictated to President Shehu Shagari how Nigeria should be managed"[69] during his tenure from 1979 to 1983.[70] This was a period of enormous profligacy that insiders knew was unsustainable. Buhari's main connection to this group was through his nephew (although slightly older), Mamman Daura. Mamman Daura became a director of Bank of Credit and Commerce International (BCCI),[71] which set up shop in Nigeria in 1979 and became the favourite bank of the ruling group, performing all manner of illegal transactions on behalf of its elite clients.

Given the insensitivity of Buhari and Idiagbon to vested interests, it is unsurprising that their rule did not last long. In August 1985 the junta's two top men were displaced in a palace coup by one of their own comrades, the Chief of Army Staff Ibrahim Babangida. It is widely believed that Babangida staged his coup because the arrests were getting close to himself and his associates, Buhari having consulted the army command with a recommendation that General Babangida be retired, further to discussions with the Nigerian Security Organization.[72] Babangida, learning that he was to be excluded from the army, in August 1985 took power himself. Being already one of the country's most experienced coup-makers, he knew just how to do it. He justified his assumption of power by reference to the abuse of civil and human rights by his predecessors. Nobody could investigate him now.

Under Babangida's eight-year tenure, corruption and crime moved onto a higher level still. The Babangida regime has been described by one seasoned academic as "an avaricious dictatorship", that resulted in the "Zaïranisation" of Nigerian society.[73]

Ethnic issues

The Biafran War of 1967–70 had its greatest effect on the relations of tens of millions of Igbos—citizens of the putative Biafra—with the Nigerian state. Victory in the civil war gave the federal government a stronger hand than ever to centralise all the payments made by oil companies, to the detriment of the regions. Oil was the main source of federal revenue, estimated at £N639 million in 1972, compared to receipts from income tax of a paltry £N150,000, itself under half the revenue from the same source in 1970–71.[74]

By evoking the spectre of Igbo disloyalty to the nation, the effect of the war was to exclude Igbos largely from getting jobs in the civil service and the army, making the federal state more than ever a foreign construct for the Easterners. Their main recourse was to find work in the private sector, including both legitimate business and its illegitimate cousins, including the drug trade. Although there are not known samples that can be considered scientifically sound, there is some suggestive evidence that indeed makes it appear that some of the vaunted entrepreneurial expertise of the Igbo has been channelled into crime. No president has ever said so, but this may be part of an ethnic division of labour: Northern elites, dominant in the armed forces since 1966, have benefited more than others from oil largesse. The Igbo, having been excluded from much state employment since the civil war, are allowed to go into business both legitimate and otherwise. This is a frequent matter of complaint by Igbo intellectuals.

To be sure, the prominence of Igbos in business, whether licit or otherwise, stems from reasons deeper than their feeling of exclusion from a country that had asserted its control over their home region by force. A wide variety of commentators has agreed that the extraordinary commercial dynamism of Igbo society has deeper historical roots, related to the lack of a traditional Igbo ruling class,[75] massive population growth leading to land shortage and pressure to emigrate, and the possibilities that colonial rule and European-style education had created for individuals to improve themselves.

An odd twist on the ethnic clustering that is typical of emigration all over the world was in the rapid appearance of a Nigerian sex industry overseas that was dominated by women from Edo State, the administrative region around the ancient city-state of Benin City. There are several versions of how it came about that a disproportionate number of women sought work in the sex business in Italy especially. A senior police officer who was himself born and brought up in Benin City told me that the sex trade to Italy began in the early 1980s when Nigerian Christians began to make pilgrimages to Rome in imitation of their Muslim fellow-countrymen who had long been accustomed to making the pilgrimage to Mecca. Pilgrims discovered the existence of the Italian fashion industry, much of it based on small family firms making attractive clothes at affordable prices. Nigerian pilgrims took to getting an Italian visa for a pilgrimage to Rome and using their stay in Italy to buy clothes in bulk, which they could take back and sell at a good profit. The pioneers of this Italian business happened to be from Benin City. As times grew hard, some women also discovered that they could make money during their stay in Italy by selling sex, investing their profits in fashion items that they could take back to Nigeria for sale.[76] In the early days of this business a short stay in Italy could be enough to launch a woman into a commercial career, but these pioneers soon controlled entry to the business, keeping it in the hands of Benin City women.

According to an Italian study,[77] the presence of Nigerians in the sex industry in Italy was hastened by the spread of AIDS in the late 1980s, as Italian men who made use of commercial sex came to fear Italian prostitutes and believed that the newcomers from Nigeria had a higher chance of being disease-free. The number of Nigerian women and girls working the streets spread from Rome to other cities. Until 1991 it remained relatively easy for Nigerian women entering the business to get a tourist visa and fly straight to Rome from Lagos. The main problem for new entrants was to raise the capital for a plane ticket to Italy. This provided a business opportunity for the first generation of Nigerian sex workers in Italy, who were now established as "madams", providers of prostitutes who lived on the earnings of their girls and often invested the proceeds in a fashion shop back home in Benin City or Lagos, using their personal connections to recruit new girls for the business. This confirmed the dominance of Benin and Edo State in the trade in sex workers to Italy. When the Italian authorities introduced stricter controls, obliging the operators to develop more roundabout routes to get new workers into the land of *la dolce vita*, it simply pushed up the price of travel from Nigeria and increased the hold of those existing operators who had the capital and the knowledge needed to run the business. So great is the dominance of Edo State that, of the 800 sex workers deported to Nigeria from Italy in 1999–2001, 86 per cent were from Edo State and 7 per cent from the neighbouring Delta State.[78]

8

GODFATHERS

When General Ibrahim Badamasi Babangida ruled Nigeria as self-styled President from 1985 to 1993, the main task of the state became to accumulate money for the man at the top, with the most obvious source being the country's oil wealth.

Babangida's innovations had an effect that lasted beyond his downfall, even after Nigeria returned to civilian government with regular elections in 1999. Ever since Babangida's time, ultimate power in Nigeria has belonged to a set of oligarchs who make money through smuggling and embezzlement. They are not united by religion or ethnicity or professional background. Sometimes they back causes that can have lethal consequences for other Nigerians, but which for them are tactical weapons in the greater strategic interest of making money; the deaths are merely collateral damage. Although this system has emerged from a history about as different from that of Russia as can be imagined, there are interesting points of resemblance between the post-Babangida system and the *sistema* of Vladimir Putin, once described by an astute critic as "a huge and uncontrolled private structure which is successfully diverting profits for its own use".[1]

Babangida is often known to Nigerians simply as IBB. In his pomp he was also called Maradona by reference to the great Argentinian footballer of that time. Just as the real Maradona was known for his ability to dribble round opponents at high speed, IBB had a remarkable talent for manoeuvre. The real Maradona was also briefly the world's most famous cheat after scoring a goal with his hand in the 1986 World Cup.

Babangida was part of a cohort of military men of Northern origin who were junior officers at the time of the 1966 counter-coup, were middle-ranking during the Murtala coup of 1975, and had reached the rank of general by the 1980s. In addition, Babangida could claim political descent from Ahmadu Bello, the Sardauna of Sokoto murdered in the first coup of 1966. The line ran via Babangida's political godfather, Ibrahim Dasuki, who had served as a private secretary to Bello.

One of the most insightful accounts of the workings of the Babangida regime was written by the Jamaican intellectual Patrick Wilmot, who knew Babangida and other senior generals socially during the 1970s boom years. Wilmot despised Babangida, describing him as small and insignificant in company, with a shifty reluctance to make eye contact.[2] Many other people, it should be said, remember Babangida as charming,[3] as he flashed his famous gap-toothed smile. Wilmot thought that Babangida had all the classic attributes of a psychopathic personality, as far as he understood this condition from a course in Abnormal Psychology he had once taken at Yale University.[4] A professor of sociology and an ardent Marxist, Wilmot worked for years as a lecturer at Ahmadu Bello University, a bastion of radicalism in the deeply conservative North and had a network of ex-students, most of them Northerners, that included several who went on to occupy senior positions in government. It was from information supplied by his alumni that Wilmot gained a degree of insight into the workings of the military elite that was unusual for a foreigner. He learned that Babangida maintained an exclusive clique around himself, and that among Babangida's "boys" a cult of homosexuality was in vogue. These were not just people who happened to be gay— the IBB boys had many of the hallmarks of a sect.[5]

Babangida...and another criminal arrives

In office, Babangida was intent on winning the support of Nigeria's elites, whatever their record. Public officials who had been convicted of fraud and embezzlement under Buhari were released and given back the assets that had been forfeited from them. Some were even given senior positions in government. Within the armed forces, outside his personal clique Babangida dispersed power to avoid the possibility of a new coup. Within the state, he obliged all senior officials to be part of his personal patronage system, "settling" political opponents, as it was said, by supplying them with money. "The settlement syndrome" was defined as "a process of sealing, blocking or shutting the mouths of political opponents with money".[6] Given his mastery of this technique Babangida needed huge amounts of money at his personal disposal to give to his cronies, bribe allies and buy off enemies. Among the many scandals of the Babangida years was the murder by parcel-bomb in 1986 of the newspaper editor Dele Giwa. It is widely believed in Nigeria that Giwa's death was connected to his investigations into elite drug-trading. Specifically, he is said to have been targeted as a result of an interview he had conducted with a former drug courier, one Gloria Okon, who had worked on behalf of principals in very senior positions of the state bureaucracy or for their families. Years later, when Nigeria staged its own truth commission, one of the country's leading human rights lawyers and one of its most senior journalists jointly petitioned the members of the Human Rights Violations Investigation Commission, popularly called the Oputa Panel, requesting this body to charge General Babangida and others with murder.[7]

Criminals and corrupt politicians need banks, preferably ones that will not ask questions about the source of their funds. In Babangida's case, his favoured bank was the Bank of Credit and Commerce International, the notorious bank that, proclaiming itself a Third World champion, had established itself in Nigeria in 1979, attracted by the smell of fraud and drug money, and had integrated itself into a practice of financial corruption and money-laundering that was "systemic and endemic".[8] As we have seen, BCCI was the bank of choice for politicians from the day it opened its doors in Nigeria. The chairman of BCCI (Nigeria) Ltd and one of its largest shareholders was Ibrahim Dasuki, one of General Babangida's closest associates, whose son was the president's aide-de-camp, one of the Babangida boys.[9] In 1988 Babangida appointed Dasuki to be the sultan of Sokoto. Known as Sarkin Musulmi, or commander of the faithful, he was seen as the spiritual leader of Nigeria's 70 million Muslims, a role inherited from the founder of Northern Nigeria, Usman Dan Fodio. Appointing Dasuki to this position was roughly equivalent to appointing Bernie Madoff as the

Pope. BCCI boomed to the extent that by 1987 it had thirty-three branches in Nigeria.[10] Other bankers, unable to get their money out of Nigeria easily, speculated that BCCI flourished on account of its political connections. Only later did it become clear that BCCI was making huge profits by converting naira to dollars illegally and channelling the money abroad. When BCCI subsequently collapsed, in what was then the world's biggest-ever bank failure, the full extent of its criminal dealings became known.

Using the BCCI network as his starting point, Babangida proceeded to set up a personalised system of financial corruption sometimes known to Nigerians as "Babangida Unlimited". Based on the private sale of oil and privileged access to the sovereign instruments of currency control, the system operated through the national oil company, NNPC, and the Central Bank.[11] Traders and market regulators noted an increase in frauds involving cargoes of Nigerian oil, whether at the direct behest of President Babangida or by others using their own initiative. Sometimes false cargoes were sold and resold several times.[12] During the Gulf War of 1990–91, when the oil price abruptly rose, Nigeria gained windfall profits that mysteriously vanished. The respected economist Pius Okigbo was appointed to investigate. Although his report was never published, Okigbo is reported to have estimated that between September 1988 and June 1994, a total of $12.4 billion had disappeared, much of it apparently through special accounts operated by President Babangida.[13] The correspondent of Britain's *Financial Times* got wind of the story and discovered that some of the money had been diverted by inflating the cost of work done by the Germany company Forestal.[14] The correspondent, William Keeling, was promptly deported.

Babangida's political trickery was a disaster for Nigeria's economy. More than ever it became dependent on oil as the old staple cash crops of palm oil, groundnuts and cocoa declined to the point of insignificance. Evidence of a boom in cocoa exports that created brief excitement among the liberal economists who held sway in Washington and London turned out to be an illusion created by over-invoicing by foreign traders as a way of getting their money out of the country.[15] Under international pressure to clean up the economy, Babangida ran his own version of austerity claiming that it was preferable to the standard World Bank/International Monetary Fund structural adjustment programmes then being applied all over Africa and that were loathed by many Nigerians as a usurpation of national sovereignty. An import licencing system for buying foreign exchange was replaced by a deregulated system called the second-tier foreign exchange market which gave banks a monopoly on the official allocation of foreign exchange. This was a gold mine for IBB cronies, with many banks coming under the ownership of "fraudsters [and] crooks" who attracted deposits that they simply "converted to their own use".[16] When the government was obliged to restore import licensing, it only created more opportunities for patronage and theft.[17]

Bank reforms carried out under guise of liberal reform thus did nothing to help the economy but did allow dishonest bankers to manipulate the exchange rate for profit.[18] The naira was massively devalued, going from parity with the US dollar to 140 to the dollar by 1994. The number of banks grew from 41 in 1985 to over 120 in 1993.[19] Bureaux de change also sprang up, and non-bank finance houses grew from zero to over 600 in just two years, in line with the liberalisation of the financial system recommended by the pundits in Washington.[20] Among the victims of austerity were junior civil servants and army officers who saw their salary eaten up by inflation as the value of the naira fell, causing them more than ever to look for opportunities to get money through soliciting bribes or other forms of corruption. Basic social services previously assured by the state became inaccessible to most people. There was an explosion of violent crime.[21] When in 1990 Nigeria sent a military expeditionary force to war-torn Liberia, it turned into a wonderful opportunity for Babangida and assorted military chieftains to perpetrate a range of frauds extending from oil smuggling to the embezzlement of the military budget.[22] The later anti-corruption chief Nuhu Ribadu claimed that the IBB government even paid off fake debts at public expense.[23]

The anthropologist Andrew Apter has written an insightful essay called "IBB=419", a slogan he once saw written on a placard held by an anti-Babangida demonstrator,[24] suggesting that Babangida himself was essentially a fraudster. This simple equation carried a lot of meaning. Nigerian politics became a theatre of prestidigitation as a government dominated by one single trickster pretended to implement conventional liberal policies but actually encouraged the growth of

parallel markets where the president and anyone else suitably equipped could make money through crime, especially in oil, petroleum
products, drugs and fraud. This was described by the political scientist
Peter Lewis as "politically-influenced arbitrage in a variety of domestic
markets".[25]

Rich Nigerians with sensitive political antennae realised that the best
place from which to manipulate power was outside the state in order
to make maximum benefit of the unofficial privatisation taking place.
This strategic positioning was reflected in the emergence of what
Nigerians call "godfathers", politicians and rich kleptocrats who preferred to operate from behind the scenes in the manner pioneered by
the Kaduna Mafia more than a decade earlier rather than to assume
public office themselves. Political godfathers did not present themselves for election but determined who won elections. They sponsored
state governors and even local government chairmen, moving in to
demand state contracts from their nominees when their man—or
woman, occasionally—was in place. Their power came from the fact
that they have "'a piece of the state' in their pockets",[26] wrote a
Nigerian academic. "What a typical godfather does is to create tension
in the political system and then present himself to members of the
public as the only person that could help others to find their ways out
of the 'dark tunnel'."[27]

Nigeria's institutions of tertiary education suffered severe damage
from application of the Babangida system. The universities were home
to people like Professor Wilmot who were equipped to analyse what
was going on and could convince new generations of students. Wilmot
himself was forcibly deported in 1988. It may be recalled that it was in
order to counter opposition from university teachers' unions, some of
the most effective opponents of military rule, that successive military
governments had surreptitiously encouraged the student cults that
mushroomed in the 1970s. University administrators, often appointed
for their loyalty to the military government rather than in regard to any
academic or managerial qualification, played off one faction against
another among the students at their institutions. Secretive confraternities were instruments in the hands of vice-chancellors concerned primarily with political control of their campuses. One campus group, the
Victor Charlie Boys, was formed under the direct patronage of the

vice-chancellor of Rivers State University of Science and Technology.[28] It was often said that the membership of campus cults and confraternities was drawn disproportionately from children from elite families, not least as they were more likely to be students in any case. The respected ex-vice-chancellor of the University of Ibadan, Professor Ayo Banjo, reported that the leaders of confraternities or cults on campus systematically targeted first-year students from rich families for recruitment as part of a long-term strategy to strengthen their social networks. Initiates were subjected to intimidation and blackmail, including even kidnapping and physical violence, in an effort to coerce them into full membership.[29]

Campus cults turned into authentic breeding-grounds of Nigerian organised crime. By the end of the decade the rivalries on the Ile-Ife campus of Obafemi Awolowo University had become so serious as to amount to gang warfare, as on 10 July 1999 a forty-strong war party from the Black Axe confraternity armed with machine-guns, including local thugs recruited for extra manpower, attacked leaders of the student union who had complained about them to the university authorities. The eight fatalities included the university's chief security officer. There were suspicions that the murderous activities of the Black Axe may have been associated with outside forces that had an interest in asserting control of the university campus. These campus warriors visited herbalists in search of amulets to protect them in their battles, bringing them into contact with networks influential in a wider criminal and political underworld.[30] A former student cult member, looking back on his experience, did not exaggerate when he noted: "it has ceased to be play. It is war".[31]

In the world of high politics, in 1993 Babangida finally ran out of space to manoeuvre and arranged civilian elections, after which he lost control of the process. He was forced to resign and on 17 November 1993, Major-General Sani Abacha pushed aside the civilian businessman whom Babangida had installed, taking power himself. Abacha, like so many of Nigeria's military leaders, had been a junior officer in the counter-coup of 1966 and had remained close to the clique of military coup-makers ever since. Nigerians, adept at word-plays and the subversion of official slogans, joked that the name Abacha was an acronym for "After Babangida, Another Criminal Has Arrived".[32]

Where Babangida had aimed to subsume all senior officials into his personal system of patronage, Abacha took the opposite approach—he attacked the revenue sources of members of the elite who even hinted at opposing him, seeking to secure all the rents from state corruption for himself and his immediate entourage. In 1994 Abacha decreed new legislation on banks that hit directly at the fortunes made by many members of the political elite[33] during the era of structural adjustment and who, together with retired military officers, constituted the bank directors and political entrepreneurs commonly known as "money bags". However, one *éminence grise* who seems to have enjoyed Abacha's favour was former head of state Major-General Muhammadu Buhari. He was appointed to head the board of a Petroleum (Special) Trust Fund, established in October 1994 to finance social and infrastructural projects using money raised from a hike in the pump price of petrol.

Plucking his rivals' sources of funds from under their noses, Abacha could not fail to amass a personal fortune in record time. He has been estimated to have plundered some $2.2 billion during his five-year rule,[34] including vast sums simply stolen from the state without any pretence at money-laundering. Much of Abacha's loot was deposited in bank accounts in Europe and the United States.[35] One of his sons pocketed no less than two billion dollars from selling off bad debts bought from Russia.[36] In 2009, long after Abacha's demise, a Swiss judge created history when he passed judgement on Abba Abacha, another son of the late general, confiscating $350 million in frozen funds held in Luxembourg and the Bahamas. This was a legal first in the demand for seizure of funds held outside Switzerland. By that time the Swiss government had already handed to the Nigerian authorities about $700 million that the Abacha family had hidden in Swiss accounts.

Abacha's financial assault on so many of his country's plutocrats was bound to have consequences. When Abacha launched a clean-up on corruption at the port of Lagos, with a view to punishing the politicians of the south-west, where opposition to him was centred, traders turned to importing goods via Cotonou in neighbouring Benin. This pushed up the price of imported goods generally. Abacha's own security people, having taken control of the port of Lagos, promptly launched turf wars with each other for control over the most valuable rents.[37]

Internationally, Abacha became most notorious for the cynical execution of the Southern politician and environmental campaigner Ken

Saro-Wiwa, carried out in such a way as to snub a public appeal for clemency from South African President Nelson Mandela, then at the height of his world popularity. When Abacha died mysteriously in 1998—allegedly from heart failure while under the influence of Viagra and cavorting with a bevy of foreign prostitutes, but most likely poisoned—Nigeria was able to revert to civilian rule.

On 29 May 1999, with barely six months to the new millennium, Nigeria became a democracy once again with the inauguration of a new republican constitution, its fourth in less than forty years of sovereign existence. This is a revised version of the country's 1979 constitution, which was itself based on the US model but with the addition of some specifically Nigerian features, such as section 34, sub-section 4, of the constitution, which criminalises membership of secret societies.

The former general and ex-military head of state Olusegun Obasanjo was sworn in as president after winning an official 63 per cent of votes cast in the presidential election three months earlier. Obasanjo could not have won—or even campaigned at all—without the support of a coterie of kingmakers, many of them ex-generals like himself. Obasanjo's political machine, dubbed the People's Democratic Party (PDP), was the creation of yet another general, Shehu Yar'Adua, who had been murdered by Abacha.

So it was that Nigeria's Fourth Republic began life as a creation of some of the military men who had run the country for most of the previous thirty-three years but who had understood that the days of direct military rule were over and that power needed to be exercised less directly. Military rule had politicised the armed forces and reduced their prestige, bringing a threat to the interests of the Northern elite that had often been the power behind successive juntas. The return to civilian rule was made possible by an unofficial agreement among Nigeria's political class on the principle known as "zoning", whereby the presidency was to alternate between the North and South of the country, with no president serving more than two terms.

In deference to pressures that elected politicians could not avoid, the new civilian government under President Obasanjo doubled the financial allocation received from the central government by Nigeria's thirty-six states and 774 Local Government Areas. The oil-producing states were now permitted to withhold 13 per cent of oil revenues for their own budget, which meant they could no longer complain that their resources were passing straight into the hands of the federal government. There were plenty of ambitious civilians eager to get direct access to the state. Elected on the PDP ticket alongside Obasanjo in 1999 was a cohort of governors and legislators who were to figure in some of the most notorious scandals of the Fourth Republic. At the same time a new class of business oligarchs emerged. While these new stars succeeded in the private sector, they remained highly dependent on good relations with the politicians. The most prominent of them was Aliko Dangote, a genuinely talented businessman who made a fortune in cement, sugar and flour milling and by 2015 was reckoned to be Africa's richest man.[38] Others of Nigeria's new business class made money in oil (inevitably), construction and banking. There was also a massive rise in service industries. Early in the first decade the South African mobile giant MTN launched a mobile phone service in Nigeria, soon contested by rivals such as Celtel and Glo. Advertising spending grew rapidly, much of it from telecoms campaigns. Banking became easier at the same time, with the result that there was a massive rise in car loans, mortgages and other facilities providing credit to Nigeria's aspiring middle class. By 2008, a quarter of Nigerians had bank accounts. President Obasanjo acquired a coterie of financial technocrats who included notably his finance minister, Ngozi Okonjo-Iweala, the first woman to serve as either finance minister (in two separate periods) or foreign minister. She was a Managing Director of the World Bank from 2007 to 2011. In Nigeria, she brought in much-needed reforms of the banking sector, making Lagos a genuine financial and business hub.

While Nigeria's Fourth Republic is a democracy of sorts, with several political parties and strident political debate, shifts of opinion and personal allegiance within parties are almost invariably associated with sums of money changing hands. Elections to public office are often marked by vote-rigging and, not infrequently, a high level of violence. In effect, democracy Nigerian-style involves plutocrats doing deals behind closed doors and offering candidates for public election who are most likely to triumph, at least in a party's heartlands, through rigged votes.

When Nigeria became a democracy once more in 1999, it was because a coterie of senior military officers who had held power for decades and made immense fortunes had decided that the political pressure to hand over power to others had become too strong to resist. At the same time, they reasoned that they had enough levers of influence that they could still protect their interests in the face of the elected politicians. They did this mostly through acting as "godfathers", described by one commentator as patron-client relations "taken to a criminal extent".[39] When in 2015 the same General Buhari who was a head of state in 1983–85 and has figured in Nigerian governments for forty years led an opposition party to victory, his first task was to confront what one commentator called "the oil management mafia".[40] This consists of a few outsiders and a small number of immensely wealthy Nigerians including military men, civil servants, foreign oil companies and politicians or combinations of them. Some of the sectors of this oligarchy have names: the Major Marketers' Association of Nigeria, the Depot and Petroleum Marketer, and the Independent Petroleum Marketers' Association of Nigeria. For years, members of these groups, plus complicit politicians, have prevented Nigeria from having a properly working oil refinery and have made billions of dollars by importing fuel, pocketing subsidies that are supposed to help the general public.[41]

Oil as loot

The academic Ike Okonta describes Nigerian politics as "a struggle for control of the country's oil largesse, which, once secured in the form of loot, is used to further and consolidate political ends."[42] Access to oil is everything, and access passes via the state. Some 90 per cent of Nigeria's export income is from oil and gas and 75 per cent of government revenue comes from taxes and royalties from the oil and gas industry.

The theft of oil by people high enough in the state apparatus to get their hands on oil contracts, and with enough friends in the oil business to negotiate shipping contracts and so on, probably started in the 1970s, when oil smuggling often enjoyed a degree of collusion from senior state officials who saw it as a way of evading the quotas imposed by Nigeria's membership of OPEC. In effect, a Nigerian president can have it both ways—he can benefit from an official state revenue from taxes and royalties on oil in conformity with laws and relevant agreements, and he can enjoy a private income by sponsoring oil smugglers at the same time. Since the return to civilian rule in 1999, oil smuggling has boomed as politicians and godfathers have sought new means of access to oil money.[43] Oil smuggling has allowed the dozens of criminal gangs in the Niger Delta, some of them having their origins in student confraternities, to gain access to senior politicians and major sources of funding. In 2004, dozens of confraternities, some of which had turned into criminal outfits, were banned by law.[44]

In 2004, a missing oil tanker laden with crude oil, the *MT Jimoh*, was discovered close to the oil capital of Port Harcourt, with the new name *MT Lord* painted over the old one. The authorities seized on suspicion of smuggling both the *Jimoh* and a Greek-owned tanker with a Russian crew, the *MT African Pride* that had also been discovered with 11,000 tonnes of stolen oil on board. This too was a false name, as the ship had previously been named *Jade*. Both ships subsequently disappeared from custody, with navy and police officials blaming each other. The chairman of a parliamentary committee, adopting a Donald Rumsfeld vocabulary, described this as an episode "that belonged to the old Nigeria",[45] implying that things had actually changed. But they hadn't.

In January 2005, two admirals of the Nigerian navy were demoted and sacked for their role in the affair.[46] Later that year fifteen Russian sailors were also convicted and sentenced to six months in prison after admitting to stealing 11,300 tonnes of crude oil. As a source close to President Obasanjo pointed out, the people who ran the big oil smuggling cartels were clearly among the country's major figures. "If the president goes after them, they could destabilise the country, cause a coup, a civil war", the source pointed out. "They are that powerful, they could bring the state down'.[47] Another analyst said: "This is an industry that makes £30 million ($60m) a day, they'd kill you, me, anyone in order to protect it".[48] This was all true enough, but it implied that the president was a good king surrounded by bad barons, whereas well-informed sources suggested the head of state was himself a beneficiary of the system.[49] One American diplomat reported a senior Shell official telling him how oil buyers paid bribes to the General Managing Director of the NNPC, to a key presidential advisor, and toothers close to the regime.[50]

The barons of oil smuggling had such influence that they were able to fend off an attempted reform of the oil and gas sector launched by the government in 2008. Oil firms, while wanting to see better conditions for investment, also feared the Petroleum Industry Bill as its central element was a restructuring of joint ventures between the NNPC and oil majors that would allow companies to raise private capital rather than rely on an annual cash injection from the Nigerian government.[51]

The current oil management system is dominated by the Nigerian National Petroleum Corporation (NNPC), a company that both regulates the oil industry and participates in it through partnerships with oil majors. Apart from being unable to stem the theft of oil, this system has been chronically inefficient as the government has consistently failed to make scheduled investments into the Shell Petroleum Development Company of Nigeria, which is 55 per cent-owned by the NNPC, 30 per cent by Shell Nigeria and the rest by other oil majors. Shell Nigeria acts as the operator for the joint venture.[52] The NNPC has not published detailed financial reports since 2005. Whereas onshore production that is reliant on state investment has remained stagnant, offshore oil production, controlled by the oil majors, has gone up by 1,287 per cent over the last decade.[53]

Oil theft is also the work of lower-level syndicates, and this type of operation has gained much greater international publicity. From the 1990s onwards militant groups, often with origins in one or other student confraternity, began to emerge with a line in radical rhetoric accusing Shell of environmental damage and of a form of colonialism, colluding with the federal government and doing nothing for local development. Oil companies with a duty to protect their personnel and their property were paying the Nigerian police or even had their own security personnel, but then risked being accused of human rights abuses and of collaborating with a brutal police force.

The first of this new generation of radical movements in the Niger Delta was the Movement for the Salvation of the Ogoni People, led by the martyred Ken Saro-Wiwa. Soon a plethora of others came into being, some of them tracing a lineage back to Isaac Boro's Niger Delta Volunteer Service.[54] The new generation of dissident groups varied in style from frankly criminal outfits, intent on making money from oil smuggling and kidnapping, to others with a genuine political agenda. The group that was most adept at presenting a bold image to international media called itself the Movement for the Emancipation of the Niger Delta (MEND). A string of Western journalists and photographers made their way to the Delta. Glossy magazines printed high-quality photos of MEND's muscular young men, sometimes with torsoes bared, wearing balaclava masks and military fatigues, cartridge belts draped over their shoulders, skimming over the creeks of the Delta in speedboats.[55] By 2008 there were no fewer than 80 incidents of piracy,[56] indicating just how adept militants had become at maritime operations.

In October 2005, a Shell official said that the company had had 50–70 employees kidnapped in Nigeria in the previous year.[57] Militant groups in the Delta area, and indeed in other parts of Nigeria too, were often recruited as political muscle by candidates for state elections, which tended to politicise them, and made them all the more dangerous when they were dropped from a politician's payroll after the campaign was over. The most tragic such case was not in the Niger Delta but in the impoverished northeast of Nigeria, where a local Islamist group nicknamed Boko Haram was picked up by a state politician for a short period.[58] Only later did it run completely wild. Many of the Niger Delta groups had a similarly chequered history, veering between crime and politics and at times engaged in low-intensity war against the police and army. Militant groups worked with small-scale local oil thieves who specialised in puncturing pipelines and scooping up oil that could be transported on small tankers to mother-ships offshore. Small-scale oil smugglers even set up homemade refineries where they could produce petroleum product from stolen crude.

Many of the hundred or more specific armed groups in the Niger Delta are descended from university confraternities, or at least modelled on them,[59] administering secret oaths of allegiance and relying heavily on violence. In the case of a cult, initiation is deemed to be for life, and individuals seeking to renounce their allegiance may be subject to drastic punishment. Some of the cults operating in the Niger Delta are reported to have initiation rituals that might include the murder of a member of the recruit's own family. Membership of such cults can range from a couple of dozen to several thousands. Some are pro-state or pro-government; some are anti-state, while others have no clear political objectives. Individual organisations can be placed on a spectrum going from groups with political aims to purely criminal associations. At various times, their main occupations might be fighting each other for turf (necessary for access to oil smuggling routes or other forms of enrichment), peddling imported cocaine, and working for politicians as enforcers. Alongside these—or, perhaps, intertwined with them, much as the original campus confraternities were intertwined with the official students' unions—are militant groups that cultivate a more conventional guerrilla image like MEND, that have conducted an armed campaign that has at times pitted them against the state and the oil companies. In June 2004, the Rivers State House of Assembly enacted the Secret Cult and Similar Activities (Prohibition) Law, which banned some one hundred named groups.[60] Others not named by the Act continued to exist and to be involved in criminal activity.

In the micropolitics of the federal and state government, the oil companies and local interest groups, shifting allegiances may cause some cults to affiliate to larger groups, and even to work as enforcers for politicians, particularly during election campaigns. When President Goodluck Jonathan—himself from the Delta Region—wanted to bring peace to the fractured area, he did so by distributing money and jobs to the militants and offering an amnesty. One of the most brutal of the former militant leaders, Government Ekpumopolo known as Tompolo, actually got a lucrative contract to manage security via a private-sector entity known as Global West Vessel Service. Amazingly, he managed to buy six second-hand warships from the Norwegian government,[61] which will no doubt serve his cause well if he were ever to change from peacekeeper to militant once more.

There is no doubt that oil companies have suffered from the activities of militants. In 2004 the Shell Petroleum Development Company was the biggest oil producer in Nigeria, with a million barrels a day. It was 55 per cent owned by the NNPC, with Shell 30 per cent, Elf 10 per cent and Agip 5 per cent. It owned 6,200 kilometres of pipelines and more than 1,000 wells, all of them vulnerable to theft or sabotage. Shell was getting about 9 per cent of its worldwide crude oil production from Nigeria, and it claimed to be losing 40,000 barrels a day through theft.[62] Estimates of the amount of oil smuggled go up and down, but by 2013 a good estimate was that about 232,000 barrels of oil were disappearing every day from facilities on land and in shallow water, at an annual cost to the state of $6.7 billion,[63] out of a total production of around two million barrels per day.

However, the activities of militant groups and illicit refiners represent only the lower end of the oil smuggling business. Crude oil can be smuggled in all sorts of ways. White-collar theft may involve pumping illegal oil onto tankers at export terminals, or siphoning crude from terminal storage tanks onto trucks.[64] Buyers might load crude from different sources onto one tanker or transfer oil between ships. In other cases, oil might be mixed in storage. One oil company employee told the BBC that his company had discovered that a vessel they were using had a secret compartment where tens of thousands of barrels oil could be redirected at the flick of a switch while the hold was being filled.[65] Whatever the technique used, the aim is to remove oil from Nigeria without paying due taxes and royalties and without it being officially registered, and then sell it on the licit market in international oil. Among the possible destinations for cargoes of stolen Nigeria crude are the United States, other West Africa countries, Brazil, China, Singapore, Thailand, Indonesia and the Balkans. The major oil-theft networks place their money in foreign banks, using bulk cash smuggling, or via middlemen, tax havens and shell companies. It appears that much of the profits made from oil smuggling eventually returned to Nigeria after being laundered.

Interestingly, the Niger Delta, where most of Nigeria's oil is drilled, has also become a prime location for piracy and the smuggling of drugs and weapons.[66] No one who knows the oil smuggling business from the inside has ever made a full statement on this matter, but the mention of drugs and arms raises the possibility that major international criminal syndicates may be dealing in multiple illicit cargoes at the same time, for example by bartering cocaine for oil. This could only be possible with a lot of money, extensive connections and knowledge of several complex smuggling trades, as well as connections to oil industry insiders. As a major study into Nigerian oil pointed out, the organisation of oil smuggling is probably not in the hands of one huge corporation but of several cells, with export operations being "probably not run by one person, family or ethnic group", and management being "more cooperative than based on command-and-control."[67] Yet it is hard to imagine that these same oil majors are not also complicit with oil smuggling inasmuch as they have interests in some of the refineries in West Africa or further afield where stolen crude is refined. Opposition to the 2008 reform of the oil production and marketing system underlines the double role of major oil companies as both victims and beneficiaries of criminality.

One of the most striking aspects of Nigerian oil-trading is the role of Swiss trading companies, which between 2011 and 2013 were the largest buyers of oil from Nigeria by means of contracts that were awarded annually, with the NNPC sometimes selling oil at below the market rate. Prominent in the Nigerian trade were such major names as Glencore, Arcadia, Trafigura and Vitol, the last two of which had opaque partnerships with the NNPC in Bermuda. Swiss companies bought 37 billion dollars' worth of oil in three years, providing more than 18 per cent of the national government's revenues.[68] It made great use of Swiss commodity traders. In 2011 Swiss traders bought up no less than 36 per cent of the 223 million barrels offered for sale by the NNPC. If Nigerian companies with a Swiss subsidiary were added to the Swiss traders, the proportion rises to over 56 per cent.[69]

For reasons arising from the system of political management that has evolved in Nigeria since the 1970s, the Nigerian state prefers to issue obscure and inefficient contracts administered via one or more middle-men, simply because this creates maximum opportunities for politicians and bagmen. It also facilitates fraud via high-level Four One Nines,[70] as it is by no means impossible for very senior officials to receive advance payment for oil cargoes that never actually materialise. In December 2013, the highly regarded governor of Nigeria's Central Bank, Lamido Sanusi, wrote a letter to President Goodluck Jonathan suggesting that the Nigerian National Petroleum Corporation was cheating the government of as much as $1 billion per month. The finance minister, angry that the allegations were leaked to the press, said that a government committee she chaired had been successful in clawing back monies from the NNPC, while the oil minister claimed that no money at all had disappeared.[71] An eventual audit by accountancy giant PwC established that the gap between the NNPC's oil revenues between January 2012 and July 2013 and the cash remitted to the government over the same period was $18.5 billion.[72]

Democrats / Kleptocrats

In October 2006, Nuhu Ribadu, director of Nigeria's Economic and Financial Crimes Commission, estimated that Nigerian governments since 1960 had stolen or wasted over $380 billion. At the time he made this statement, his agency was investigating no fewer than two-thirds of the country's 36 state governors for corruption,[73] and altogether his agency investigated 31 of 36 governors for corruption totalling 46 billion naira.[74] The scale of official law-breaking was acknowledged by no less an authority than Olusegun Obasanjo, three times head of state, when he remarked that Nigerian leaders have "broken the law [and] breached the constitution as a matter of routine".[75]

One of the most important acts taken by President Obasanjo during his first elected presidency, in 2002, was to issue an executive order that 13 per cent of state revenue should be retained by the state for development purposes, with the result that some state governors in Nigeria's South had control of budgets larger than those of entire West African countries. Henceforth, any presidential candidate needed the support of the governors of the oil states because of the vast resources they controlled. Conversely, any would-be governor of an oil state would need more than ever the support of a national political machinery. Thus did the governorships of Nigeria's four oil-producing states become some of the most lucrative (and most venal) positions in Nigerian politics. Meanwhile poor states, especially in the North, receive far less. All this has produced a logic that emphasises regional differences more than before.

The most notorious of all the oil state governors is Diepreye Alamieyeseigha. Born in 1952, Alamieyeseigha briefly worked as a civil servant after leaving school and then served for twenty years in the air force. Alamieyeseigha was one of those swept into power in the 1999 elections, becoming governor of Bayelsa State on behalf of the ruling PDP. With Baylesa producing 30 per cent of Nigeria's oil, and the state government permitted to retain 13 per cent, Alamieyeseigha was able to use his governorship to divert vast sums of money that he deposited in banks in an array of European countries, with Barclays, the Royal Bank of Scotland and UBS being among his favourites.[76] He bought an oil refinery in Ecuador as well as properties in London, California and South Africa. Calling himself the "Governor-General of the Ijaw Nation", in reference to Nigeria's fourth-largest ethnic group, Alamieyeseigha was successfully re-elected as governor of Bayelsa in 2003 with active support from the Vice-President of Nigeria, Atiku Abubakar, who was the real manager of the PDP machine and himself a major businessman. Alamieyeseigha's deputy governor was one Goodluck Jonathan.

Diepreye Alamieyeseigha was detained in London on charges of money-laundering in September 2005. At the time of his arrest, police found about one million pounds in cash in his London home, and later some £1.8 million in cash and bank accounts. His properties in London were worth an alleged £10 million. His family had also banked large quantities of cash during his term of office.[77] He was released on bail pending trial but on Friday, 18 November 2005 he boarded a Eurostar train to Paris and then made it back home, where hundreds of supporters welcomed him back to his official residence at Creek House in Yenagoa.[78] Government officials said he escaped disguised as a woman, although he claimed it was the work of God.

Alamieyeseigha was then impeached and charged in Nigeria with illegally operating foreign accounts in London, Cyprus, Denmark and the United States. It was his conviction that brought the state governorship to his deputy, Goodluck Jonathan, paving the way for his unlikely rise to the presidency. Alamieyeseigha was released from prison in 2007, two days after receiving a two-year sentence, having already served two years on remand. In 2013 President Jonathan issued a presidential pardon to his former boss Alamieyeseigha because he had been "remorseful", presidential adviser Doyin Okupe said.[79] "What is eminently wrong, you know, in giving a remorseful sinner pardon?" Okupe asked.[80]

By 2014, Alamieyeseigha was eyeing a seat in the national Senate. This was a well-worn route for felons. A former senior police officer who had himself made it to the Senate, Nuhu Aliyu, once noted that some of his Senate colleagues were professional criminals. Another former police chief once declared himself surprised to find in the Senate someone he had sent to prison, whom he thought was still under lock and key.[81]

While state governors have provided some of the most sensational and blatant stories of corruption from the vast democratic kleptocracy that Nigeria has become, it would be wrong to overlook the more discreet role of foreign companies, as always prepared to offer inducements for state contracts. A US court imposed a fine of half a billion dollars on the KBR company, a subsidiary of the oil services giant Halliburton, for bribing Nigerian officials to the tune of $180 million between 1995 and 2002. During almost exactly that same period KBR's parent company, Halliburton, was chaired by the former

Defense Secretary and later Vice-President, Dick Cheney. In similar mode, Siemens was convicted by a German court for maintaining a secret bribery fund of over $1 billion that it used to bribe Nigerian officials.[82] This suggested that the dash system of the 1950s had grown to levels undreamed of.

It seems that the corruption of several generations of politicians, military and civilian, has damaged the legitimacy of the Nigerian state and of almost all the people associated with it, as well as many of the companies that have done business with it. It has also subverted the honour codes of proud groups of people. As long ago as the early 1980s, an eminent Igbo writer noted that "the northern Muslim has lost much of his reputation" in regard to the reliability of the spoken word. A northern Muslim, he said, "can now call on Allah or swear by the Koran nearly as glibly as the Christian invokes God and the Bible".[83]

9

THE BUSINESS OF CRIME

By 2003, about 15 million Nigerians were living outside their country.[1] By 2015, in the Chinese city of Guangzhou alone there were hundreds of thousands of Africans, many of them Nigerians.[2] Each Nigerian community abroad has its own characteristics reflecting both different types of cultural connection and different periods of emigration. In the United Kingdom there is a disproportionate number of Yorubas, reflecting the fact that Lagos and its hinterland was an early hub of Anglo-Nigerian relations and that Yoruba students were travelling to Britain from an early date. In the United States, where the bulk of Nigerians arrived rather later, Nigerian communities seem to be disproportionately composed of Igbos. Houston, the oil capital of Texas, has a particularly large Nigerian population. In Dubai and the Middle East one is more likely to meet Fulani and Hausa, from Northern Nigeria.

Wherever they head, most Nigerians going abroad need to make money to survive and to provide for their families back home, and indeed this is the prime reason for leaving their country in the first place. In most cases people look for whatever work they can find, as is clear from a description of the difficulties experienced by, for example, some of the 2,000 Nigerians who were living in Mumbai by the start of the present century. As in quite a few Nigerian expatriate communities, many of them work in the import-export business and some trade drugs or busy themselves with Four One Nine frauds or indeed dabble in all of these.[3] Probably most emigrants go abroad with little idea of how they will actually make money, and only later do some discover that the easiest way is through some form of illegality. From Abidjan in Côte d'Ivoire there are reports of whole communities of Nigerians, mostly Igbo, working on Internet-based fraud.[4] There are Nigerian fraudsters in Australia,[5] and indeed in probably just about every country on earth. In South Africa, Nigerian immigrants established themselves in the drug trade especially with extraordinary speed.[6] By 2009, South Africa was a major centre for Nigerian fraudsters, some of whom had managed to bribe officials at the Companies and Intellectual Property Registration Office. Nigerian scammers were able to mimic leading companies and, for example, to receive tax refunds from fake accounts and to intercept cheques.[7] Needless to say, there are very many Nigerians who do not engage in criminal activity. In the world's richest countries there are many Nigerians working in law, banking, academia and many other conventional sectors of business and the professions.

Everyone who has grown up in Nigeria has acquired a deep experience of pervasive state corruption. Practices of deception are simply a fact of life, like malaria.[8] Nigeria's Fourth Republic has built on the culture of deception that grew so massively during the Babangida and Abacha years. More than fifty years ago, one Nigerian writer thought that the notion that "the attainment of material riches is the supreme object of human endeavour" had become so widespread that it "largely pervades Nigerian society".[9] In 1996, the academic Claude Ake called Nigeria "a society of beggars, parasites and bandits."[10] Wole Soyinka has described the Nigerian character as formed by "an incongruous juxtaposition of tragedy and the parody of real life".[11] All this is in the psychological baggage that Nigerians take abroad with them.

Crime as a career

To earlier generations of Nigerians, the most obvious path towards progress, development and self-improvement lay through education. Under military government, many ambitious young men aspired to a commission in the armed forces, an obvious locus of power, only to find that the very top levels were suffused with factions and political in-fighting that blocked the way to talent. After the calamitous fall in oil prices of the early 1980s, prospects of formal employment were poor for the formidable numbers of graduates now being produced by Nigeria's universities and schools. The problem has in some ways become still more acute over time. Various individuals, corporations and religious bodies have established private universities to the extent that by 2008 the Nigerian Universities Commission recognised almost 100 universities, 100 polytechnics and 150 technical colleges. Demand for one of the estimated 148,000 annual university places remained fierce, despite the fact that the expansion in numbers had damaged students' job prospects, with graduate unemployment estimated at about 60 per cent at that time.[12] Nowadays it is said that in Igboland, renowned as a nursery of entrepreneurial talent, where Western education was received enthusiastically at an earlier period, many adolescents prefer to apprentice themselves to a trader or manufacturer rather than continue in education.

Some graduates become employed in criminal activity, usually smuggling or white-collar crime, but even armed robbery—in Kwara State, the police claimed in 2006 that most of the armed robbery suspects they had arrested in the first half of the year were students at tertiary institutions.[13] Four One Nine frauds are another option. Wole Soyinka has called Four One Nine "a national affliction of epidemic proportions" arising from "predator cultures".[14] He has described how he himself was scammed in the 1990s by "the daughter of an illustrious class alumnus". Nor was this a unique case, as "another scion of an 'Old Boy', trading on his father's name actually took me personally for a tidy sum in the cause of a non-profit Foundation that he claimed he was establishing in honour of his father's memory".[15] In this second case, the scammer had ambitions to become a state governor.[16] According to Soyinka even Nigeria's Central Bank could be involved in Four One Nine scams,[17] which is entirely credible in view of the abuse of this institution by Babangida and Abacha. The NNPC too has "figured prominently in a string of 419 scams that are evidently ran [sic] or abetted by senior employees of the company".[18] Military officers too, we have seen, may be complicit in oil smuggling.[19]

In keeping with the emergence of crime as a career choice, there are even private colleges in Lagos offering courses in credit card fraud and advance-fee fraud. One such establishment visited by an investigative journalist in 2009 was charging 70,000 naira for a three-month course. "The training was mostly at night", the journalist noted, "at an innocuous-looking cybercafé inside an uncompleted three-storey building directly opposite the Isolo Public Library along Holy Saviour College Road".[20] The tutors also offered advice on migration and fake visas, in return for a fee, naturally.

The original model of advance-fee fraud, in which the first move is a letter offering some sort of business proposition has over time become supplemented by a range of related frauds, including cybercrime and online dating frauds. Whatever the precise type of fraud, it may be perpetrated at a number of levels, going from the unemployed youngsters known as Yahoo Boys who send out fraudulent emails from Nigerian cyber-cafes, often at night when the fees are lower, all the way up to senior state officials and their associates perpetrating contract frauds worth millions of dollars. Some frauds are entirely individual, while others may include several perpetrators working together both in Nigeria and abroad. A study of Yahoo Boys reveals that many of them use traditional medicine or juju, known to them as Yahoo Plus, in an effort to boost success. Some may even use medicines made from human body parts obtained from traditional priests. This is known as Yahoo Plus Plus.[21]

One reformed fraudster has written a memoir describing in detail how he acquired the spiritual power that could make him succeed. Iyke Nathan Uzorma, born in Imo State in 1964, claims to have undergone a spiritual journey that began in his childhood. In adult life, he joined a cult called Okonkor and learned how to go into trance and make contact with the spirit world. "I was empowered by higher spirits to be making money through occult manipulations", he wrote. "Consequently, I had a mystical handkerchief (Lakshmi Jacha) prepared with the blood of a hunch-back man, with which I made 1,000.00 [nairas] daily". There were various rules attached, including that he must spend the money only on himself, that the money must be destroyed if not used on the day of its acquisition, and that he would have to kill a pigeon every ninety days and use its blood to revive the powers in the handkerchief. By his own admission, among those he succeeded in cheating out of money were a banker in Port Harcourt, a businessman in Kano, an army officer in Lagos and businessmen from Britain and the United States. He converted to Christianity and became a popular writer and preacher.[22]

A small study done in the university town of Ile-Ife in the mid-2000s surveyed forty self-confessed Internet scammers. These were low-level operators, more or less fitting the description of Yahoo Boys. The study found that half of the sample were in their early twenties, and 40 per cent in their late twenties. No less than 95 per cent were undergraduate students, 80 per cent were Christians, and 95 per cent were male.[23] The study reported that many scammers had moved from conventional advance-fee fraud into the lucrative new fields of online dating and other forms of Internet-based deception. Some of them claimed to work in collaboration with law enforcement officers.[24] It appears that fraudsters at this low level, working in Nigeria itself and probably without an extensive international network of contacts, generally have to sell any leads they make to someone more advanced in their line of business with the experience and the connections to turn a lead into a successful fraud.

The character of the Internet is ideal for advance-fee fraud, as it is anonymous, has no controlling centre, and is relatively safe from legal action due to its international nature. It must also be said that many Nigerian scammers seem to have a talent for computer work. Some have become so adept at cyber-crime that in 2005 the US Secret Service was reportedly detecting some 30,000 cyber-crimes monthly with a Nigerian origin.[25] Two years later the US Internet Crime Complaint Center rated Nigeria third in this category worldwide.[26] Some useful details of Nigerian cyber-crime may be gleaned from evidence presented in successful prosecutions. In the United Kingdom, there have been some successful prosecutions of Nigerian cyber-scammers. On 1st January 2009 Adewale Taiwo was sentenced to four years' imprisonment by Hull Crown Court for conspiracy to defraud between June 2004 and February 2008.[27] One Nigerian phishing scammer, Olajide Onijkoyi, 29, was convicted in December 2013 after stealing £393,000 from 238 victims. He was working in association with other Nigerian cyber-criminals based in the United Kingdom, who together stole more than £1.5 million from hundreds of students. The police recovered chat logs on Onijkoyi's computer showing that he was conspiring with other cyber-crooks from Russia, Lithuania and elsewhere to hack computers and defraud bank accounts.[28] As a consequence of Nigeria's reputation for cyber-crime and fraud generally, some companies refuse to accept credit cards issued by Nigerian banks, while some Internet servers systematically block all e-mails from Nigeria. There are also companies that refuse to ship goods to any address in Nigeria.

It appears that in some countries the number of Nigerian immigrants or residents who have tried their hand at advance-fee fraud at some point or other is very substantial. A detailed study carried out in the Netherlands notes that "the majority of young Nigerian men in the Netherlands are occupied with 419 fraud",[29] particularly in the Zuid-Oost district of Amsterdam that is home to many West African immigrants.[30] Within the Nigerian community, the study finds, "the involvement of young men in this form of crime seems to be the rule rather than the exception".[31] Those concerned often also engage in drug-trading, pimping and identity theft as well. In this case, and no doubt in many other Nigerian communities abroad, there is a well established *hawala*-style informal banking system that enables people to transfer money to Nigeria outside formal financial channels,[32] contributing to the $5.39 billion per year that Nigerians are estimated to remit to their homeland annually. In the United Kingdom, a study found that "the vast majority" of the proceeds of financial frauds were sent back to Nigeria, often to be invested in property.[33] Another Dutch study succeeded in interviewing three Nigerian Four One Nine fraudsters, all aged in their thirties. All three had been in the Netherlands for over ten years, although one had no residence permit, and all three were highly educated. As well as doing advance-fee fraud, all three also traded in cocaine.[34]

Roughly similar sorts of figures to those from Amsterdam have been recorded in other countries with much larger Nigerian communities, such as the United States, where in 1984, the national customs service estimated that more than three-quarters of the Nigerians living in the country were involved in fraud.[35] In 2001 the US Secret Service reckoned that a quarter of the major fraud investigations it undertook involved Nigerians.[36] Some recorded cases of Nigerian fraudsters in the US reveal impressive levels of skill and sophistication. Some fraudsters maintain as many as forty identities and use them to perpetrate cheque and credit card fraud, laundering their gains by buying second-hand cars or luxury goods for export to Nigeria. Some also trade drugs.[37] According to a US law enforcement officer with long experience in the matter, African criminal networks in general are often underestimated by police agencies the world over "because Africa is the poorest continent, so it is assumed the people there are uneducated and sophisticated....Many of those involved overseas in these criminal networks are the opposite. If you've spent any time working these organisations, you'll become shocked by how many computer programmers, accountants, engineers and business degree holders there are among your investigative targets."[38]

Although the Nigerian community in the Netherlands has never been very large, by 2003 Amsterdam had become a significant operational centre for Nigerian advance-fee scammers, probably because of its combination of excellent infrastructure and banking facilities and an international airport with a direct connection to Lagos. The Four One Niners used Amsterdam as a centre from which to contact a "mark" or a *"mugu"* in other countries, and the Amsterdam police at that time were being notified of a successful Four One Nine fraud about once every two weeks.[39] One police expert informed this author of three Japanese businessmen who over the space of three years had handed over some £2.1 million to a team of Nigerian fraudsters. Some estimates are that advance-fee frauds by West Africans in the Netherlands—not Nigerians exclusively—amounted to almost €21 million by 2002,[40] by which time the Dutch police were reported to estimate that Four One Nines worldwide were worth some $2.5 billion.[41] For many years, the Dutch police were rather dismissive towards people reporting themselves as victims of advance-fee fraud, believing that they had only themselves to blame for their misfortune. However, the police eventually came to realise that investigating Four One Nines could provide leads to other sorts of crime, as Nigerian fraudsters were often also active in drug-trading especially. As a result, in 2007–08, the Dutch police decided to target advance-fee fraud. In that period they detected some 2,500 foreign victims of about 150 fraudsters based in the Netherlands. The police estimated that foreign fraudsters based in the Netherlands, 90 per cent of them Nigerians, had made as much as €150–200 million.[42]

No doubt because of this enhanced attention from the police, most Nigerian scammers left Amsterdam and moved to Madrid. It was noticeable at that point that a new fraud began appearing online, consisting of an announcement sent via email to a recipient who was informed that she or he had won the Spanish national lottery. The notification included an invitation to contact the sender of the message. Those who responded would find that, before their supposed winnings could be transferred to them, they would need to pay some administrative fees. The Spanish police were soon alerted to the existence of this scam on their territory, and in early 2008 arrested 87 Nigerians suspected of defrauding at least 1,500 people to the tune of €20 million.[43] Subsequently, the estimate was considerably increased, to a figure of 20,000 people defrauded in the Spanish lottery scam to a value of €100 million per year. Police seized €218,000 in cash, nearly 2,500 mobile phones, 327 computers and 165 fax machines.[44]

Clearly, advance-fee fraud scams have moved on from the first international efforts in the 1980s, which generally proposed a too-good-to-be-true business opportunity, to more subtle temptations. Not all victims are greedy, as a number of charities, for example, have been stung with emails from law firms suggesting that they are eligible to receive a bequest from the will of a deceased person. Increasingly, scammers use Internet dating sites to prey on the lonely and the love-lorn, conning them out of their savings to pay for a fiancé whom they have never met and never will meet. Among the cruellest of the new-generation scammers are those in Nigeria itself who pose as talent scouts, preying on young footballers who dream of playing for one of the big European clubs. They simply con people into sending them money purportedly as a registration fee, and then disappear with the cash.[45]

The creation of trust is the all-important ingredient, and in this Nigerian scammers are in the top class. Anyone who is successful in the advance-fee fraud business has to have an excellent understanding of psychology. Some individual case-studies illustrate this very clearly, such as the case of an American psychotherapist, no less, who was duped into a fraud in 2001–2003 by Nigerians who drew him in by paying money to him in the first instance, using pirated cheques, and causing him to solicit money himself under false pretences. The American was tried in 2005 in a Boston court and received a soft sentence when the judge recognised that he had acted more out of naivety than greed.[46] There are also intended victims who delight in pursuing the perpetrators of scams. There are several websites run by European and North American anti-scammers who try to turn the tables in an online battle of wits by getting Nigerian scammers to place pictures of themselves on the Internet in ridiculous poses, as a way of humiliating them.[47] One British anti-scammer, Mike Berry, was aged 41 when he started his Four One Nine-busting activities in 2003. Ten years later, he reckoned he had dealt with some 4–5,000 scammers during his career as an online vigilante.[48]

Nigerian scammers, whether based in the country itself or abroad, do not operate in large, stable groups. Some, we have seen, may have a relationship to a more senior fraudster, a "chairman" who buys leads from them if they manage to get a reply to one of their mails. In most cases they operate through a network of social contacts that, as a study of 98 advance-fee fraud victims notes, is itself like a human Internet.[49] While successful fraudsters need to work extraordinarily hard, scouring the Internet for names and addresses and researching death announcements, for example, with a view to targetting the recently bereaved, most are essentially opportunists,[50] who will pursue any type of opening that presents itself, for example with regard to fraudulent insurance claims. Nevertheless, some Nigerian-based scammers have established veritable family businesses. One study reported the existence of a Nigerian fraudster who claimed that his family had been in advance-fee fraud for fifteen years and that his ill-gotten gains supported dozens of people. "We have the letter writers and the people who create the official documentation, the people who talk to our clients on the phone, the people who arrange travel and meetings and tours of government offices in Africa, Canada, Japan and the United States",[51] he bragged. The criminal underworld in Lagos especially is diverse enough to support many kinds of criminal activity. The city's Oluwole market, for example, is a place where forgers offer a range of false documents.

The Kings of Four One Nine

Measures taken against Nigerian money-laundering, by the United States especially, were creating severe financial problems to the country in the early months of this century. In June 2001 the Financial Action Task Force placed Nigeria on a list of uncooperative countries in the fight against money laundering. By 2002 Nigeria's reputation for financial insecurity was such that the US authorities issued an advisory notice to banks in its own country warning them about doing business in Nigeria.[52] The Nigerian government, keen to create a better financial environment, responded by enacting new legislation on money-laundering, and in April 2003 it set up an Economic and Financial Crimes Commission (EFCC). Although President Obasanjo seems to have set up the EFCC with little sense of purpose other than to show goodwill to the outside world, the director of the agency turned out to be an individual of extraordinary courage and ability. This was Nuhu Ribadu, son of a prominent politician in Nigeria's First Republic.

Ribadu was determined to take on corruption in his country, and found Four One Nine fraudsters an ideal place to start. Many of them were well known, and enjoyed immunity from prosecution only because they kept police chiefs bribed.[53] Ribadu launched a wave of prosecutions, laying bare some of the biggest frauds ever perpetrated.

The most mind-boggling of Ribadu's investigations concerned the Banco Noroeste scam, which had lasted from 1995 to 1998 and had delivered an astonishing $242 million, making it the third-biggest bank theft of all time[54] and the biggest single bank fraud at that point.[55]

It all started on a fateful day in March 1995 with a fax addressed to Nelson Sakaguchi, a Brazilian banker who ran the Cayman Islands branch of Brazil's Banco Noroeste. The fax was sent on behalf of a group of people whom Sakaguchi had met on a business trip to Nigeria the previous year, when he had gone to West Africa in search of new business. During his Nigerian trip an acquaintance had introduced him—so he believed—to the governor of Nigeria's Central Bank and to the deputy governor in charge of foreign operations, accompanied by one Mrs Agbakoba. The fax that Sakaguchi now received was an invitation from this group to participate in building a new international airport in Nigeria. They claimed that they knew the right people to secure the contracts that would be needed for construction work. The March 1995 fax delicately suggested that awarding contracts for Nigeria's new international airport would entail some up-front commission payments—bribes. Knowing how business was done in Nigeria, Sakaguchi agreed.

What Sakaguchi did not know was that all of this trio were impostors. The people behind the fraud were Emmanuel Odinigwe Nwude, who played the role of the Central Bank governor, and Ikechukwu Christian Anajemba, who took the role of the deputy governor. The woman in the trio was in fact Anajemba's wife, Amaka.

Sakaguchi later claimed that he had already lost millions of dollars in currency trades with his bank's money and that he thought the Nigerian contract would give him a way to pay back what he had already lost—the classic gambler's delusion. Borrowing money from his own bank, he travelled to London to meet the purported principals of the scheme. In London he paid one of them £35,000. In May and June 1995, he transferred an additional $4.65 million to Nigeria in seven instalments, all of it money that actually belonged to the Banco Noroeste.[56]

In return for these upfront payments, the fraudsters provided Sakaguchi with a contract from the Ministry of Aviation. Needless to say, it was actually a forgery. They then hit on a brilliant idea to milk more money from him. Writing on headed notepaper, the conspirators claimed to represent a contracts review panel that had determined that, since Sakaguchi's contract with the Aviation ministry (number FMA/132/019/82) had not been honoured, he was eligible to be reimbursed to the full value of the contract, some $187 million, plus interest. However, before he could be reimbursed, there were something called "fluctuational charges" that had to be paid. This he did. Even after those charges had been paid, further stumbling-blocks emerged—a minister had to be bribed; a document had to be obtained certifying that Sakaguchi's precious contract complied with the requirements on local participation; and so on. Always there was just one more administrative fee before the money could be released. From 1995 to 1997, Sakaguchi kept the money transfers going.

The whole scheme was discovered in 1998 only because at that point the Spanish bank, Santander, was preparing to buy Banco Noroeste. Santander ordered a due diligence inquiry by Price Waterhouse, which discovered a vast hole in the accounts that seemed to be connected to transfers to Nigeria. Sakaguchi was dismissed from his employment and headed for Nigeria to try and get redress. He tracked down the businessman who had originally introduced him to the fraudsters. This person, claiming innocence, took Sakaguchi to the most famous oracle in the whole of Igboland, Arochukwu, in an attempt to discover the truth. It emerged that all the fraudsters were from Anambra State, and, as we shall see, there are actually good grounds for thinking that they might indeed have had dealings with such a famous oracle as Arochukwu.

One of the trio of fraudsters, Anajemba, was murdered in mysterious circumstances in 1998. His two main accomplices, his widow Amaka and Nwude, remained at large. Both invested heavily in property with the proceeds of their enormous scam, while Nwude bought himself a shopping-mall and became a board member of the Union Bank, one of the biggest in Nigeria. Nwude was recorded as using an Indian businessman resident in Nigeria and another associate who owned a bureau de change to launder money for him.

Work by Nuhu Ribadu and his staff at the EFCC enabled others to begin reclaiming some of the stolen funds. Former Banco Noroeste shareholders engaged a Miami lawyer to trace the money, and their lawyer eventually tracked down millions of dollars in bank accounts belonging to the scammers. The group initiated legal proceedings, civil or criminal, in various states of the United States and in Switzerland, the United Kingdom, Hong Kong and Nigeria and succeeded in freezing various of Nwude's bank accounts. Knowing how unreliable the Nigerian system of justice was, their strategy was to litigate outside Nigeria and then use court decisions to enforce decisions in Nigeria. By these means they were able to recover some of the stolen money.

Another fraudster exposed by Nuhu Ribadu was Maurice Ibekwe, whom we have already mentioned in connection with his first major fraud, in Libya in the 1980s.[57] Returning to Nigeria after his Libyan sojourn, Ibekwe became an enormously successful scammer. Among his victims was a German businessman named Klaus Münch, the head of a family-owned electronics company. Using a false identity and claiming to be the accountant-general in the then Ministry of Transport and Aviation, Ibekwe offered Münch a $30 million contract for the supply of computers, monitors, radar system accessories and other equipment for the Nnamdi Azikwe International Airport, a new hub that allegedly was to be build in Abuja. In 1993 Ibekwe succeeded in extracting from Münch payments of more than $300,000 and DM 75,000.[58] Like many successful fraudsters, Ibekwe invested part of his winnings into having himself invested with an honorific title in his home area, Imo State. Armed with the prestige this gave him, he moved into national politics, and in the elections of 1999 that restored democracy to Nigeria he succeeded in getting himself a seat in the House of Representatives. From there he managed to become appointed as chairman of the Police Affairs sub-committee of the House of Representatives, a wonderful shield against prosecution and a platform for future scams.[59]

Perusing the records of these master-scammers makes it clear just how credible their stories could be. Fred Ajudua, a major Four One Nine con artist, cheated a German woman named Frieda Springer-Beck, who was running a small company in Bavaria that she had inherited from her husband, who had died in a road accident. Widows are a favourite target of skilled Four One Niners, not only because they are probably in a highly emotional condition if their bereavement is recent, but also because they are vulnerable to stories concerning their late partner. This was exactly the case with Springer-Beck, who in 1993 received a letter purporting to come from a Nigerian law firm concerning an investment by her late husband that was described as being worth more than $24 million. The initiator of the letter, Ajudua, a lawyer, informed her that the investment would be forfeit if she did not take action needed to claim it. She took the first of several flights to Lagos, met Ajudua, and ended up paying him more than $350,000 that she believed to be fees required before she could touch her late husband's non-existent investment. Springer-Beck had been conned, but she turned out to be an unusually tenacious woman, spending much of the next twelve years trying to get her money back and even moving to Nigeria to get better access. After Nuhu Ribadu had begun work, she was able for the first time to get some serious help from the Nigerian authorities, and in 2005 settled out of court with her tormentor.[60] At the time of his settlement with Springer-Beck Ajudua was considering embarking on a political career, like his wife Pat, who was already a member of the Delta State House of Assembly.[61] Ajudua is also known to have cheated a Canadian business-man for $285,000, among other achievements. He had been active in the USA, and in 2001 the US authorities had frozen one of his bank accounts in New York, through which no less than $30 million had passed, some of it en route to Nigeria, and some going to Asia for the purchase of drugs. When he was eventually cornered by the EFCC in Nigeria, Ajudua escaped to India.[62]

Although top Four One Nine scammers may work with associates on specific operations like the tricking of the Brazilian banker Nelson Sakaguchi, there is no evidence of the existence of permanent, corporate-style groups of Four One Niners. What is abundantly clear is that Nigerian fraud takes place at various levels, and that at the top level it may take place with the collusion of senior officials, lawyers and bankers. In June 2015 Nigeria's EFCC arrested six senior Central Bank officials and sixteen bank staff from the private sector in connection to an alleged $33 million racket wherein boxes of new bank notes supplied by the Central Bank to commercial banks in fact contained bits of newspaper cut to size and hidden under a top layer of genuine notes.[63] It suspected that the scam had been going on for years, in an updated version of the old "black money" scam used in Southern Nigerian markets seventy years ago.

At the top level, the very biggest Four One Nine fraudsters are excellent actors, with an ability to play the part of very senior state officials and to manipulate the symbols of state power in a manner to convince a foreign businessman or banker.[64]

Drugs

Those Nigerians who entered the international drug trade in the 1970s and 1980s had, as we have seen, a competitive advantage for some years in that customs officials in the consuming countries of Europe and North America were simply not expecting cocaine and heroin smugglers from West Africa. Some of the more successful smugglers, having made a massive profit on just a few small cargoes were able to build the financial capital necessary to invest in large quantities, and above all to acquire the contacts and operational expertise required for working in a complex international business that was one of cut-throat competitiveness, sometimes quite literally. Some Nigerian individuals and groups proved themselves able to collaborate with such redoubtable outfits as Colombian drug cartels and Neapolitan Camorra families, offering business services to organisations that are generally larger and more hierarchical (as well as more violent) than their own. Nigeria itself is home to what a US government official called "a vast commercial sector, immune to most regulations and well suited to illegal activities".[65]

Nigerian criminals working overseas excel in inserting themselves into a social milieu, identifying and exploiting market niches. This form of flexible organisation based on constantly forming and re-forming professional relationships from a wide pool of social acquaintances resembles a so-called "adhocracy", a management system able "to fuse experts drawn from different disciplines into smoothly functioning ad hoc project teams".[66] This form of business organisation is regarded by some analysts as particularly well suited to the modern business environment. These networks have the advantage of adapting to circumstances—one US investigator in Thailand noticed that many of the Nigerian drug couriers he helped to arrest "reported having been previously solicited for information relative to their arrests by either organisation members or organisation associates. The collecting of intelligence from these couriers was done either directly through prison visits or using trickery".[67] In other words, such networks may have a counter-intelligence capacity.

In the general atmosphere of corruption and manipulation that characterised General Babangida's years as head of state, from 1985 to 1993, the country's role in the global narcotics trade grew. Nor was Nigeria alone in West Africa. From the late 1970s, there were reports of individuals from various countries in the region importing narcotics for eventual re-export. Many traffickers appear to have been acting on their own initiative or at any rate without the support of extensive networks. Some powerful external interests also discovered the commercial potential of small West African states that attracted little international attention, and whose authorities could be bought or manipulated. Some Lebanese networks had used West Africa to move narcotics to the United States for decades, and this has developed into some sophisticated schemes linking Lebanese communities in North and South America, West Africa and Lebanon itself. It is often thought that the militant group Hizbollah takes taxes from such Shia-dominated groups. In Sierra Leone, there was a sudden influx of heavy-duty mobsters from the Soviet Union in the mid-1980s, some of them with connections to Israeli intelligence.[68] The most formidable of the newcomers was Marat Balagula. He and his colleagues used Sierra Leone as a freeport facility, smuggling in diamonds from the USSR and swapping them for heroin from Thailand for onward transmission to the

USA. Balagula moved to the United States himself and became a pioneer of Russian mafia influence, serving a prison sentence there before his murder in March 2008. They also managed President Joseph Momoh's election campaign.[69]

Trafficking networks with high-level government connections emerged in other countries too. One example involved a group of Ghanaians and a diplomat from Burkina Faso, the latter providing members of the syndicate with diplomatic passports. This team imported heroin from Mumbai to Abidjan for onward transmission to Europe. One of the Ghanaians involved, a certain Emmanuel Boateng Addo, revealed some details of this operation in 1993 after his release from a French prison.[70] The Burkinabe diplomat at the heart of this syndicate was also a close associate of Charles Taylor, subsequently to become president of Liberia. Other West African heads of state said by police sources to have been implicated in drug smuggling include the late president of Togo, Gnassingbé Eyadéma.[71] These and other West Africa countries over the years became home to Nigerian traffickers, who used them to import narcotics for storage and repackaging for onward transmission.

From the early 1990s South Africa became one such base, as it offered the advantages of an excellent transport infrastructure and a good banking system as well as a substantial domestic market for drugs. Before 1990, the drug trade in South Africa was largely confined to mandrax and locally-produced marijuana. The South African police, preoccupied by political matters, ignored the risk posed by international traffickers, who flocked to the country from Eastern Europe and Nigeria especially. By 2005, there were between 40,000 and 100,000 Nigerians living in South Africa, as many as 90 per cent of them illegally. The drug dealers among them were described as "the most prolific of the organised crime groups operating in the country".[72] Nigerian traders also established operational centres in Cotonou and Abidjan, which were home to Beninese, Ivorian and other nationals who had entered the narcotics business. In March 1998, the US government described Nigeria as "the hub of African narcotics trafficking", noting also "traffickers' expansion into bulk shipments into Nigeria's neighbours".[73] After Nigeria had dispatched a peacekeeping force to Liberia in 1990, under the auspices of the Economic Community of West African States (ECOWAS), some members of the Nigerian expeditionary force developed interests in the narcotics trade. Their control of Liberia's seaports and of its international airport provided ideal transport facilities. A further attraction was Liberia's use of the US dollar as an official currency.[74] The Nigerian military, in power almost continuously for three decades, had by this time developed a high degree of impunity. In 1998, NDLEA director Musa Bamaiyi complained that his agents were not allowed to search military barracks, despite the fact that, according to him, "a lot" of military officers were involved in the drug business. He had sent a list of names of military suspects to the presidency.[75] Bamaiyi, generally well-regarded by international law enforcement agents with whom he collaborated, had himself served in the Nigerian peacekeeping contingent in Liberia.[76] Being also a brother of his country's chief of army staff, he was particularly well placed to make such a judgement about Nigerian military involvement in drug trafficking.

Nigerian traders had become truly global. In Moscow, according to one veteran journalist, "the Central Asians…were being displaced from 1997 onwards by Africans, especially Nigerians, who have established efficient and well-concealed networks for selling heroin and cocaine in Moscow's student living areas and university residences".[77] Nigerians were particularly prominent in the North American heroin trade until being displaced in recent years. In 1999, the US Department of Justice said it was looking for two Nigerians who were said to be running a network importing "up to 80 per cent of the white heroin entering the USA from southeast Asia".[78] This high figure is less noteworthy than might appear at first sight, as the US market for Asian heroin had by then lost ground to imports from Latin America. In 2002, Dutch customs officers, in a controlled experiment, for a period of ten days searched every Nigerian arriving in Amsterdam from Aruba and the Dutch Antilles, a route used by many of the 1,200 drug couriers arrested annually at Schiphol airport. They found that of the eighty-three Nigerian passengers using this route during that period, no fewer than sixty-three were carrying drugs.[79] In the same year, Nigeria's NDLEA arrested two Nigerians and one foreigner with 60 kilograms of cocaine, the agency's largest-ever cocaine find, on board a Brazilian vessel at Tin Can Island wharf in Lagos.[80] Substantial though this haul was, perhaps its chief significance lies in the evidence it presents of direct seaborne transport from Latin America.

There was evidence that knowledge of the drug trade was being passed from one generation to the next. In 2002, a twelve-year old Nigerian boy with US citizenship was reportedly arrested at New York's John F. Kennedy airport with 87 condoms of heroin. He was the son of one Chukwunweike Umegbolu, who had been convicted in 1995 for his part in importing more than $33 million of heroin in a period of more than a decade.[81]

By the mid-1990s, thus, some Nigerian drug traffickers in particular had not only developed the means to invest in bulk shipments of narcotics, but had also become fully global, having business associates in both producing and consuming countries as well as other facilities in countries outside Nigeria. The social basis of Nigerian crime networks meant that it was possible for a single drug dealer to have a network of business connections worldwide, quite often based on people from his or her home village. Thus, a middle-sized Nigerian network could offer a drug transport service to other, larger networks, such as the Latin Americans, offering prompt door-to-door delivery anywhere in the world. The same was true on a smaller scale of traffickers from other West African countries, notably Ghana. By the same token, non-African traffickers had become interested in the commercial advantages offered by West Africa. A senior US anti-drugs official, Robert S. Gelbard, described Nigerian drug networks as "some of the most sophisticated and finely-tuned transshipment, money-moving and document-forging organisations in the world". He pointed out that "they are sought out by both Asian and Latin American drug producers" on account of their commercial skills.[82]

The Nigerian drug trade is characterised by a distinctive business structure that has developed over decades, and which gives depth to the emerging cooperation with traders from other countries and continents. The typical Nigerian modus operandi stands in contrast to the more corporate-style structure of classic American organised crime groups that have exerted such a powerful influence on popular ideas about how organised crime works via films like *The Godfather* or the TV series *The Sopranos*.

A senior officer of Nigeria's National Drug Law Enforcement Agency has described[83] how the Nigerian narcotics business, dominated by people from the southeast of the country, is organised into distinct fields of professional expertise. "Drug barons" are those who have the capital and the overseas contacts necessary to buy a substantial quantity of drugs at source in Asia or South America. In this informant's view, a Nigerian drug baron requires at least three assets. First, he, or she, needs to be able to buy drugs cheaply at source. As we have seen, from an early date, there were Nigerians who travelled to producer countries in South America and Southeast Asia to buy drugs. In 2003, some 330 Nigerians were said to be serving prison sentences in Thailand for drug-related offences.[84] Hundreds of Nigerians were living in Bangkok, notably in the city's Pratunum district that was home to a substantial African community. Many of these people were occupied in the textile or jewellery trades, but a significant number were alleged to have interests in crime.[85] There is even a small Nigerian community in Afghanistan. A drug baron who lives in one of these locations or has stayed there long enough to build excellent local contacts is well placed to buy heroin. Sometimes, a baron who has the wherewithal to buy a large quantity of cocaine or heroin at source may sell this to a syndicate of smaller operators pooling their resources for such a major purchase. In December 1997, John Ikechukwe, a Nigerian who had emigrated to South Africa and become rich working the South American route, was murdered after cheating some fellow-traders in such a scheme. According to the South African police, twenty-eight Nigerians were killed in Johannesburg alone in the first quarter of 1998.[86] A second requirement for a drug baron is a good contact in the receiving country, generally North America in the case of heroin, or Europe in the case of cocaine. North America and Europe have substantial Nigerian communities. Even if most of these people live blameless lives, earning their living in respectable occupations, the existence of this diaspora nevertheless constitutes a medium in which traffickers can move. Many Nigerian drug barons keep a very low profile in order not to attract attention. The third necessity for a drug baron is a substantial supply of capital to finance operations. This poses little problem to anyone who has already made a couple of successful transactions. An example is Ekenna O, first arrested in 1995 and sentenced to one year's imprisonment, and rearrested in October 2005. At that point, his assets were over 500 million naira, or $4.16 million. He owned three properties in Nigeria and several companies.[87]

For purposes of transportation, a drug baron works with a second layer of operators, known as "strikers"'. A striker is a logistician with expertise in a field necessary for effective smuggling of illegal drugs, such as transport, document forgery and the recruitment of couriers. Many strikers are middle-aged, from their late thirties upwards. A striker knows exactly who is the best person to approach for forged documents or who is an expert packer of drugs. He receives a fee for performing this type of service on behalf of a baron, and will typically work with several such barons while remaining essentially self-employed. A striker is quite likely to be a former courier who has entered the business at the lowest level and worked his way up, acquiring an excellent network of contacts.

One of the striker's most important tasks is the recruitment of couriers, and one of the features of the Nigerian system that makes effective police detection so difficult is that the use of independent specialists provides a vital cut-out between the top level of operation and the humble courier. After one project has been completed, a baron may initiate a new one using a different striker and different couriers. Couriers recruited to carry drugs from country to country generally have had no contact with the baron who has financed their operation and may not even know the true name of the striker who recruits them. A courier is normally ignorant of the name, or even the very existence, of the baron who is the real initiator of a drug transaction. If a courier is arrested, he or she therefore cannot be prevailed upon to give vital information to police officers. For this reason, strikers often try to recruit a stranger as a courier, although friends and family may also be approached. A Nigerian striker based in South Africa, for example, may recruit South African nationals, or even better, South Africans with British passports. Gambia is a transit point used by Nigerian drug traders, not least because the existence of a tourist trade makes it easy for a courier to travel with a planeload of tourists, or to recruit a holiday-maker and persuade or trick them into acting as a courier. The favourite recruits for strikers based in Nigeria itself are fellow-countrymen who have residence permits for European or North American countries, or Nigerians who possess foreign passports, the more prestigious the better. The preferred destination for couriers in the mid-2000s was Spain, on account of its relatively lax residence rules. An applicant could get a temporary residence permit after just six months, which made him or her far less likely to be searched on entry as it is assumed that adequate checks have been made. Thus, between January 2006 and 5 September 2007, out of 273 people arrested in Nigeria on suspicion of exporting drugs, 29 per cent were heading for Spain.[88] Having recruited a courier, a striker will stay with the person until the point of departure, a period often between a couple of days and a week, to make sure they don't lose their nerve. In some cases, couriers are escorted to an oracle during this period to swear an oath of loyalty. Relatives or home-boys who have been recruited, and made to swear a solemn oath of this sort, do not easily betray their associates. They can also speak on the phone in "deep" dialects of African languages, difficult for foreign police services to interpret if the conversations are intercepted.

The lowest level of transportation is the couriers or mules, mostly people in desperate need of money. Couriers recruited by Nigerian barons, via a striker, usually carry a small parcel of drugs on their person, in return for cash payment. There are also freelancers, individuals who try their luck at buying and smuggling drugs on their own. The 21-year old Iwuchukwu Amara Tochi was one such unfortunate who was hanged in Singapore on Friday 26 January 2006 after being caught in possession of 727 grams of diamorphine. He was just eighteen at the time of his arrest. He had gone to Asia in the hope of pursuing a career as a professional footballer, but had been recruited as a courier by a fellow-Nigerian for a fee of $2,000.[89] Of 316 people arrested at Lagos international airport in possession of cocaine or heroin between January 2006 and 5 September 2007, according to a Nigerian police report, no less than 69 per cent were so-called "swallowers", persons who had ingested condoms filled with hard drugs.[90] Only 31 per cent had packed them in baggage. Of the fifty-five people arrested at the same airport for similar reasons in the third quarter of 2007, most were in their thirties. According to police analysts, this is a vulnerable age because it corresponds to people losing the support of their parents and having to make major life choices. A convicted courier, after serving ten years in prison said: "It's a chain of barons at the top, agents in the middle and we couriers at the bottom of the ladder. The barons are invisible to the agents and couriers".[91]

The employment by Nigerian drug traders of large numbers of couriers carrying small parcels of cocaine or heroin endows them both with a high degree of "vertical" integration of their marketing channel from purchase to sale, and with the means to penetrate any customs service in the world. However, this method carries a high risk of arrest for those who actually transport drugs through customs controls. The number of West Africans sitting in jails all over the world after being arrested in possession of illegal drugs is probably disproportionate to the volume of narcotics seized, in consequence of the human-wave tactics often used by drug barons.

In the present century, some Nigerian traders have not only joined the major league of those who are able to transport cargoes of hundreds of kilograms or even more than a tonne, but they have also formed groups with a rather higher degree of permanence than the older adhocracies. The first recorded case of a Nigerian smuggler transporting heroin in bulk is that of Joe Brown Akubueze, who imported some 250 kilograms of heroin from Thailand by sea, packed in water coolers, in December 1993. He was arrested in Nigeria after a tip-off, and sentenced by a court to 115 years in prison, of which he served ten years before being released.[92] In retrospect, this was an early indicator of a move towards very large shipments by air and sea, although the classic Nigerian courier trade still remained as strong as ever until quite recently. From the late 1990s, there were growing reports of "very large consignments" of drugs heading to West Africa "by ship or commercial containers", according to a police officer working for the United Nations.[93] On 31 January 2008, 2.4 tonnes of cocaine were on board the *Blue Atlantic* when it was intercepted by the French navy off the Liberian coast, en route to Nigeria.[94] Cargoes of comparable size have been detected in or close to the offshore waters of Cape Verde, Senegal, Mauritania, Guinea-Bissau, Guinea, Liberia, Sierra Leone, Ghana and Benin. In many of these seizures, Nigerian traders were involved as part of an international syndicate, suggesting that multinational groups exist. In 2006, Nigeria's drug police, the NDLEA, was reported to have seized no less than 14.2 tonnes of cocaine located in a container on a ship, the *MSV Floriana*, berthed at Lagos's Tin Can Island port. According to press reports, the ship had originally come from Peru via the United States and Cameroon. However, several features of this case as reported by the press are puzzling.[95]

Foreign drug importers, often Latin Americans, often seek partnerships with Nigerian drug traffickers who have longstanding connections in South America. In time, multinational groups have formed in which Nigerians may work with Latin Americans and Europeans, including Russians, as well as other West Africans. When Gambian and British officials seized two tonnes of cocaine in Gambia in May 2010, Nigerians were among those arrested.[96] US officials arrested at least one Nigerian among a mixed group of Europeans, Africans and Latin Americans involved in a lengthy negotiation for a multi-tonne cocaine shipment in Liberia. Among those who appeared before a US court in 2011 in connection with this affair was a Nigerian, Chigbo Umeh. Umeh had got into the drug trade in the early 1990s, when he was a college student in Lagos. He began helping Nigerian friends in the United States to smuggle heroin from Afghanistan through Nigeria into New Jersey and soon became a professional drug dealer, serving a six-year term in a US prison before his eventual conviction for the huge Liberian deal.[97]

When a Latin American group wants to export drugs to West Africa and needs local services, including political protection, safehouses and so on, they often approach resident Nigerian traders who are already well established regionally. The Nigerians are often paid in kind for logistical services rendered at the West African stage of the operation, provided with parcels of cocaine. The Nigerians can then use this to operate their traditional courier service to European markets. In December 2006, 32 cocaine mules traveling from Guinea-Conakry via Morocco were arrested at Amsterdam airport. No fewer than 28 of the 32 were Nigerians.[98] As we have seen, in the Niger Delta, local militias smuggling crude oil to tankers moored offshore are said to be paid not only with cash and weapons, but also with cocaine.[99] Some of the cocaine imported into Nigeria in this process is consumed by foot soldiers in the militias, and towns like Warri and Port Harcourt have now become drug centres.

In more recent times a major heroin trade has emerged linking producers in Pakistan and Iran with East Africa. Cargoes of up to a tonne of heroin are taken by dhow over the Indian Ocean, following trade routes two thousand years old. In East Africa Nigerians figure among the leading wholesalers who buy these goods for onward transport to consumer markets.[100] Nigerian traders are also active in transporting heroin from Kano to Saudi Arabia.[101] By 2015 it was said that meth-amphetamines were being manufactured in Nigeria primarily for export to Japan and other East Asian destinations.

However, in view of the extensive literature on illicit recreational drugs, it is striking that there is far less said and done about a plague probably more harmful to Nigeria's population, namely the 60 per cent of pharmaceutical drugs that, among drugs on sale in Nigeria in 2003, were said to be counterfeit, substandard or expired. Many counterfeit drugs are imported from China or India or made in the great market at Onitsha. The selling of patent medicines is a long established trade in the South of Nigeria. When in 2001 the National Agency for Food and Drug Administration and Control acquired a dynamic director in the person of Dora Akunyili, one of Nigeria's biggest fake-medicine dealers tried to have her killed. He was eventually sent for trial by the Supreme Court.[102] Some pharmaceutical companies had even resorted to doing clinical tests in Nigeria where monitoring was far less strict than in the developed world, a theme in the novel *The Constant Gardener*.[103]

Sex work

On 4 May 2006, a young woman calling herself Jennifer arrived at Amsterdam's Schiphol airport on a direct flight from Lagos. On passing through security, she presented a false passport but she could not be deported as she claimed to be under 16. Dutch gendarmes took her to a detention centre, as is standard practice. The very next day Jennifer received a phone call from a Nigerian in Germany. Shortly afterwards she disappeared, caught up by a Nigerian smuggling gang that special-ised in bringing girls like her from Nigeria and sending them to work in the sex industry in Italy.

It emerged that the person who called Jennifer from Germany was one Solomon Osaikhwuwuomwan, who had previously been investi-gated no less than five times for suspected people-smuggling.[104] Dutch police monitored his contacts by placing a bug on his BMW car and tapping his phone, and by these means they learned of his association with a fellow-Nigerian called Gilbert Ektor, who was living in the United Kingdom. Eventually the police found that these two were part of a wider criminal network extending to Italy, France, Belgium and Nigeria itself, some of whose members had been in the people-smuggling business for ten years or more. Ektor, based in the UK, was the chief European coordinator and was often referred to in tapped calls as "chairman". The system worked as follows: a girl arriving at Schiphol would be taken to a detention centre and then contacted by Osaikhwuwuomwan. He would eventually help her abscond from the detention centre and take her by car to Paris, where she was received by a female member of the group who then put the girl on a train to Italy. There, another member of the ring was in contact with Nigerian "madams", brothel keepers and whoremongers, many of whom were themselves ex-streetwalkers. The madam who received a new girl for her stable then remitted a fee to Osaikhwuwuomwan and Ektor via Western Union, and these two repatriated their profits to Nigeria via an underground banking network.[105] Various members of the group specialised in such matters as finance, transport and housing. One had the task of obtaining forged documents that he had made in Amsterdam by a Surinamese national, and another specialised in making "legends" for the girls that they could use as the basis for the stories they told to policemen and officials to disguise their true intentions.

Jennifer was just one of many girls and young women smuggled by a single network that was well organised and efficiently run. Most of the players, and all of the principals, were from the same state in Nigeria: Edo State. Indeed, so close was the bonding between expatriates from Edo State that Ektor was a member of a club that called itself the Edo Topmen Group, which held regular meetings, with a dress code in force.[106] The chief suspect in the whole people-smuggling ring was one Enadeghe Kingsley Edegbe, born on 10 August 1964 in Benin City, the capital of Edo State. Edegbe was the owner of a massive house in his home town and ran a travel agency as cover for his pimping activities. When he was arrested in Nigeria in October 2007, Edegbe had in his possession material for coaching girls for the sex business, wigs, and other tools of his trade. Several girls interviewed by the police in connection with the business had Edegbe's phone number stored in their phones.

The trade in sex workers that is said to have been pioneered in Rome in the 1980s[107] has spread further afield and developed a distinctive business model. There is no doubt that the trade in sex workers from Nigeria to Europe is dominated by people from Edo State, just one of Nigeria's 36 states.[108] A Nigerian "madam" in Italy is most likely herself to be from Edo State and to have worked in the sex business, graduating to a management position that enables her to make good profits. As we have seen, these are often invested in clothes for export to a boutique in Nigeria where they can be sold for profit but which also provides a convenient legal front for the whole enterprise. Each madam is in need of girls or young women from home to refresh her stable of workers, as entrants tend to last only four or five years before becoming worn out, sick, drug addicted or otherwise useless. The madam will then contact a known recruiter in Benin City, known as an "Italo sponsor", who is known for his or her role in the provision of sex workers for the Italian market. The sponsor then goes in search of a girl who wants to work in Italy. Supply is not a problem, as the small towns and villages of Edo State are full of girls from poor families who are under strong social pressure, even from their own parents, to go to Italy to earn money that they can send home. Many sponsors have good contacts with the traditional rulers who are particularly influential in Edo State. Having identified a new recruit, a sponsor will negotiate an agreement with the girl's family that typically involves a promise by the sponsor to pay for the girl's travel to Italy and introduction to a madam, incurring a debt that is often in excess of $50,000. A Dutch study published in 2012 found that women typically had to pay off bonds of €30–60,000.[109] According to a deputy Superintendent of Police in Benin City, sometimes a lawyer may be asked to draw up a formal agreement binding the girl to her sponsor until such time as she is able to repay her debt.

Whether or not a lawyer is involved, an agreement will always be sealed by a visit to a shrine and performance of a ritual often referred to as a voodoo ceremony. The reference to voodoo is technically incorrect, as this is a New World religion, best known from Haiti, that derives from the *vodun* religion found along the coast of the West African countries of Togo and Benin, from where it was taken to the Americas by slaves centuries ago. *Vodun* or voodoo are not religions found in Nigeria's Edo State. Although it is therefore incorrect to refer to voodoo ceremonies in Benin City, the term has nonetheless gained currency among some Nigerians and among European police officers dealing with Nigerian people-smugglers and pimps.

One personal account of a "voodoo" ritual applied to a candidate sex worker is as follows:

> I received scratches between my breasts, on my back, on my forehead and on my legs. They were made with a razor blade. A sort of black powder was rubbed in. It was then taken out, mixed with blood, and I had to drink it....I was tied up while this happened. A man stood by with a club and threatened to hit a picture which would cause pain to me. The picture was bewitched.[110]

Following the swearing of an oath to seal the bargain between the sponsor and the would-be sex worker, the girl may be entrusted to a transport specialist known as a "trolley" who is responsible for transporting her to her destination with the madam who has commissioned her recruitment. Recruits may be provided with a passport to leave Nigeria but are coached to declare themselves to be without papers on arrival in Europe. A member of the trafficking gang may travel with them incognito and take the passport back to Nigeria for further use. Girls are provided with the phone number of a person in Britain or the Netherlands to contact on arrival.[111] Once they have arrived in Italy Nigerian sex workers are contracted to a madam who normally works with a male enforcer, also Nigerian, who is known in the jargon of the trade as "Madam's black boy". Women are normally required to work on the streets, where madams will pay Italian criminals 200–250 euros per month for a kerbside pitch.[112] In recent years the usual rate for sex in Italy has been some €10–15 per time, meaning that a sex worker with a debt of €50,000 will need to have sex up to 5,000 times to earn her freedom. Often, though, a sex worker caught in this system may have to pay her madam for lodging and clothes, meaning that she retains only a small part of her daily earnings, and it may take more than 5,000 sexual contacts before she has paid off her bond and become a free agent once again. At this point, a former streetwalker may try to set up as a madam on her own account, but more often she may be physically exhausted and may want to return to Nigeria with the meagre sum she has earned. Madams are in contact with one another to manage their girls.

The system thrives on the fact that recruits for the sex industry are not actually trafficked—meaning, taken against their will—but are socially obligated to take part in a very exploitative business. The fact that madams, trolleys and sponsors as well as the girls and women they recruit all come from the same region is important, as it reinforces the social control of the managers. For example, in June 2009 a Nigerian woman staying at a hostel for immigrants in the Spanish city of Ceuta, an enclave on the coast of Morocco, made an official complaint after another migrant, a Nigerian man, had tried to force her into prostitution as a way of paying the debt he claimed that she owed after he had helped her to enter Spain. A few days later, her family home in Nigeria was burned down as revenge for her complaint[113]—an example of how migrants to Europe can still be intimidated and controlled through their places of origin. By means like these, many sex workers are affiliated to powerful secret societies, among them the Owegbe society, through which they flaunt their social connections and wealth. It is said that those who cross the path of a member risk being detained at the Criminal Investigation Department of the police in Benin City, so extensive are the connections of these societies.[114] A secondary school teacher in Benin said: "It's very easy for a member to deal with you. She goes to the CID and tells a policeman: You have to handle one fellow for me, officer. I am an Akatarian". "Akatarian" is the popular term in Benin for one who has been to Europe, particularly Italy, and made so much money. The Akatarian girl gives the officer the address of the "offender" and some dollars and he does her bidding".[115]

The traffic in girls and women for sex-trafficking is very well organised. Some groups are reported periodically to insert a spy into the asylum system in order to acquire intelligence that enables them to hone their techniques to counter those of the immigration authorities.[116] One police team in the Netherlands even found an exercise book containing instructions on how to pass oneself off as a Liberian.[117] Some girls had learned their lessons so well that that on arrival in the Netherlands they asked for application of the B9 administrative rule.[118]

In recent years the organisation of Nigerian workers abroad has extended to other forms of unfree labour. In southern Italy labour markets are often controlled by Ndrangheta crime gangs, the source of a wave of violence against African farm workers so fierce as to attract specific condemnation from the Pope in 2010.[119] Moreover, although Italy remains the hub of Nigerian sex work in Europe, it is only one market, as similar cases have been reported from many other countries in Western Europe. In 2015 the UK's first independent anti-slavery commissioner, Kevin Hyland, stated that hundreds of Nigerians were being illegally trafficked to the UK where they faced sexual exploitation or being forced into domestic servitude. He reported that more than 2,000 potential trafficking victims had been referred to the authorities in 2014 of whom 244 were from Nigeria, although he thought this figure was a vast underestimate. Nigeria was consistently in the top "top one or two" of the countries concerned, with an amazing 98 per cent of those trafficked from Nigeria coming from the state of Edo.[120] In 2011, a Nigerian named Anthony Harrison, who had himself claimed political asylum in the UK in 2003, was convicted of trafficking people for sexual exploitation and other offences. He was part of a smuggling ring that had brought children illegally to the UK to be re-exported to work in the sex industries of Spain and Greece, including two girls aged 14 and 16 when they were brought to Britain two years earlier. Both were from Edo State and were described in court as "vulnerable girls from small villages in Nigeria, with limited education and little exposure to the outside world." One of the girls told police that it was her uncle who had delivered her into the hands of smugglers. She had undergone rituals including being stripped naked, cut with razors and locked in a coffin for hours.[121]

In October 2006 the Dutch police embarked on a major investigation known as Operation Koolvis. They discovered that the girls sent to Europe had been taken to a shrine and made to swear an oath in front of what they called Ayelala priests.[122] In other cases they had sworn an oath to Isango, the protector-deity of women.[123] It was clear that local shrines played a key role both in recruiting girls for the European sex industry and in keeping them under the discipline of their managers. According to the Nigerian police, traffickers in Spain were sending samples of hair from their girls and nude pictures to home for oathing at a shrine. This is regarded as being as effective as their actual presence. The priests kept samples of pubic hair in parcels that were recorded in a register.[124]

Only the best organised people-smugglers are able to take girls by air to Europe, which requires a sophisticated network. In many other cases girls travel overland across the Sahara, often failing to reach

Europe but ending up in sex work in the Sahel or North Africa. Here, too, Nigerians are often present at the various locations on the migrant routes to North Africa and Europe, where those who are well established may specialise in arranging further transport and other facilities for newcomers, in return for a fee. This is West Africa's overland migrant trade, that often ends up in a port on the North African coast. One of Nigeria's top investigative journalists, Emmanuel Mayah, for thirty-seven days travelled a total of 4,318 kilometres across seven countries and the Sahara desert in the company of African migrants on their way to Europe. He described how a people-smuggler known as Rajah—one Lawrence Eyohomi—engaged the services of a spiritualist from Edo State when the party arrived in Cotonou. Eyohomi was introduced as "a prophet". He made long prayers for safety on the road ahead. He then made the travellers swear an oath on his fetish. He spoke in the Bini language used in Edo State, invoking the deity Osunene. He made some incisions on the knuckles of the travellers. The girls, destined for sex work, also underwent other rituals that involved taking samples of their pubic hair and nail clippings.[125]

Because of the importance of "voodoo" rituals in creating bond-slaves, some Christian pastors have specialised in trying to free victims from the psychological effect of the oaths they have sworn. Tom Marfo is a Ghanaian pastor who has lived in Amsterdam since 1994 and who has specialised in freeing girls held in bondage. He claims that in the Bijlmer district of Amsterdam women are sometimes paraded in the open air to be bought by buyers from Belgium or Luxemburg. Marfo is highly regarded by the Dutch authorities and has received various awards for his work. Amsterdam is also home to a Nigerian pastor, Moses Alagbe, who is engaged in similar work.[126]

By the beginning of this century an Italian ambassador to Nigeria reckoned that there were 20–30,000 Nigerian women working in the sex business in Italy.[127] However, the business goes on in many other parts of the world. Some girls promised jobs in Europe end up in brothels in Mali, Morocco or any other country on the overland route to Europe, often under very harsh conditions. Women were also trafficked from Northern states to Saudi Arabia. In South Africa, a sting operation conducted by the police in 2004 identified "a single Nigerian syndicate" that was taking minors from rural areas of South Africa for prostitution in the cities. The syndicate was found to have about 160 youngsters, mostly girls, working in brothels. Some had been encouraged to develop a crack habit to enforce their enslavement.[128] By 2007, the International Labour Organisation reckoned that somewhere between 700,000 and two million children and women were being trafficked annually across international borders in an industry worth some $12–17 billion per year.[129]

Girls and young women who go to Europe to work in the sex trade may be no more unfortunate than other young people who are required to do street work in Nigeria itself. A study in 2000 by two Nigerian researchers who examined 1,400 schoolchildren and 700 working children in seven locations found that 19 per cent of schoolchildren and 40 per cent of street- and working children had been "trafficked". However, the researchers were using a very broad definition of the term "trafficking", which usually means the physical transportation of a person against their will. In this case the researchers seemed to be indicating that a large percentage of street children in Nigeria were working for others, who took most or all of their earnings. There were said to be professional agents who were responsible for recruiting children for work of this sort.[130]

Trafficking people for sex or other types of work can also be mixed with the sale of children for adoption. In Imo State, police actually discovered a "baby factory" in 2013. It was a house in which seventeen pregnant teenage girls were living with eleven babies who were being bred for sale by the woman who ran the place. The pregnant girls claimed they received food only once a day and were not allowed to leave the home. All had been made pregnant by the same 23-year old man, who was arrested. It is said to be not uncommon for such "baby factories" to be found in southeastern Nigeria.[131]

Organisation

We have seen that in the drug trade and the people-trafficking business there are distinct signs of a dominant business model. The evidence, fragmentary though it is, suggests that the people-trafficking business is rather more tightly organised than drug-trading usually is, probably because this is necessary to keep control of human merchandise rather than inanimate cargo. As for the fraud business, this is so vast and diffuse as to defy the concept of a business model, although some successful fraudsters do clearly work in teams at least for short spans of time. At the lowest level, vast numbers of individual Yahoo Boys patiently send out their emails on their own, engaging others with more experience in the business only if they get a hit on a mark or a *mugu*, as a victim is known in the trade.

Among law enforcement officers concerned with Nigerian crime there is a permanent debate as to the extent to which successful fraudsters may also engage in other forms of crime.[132] This indeed seems to happen at all levels, from struggling to get by in a foreign country to masters of fraud like Fred Ajudua, who seems to have been both a major fraudster and a major drug smuggler. Probably a very rough rule of thumb is that the greater the success in a given field, the greater the tendency to specialisation, but there are clearly many exceptions to this. For the most part, Nigerian criminals remain opportunists *par excellence*. Their flexibility is a big part of their success.

Certain ethnic or local groups dominate particular trades, most obviously in regard to the overwhelming role of people from Edo State in the provision of sex workers to Europe. Yet the women-smuggling groups, while based in dense social networks, are judged by Italian researchers, who clearly have their country's own organised crime gangs in mind as a model, not to form a "structured organisation according to a strongly hierarchical model (as the Italian mafia organisations)", but to be composed of "numerous criminal groups linked to each other on a horizontal plane, characterised by strong flexibility, high level of specialisation, [and] a system of network links which is not easily visible from the outside".[133]

In regard to the Nigerian narcotics trade, there is a general consensus among observers that this is dominated by Igbo people. Among Igbos themselves, it is sometimes said that most narcotics traffickers come from one particular Local Government Area out of the 774 in Nigeria. One researcher who did an informed survey of the origins of 104 drug traffickers arrested at Lagos airport in the twelve months from mid-2012 found that some 78 per cent of those arrested were from the federal states of Abia, Anambra, Enugu and Imo, the Igbo ethnic heartland, which contains about 10 per cent of Nigeria's total population. Of these, Anambra was in front by a long way, with 41 per cent. The sample is too unscientific to carry great weight and informs us only about a small number of drug couriers, as opposed to those higher up the business chain, but it is nonetheless suggestive.[134] Surveys of Nigerians imprisoned for drug offences in Europe, America and Asia generally also suggest that Igbos are disproportionately involved in this business.However, it should be repeated that this is purely anecdotal evidence.

There seems to be little publicly available information on Nigerian criminal activity in Saudi Arabia, Dubai and other Middle Eastern hubs other than occasional press items, and yet there are reasons to suppose that many of the Nigerians who trade drugs or engage in other serious crime in those countries are more likely to be of Northern Nigerian origin than those who ply their trade in Europe or America. Recent reports from the British police[135] suggest that criminals from Northern Nigeria are beginning to make their presence felt in London, traditionally home to Yoruba expatriates particularly.

A degree of ethnic specialisation in illicit business is to be expected, as this is a pattern that extends to many branches of business activity in Nigeria. In many legal businesses too, an individual entrepreneur, when he or she needs assistance, often turns to someone from their home area. This may be someone to whom they are related either closely or more distantly, or it may be someone who has property in the same village of origin, or a former school classmate. Entrepreneurs compete with one another but are also able to cooperate when circumstances require.[136] Social networks that refer to a village of origin are sustained even when people live in Lagos or further afield, with the village remaining a moral point of reference. It is for this reason too that when an important bargain is made, including in regard to commerce or politics, the parties to the deal may swear a solemn oath on a traditional oracle. A US investigator with long experience of West African crime groups notes that "like the legitimate businessmen, they conduct themselves as independent small traders, using family connections scattered around the globe to pursue their criminal enterprise."[137] The same source describes Nigerian law-breakers as forming "loose, fluid, alliances, driven by specific criminal projects. Though the associations always remain and can be drawn upon at any time, the actual work of completing a specific criminal project leads to the development of temporary relationships to complete the project at hand". Thereafter, "the business alliances often dissolve as each criminal task is completed".[138]

Igbos themselves often explain their prominence in business by reference to the civil war of 1967–70, alleging that they have subsequently had a semi-detached status within Nigeria that obliges them to seek their livelihood outside the ambit of the state. Many Igbo businesspeople recall how, after the civil war of 1967–70, bank accounts held by Igbos were closed down by the government, and account-holders compensated with a paltry sum. One businessman complained that after the civil war, Igbos had been "boxed into a corner", as he put it, excluded from state employment at a senior level and access to government contracts, and thereby forced into unconventional businesses including advance-fee fraud and drugs,[139] possibly the second- and third-biggest sectors of the Nigerian economy after oil.[140]

However, the Igbo ethos of enterprise also has older roots. Igboland was once renowned both for the productivity of its agriculture and for its prominence in the Atlantic slave trade. The establishment of colonial government and missionary education in the early twentieth century became an avenue of economic advance and social promotion for Igbos, whose political organisation was traditionally republican, without powerful chiefs or any aristocratic class. The population of Igboland has increased dramatically, but the exhausted soil can no longer support even those who stay behind and farm. Still, it remains the ambition of many Igbo men to make money and buy land and build an impressive house in their home village as a mark of their success. There are many stories of people who have made money by whatever means returning to their home villages as heroes, investing in the purchase of traditional titles as a means of acquiring respectability. "Rich cocaine pushers" who hold extravagant parties to celebrate the acquisition of a chieftaincy title are widely regarded as being a recognisable social type.[141] According to Nigerian police officers, those Igbos who dominate the drug trade do not normally choose this career in order to become professional criminals in the Western sense, but primarily as an avenue to wealth and social esteem.

James Cockayne[142] divides definitions of transnational organised crime into three broad categories, according to whether attention is directed primarily to a set of activities, or to specific hierarchical entities, such as the Sicilian Mafia or the New York crime families, or to the transnational effects of criminal activities. Nigerian crime networks least resemble organised crime when the latter is considered in terms of hierarchical, stable structures of the sort that the general public probably thinks of most readily in this context, largely thanks to television dramas and movies like *The Godfather*.

Nevertheless in recent times one major police force in North America claims to have detected a fully structured crime network dominated by a single organisation,[143] the Black Axe, that is based on one of the campus cults that emerged in Nigerian universities in the 1970s. The Black Axe is said by some sources[144] to be a fully organised mafia-type organisation. In this case it is suspected of being linked to the transferral of no less than half a billion US dollars' worth of proceeds of crime in just one year.[145]

An indication of the coherence of the Black Axe and of its close relative, the Neo Black Movement, is the administration of an oath to members. Here is what one leading member texted to others in a communication intercepted by police:[146]

> Your thumb were been cut, and blood came out! And u took an oat! "If I ever betray…., let this kokoma squeeze life out of me". Ur name was involved and u said it with ur mouth, as at that moment u ve enter into agreement with….Dear………, I plunge you nvr forget the oat u took! Take a deep breath and analyze all the words u said with ur mouth! Be reminded that….as word is an entity, jst like naming countries eg Nigeria in it's true sense it is the people that makes an entity, it is the people that exist not an entity, so when u say……it means iz members not as word. Hence if u betray……kokoma will squeeze live out thee. Let's be guarded………oba akenzua, djn…….

The word *"kokoma"* is used by the Neo Black Movement, one of Nigeria's major campus cults. It appears to be used as an alternative identity by the Black Axe, founded in Benin City in 1977.[147] It is also notable that the text includes the words *"oba akenzua"*. This is the name of the traditional ruler of Benin City from 1933 to 1978.

In Nigeria itself the main campus cults maintain their importance. In May 2015 the Nigerian police paraded eleven suspected leading members of cult groups suspected of committing a range of serious crimes in

Edo State as well as some 68 foot soldiers. They included members of the Eiye Fraternity, Black Axe, and others. Many of them were well established in professional careers, such as engineering. According to the police commissioner for the state, the suspects were being "interrogated for their conspiratorial involvement" in the murder of ten people in Edo State in just one month. The police seized cult objects, membership cards of different political parties, passport-size photographs of people marked "RIP" and weapons from some of the suspects.[148]

10

COSMIC POWERS

Most Nigerian criminals believe that spiritual power can have a posi-tive effect on their own careers as well as being a means to exploit others. Iyke Nathan Uzorma, the Four One Niner with a magic hand-kerchief whom we have previously met, whose power had to be sus-tained with blood from an animal sacrifice every three months, believed that he actually came to crime via the spirit world. Every computer fraudster who uses Yahoo Plus juju has to buy his medicines and amulets from a traditional healer, bringing the world of healers and spiritualists in contact with that of professional criminals. One US law enforcement officer records apprehending a Nigerian drug trader in Bangkok who responded: "You can't arrest me because you can't see me. I'm invisible!". He was carrying a small yellow book called *The Golden Key* that contained spells to be used for different forms of protection, including invisibility.[1]

The use of religious institutions for criminal purposes does not involve traditional cults only. More than twenty-five years ago, US narcotics officers found a Nigerian drug courier who had travelled from Lagos to New York with a stomachful of drugs wrapped in condoms. He collapsed and died when he completed his journey to Chicago. One of the capsules had burst, effectively killing him with a drug overdose. The courier had been hoping to achieve a successful run by using candles obtained from a Chicago branch of a Nigerian church, the Celestial Church of Christ, that had been blessed in order to make them spiritually effective. US officials said that the use of the ritual "seriously baffled" them.[2]

Nor is it only the lower class or the uneducated part of the population that believes in the power of spiritual forces. The anthropologist Wale Adebanwi, in his study of one of Nigeria's most sophisticated political and cultural elites, found that "[m]ost of my informants believe absolutely in the efficacy of sorcery, witchcraft and magic".[3]

Cults and shrines

It is helpful to consider the political and social importance of traditional religious institutions, especially in the light of an article published by the Nigerian academic Peter Ekeh in 1975 on what he called "the two publics" in Africa.[4] Ekeh's article is often regarded by Nigerian intellectuals as a foundational text, no doubt because it articulates an opinion held by many of them.

Ekeh argues that most countries in Africa have two distinct public spheres. One of these is that constituted by the institutions created in colonial times, such as a national government, a national press, a parliament and so on. This space is rather sterile. The second sphere is a local one that is based on institutions and practices that are indigenous. It is intimately bound up with kinship and ethnicity. It inspires deep emotional attachment. It is obvious that Ekeh's vision of a two-fold division of public space draws heavily on his own Nigerian background and that it corresponds to the history of Indirect Rule.

According to another Nigerian academic, Ogbu Kalu, an expert on religion, the crisis of legitimacy experienced by Nigeria's military governments in the late twentieth century was accompanied by what he called "the villagization of the modern public sphere".[5] What he meant was that traditional religious and cultural institutions, often located in rural areas and rooted in the finely-grained world of the village, have sometimes become platforms for the mobilisation of economic and social power in the modern sector of the economy. Kalu attributed this re-emergence of indigenous cults to "the intensity of the material and psychological scourges caused by the legitimacy crisis".[6] Building on Peter Ekeh's idea that Nigeria has two public spheres, one national and the other local, Kalu argued that Nigeria's whole political culture "like a virus, feeds on the red blood corpuscles of the primal world".[7] A politician may dip into this "primal" culture in order to establish a relationship with a power-base that carries an emotional charge that is hard to find elsewhere. This technique was used by the sinister, sunglass-wearing General Sani Abacha in his effort to stay in power while dispensing with the support of rival national leaders.

Conversely, by way of traditional religious institutions, an otherwise obscure local notable may offer political and spiritual services to a general or some other player in national politics, thus gaining access to a share of the immense power and wealth associated with control of the state. The warlords of the Niger Delta have achieved this since the 1990s, bringing their local spiritual beliefs and religious regalia with them as they become players in global politics. Houston oil men and Washington bureaucrats struggle to understand how the world price of oil can be affected by the antics of Niger Delta warlords sporting juju amulets as well as AK-47s. Northern Nigeria has a rather different story to tell, as we have already considered in various contexts. In the North, Islam has traditionally been both an ideology of government and a lubricant of commercial relationships. While Northern elites have been fully engaged in Nigerian state corruption for decades, Northern society has not produced criminal networks able to excel in global markets. Dissatisfaction with the prevailing order expresses itself more often in Islamist reform movements, and less often in the form of criminal networks operating on the margins of politics and mainstream society, with roots in Nigerian diasporas overseas.

If we look closely at the particular shrines and oaths used by women-smugglers and Four One Niners, it is indeed apparent that many of these can be described as traditional in origin. For example, one Internet fraudster who had himself been scammed online by an anti-Four One Nine activist in a cyberspace battle of wits, threatened his British tormentor with vengeance from deities whom he named as Ogun, Isango and Ayelala.[8] All three are often invoked by the people-smugglers of Edo State as well, and all three are well known. Ayelala, for example, is a deity popular all over Western Nigeria, widely considered as a truth-telling juju that can be invoked to punish those who offend against popular notions of law and order. In a recent survey, 52 participants were asked whether Ayelala should be incorporated into

Nigeria's criminal justice and political systems, to which an impressive 94 per cent of those surveyed agreed.[9] In other words, when pimps and Ayelala priests require young sex workers to swear an oath to this deity, however shocking it may seem, they are actually invoking a known and respected spiritual force that is considered a guarantor of probity and upright behaviour to uphold the solemn agreements they have made with the girls and young women who are to be taken abroad as sex workers.[10] In Benin City, the cult of Ayelala is so popular that it has become an alternative to the official state system of justice.[11] People go far more readily to a shrine of Ayelala than to the police if they have had their houses robbed, and they are far more likely to get their goods back, as Ayelala inspires respect and fear even among criminals.

Cults like these are survivals from before colonial times, when systems of government throughout many of the territories that were to become Nigeria were articulated by networks of innumerable shrines, oracles and cults. In areas that had little in the way of central institutions, small communities maintained links with one another and across lineages by means of age-grades and secret societies. The main oracles wielded extensive power in the form of judicial authority. This was sometimes true even of Northern Nigeria, although many of the local cults in that region had been made subordinate to the orthodox Sunni Islam that was the mainstay of government from the early nineteenth century.

In what is now southeastern Nigeria, religious institutions were for centuries centrally involved in systems of long-distance trade. People condemned to slavery by the judicial powers of Igbo oracles were a main source of slaves recruited for sale to the coast.[12] Some people were even enslaved in this way with the help of their own families, for example if they were held guilty of a crime or a serious ritual transgression. The historian Paul Lovejoy has estimated that of some 850,000 slaves from the Biafran hinterland that were landed overseas from 1640 to 1800, 67.75 per cent were from Igboland.[13] Slave exports from the area continued at a lower level throughout the nineteenth century.

By the time the British took control of Igboland, in the whole region there were perhaps half a dozen shrines of real significance. The most important was the so-called Long Juju of Arochukwu, also known as Igbiniukpabi.[14] According to a later Nigerian historian, "The

Aro Long Ju Ju was recognised as the supreme god by practically all the numerous village communities from the Cross River to the Niger".[15] In 1901–1902, the British launched an expedition whose main aim was to destroy the Long Juju in the belief that this would weaken slaving networks and establish British rule.[16] However, the oracle was subsequently restored in secret by a local notable. By 1912 the colonial government had learned of its re-establishment and destroyed the oracle a second time, but it was again restored and was functioning again in 1915 at a new location.[17] An assistant district officer writing a report on the area in 1933 noted that, at the time of its first destruction thirty-one years earlier, the fame of the Long Juju was so extensive as to have reached Sierra Leone and even Congo.[18]

British colonisers liked to think that abolition of the slave trade and of the institutions that fed it was at the heart of their mission to civilise West Africa, but in the early days of colonial rule they did not well understand the nature of enslavement, believing that slaves were taken through raiding and that slavery would disappear with the imposition of a *pax britannica*. They paid less attention to the judicial role played by oracles that made them so central to the functioning of society. The Long Juju proved itself so stubbornly resistant because it was both a commercial asset and a central element of the judicial system of a large area. The colonial government, believing that judicial functions should be entrusted not to religious institutions like this but to a native court established for the purpose, appointed chiefs to rule in conformity with the doctrine of Indirect Rule. However, the famous Women's War of 1929 in southeastern Nigeria made clear to the British authorities just how ineffective Indirect Rule was in this area. Four years after the Women's War, the same assistant district officer whom we have quoted on the history of the Long Juju observed that Aro had become "yet another area wherein an artificial judicial body came into being, a body having behind it, in native eyes, no sanction but force as represented by the District Officer, and the Police".[19] Jumping forward six decades, we may note that this is the very same oracle that the Brazilian banker Nelson Sakaguchi visited when he was trying to recover money stolen from him in the stupendous Banco Noroeste scam.[20]

If local oracles continued to function clandestinely and to fulfil a judicial function unrecognised by the colonial government, it was because they were perceived as having an ability to communicate with the invisible world. The oracles also performed many other roles for which the colonial system was not competent, such as divining the future, communicating with ancestral spirits, dealing with problems of premature death and infertility, and so on. When it came to colonial justice, people had a generally low opinion of the government's use of imprisonment as a form of punishment for wrongs committed.[21]

Shrines and oracles remained connected to a comprehensive parallel system whose influence was felt in social and economic matters. The world of traditional religion even had a geographical aspect, as the government built roads to encourage commerce, but certain types of trade that operated outside the purview of the colonial authorities continued to pass along bush paths. "While the produce trade 'flowed' along the newly made roads", Afigbo notes, "the slave trade and oracle business 'flowed' along the old and tried bush tracks."[22]

The Okija shrine

One of the most instructive public investigations of the workings of a shrine in modern times concerns the Okija shrine, situated in the Ihiala Local Government Area of Anambra State, in Nigeria's southeast. The Okija shrine became exposed to public scrutiny through the national press after a number of shrines situated in Umuhu Okija village were raided by fifty or more officers of the Nigerian police, including from the Special Anti-Robbery Squad, in August 2004.[23] By exposing the inner workings of this particular oracle, the raid on the Okija shrine threw light on a far wider system that is usually exempt from scrutiny.[24] It is therefore interesting to look more closely at the history and operation of the Okiija shrine, one of hundreds operating throughout Southern Nigeria, with a view to tracing the evolution of others of similar type.

The Okija village consists of some thirty hamlets, of which two had major shrines in 2004, in addition to other related shrines in the area, some twenty in all. The main Okija shrine is situated in a small wood, described by the press as the "forest of horror" or "the evil forest", although it could also be called a sacred grove, a small enclave of wilderness in a quite densely populated area. The reason for these gothic descriptions is that the police found in the small woodland surrounding the main shrine some twenty human skulls and the remains of dozens of corpses strewn at random, some of them dismembered, some lying in coffins, others draped by the side of the path.[25] A nearby building contained various religious fetish objects and a pit with a crocodile.[26] By most accounts, the stench of decomposing bodies was appalling. Some commentators assumed that the Okija shrine had been used for human sacrifices.[27] However, almost every relevant source, including police officers and a local Anglican or Catholic cleric,[28] confirmed claims by the shrine officials themselves that the Okija shrine had a quasi-judicial function, although it also served other purposes as well. The bodies surrounding the shrine were those of people who were considered to have died badly and had been brought to the shrine for that reason.

In connection with their grisly discovery the police arrested a number of people whom they suspected of being officials of the Okija shrine, most of whom appeared to be from one extended family. Eventually, the police paraded before the press in Abuja thirty-one suspects arrested in connection with the discovery of eighty-three corpses including sixty-three headless bodies and twenty skulls.[29] Police officers took a cautious view of their discovery, refusing to speculate and restricting themselves to remarks concerning charges that included unlawful possession of human heads, obtaining goods by false pretences, misconduct with regards to corpses, and unlawful trial by ordeal.[30] Sections 207 and 208 of Nigeria's criminal code forbid the possession of corpses.

The police regarded the operation as highly successful and prestigious. Within a month of the initial raid, the shrine had received the visit of Nigeria's most senior police officer, the Inspector General of Police, Tafa Balogun, at the head of no less than 500 policemen, with 60 journalists in tow.[31] The Anambra State police commissioner, Felix Ogbaudu, who also received a good deal of favourable publicity from the event, gave a number of interviews in which he scoffed at suggestions that the alleged mystical powers of the shrine could be used against him, enhancing his image as a no-nonsense officer. "When I was going, people were phoning me saying 'Oga be careful o. That juju is very dangerous o. Don't joke with it'. As far as I am concerned, these are common criminals looking

for what to eat and the gullible ones amongst us always fall prey to them",
he said.[32]

Officials of the Okija shrine insisted that the bodies found at the site
were not the remains of people who had died in the sacred grove, and
that they had been brought to the shrine from elsewhere. They said that
people who were party to a dispute, often people in business together
or parties to a land dispute, came to the shrine in search of justice, and
were made to swear oaths in support of their plaints.[33] If a plaintiff
came to the shrine alone, the priests might summon other parties to
the case to appear, in much the same way as a regular court of law. If
one of the litigants subsequently died, he or she would be regarded as
having been punished by the shrine deity, and his family would be
obliged to bring the corpse to the shrine. "You know that when you
offend the gods, you die. And the corpse must be brought here", one
shrine official was reported to have said.[34] Other shrine priests confirmed this, claiming that the corpses had not been killed for ritual
purposes—with the implication that body parts were required for
making juju—but that they were the remains of individuals killed by
the deity as punishment for offences. They said the relatives brought the
corpses to the shrine to placate the deities, fearing that if they did not
do this, the angry gods would kill the next of kin of the deceased in
revenge.[35] As it happens, a government inquiry into a chieftaincy dispute had looked into some of these matters in 1963, so it is possible to
get some confirmation from historical sources. Elders questioned at
that time agreed that claimants to leadership status in the village in
former times had been required to make war against a neighbouring
village to show their bravery, and they would prove their feats by bringing home human heads. One of those consulted in 1963 thought that
this custom would surely be resumed if the government ceased to be
involved in such matters.[36]

The Okija shrine was historically part of the system dominated by the
Long Juju of the Aro. After the establishment of colonial rule in the area,
priests of the Okija shrine still tried to follow tradition in most respects
except for what was officially termed "repugnant usages and practices",
meaning "such things as entail human sacrifices, ritual murder, the sale
and purchase of human beings".[37] In the years after Independence, the
shrine grew in importance, overshadowing its once famous elder brother,

the Long Juju of the Aro. It also began to attract the attention of professional criminals. In 2004 the president of the Okija Town Union said that in the previous ten years the shrine had been hijacked by advance-fee fraudsters and other unsavoury characters, who had turned it into a money-making venture.[38] This allegation certainly fits with the claim that one of those whose corpse was deposited in the forest surrounding the shrine was a certain Victor Okafor, described as one of the top Four One Niners in Nigeria. He had died in a car accident that was widely thought to have been caused by the intervention of spiritual forces.[39] Okafor, himself a native of the Ihiala Local Government Area where Okija is situated, was said to have dropped out of secondary school and taken to a life of crime, becoming part of a gang of armed robbers in Onitsha in the 1980s. In 1989 he moved to Lagos. Within a few years, he had become fabulously rich, reportedly from Four One Nine frauds. As successful entrepreneurs often do in Igboland, he invested some of his money in prestigious titles, thus acquiring the name "Ezego". He is said to have acquired many properties, a fleet of luxury cars, and two shopping-malls in Lagos. He gave lavish parties attended by politicians and senior military officers, but in 1997 he fell foul of politics when he was arrested for illegal arms trafficking.[40] His last involvement with the Okija shrine is said to have resulted from a business relationship with Chuma Nzeribe, an *éminence grise* of Anambra State politics, who had made money in Italy under obscure circumstances and been deported from that country before being employed by the Anambra State government to organise a private army of thugs known as the Bakassi Boys on behalf of the state governor whom he served. One of the Okija priests confirmed that Okafor had visited the shrine in connection with a business dispute.[41]

Among those who frequented the Okija shrine were not only criminals, but also politicians. Chinwoke Mbadinuju, the Anambra State governor from 1999 to 2003, obliged members of his cabinet to swear an oath of loyalty at a shrine in his district, almost certainly the Okija shrine.[42] Mbadinuju's government became notorious for its venality and for its enlistment of the Bakassi Boys.[43] This was originally the name of a vigilante group that had enjoyed great popularity in a neighbouring state,[44] but which degenerated into a gang of political thugs after their recruitment by Mbadinuju.[45] Governor Mbadinuju was beholden to the super-rich oil magnate who had funded his election campaign—an example of what Nigerians call a "political godfather". Soon after his election, Governor Mbadinuju had serious disagreements with this financial backer, chiefly over the allocation of government contracts, one of the main sources of enrichment for members of the country's plutocratic class.

Another governor who obliged his cabinet to swear an oath at the Okija shrine was Orji Uzor Kalu of Abia State,[46] who took this step at the behest of his mother, Eunice Uzor Kalu, the boss of a political machine known as Reality Organization. Mrs Kalu was regarded as the real power behind her son's governorship[47]—in effect, a "political godmother" in addition to being the biological mother of the state governor. One former aide described Governor Kalu's government as "satanic", revealing that Governor Kalu retained the services of the chairman of one of his state's Local Government Areas as a coordinator of shrine activities, with the title Grand Commander of the Faithfuls.[48] There were rumours that still more illustrious political figures had visited the Okija shrine, including two former military heads of state.[49]

Behind these assorted godfathers and governors lay a titanic national struggle for influence between President Obasanjo and his deputy, Atiku Abubakar, who had his eyes on the top job. After Mbadinuju had run into difficulties with his godfather, he lost influence in the ruling PDP and was dropped as a candidate for the 2003 elections, replaced by a little-known medical doctor, Chris Ngige. Ngige was elected only by ballot-rigging, as Obasanjo later admitted. Ngige was supported by his own political godfather, one Chris Uba. The latter was a frequent visitor to the residence of President Obasanjo where his brother, Andy Uba, worked as a top presidential aide, participating in high-level meetings on oil matters. He was said to be a brother-in-law to Obasanjo. Learning from the bruising experience of the last incumbent, the godfather Chris Uba extracted from his front-man, Governor Ngige, a letter of resignation that Uba kept as an insurance policy. He also kept a video of Governor Ngige in the act of signing this letter.[50] As Uba had anticipated, within weeks of the election he began to encounter serious differences with his protégé, Ngige, in regard to the award of state contracts, repeating the type of conflict the previous governor had had with his godfather. On 10 July 2003, Uba resorted to kidnapping Governor Ngige and duly announced his resignation to the press, confirmed by showing the pre-signed letter. Ngige was made to swear an oath at the Okija shrine as a way of disciplining him.[51] According to some sources[52] he was accompanied to the shrine by his godfather, Chris Uba, and by Chuma Nzeribe, the controller of the Anambra State Bakassi Boys and a member of the state House of Representatives. The Ngige kidnap saga has its roots in the tension between the extensive powers bestowed on state governors under the constitution adopted on Nigeria's return to civilian rule in 1999 and the reality of a political system that is based on patronage systems oiled by huge sums of money and enforced by the gangs of murderous thugs employed by some state governors.

After his kidnap, Ngige turned from Obasanjo to Vice-President Atiku Abubakar in search of protection.[53] At this point Nigeria's top policeman entered the story. This was Inspector-General of Police Tafa Balogun, the first university graduate to occupy that post. Balogun himself had his own godfather, former police chief Mohammadu Gambo, as well as enjoying support from some traditional rulers in his home area.[54] Balogun was also a protégé of Vice-President Abubakar,[55] and it was he who, seeking to assert the superiority of the Abubakar political faction in Anambra State, organised the police raid of August 2004. In other words, the raid on the Okija shrine was part of a high-level political tussle that had little to do with maintaining or suppressing the practices at the shrine. The struggle concerned in the first instance the governorship of Anambra State and, beyond that, struggles between rival clientelist systems answerable respectively to the head of state, President Obasanjo, and his vice-president, Atiku Abubakar. Ultimately Obasanjo could be said to have won the contest, as Abubakar never did get a run at the presidency, and Obasanjo exacted revenge on Inspector-General Balogun by securing his eventual conviction for embezzlement.[56]

The consultation of the Okija shrine by such figures as the criminal Okafor, the enforcer Nzeribe, as well as governors Ngige and Kalu, indicates the importance of the shrine for serious money-makers and power brokers, all members of Nigeria's political and plutocratic classes, as well as giving substance to the allegation that the shrine had been taken over by Four One Niners. However, there is much in this story that is not so new, as prestigious oracles have always been associated with commerce. It is clear that the existence of the Okija shrine had in fact been well known in Anambra State and beyond even before the police raid, and that it was by no means a unique institution of its type. Several newspapers reported claims that there were similar shrines in many parts of the country, actually printing the names of some of them.[57] Anonymous police sources told the press that they had been aware that the shrines were habitually visited by people who went there to confess their misdeeds.[58]

Litigants at the Okija shrine are reported to have paid sometimes very large sums, even hundreds of thousands of naira, the equivalent of thousands of dollars, to the chief priest of Okija in support of their cases. Litigants who subsequently died, and whose corpses were brought by their families to the forest, had their goods confiscated by the shrine. This meant that very considerable amounts of money were involved in the shrine's affairs. Registers maintained by the shrine secretary[59] and found by police at the shrine allegedly contained over 5,000 names of people who had visited the place. When the registers' contents were eventually revealed in the press, they indicated that most patrons were from the southeast of the country and that they included doctors, lawyers, engineers, politicians and company directors. Contrary to priests' claims that the fees were paltry, the lowest recorded payment was 5,000 naira ($25 at 2004 values). The highest charge recorded was over 100 times that amount.[60] Police Commissioner Ogbaudu stated that he knew of one person who claimed to have paid 800,000 naira ($6,000).[61] A shrine priest "admitted that his family resides in Lagos where he owns houses and other businesses", suggesting that the shrine could provide a good living.[62] Close to the shrine were modern bungalows apparently built with the proceeds, one of them incongruously sporting a sticker on the door stating "I'm proud to be an Anglican".[63] If each of 5,000 clients were to have paid the equivalent of $100 dollars—a very conservative estimate—it would imply total fees of a half a million dollars paid over an unspecified period, excluding goods confiscated in kind and payments that went unrecorded in the registers. This financial aspect of the shrine drew some withering comments from Commissioner Ogbaudu, who maintained that the shrine priests were simply fraudsters who gull people out of their money. He claimed that shrines were used for extortion, sometimes of large amounts.[64] Ogbaudu said of the priests "they are just ordinary 419ers".[65]

Shrines in southeast Nigeria continue to have vestiges of their former roles in commerce, governance and healing. Hence, the 4 August police raid at Okija led to pressure on some banks, as some of the shrine's adepts and beneficiaries withdrew money that was connected with the shrine and that they feared they might now lose.[66] Some of those who believed they had prospered from the shrine's "money potion", the charms it provided for the prosperity of clients, were afraid that its power might now wither. Many of those concerned were reported to be traders from Anambra State who had become wealthy after visiting the shrine. Businesspeople with connections to the shrine were also afraid that the scandal might cause the authorities to begin looking into their financial affairs and their tax records. This was consistent with the view expressed by some that the raid was politically motivated in the sense of being intended to put pressure on the Igbo business community.[67] The legal status of Okija and similar shrines is somewhat unclear. The law forbids certain types of behaviour associated with shrines like Okija, giving grounds for the police to make arrests, but the constitution also recognises freedom of religion and association. Issues of culture, morality and politics become entwined.

The unclear status of many shrines and the ambivalence of popular attitudes towards them, even as they wield great social influence, create a dilemma for politicians. They may wish to patronise shrines as sources of power both spiritual and political, but they cannot be seen to do so for fear of being labelled as uncivilised, primitive or even satanic. Thus, the Igbo politician Chukwuemeka Ojukwu, the one-time leader of Biafra, reacted to the 2004 raid on the Okija shrine by lamenting that nothing had been done to stop the rituals practised there, which he referred to as "these kinds of primitive acts".[68] Ojukwu also condemned the use of shrines for political purposes, but in doing so he made a point of naming some other traditional religious organisations, Ogboni and Ekpe,[69] the former of which is current among the Yoruba people and the latter among the Ibibio. He seemed to be making the point that, while he supported the police and the rule of law, such practices as occurred at the Okija shrine were not unique to Igboland. Cases as sensational as the exposure of the Okija shrine have indeed occurred from time to time. In 1996, some businessmen in Owerri, Imo State, were alleged to have been using a hotel as a centre for ritual murders calculated to bring them financial success. The discovery had caused major disturbances, including the burning of several religious edifices.[70]

A roughly comparable incident had occurred in Kaduna State in 1994, where police had discovered ten human heads and three corpses.[71]

One of those arrested at the Okija shrine waxed indignant at the raid: "This is our culture", he was reported as saying.[72] A roughly similar position was taken by the secretary-general of the leading Igbo cultural organisation who claimed that the raid was designed to make the Igbo people appear as cannibals, and suggested that the police had more important things to do,[73] although other spokesmen for the same organisation took a more cautious position.[74] A local ruler, the Igwe of Okija, also protested at the damage done to the image of the local community, convening a press conference in his palace during which he protested that "Okija people are no barbarians, we are no cannibals".[75] In general, some people considered the matter an issue of freedom of worship, others thought it concerned the respect owed to tradition, and others applauded what they saw as the destruction of primitive institutions.

Something resembling the embarrassment that Igbo politicians and intellectuals felt on learning of the exposure of the Okija shrine may also occur at a national level whenever the reality of governance in Nigeria is compared to the theory. Nigerian governments generally take great pains to maintain the outward symbols of statehood, as these are vital for continuing international recognition of their sovereignty. Yet they may also make extensive use of informal methods of governance that have no legal standing or that even involve breaking the law, as is the case in state corruption. The importance of keeping up appearances was well stated by none other than Inspector-General of Police Balogun, who said in 2004 that "Nigeria is a distinguished member of the international community and as such we must, at all times, conform and be seen to conform with all norms, conventions and rules that are sine qua non to peaceful living and respectable human coexistence."[76] This was shortly before his conviction on charges of embezzlement and fraud.

Law versus reality

The mismatch between the legal and constitutional theory of how the Nigerian state works, on the one hand, and, on the other hand, its reality, is nowhere more contested than in matters of religion.

Broadly speaking, European missionaries attempted to convert people to Christianity wherever possible from the middle of the nineteenth century. This was mostly in Southern Nigeria. In the North, the colonial authorities restricted the work of Christian missionaries out of deference to the sultanate of Sokoto, the successor of the caliphate that had operated there in precolonial times. In Muslim-majority areas, clerics preaching various interpretations of Islam, sometimes associated with foreign centres of learning in North Africa, occasionally made their appearance. In any case, colonial officials attempted to impose a formal separation between religion and politics that they believed to be necessary for the proper exercise of government, even as shrines continued to have vestiges of their former roles. The combined effect has been a sharp change in the nature of Nigerians' relationship with the invisible world, so important both to their personal well-being and to their systems of governance.

An appreciation of the changing role of religious institutions and in the relationship between people and the invisible world is useful in understanding the nature of corruption in Nigeria, which is more than the use of entrusted office for private benefit, as it may be loosely defined. Corruption in Nigeria is described by one commentator as "a complex interplay between indigenous and foreign understandings of appropriate government conduct".[77] In Nigeria, the same author adds, activities often classed as corruption are actually the product of three factors: first, patron-client relations; second, the use of technocratic and academic paradigms that are ill-adapted to reality; and, third, the actual history of governance in Nigeria.[78] In short, corruption in Nigeria is a shorthand term for a complex situation in which the reality of governance differs from the legal framework that formally constrains the operations of government. It is precisely in this gap that political power is generated and vast fortunes are to be made.

This gap between the legal universe and lived reality is also a moral and even a spiritual one. That this should be so stems from the fact that power has been conceived throughout Nigeria's history partly in spiritual terms and the spiritual domain is one in which power is actively contested. There have been some general trends in Nigeria's longer history that are relevant to mention in this context. Most importantly, there has been a tendency over time for the spirit world to acquire a dual character that it did not traditionally have. This was largely due to the influence of missionaries who regarded the god of Christianity as absolutely opposed to the indigenous deities that it construed as forms of satanism and paganism. As a result, there has been a tendency for spirits to be considered as either good or evil, rather than as morally neutral entities that can be channelled by religious actors for specific social purposes. Christians and Islamic reformists have tended to demonise older concepts of the spirit world. As a very broad rule, Nigerians nowadays experience greater difficulties than they once did in engaging with the spirit world and domesticating the spirits they believe to reside there.

For the many born-again Christians in Nigeria, the ritual activities at the Okija shrine and other similar sites appear to be nothing less than satanism, and the fact that leading politicians and criminals have been associated with the shrine are signs that Satan is active in politics and business. Bishop Alexander Ezeugo Ekewuba of Overcomers Christian Mission,[79] one of the myriad new churches in Nigeria, refers to shrines in the southeast of Nigeria as "places raised by Satan to deceive people so that they can serve him....These are satanic places in our land that bring curses on our people and hinder the presence of God in our midst."[80] In his view, it is the continued existence of such shrines in Igboland that is the cause of Igbos' political misfortunes and the reason why they live scattered among other Nigerians rather than in their own ancestral territory.[81]

For shrine devotees, on the other hand, the logic is the exact opposite: the country's misfortunes derive from the fact that people have broken faith with the customs of their ancestors. One of the Okija priests, Edinmuo Ndukwu, interviewed in jail by the press,[82] described himself as "an ardent pagan", who was simply following the practices he had learned from his father. He regarded Christianity as a foreign religion. Ndukwu maintained that those whose corpses lay at the shrine had died because they had told lies and sworn false oaths. He pointed out that the shrine could bring prosperity to people, and was not purely destructive. Another shrine priest, who regarded himself as an Anglican as well as an adept of the Okija deity, said that the traditional religion caused people to speak the truth, whereas the church thrives on falsehood.[83] Several shrine priests claimed that it was possible to be both Christian and a shrine adept on the grounds that we should give to Caesar what is Caesar's, and to God what belongs to God.[84] "Caesar is the idol and God is the Almighty", said one, suggesting that the shrine is indeed seen as a manifestation of a yet higher power, and that the Christian god has been assimilated into the indigenous cult.

I have referred elsewhere[85] to the condition here described as a "spiritual confusion". The forms of communication with the spirit world once controlled by shrines have essentially become privatised. They are at the disposal of clients who have the means to pay for them, and have escaped institutional control. It is in this form that they have also been taken overseas by Nigerian migrants: it is interesting to note that Inspector-General of Police Balogun referred to the famous Boy Adam case in Britain,[86] citing it as an example of the type of police investigation to be emulated in cases involving violence perpetrated in the name of such religious communication.[87] Other cases involve the widespread practice by Nigerian people-smugglers and fraudsters worldwide of using local cults and shrines as mediums for enslavement, as they have been for centuries.

While the role of shrines such as Okija has changed considerably over the last century, one thread of continuity is the presence of death in various guises. Before the institution of colonial rule, such shrines were closely associated with the social death[88] of enslavement, a common punishment for offences including witchcraft. The shrine continues to function as a place of spiritual death, the repository for the corpses of those whose spirits cannot be accommodated in an ordinary funeral ceremony, and which have to be consigned to the wood surrounding the shrine, where unquiet souls can be kept from troubling their living relatives. It can be a medium for physical death, through the belief that people who have sworn false oaths may be killed by the deity, as Victor Okafor is said to have been. There are stories of shrine officials carrying out such punishments by the use of amulets or poison.

The shrine's power is likely to continue for as long as the Nigerian state is unable to deliver certain forms of justice to its people, as even opponents of traditional religion recognise.[89] The idea of truth-telling jujus remains very widespread in Nigeria, for example in the popular videos produced by the mighty Nollywood film industry, which routinely deal with stories of crime and misconduct in which the wrongdoers are brought to book by spiritual powers, but in which those very same powers may also be used for nefarious purposes usually described in English as witchcraft or satanism.[90]

In many respects, the student confraternities that arose in such profusion from the 1970s, popularly known as campus cults, are part of the same history as traditional shrines. Once student associations had become not only politicised but also militarised, it was a short step to their being used for instrumental purposes in personal quarrels. Wole Soyinka notes the case of a university vice-chancellor who used one student confraternity as a personal strong-arm squad to attack faculty members,[91] probably referring to the Victor Charlie Boys in Rivers State. By 2002, there were reports of former cult members being recruited by a state governor in the southeast, where shrines and secret societies play a key role in a particularly thuggish political system.[92] Some confraternities were the basis of criminal gangs that work as political thugs during election campaigns and outside the campaigning season make money from oil smuggling and kidnapping. Some cultists, having made connections with politicians and other powerbrokers during their time in student politics, have themselves gone on to pursue careers in politics, government or the professions, while retaining their membership of their society. This means that some campus cults have developed into networks of influence that pervade wider sections of society. Members of the Black Axe and some other groups are to be found as far away as Europe and North America, where they are heavily involved in crime.

In Northern Nigeria, dissatisfaction with the established order and with state corruption has far more commonly taken the form of radical Islamic movements of renewal. The most important one of these in recent times was Izala, founded in 1978. It was followed by a series of movements, including Maitatsine and Kalo Kato. The most recent is Boko Haram, which began life as an Islamic renewal movement before becoming politicised after it was enlisted to support a candidate in the 2003 elections for the governorship of Borno State, which connected Boko Haram to elite political struggles. Thereafter, Boko Haram's increasingly fraught relationship with the police led to the "Battle of Maiduguri" in 2009, in which the Boko Haram leader, the cleric Mohammed Yusuf, was killed.

In all cases, North and South, we may see how political dissent can take particular forms that are shaped by local histories and how politicians struggle to enlist or co-opt dissident movements, particularly during election campaigns. Senior politicians and officials may, in addition to the public office that they hold, themselves have a status within formal but nonetheless unpublicised organisations, ranging from traditional shrines to international networks such as the Freemasons or the Rosicrucians. Such networks are considered not only as useful means for dispensing political patronage but, in many cases, also as channels for attaining esoteric power.

Generally speaking, Northern power brokers have had disproportionate access to the Nigerian state since Independence, and much of the loot derived from the oil business has gone into their capacious pockets. Northern Nigerians do not appear to become professional criminals to the same degree as in the South, and crime does not provide an alternative livelihood in the same way that it does in parts of the South. To the many Northern Nigerians who are brought up within Muslim tradition, such corruption is considered in religious terms. Thus, the Islamist scholar Sheikh Ahmad Gumbi identifies Nigeria's most fundamental problem as the establishment by colonial rulers of "a government that was based on demand and receipt of gratification", for which the appropriate rectification is to search for a strain of Islamic purity.[93] New religious movements in both North and South Nigeria represent campaigns not only of spiritual renewal, but also for the creation of spaces of autonomous action free from the moral complexities engendered by Nigeria's politics over the last half-century.[94]

Religion and self-fashioning

Police in Thailand who in the 1990s arrested a Nigerian drug-dealer found the following prayer written on a piece of paper in his room:[95]

> Almighty God in Heaven, I have the right to be rich. I have the right to be a millionaire, and no country has the right to pass laws that interfere with my reaching my goal of being rich. Any laws that are designed to keep me from this goal, are illegitimate.

This theology of abundance has become widespread in Nigeria, especially through the new generation of pentecostal churches. It is not difficult to see why it may be particularly attractive to those who take up crime as a career. The conviction that they are spiritually empowered is often an important part of the often-noticed dynamism and resilience of Nigerian criminals.

By the same token, criminals who regret their choice of career may articulate their new feelings through some form of religious transformation. Thus, an Internet fraudster called Samuel Johnson who specialised in scamming lonely American and European women on dating websites, earning himself the nickname "King of Dating", confessed to his activities in public at one of Lagos's biggest pentecostal churches, led by the famous evangelist T.B. Joshua. Johnson stated that social media, notably Skype and Facebook, had made his business much easier. Johnson, originally from Edo State, said that he got into Internet fraud after joining the notorious Black Axe confraternity at the age of nineteen, while he was a student at the University of Port Harcourt. He described having undergone a brutal initiation ritual. He claimed that his personality changed from that moment: "It was like I had two people living inside me, I became very aggressive. I had this urge to steal and started stealing from people. I also started smoking and drinking excessively". Another member of Black Axe coached him in Internet fraud, but he also claimed to receive instructions from a voice inside his head. Johnson declared to have got tens of thousands of dollars from some victims, and sometimes as much as $250,000. Sums this big are obtained by charming a victim online, often promising marriage, and then spinning a disaster story that requires the wealthy victim to put up the money to help her supposed lover. As to his conversion, Johnson claimed that this started with a dream that eventually led him to seek out T.B. Joshua.[96]

Nigeria continues to produce stories of rags-to-riches success that almost defy rational explanation. Consider the case of the quasi-diplomat and businessman Deinde Fernandes, one of Nigeria's richest men. Born in Lagos in 1936, he is said to have begun his international career in the 1960s. Travelling to Mozambique, he somehow succeeded in becoming an advisor to President Samora Machel. He even took part in the ultra-sensitive diplomatic talks that led up to the Nkomati Accord signed by Mozambique and South Africa in 1984.[97] In those days Fernandes was also known to officials of the African National Congress (ANC), the exiled South African liberation movement that had an office in Mozambique. In 1987 an ANC representative reported to the ANC secretary-general: "Nigerian Chief Fernandes is said to be still attached to the Mozambican mission at the UN but has not been in his office there for months. He is apparently angling to be appointed Mozambican ambassador to Canada...He is also said to be involved in a deal with [President] Chissano's brother to take over a state farm in Maputo province, but the President is apparently not happy about it".[98] At other times, Fernandes is reported to have served as a diplomat on behalf of the governments of Dahomey, Swaziland, Angola and the Central African Republic. Somewhere along the way, he became extraordinarily wealthy. He briefly gained worldwide attention when he claimed to have provided funding to Nelson Mandela, at that time still the president of South Africa, in connection with an oil contract—a claim which was greeted with some scepticism if not alarm.[99] Fernandes claims to have received various titles including Baron Dudley (conferred in Scotland) and Garsan Fulani of Kano, a title bestowed on him by the Emir of Kano.[100] A recent search did not locate any record of a Scottish baronage with this title.

As in earlier times, many Nigerians continue to believe that wealth is connected to mystical powers, and that a rich person is one who has effective knowledge of money's true source.[101] They continue to believe that wealth can be accessed through relationships with powerful people—a simple statement of reality—but also through networks that combine the human world with the spirit world. This reinforces the eminently reasonable supposition that hidden mafias and cults have the power to give wealth to those they favour.[102]

11

NIGERIAN ORGANISED CRIME

All through this book, I have avoided choosing any single definition of organised crime from among the many dozens offered in the literature of criminology. It is time to explain why.

The concept of organised crime emerged in the United States, where it originally reflected the government's interpretation of patronage networks among Italian immigrants involved in crime. In the 1950s and 1960s there was considerable debate on how to understand the Mafia in America, in either its Sicilian or Italian-American variants.[1] A legend was born.

Since then, the phrases "organised crime" and "mafia" have gained a greater or lesser degree of acceptance in relation to many countries. Yet the type of organisation and activities designated by these words differ from one place to another. The original Mafia, rooted in Sicily, developed by enforcing contracts where state law was ineffective.[2] The Sicilian Mafia occupied a niche within the politics of the Italian state during the country's unification in the late nineteenth century, and in the Cold War period this developed into a position in regard to national politics. One writer on the subject describes the Mafia as "a shadow state, a political body that sometimes opposes, sometimes subverts, and sometimes dwells within the body of the legal government".[3]

In Russia, since the Cold War there has been much talk of the existence of a Mafia or even, in Russianised form, a Mafiya. Organised

215

crime groups were relatively unimportant during the heyday of Soviet government but gained political purchase during the upheavals of the 1980s and 1990s as enforcers of contracts in new markets.[4] "What was organized crime in the Soviet Union?", a leading Russian commentator asks. "At least after Andropov's time [1984], it began to be part of the system, under the control of the KGB. The only people who the bandits were afraid of were the state security officers. And this evolved into its present-day form".[5] Under the presidency of Vladimir Putin, organised crime has become a key component of Russia's politics and even of its government.[6]

Similar examples could be taken from a wide range of countries. Hence, if we accept that something that can reasonably be called "organised crime" exists in many places, it is nevertheless apparent that this thing called organised crime takes quite different forms, according to the particular historical and political context in each case. It is for this reason that it seemed best not to begin a study of Nigeria by adopting one of the many definitions of organised crime offered by the relevant literature, which are derived mainly from the study of Europe and North America,[7] and then testing its relevance to West Africa, but to proceed the other way round. In other words I have assumed throughout this book that the scale and ubiquity of Nigerian crime make it obvious that this is in some sense organised, and it has been with this in mind that I have traced its unique historical trajectory.

In telling the story of Nigerian organised crime, some of its features have become obvious. First, there does not appear to have been any general perception until after the middle of the twentieth century that crime might pose any particular or deep-seated problem in Nigeria. There is one major exception to this observation, namely with regard to the trade in people. People-trafficking and people-smuggling in the twentieth century reflect the deep historical legacy of slavery and the slave trade. Many parts of the territories that were incorporated into Nigeria when the country was founded in 1914 had been involved in large-scale slave-raiding and slave-trading for centuries, both across the Atlantic Ocean to the Americas and over the Sahara to North Africa. The Sokoto caliphate was one of the world's last major states based on slavery before its conquest by the British. Despite the abolition of slavery by the colonial administration, by the 1930s it had become apparent that many of the networks and practices that had developed around slavery over centuries had remained intact. They are still visible in the way that people-smuggling is organised today.

A second obvious feature of organised crime in Nigeria is its association with state corruption. This became an issue from the moment that nationalist political parties, led by people who did not possess vast personal fortunes and who did not represent any clearly established economic class, had gained a foothold in government at Regional level following implementation of the 1951 Macpherson constitution. Politicians in all three of Nigeria's Regions took to signing government contracts in return for kickbacks in order to generate funds for themselves and their parties, and the contractors, which in those days were nearly always foreign companies, were pleased to play this game. A survey of documented corruption scandals going back to the mid-1950s shows a pattern of private accumulation by those in a position of power in collaboration with foreign interests, often by means of manipulating the mechanisms for importing and exporting goods or money.[8] Ever since that time political corruption carried out through state institutions has been inseparable from the interests of foreign companies and, occasionally, their associated governments.

State crime

Given the importance of the state in the story of Nigerian crime, we need to think about how to address systematic and large-scale law-breaking by senior state officials. In Western philosophical and legal traditions, the state has often been considered as external to society, a Leviathan to which the citizenry is bound by means of a social contract. The state being the fount of law, it is hard to see how it can itself be subject to the law. As one eminent criminologist puts it, "governments and their agencies do not commit crimes, but only because the criminal law does not take cognizance of them as criminal actors."[9] Over time, however, the law has come to be considered in the West in less elevated or even metaphysical terms than it was in the days when kings were held to be God's representatives on earth, with a divine right to rule. Instead, the law has come to be seen as a set of rules produced by a society that organises itself.[10] This makes it easier to conceive of a state itself becoming liable to condemnation for breaking the rules it articulates and for offending the basic rights of the people under its authority, for example by ordering and implementing a campaign of murder or torture.

In his 1988 presidential address to the American Society of Criminology, William J. Chambliss defined state crime as "acts defined by law as criminal and committed by state officials in the pursuit of their job as representatives of the state".[11] He went on to specify that "state-organized crime does not include criminal acts that benefit only individual officeholders, such as the acceptance of bribes or the illegal use of violence by the police against individuals, unless such acts violate existing criminal law and are official policy". An individual civil servant or minister who commits a crime for personal benefit may be regarded as a criminal like any other. The concept of state crime imposes itself when the civil servant in question commits a criminal act that may be interpreted as part of a policy or practice having some wider element of official sanction, like, for example, the infamous Watergate burglary committed by a team acting in the political interest of the head of state. It is necessary, therefore, to distinguish between crimes committed by the state as an institution and "harmful acts carried out by state officials for their own benefit", which may more properly be called "governmental crime".[12] In practice, both types of offence are likely to be considered under the rubric of state crime.

The question, then, is to know whether the acts of state officials who break the law are performed in a purely personal capacity or whether they are perpetrated on behalf of the state itself or of a more or less organised network within the state, such as a political party. It should be said that the situation has changed in recent decades in the many parts of the world where states have come to be little more than a hollow shell, wherein real power lies not in the official organs, but in personalised networks extending both inside and outside the formal state structure, articulated by a central figure such as Serbia's Slobodan Milosevic or Iraq's Saddam Hussein.[13] There have been so many such cases in recent decades that they can be considered as evidence of a profound shift. Financial globalisation and the increasing speed of communication have created new channels for the accumulation of wealth and the representation of power. At the same time, financial deregulation "has enormously increased the scope and profitability of transnational organized crime".[14] Criminal markets, until quite recently "small and isolated",[15] have become integrated into the legal economy, creating a grey zone between legitimate and criminal business, or rather a grey area where they become difficult to distinguish from each other. An influential sociologist describes this process as the "perverse integration" of a substantial number of countries into international relations of production that have changed enormously since the third quarter of the twentieth century,[16] while an investigative journalist considers it the construction of what he calls simply "a looting machine".[17]

If we try to fit Nigeria into this analysis, we may note that British officials from the onset of colonial rule, using British criteria that they wished to impose universally, regarded the personal prerogatives enjoyed by local rulers as evidence of corruption. From the implementation of Indirect Rule until today, much of the routine law-breaking by state officials that has gone under the general name of corruption has come to constitute the fabric of the state itself.[18] As mentioned earlier in this book, Andreski invented a new word to describe Nigeria's First Republic, namely as "the most perfect example of kleptocracy", in which "power itself rested on the ability to bribe".[19] The fact that corruption is so frequently lamented by Nigerians themselves is a sign that most of them do not accept as fully legitimate the form of governance called kleptocracy. However, the common attitude to state corruption is highly ambivalent, as many Nigerians simultaneously condemn it and aspire to profit from it by obtaining for themselves a sliver of the wealth that it spews forth.

So routine are fraud and embezzlement by officials of the Nigerian state that we sometimes have to remind ourselves that such behaviour is not permitted by the law of the land. Practices of fraud and embezzlement have had a high degree of consistency and coherence over decades, regardless of the formal provisions of the law, as they have in many African contexts.[20] One former South African state official, noting the degree to which the state in Africa has become an instrument for the accumulation of personal wealth, concludes that "the overall result is an overlap between criminal activities and the institutions of the state itself".[21] However much they steal, Nigerian state officials do not act solely for purposes of criminal gain. Many also have genuinely political motivations and act as part of organised political factions. This means that their activities have aspects of both state crime and organised crime but do not fit standard definitions of either.

In considering the effect of the political corruption that afflicted Nigeria from the 1950s onwards, it is helpful to recall the finding made in 1928 by one of America's greatest judges, Louis Brandeis, that "If the Government becomes a lawbreaker, it breeds contempt for law; it invites every man to become a law unto himself; it invites anarchy".[22] This judgement is borne out by Nigeria's experience, in which, from late colonial times onwards, serious and organised law-breaking was routine among many of the very people who also formed the government. Under successive military regimes and with the emergence of a major oil industry, state corruption in Nigeria reached huge proportions. Many ordinary citizens indeed came to disrespect the law of the land as Brandeis had predicted. Yet, when it comes to asking why the rule of law is so disregarded in Nigeria, there is more to it than this. The British tradition of law that was imposed through colonial rule is different in form and substance from the traditions of justice that had prevailed in precolonial times in the territories that came to form Nigeria. Generally, these older traditions were not based on written law at all. Writing was not in use other than in the courts of the Northern emirs and in a few other places. And much Sharia law was in fact customary in nature rather than codified. Both Sharia and customary courts operated in the Northern Region under British rule. The administration of justice was inseparable from religion, whether in the form of Islam or that of the shrines and oracles that abounded in the South.

All over Nigeria, many practices and institutions that had been associated with governance and justice in earlier times lived on under Indirect Rule, officially or underground, and came to play a significant role in society and politics after Independence in 1960, often without constitutional provision. During the twentieth century traditional shrines and initiation societies came to acquire a highly ambivalent position in regard to the state and the rule of law, being patronised both by politicians and by professional criminals, but also being considered as authentic sources of justice. Obscure rural sites like the shrine at Okija, which we have examined in some detail,[23] may become nodes of interaction for criminals and politicians with global interests. Others have pointed out that when traditional cults like this are used for state politics, they lose many of the checks and balances that formerly restrained them. In the words of one analyst, "traditional cults are used in modern public space without the due moderation and boundaries because the modern space is supposed to be an unlimited and unbounded space."[24] Meanwhile, new types of initiation society have sprung up, especially on college campuses, and a handful of these have become vehicles for the organisation of crime on a large scale, both at home and abroad.

These episodes in Nigeria's history did not occur in a vacuum. When the bubble of Nigeria's oil economy burst in the early 1980s, large numbers of people, including many with college diplomas, went abroad, introducing Nigerian-style crime to the rest of the world. This was at a time when many fields of legitimate activity in politics and business were actually becoming more closely associated with crime all over the world, sometimes to the extent that they have become hard to distinguish from one another. This process is best traced to the beginnings of modern financial globalisation in the 1970s, but the end of the Cold War was also of huge importance as it enabled political elites and secret services with no ingrained respect for law to make common cause with existing crime barons throughout the former Soviet bloc. The collapse of the USSR enabled the establishment of huge new markets, sometimes where none had previously existed, thereby creating opportunities for well-placed individuals to make huge fortunes overnight.

All over the world, including in the historic democracies, political campaigning has become massively expensive. Politicians find themselves required to raise colossal sums of money, far more than they could hope to receive from individual subscriptions or even from corporations seeking access to future governments. Under pressure to raise funds, they may, knowingly or not, accept contributions from people or businesses engaged in illegal activity who require political protection. Incumbent politicians may make arrangements with certain companies or individuals that provide them with slush-funds in return for political favours. Many top companies appear to maintain an off-budget treasury that may be used for illicit purposes,[25] the biggest of them both generating these funds from deals made in places with weak law enforcement and using them to finance political accommodations.

Western politicians have tolerated rule-breaking and even law-breaking by banks in the hope that the provision of credit in any form would stimulate national economies, creating wealth and therefore making the same politicians more electable. This in turn has permitted mind-bogglingly large international transfers of money that are hard or impossible to regulate.

So, corruption and fraud have increased in scale worldwide, but above all their strategic importance has been enhanced as politicians insert themselves in complex arrangements with financiers and captains of industry that can generate enormous pay-offs.[26] There is an intimate connection between the emergence of a grey area between banks, businesspeople, and politicians in the West, on the one hand, and Nigeria's type of crime and state corruption. This is true not only in the sense that opaque oil deals and public contracts in Nigeria may serve to enrich major companies based elsewhere, but also for the reason that today's biggest fortunes are often made less from the manufacture or production of physical commodities than from the promise of future profits, obtained by shaping markets in such a way as to attract investors. This is possible only in an environment where confidence in the future is sustained by durable institutions, including organs of state, banks and insurance companies, that permit the infinite generation of credit. Hence, a successful and wealthy criminal entrepreneur or a corrupt politician in a country with poorly developed institutions may develop an ambition to access the facilities of a developed state on a permanent basis. This is one of the main reasons for the huge illicit flows of capital from Nigeria to bank accounts in more stable environments, especially in Europe and the United States, said to amount to almost $16 billion annually.[27]

In short, a fundamental shift in the way the world works has changed the relationship between politics and crime everywhere and has led to a change in the nature of grand corruption. Countries with weak state institutions and an abundance of minerals play an important part in the resulting calculus. Yet, even if this pattern is recognisable in many places, Nigeria seems to be in a category of its own. The patterns of state corruption in Nigeria are not uncommon in countries where large mineral reserves are worked by multinational companies. What is most unusual is the success of Nigerian criminals in specific illicit markets, notably drugs and fraud. We need to investigate what makes Nigerians so distinctive in this field.

Why Nigeria?

Colin Powell's quip that scamming is a part of Nigerian culture, quoted in the introduction to this book, is entertaining but it should not be accepted as an explanation.[28] No respectable social scientist would use the concept of culture to designate a straitjacket of ideas and behaviour that leaves individuals no room for escape. Nevertheless, Powell's insight is a sharp one inasmuch as it sums up a question that cannot be avoided. The emergence of a multinational "looting machine" is not unusual in countries that produce minerals, but Nigeria is exceptional in producing substantial numbers of criminals able to participate successfully in global illicit markets. Why is Nigeria special in this regard? Does culture play a role, as many people think?[29] Cultures offer repertoires of behaviour that are constantly changing but that have historical roots. The most persuasive analysts insist that cultures of corruption have to be studied in historical depth if we are to understand how they work and how they evolved.[30] Although culture is a concept regarded with deep suspicion by social scientists, it seems impossible to avoid asking to what extent Nigeria's contemporary culture of corruption is rooted in precolonial concepts of honour and gift-giving and how far it is the product of more recent, external, influences.

In matters of public administration, European criteria and norms were transplanted to West Africa in colonial times and assimilated by indigenous populations to varying degrees, becoming mixed with existing notions of proper behaviour. The same is true of commercial behaviour. For while precolonial Nigerian societies used money, they did not have capitalism. Money exchange was inseparable from a range of other obligations moral and religious, with only slave exporting taking place outside the prevailing moral nexus. Haggling was normal in market transactions given the lack of standardised weights and measures. Moreover, precolonial societies formed what a Nigerian commentator calls "a raiding complex, i.e. sanctioned external stealing".[31] The eminent human rights lawyer Gani Fawehinmi relates how communities in precolonial times "waged wars with the main objective of subjugating other communities and extracting slaves".[32] He believes that this has been one of the roots of subsequent corruption.

During the early period of colonial rule throughout Africa, until the 1930s, it has been said that "Africans and their leaders were concerned with honour in its older forms, practising gift-exchange and rarely distinguishing between public and private wealth, at a time when rulers had lost many sources of revenue, numerous activities were for the first time monetised, and bureaucratisation multiplied opportunities for impersonal extortion."[33] The Nigerian agents of Indirect Rule all carried inside their heads traditional ideas of honour and gift-giving and the habit of capturing wealth by creating margins on transactions, "configuring value scales rather than reducing them all to number."[34] What one writer termed "the objective rationalized standards of probity" in the modern sector were "essentially outside the scope of traditional ethics and so remain incomprehensible to the villagers."[35] Yet the same villagers admired the attributes of success, especially the consumer goods associated with both public administration and missionary education. Colonialism opened vast new areas of social and economic space where traders and entrepreneurs, licit and otherwise, often continued to organise themselves in ways rooted in local history rather than in the form of the Western-style business firm or corporation. Successful people often continued the old practice of investing in membership of a secret society as a way both of expressing and consolidating their achievement, but, no longer being able so easily to recoup their costs from a new entrant, were obliged to look for new sources of income instead.[36] Indirect Rule led to "a superficially competent Government acting through African subordinates", Margery Perham thought.[37] However, these African agents of colonial rule became, "by our use of them a class whose interests and standards separate them from the mass of the people". Perham's considered opinion was that this led, at worst, "to gross hidden oppression which may not stop short—I write advisedly—of torture and murder".[38]

While the survival of precolonial notions of honour and gift-giving have contributed to the rise of Nigeria's particular brand of political and state corruption, there has never been anything inevitable about this process. It has come about through the actions and inactions of individuals, especially powerful ones. This is what the great novelist

Chinua Achebe meant when he wrote that "the trouble with Nigeria is simply and squarely a failure of leadership".[39] Accordingly, it is interesting to consider whether it is possible to identify specific individuals who have had a crucial effect in bringing about the situation that now prevails in Nigeria.

Let us consider three such people. The first is Lord Lugard (1858–1945), the British imperial soldier and administrator who created Nigeria. It would be ludicrous to blame today's organised crime on Lugard. He cannot possibly have foreseen the distant consequences of decisions he took a century ago. However, there is a consensus among Nigerians that his decision to amalgamate the various colonial territories centred on the Niger valley into a single administrative unit created a massive set of problems that endure to this day. These problems were made still more complex by Lugard's elevation of Indirect Rule from an instrument of government into a dogma. A second person who played a role of historic importance in the evolution of Nigeria's distinctive brand of organised crime is Felix Okotie-Eboh (1919–1966), the federal Minister of Finance in Nigeria's first post-Independence government. He was the chief organiser of financial corruption at both national and Regional political level and the main builder of a system that still bears the marks of his handiwork. A third is Ibrahim "IBB" Babangida (born 1941), the veteran coup-maker and military politician under whose watch Nigeria's tradition of political corruption became an integrated system.

All of these three, of course, had internalised ideas and attitudes that reflected the times they lived in. The colonial state in Nigeria, as in much of tropical Africa, was a gatekeeper[40] that regulated the access of African populations to international networks of commerce and exploited its own position in order to extract rents or taxes that could be used for its own support. The colonial government employed a large part of this revenue to pay salaries and allowances to its officials in conformity with the regulations in force. As Nigerians took over this system in the process of decolonisation, successful individuals who amassed wealth through state corruption generally did so by invoking communal responsibilities, with the result that "in so far as a successful individual is seen to contribute to the welfare of his community, he is not seen as corrupt".[41]

The ambiguity of popular attitudes to public corruption has been noted by many observers from the time that the system emerged in the 1950s. "We have all been known as prospective '10 percenters'", one journalist wrote. "Money, it's widely believed, can do anything in this beloved country".[42] In 1974, a British High Commissioner wrote that "It is no longer correct to speak of the problem of corruption in Nigeria. This is a corrupt society". The only exceptions, he thought, lay in the higher levels of the judiciary and "the more reputable of the churches".[43] Nevertheless, some Nigerian writers maintained that, although corruption existed at every level of the civil service, it was "still the exception rather than the rule" at that time.[44] This could no longer be said after the Babangida government had integrated corruption into a coherent system at the same time as the relationship of political corruption to business and organised crime was in flux all over the world.

Nigeria's modern political history, and more precisely its history of crime and corruption, is closely related to its role as an oil producer. It is often noted that oil production tends to have economic and financial consequences that may encourage corruption and strife. The main reason for this is that oil provides rents that can be captured by local elites only through tenure of state power. In Nigeria, as in the other oil-producing countries of West Africa, political elites nourished by oil have found it hard "to sustain cooperation for a prolonged amount of time". Rather, "they endure in a condition of 'turbulent equilibrium' that is more akin to that of Mafia formations than secure ruling classes."[45] This has contributed to the impression that party politics in Nigeria resembles war by other means.[46] Under military rule, the lack of parties reinforced the tendency for cliques to organise themselves informally in an attempt to exercise influence. One respected analyst goes as far as to say that Nigeria has no state, in the strict sense, but only a contested terrain, in which politics is *constituted as warfare*.[47] "We pretend that we are playing politics", he adds, "when, like Mafia families, we are actually waging a violent struggle for a lucrative turf".[48] These comparisons with a mafia are telling. Nigeria's political elite, while composed largely of people with political and analytical skills, nevertheless periodically takes the country to the verge of catastrophe, as rival groups pursue their individual course.[49] The clash of interests that leaves little room to articulate a national interest leads to the question posed by a British diplomat, who wrote: "One ends up by asking oneself....Who is the government of Nigeria? Is there a government of Nigeria? Are things decided or do they just happen?"[50]

Some similar tendencies are noticeable among less elevated citizens, who find that attachment to particular networks rather than membership of a generalised civil society is the best way of obtaining a slice of the national cake that is the goal of most political activity. When it comes to debating reform and ideology, ever since the collapse of the fantastic Nigerianism that was in vogue in the 1970s, the dominant language has been a religious one. In Northern Nigeria, movements aimed at remaking society have typically taken the form of Islamic renewal, from the Izala society to Boko Haram, although the latter has lost its reformist ambitions as a result of prolonged war against the state, and seems to have become nihilist in its orientation. In areas with a strong Christian tradition, religious renewal takes the form of new churches and religious movements endowed with a strong sense of breaking with a ruined past.[51]

This sense that history has to be remade if Nigerians are to function properly is widespread. Wole Soyinka, writing specifically on the subject of the student confraternities that have degenerated into delinquent groups and even into criminal conspiracies, refers to the "cheap alibi" that is characteristic of Nigerian criminals: *"we are thus because of how we started, which is no fault of ours"*.[52] It is quite common to hear fraudsters justify their activities on the grounds that they are simply plundering the West as it once did to West Africa, from the days of the slave trade onwards. The law is derided as a colonial project, ignoring the fact that as a sovereign state Nigeria is responsible for its own law. Ever since the beginnings of the drug trade, Nigerian drug dealers have claimed that illegal markets, and crime more generally, are "the only way to redistribute wealth from the north to the south", arguing that "mainstream commercial channels are effectively occupied".[53]

The attitude that a faulty past legitimates disrespect for the current law has also been widespread among politicians. When nationalists began to occupy key posts in government in the 1950s, they often did not regard themselves as bound by the rules of the colonial state, or even by its laws, and had little compunction in using its resources for their own projects, both political and personal.[54] Many West African nationalists, like Ghana's Kwame Nkrumah, considered colonial regimes to be themselves corrupt insofar as they exploited colonies for the development of their home countries. Nkrumah used the metaphor of the colonial state as an elephant, crashing through the bush and eating its fill. Since this great beast was outside society, it could be killed and eaten by anyone.[55] Ken Saro-Wiwa is one of the striking number of Nigerian writers to have dwelled on this matter, describing the preoccupation of politicians in the early nationalist period with seizing the maximum possible share of the national cake in a process notable for its opportunism and cynicism.[56] Decolonisation obliged British businesses to compete with others for government contracts, at the same time creating new opportunities for businesses from further afield. What was then known as "the dash system", by which contractors and officials entered into convenient but corrupt understandings, was fully in place by the time of Independence.

The decisions taken by particular leaders at key junctures, the incidence of military coups and a civil war were all particular to Nigeria. They combined to shape a generation of young emigrants literate in English who started to leave the country en masse in the late 1970s, many of them well-educated. The new diasporas that sprang up in many places introduced criminal practices learned in Nigeria at new locations all over the world. They had been nurtured on the grandiose quasi-ideology of Nigerianism, founded on a vision of the country's inevitable greatness. The emigrants of that generation were overwhelmingly from Southern Nigeria, where a social revolution inadvertently stimulated by colonial rule and missionary education in colonial times had created an aggressive spirit of enterprise and ambition that had no popular equivalent in the North. It seems that successive governments of Nigeria were content to allow these unemployed young people to emigrate and even encouraged it. For, although the emigration of some of the country's brightest young people was a blow to the country's development, to a set of short-sighted and sometimes poorly educated military leaders it seemed preferable to having them agitate for reforms at home. As time went by, educated emigrants were increasingly likely to have joined as students one of the dozens of confraternities or campus cults that sprang up in the 1970s and 1980s. A handful of these societies have turned into genuine criminal conspiracies.

These are among the factors that have formed a distinctively Nigerian type of criminality that differs even from that found even in other oil-producing African ex-colonies.

Nigerian crime in globalisation

Within the world's financial system it has often become difficult to discern any difference between money earned from legitimate business, transfer pricing by multinational companies, money generated by kickbacks and corruption, and even income from drug trafficking or other organised crime. Money from all these sources moves through the same banks.[57] Some of the world's longest-established organised crime groups, such as the Sicilian Mafia and the New York crime families, have for over half a century been developing global strategies in which the sovereign status of a partner or client may be a valuable asset. They are simply imitating legitimate business corporations that have been using the legal niches provided by sovereign status for over a hundred years.[58] Today, the number of organised crime groups using such techniques has greatly increased.

The prominence of organised crime in global markets gives rise to the claim, which has become a central plank of US foreign policy, that the civilised world is threatened by an unprecedented alliance of politically-motivated terrorists and organised criminals. This is not untrue, but it is a very partial view of reality. First, it underestimates the degree to which business, organised crime and politics have become integrated through their mutual interests. A French magistrate who investigated fraud in her country's leading oil company found that it was not organised crime as such that was at the heart of the global system of corruption and malfeasance she encountered, but otherwise respectable organisations, including the state itself. "I do not see an evil hydra of crime, terrible and multiform, attacking a besieged fortress", she wrote, "but a respectable and well established power that has integrated grand corruption as a natural dimension of its exercise".[59] Second, the idea of organised crime as a global threat exaggerates its homogeneity. Organised crime has showed itself very successful—perhaps even more so than multinational businesses—in integrating local identities and practices into organisations with a global reach. Nowhere illustrates this better than Nigeria. Nigerian practices of organised crime notably in regard to fraud and embezzlement were well developed locally just at the point where global criminal activity exploded in the late twentieth century, with a profusion of new markets.[60]

Nigerian criminals have shown themselves highly successful in many of their chosen fields. One of the tests whether the activities of a particular group can properly be considered as organised crime is if it is able to adapt, passing from one sort of activity to another when market conditions change and circumstances require it. Here, the top Nigerian networks and operators have passed the test, sometimes moving from the smuggling of legitimate products into illicit ones, or from fraud into drugs, and from crime into politics, proving themselves able to cooperate internationally with the top players in their field. Nigerian organised crime is not created by culture, but it does arise from a particular history.

Where else could it possibly come from?

APPENDIX

List of cult groups banned under the Secret Cult and Similar Activities Prohibition Law 2004.*

Agbaye
Airwords
Amazon
Buccaneers (Sea Lords)
Barracuda
Bas
Bees International
Big 20
Black Axe
Black Beret Fraternity
Black Brasserie [sic]
Black Brothers
Black Cats
Black Cross
Black Ladies
Black Ofals
Black Scorpions
Black Sword
Blanchers
Black Bras
Blood Suckers
Brotherhood of Blood
Burkina Faso: Revolution
    Fraternity
Canary
Cappa Vandetto
Daughters of Jezebel

Dey Gbam
Dey Well
Dolphins
Dragons
Dreaded Friends of
    Friends
Blood Hunters
Eagle Club
Egbe Dudu
Eiye of Air Lords
    Fraternity
Elegemface
Executioners
Fangs
FF
Fliers
Frigates
Gentlemen's Club
Green Berets Fraternity
Hard Candies
Hell's Angels
Hepos
Himalayas
Icelanders
Jaggare Confederation
KGB
King Cobra

KlamKonfraternity
Klansman
Ku Klux Klan
Knite Cade
Mafia Lords
Mafioso Fraternity
Malcolm X
Maphites/Maphlate
Mgba Mgba Brothers
Mob Stab
Musketeers Fraternity
National Association of
    Adventurers
National Association of
    Sea Dogs
Neo-Black Movement
Nite Hawks
Night Mates
Nite Rovers
Odu Cofraternity
Osiri
Ostrich Fraternity
Panama Pyrate
Phoenix
Predators
Red Devils
Red Fishes

* Osaghae et al, "Youth Militias, Self Determination and Resource Control Struggles in the Niger-Delta Region of Nigeria", 2007, p. 22.

Red Sea Horse
Royal House of Peace
Royal Queens
Sailors
Scavengers
Scorpion
Scorpion Fraternity
Sea Vipers

Soiree Fraternity
Soko
Sunmen
Temple of Eden
    Fraternity
Thomas Sankara Boys
Tikan Giants
Trojan Horses Fraternity

Truth Seekers
Twin Mate
Vikings
Vipers
Vultures
Walrus
White Bishop

NOTES

INTRODUCTION

1. *Opgelicht*, TROS-TV, Nederland 1, 9 May, 3 October 2006.
2. Ibid.
3. *The Times* [London], 21 July 2005, p. 40.
4. BBC News, "Spain Holds Lottery Scam Suspects", 17 April 2008.
5. IPOL, *Nationaal Dreigingsbeeld 2012: Georganiseerde criminaliteit* (Dienst IPOL, Zoetermeer, 2012), p. 139.
6. Quoted in Henry Louis Gates, "Powell and The Black Elite", *The New Yorker*, 25 September 1995.
7. There is no generally accepted definition of organised crime: Nikos Passas, "Introduction", pp. xiii-xix, *Organized Crime* (Dartmouth Publishing Co., Aldershot, 1995). See Chapter Eleven for further discussion.
8. National Archives of Nigeria [NAN], Ibadan, Oyo Prof.1, 4113: "Crime and its Treatment"; report to the Governor by Alexander Paterson, February 1944.
9. http://archiveswiki.historians.org/index.php/National_Archives_of_ Nigeria [accessed 26 July 2015].
10. http://www.archives.gov/dc-metro/college-park/
11. http://www.nationalarchives.gov.uk/

1. RULES OF LAW

1. Ogechi Ekeanyanwu, "Zungeru, Town of Amalgamation, in Shambles", *Premium Times*, 16 March 2013, http://www.premiumtimesng.com/arts-entertainment/125291-zungeru-town-of-amalgamation-in-shambles.html [accessed 1 May 2015].
2. Helen Callaway and Dorothy O. Helly, "Crusader for Empire: Flora Shaw/ Lady Lugard", in Nupur Chaudhuri and Margaret Strobel (eds), *Western*

Women and Imperialism: Complicity and Resistance (Indiana University Press, Bloomington and Indianapolis, 1992), pp. 79–97.

3. Written as Ibo in older texts.

4. "Introduction", in A.H.M. Kirk-Greene (ed.), *Lugard and the Amalgamation of Nigeria: A Documentary Record* (Frank Cass, London, 1968), p. 27. A recording of Lugard's amalgamation speech may be heard at https://www.youtube.com/watch?v=C5Xom7T6-yU [accessed 13 May 2015].

5. Quoted in Henry L. Bretton, *Power and Stability in Nigeria: The Politics of Decolonization* (Frederick A. Praeger, New York, 1962), p. 127.

6. Quoted in James Booth, *Writers and Politics in Nigeria* (Hodder & Stoughton, London, 1981), p. 23.

7. Attributed to Sir Ahmadu Bello.

8. I.F. Nicolson, *The Administration of Nigeria 1900–1960: Men, Methods and Myths* (Clarendon Press, Oxford, 1969), p. 8.

9. Sir F.D. Lugard, "Report on the Amalgamation of Northern and Southern Nigeria", in A.H.M. Kirk-Greene (ed.), *Lugard and the Amalgamation of Nigeria*, p. 67.

10. Ibid.

11. Ibid.

12. G.H. Findlay, report on the reorganisation of the Colony, 1927, cited by L.C. Gwam in his catalogue to the colonial archives at the National Archives of Nigeria, Ibadan.

13. John Iliffe, *Honour in African History* (Cambridge University Press, 2005), p. 121.

14. Lugard, "Report on the Amalgamation of Northern and Southern Nigeria", p. 68.

15. Ibid., p. 67.

16. Ibid., pp. 68–9.

17. Margery Perham, *Native Administration in Nigeria* (1937; 2nd impression, Oxford University Press, 1962), pp. 73–4.

18. Ibid., p. 43.

19. Robin Horton "Stateless Societies in the History of West Africa", in J.F. Ade Ajayi and Michael Crowder (eds), *History of West Africa* (2 vols, Harlow 1985), I, p. 87.

20. Lugard, "Report on the Amalgamation of Northern and Southern Nigeria", p. 72.

21. Sir Bernard Bourdillon, *Memorandum on the Future Political Development of Nigeria* ("confidential", Government Printer, Lagos, 1939), p. 4. Copy in the National Archives of Nigeria, Ibadan, at MN/B4A.

22. Frederick Lugard, *The Dual Mandate in British Tropical Africa* (1922; 5th edn, Frank Cass, London 1965).

23. Michael Crowder, "Indirect Rule: French and British Style", *Africa*, 34, 3 (1964), pp. 197–205.

24. Hubert Deschamps, "Et maintenant, Lord Lugard?", *Africa*, 33, 4 (1963), pp. 293–306.

25. William Malcolm Hailey, *An African Survey* (Oxford University Press, London, 1938), p. 272.

26. Ibid., p. 273.

27. Rémi Brague (trans. Lydia G. Cochrane), *The Law of God:The Philosophical History of an Idea* (University of Chicago Press, Chicago and London, 2007).

28. Obafemi Awolowo, *Awo: The Autobiography of Chief Obafemi Awolowo* (Cambridge University Press, 1960), p. 12.

29. Simeon O. Eboh, "Law and Order in the Society:The Nigerian Experience", *The Nigerian Journal of Theology*, 18 (2004), p. 23.

30. Ibid., p. 24.

31. Biko Agozino, "Crime, Criminology and Post-colonialTheory: Criminological Reflections on West Africa", in James Sheptycki and Ali Wardak (eds), *Transnational and Comparative Criminology* (Glasshouse Press, London, 2005), p. 125.

32. Lugard to Lady Lugard, 13 Nov. 1912, quoted in Kirk-Greene, "Introduction", p. 13.

33. Stephen Ellis and Gerrie ter Haar, *Worlds of Power: Religious Thought and Political Practice in Africa* (Hurst & Co., London, 2004), p. 14.

34. Marcel Gauchet (trans. Oscar Burge), *The Disenchantment of theWorld:A Political History of Religion* (Princeton University Press, Princeton, NJ, 1999).

35. Awolowo, *Awo*, pp. 8–9.

36. Frank Hives and Gascoine Lumley, *Ju-Ju and Justice in Nigeria* (1930; Penguin edn., Harmondsworth, 1940), p. 111.

37. Obafemi Awolowo, *The Path to Nigerian Freedom* (Faber & Faber, London, 1947), p. 97.

38. Ibid.

39. Perham, *Native Administration in Nigeria*, p. 71.

40. Ibid, p. 76.

41. Iliffe, *Honour in African History*, p. 214.

42. A.A. Lawal, *Corruption in Nigeria:A Colonial Legacy* (University of Lagos, 2006), text of an inaugural lecture on 7 June 2006.

43. David Pratten, *The Man-Leopard Murders: History and Society in Colonial Nigeria* (Edinburgh University Press, Edinburgh, 2007), p. 88.

44. Ogbu U. Kalu, "Missionaries, Colonial Government and Secret Societies in South-Eastern Igboland, 1920–1950", *Journal of the Historical Society of Nigeria*, 9, 1 (1977), pp. 75–90.

45. National Archives of Nigeria, Ibadan [NAI], M.L.G. (W) 17887, "Reformed Ogboni Fraternity": Otu Edu to Chief Commissioner, Western Province, et al., 1 April 1950.

46. Pratten, *The Man-Leopard Murders*, p. 88.

47. Ibid., p. 86.

48. Record of the second meeting of the colonial Local Government Advisory Panel, 22 Oct. 1948, in Martin Lynn (ed.), *British Documents on the End of Empire. Series B, Country Volumes, Volume 7* (vol. I, the Stationery Office, London, 2001), pp. 162–4.

49. David Pratten, *The Man-Leopard Murders*, p. 97.

2. WONDER-WORKERS

1. NAN, CSO 26/03765, vol. 1, "Charlatanic Correspondence": minute by staff officer of the Inspector-General of Police, 12 July 1922.

2. Robin Horton, *Patterns of Thought in Africa and the West: Essays on Magic, Religion and Science* (Cambridge University Press, 1997).

3. NAN, CSO 26/03765, vol. 1, "Charlatanic Correspondence": minute by staff officer of the Inspector-General of Police, 12 July 1922.

4. Ibid.

5. Pratten, *The Man-Leopard Murders*, p. 96.

6. NAN, CSO 26/03765, vol. 1, "Charlatanic Correspondence": Macgregor to Governor, 14 August 1925.

7. Ibid.

8. Ibid.

9. Ibid.

10. NAN, CSO 26/03765, vol. 1, "Charlatanic Correspondence": Churchill to Sir Hugh Clifford, 18 May 1922.

11. NAN, CSO 26/03765, vol. 1, "Charlatanic Correspondence": P. Crentsil to N.A. Mensah, 18 December 1920.

12. Harvey Glickman, "The Nigerian '419' Advance Fee Scams: Prank or Peril?", *Canadian Journal of African Studies*, 39, 3 (2005), p. 472, hints at a similar episode having taken place some years earlier.

13. NAN, CSO 26/03765, vol. 2, "Charlatanic Correspondence": O.A. Johnson to Inspector General of Police, 7 Dec. 1921.

14. NAN, CSO 26/03765, vol. 2, "Charlatanic Correspondence": Director of Posts and Telegraphs to Chief Secretary, 22 November 1948.

15. Ibid.

16. Pratten, *The Man-Leopard Murders*, p. 200.

17. Ibid, p. 377, note 137.

18. Marius Nkwoh, *The Sorrows of Man* (Okolue's Bookshop, Enugu, 1963), pp. 57–58.

19. A.E. Afigbo, *The Abolition of the Slave Trade in Southeastern Nigeria, 1885–1950* (University of Rochester Press, Rochester, NY, 2006), p. 67.
20. Nkwoh, *The Sorrows of Man*, pp. 57–8.
21. Ibid.
22. C.O. Okonkwo, *Okonkwo and Naish on Criminal Law in Nigeria* (1964; Sweet and Maxwell, London, 2nd edn, 1980), p. 310.
23. NAN, CSO 1/33, despatches from the Secretary of State, vol. 251: circular from the British Consulate-General, San Francisco, 3 November 1947.
24. Pratten, *The Man-Leopard Murders*, pp. 132–34.
25. W.R. Crocker, *Australian Ambassador: International Relations at First Hand* (Melbourne University Press, Carlton Victoria, 1971), p. 117.
26. National Archives and Records Administration (NARA II), Maryland, RG 84, records of the US consulate, Lagos, 1950–55, box 2: Erwin P. Keeler to Department of State, 29 September 1953, where his third name is given as Ewafor.
27. http://en.wikipedia.org/wiki/Nwafor_Orizu#cite_note-amamb-3 [accessed 1 June 2013].
28. NARA II, RG 84, records of the US consulate, Lagos, 1940–63, box 1: C. Porter Kuykendall, consul-general, to Secretary of State, 16 May 1949.
29. Ibid.
30. Stéphane Quéré, "Les clans criminels nigérians" (diplôme universitaire, Université de Paris II Panthéon-Assas, 2001), p. 39.
31. The National Archives of the United Kingdom, Kew, Colonial Office, CO537/5780: enclosure with Macpherson to Griffiths, 18 August 1950.
32. *Nigerian Catholic Herald*, 22 February 1952. Copy in NARA II, RG 84, records of the US consulate, Lagos, 1950–55, box 1, "Religion—Church": enclosure with A.W. Childs to Department of State, 28 February 1952.
33. NARA II, RG 84, records of the US consulate and embassy, Lagos, 1940–63, box 6: "Fraudulent Schemes".
34. *Daily Service*, 4 October 1957, p. 12.
35. Ayodeji Olukoju, "Self-help Criminality as Resistance? Currency Counterfeiting in Colonial Nigeria", *International Review of Social History*, 45, 3 (2000), pp. 385–407.
36. James Buchan, *Frozen Desire: The Meaning of Money* (Farrar, Straus, and Giroux, New York, 1997), esp. pp. 96–107, 120–6.
37. Richard Seaford, *Money and the Early Greek Mind: Homer, Philosophy, Tragedy* (Cambridge University Press, 2004).
38. Philip Goodchild, *The Theology of Money* (SCM Press, London, 2007), pp. 12–13.
39. Cf. David Graeber, *Debt: The First 5,000 Years* (Melville House, Hoboken, NJ, 2011).

40. Ellis and Ter Haar, *Worlds of Power*, pp. 51–56.
41. Paul Osifodunrin, "Escapee Criminals and Crime Control in Colonial Southwestern Nigeria, 1861–1945", *IFRA Research Review*, 1 (2005), p. 61.
42. Toyin Falola, "Money and Informal Credit Institutions in Colonial Western Nigeria", pp. 166–67, in Jane Guyer (ed.), *Money Matters: Instability, Values and Social Payments in the Modern History of West African Communities* (James Currey, London, 1995), p. 166.
43. Ibid., p. 165.
44. Ibid., pp. 165–6.
45. Cf. Jane I. Guyer, *Marginal Gains: Monetary Transactions in Atlantic Africa* (University of Chicago Press, Chicago and London, 2004).
46. J.D.Y. Peel, *Religious Encounter and the Making of the Yoruba* (Indiana University Press, Bloomington, IN, 2000), p. 66.
47. Ibid., pp. 69–70.
48. Iliffe, *Honour in African History*, p. 121.
49. NAN, CSO 26/03002: Report on the Nkanu Patrol, 1923, by Lt-Gov. Col. H.C. Moorhouse, 11 Oct. 1923.
50. Afigbo, *The Abolition of the Slave Trade in Southeastern Nigeria*, p. xiii.
51. P. Amaury Talbot, *Tribes of the Niger Delta: Their Religions and Customs* (1932; Frank Cass, London, 1967), p. 289.
52. Elechi Amadi, *Ethics in Nigerian Culture* (Heinemann Educational Books, London, 1982), p. 44.
53. Ibid.
54. NAN, CSO 26/29017: intelligence report on the Aro by T.M. Shankland, 1933.
55. NAN, CSO 26/29001: intelligence report on the Achalla group, Onitsha division, by W.R.T. Milne, 1933.
56. NAN, CSO 26/29017: intelligence report on the Aro by T.M. Shankland, 1933.
57. Ibid., p. 13.
58. Talbot, *Tribes of the Niger Delta*, p. 289.
59. Afigbo, *The Abolition of the Slave Trade in Southeastern Nigeria*, p. 46.
60. NAN, CSO 26/03002: Report on the Nkanu Patrol, 1923, by Lt-Gov. Col. H.C. Moorhouse, 11 Oct. 1923.
61. Laurent Fourchard, "Prêt sur gages et traite des femmes au Nigéria, fin 19ᵉ-années 1950", in Bénédicte Lavaud-Legendre (ed.), *Prostitution nigériane, entre rêves de migration et réalité de la traite* (Karthala, Paris, 2013), pp. 15–32.
62. Iliffe, *Honour in African History*, p. 269.
63. Pratten, *The Man-Leopard Murders*, pp. 158–67.
64. NAN, CSO 26/28994: "Slave Dealing and Child Stealing": Secretary, Southern Provinces, Enugu, to Chief Secretary, 14 June 1934.

65. Ibid.
66. Afigbo, *The Abolition of the Slave Trade in Southeastern Nigeria*, pp. 57–67.
67. NAN, CSO 26/28994: "Slave Dealing and Child Stealing": letter from O.W. Firth, 25 Feb. 1933.
68. Ibid.
69. NAN, CSO 26/28994: "Slave Dealing and Child Stealing": Secretary, Southern Provinces, Enugu, to Chief Secretary, 23 Nov. 1933.
70. NAN, CSO 26/28994: "Slave Dealing and Child Stealing": comments by Chief Secretary, 4 Feb. 1935.
71. A.E. Afigbo, "The Eclipse of the Aro Slaving Oligarchy of South-Eastern Nigeria, 1901–1927", *Journal of the Historical Society of Nigeria*, 6, 1 (1971), p. 16.
72. NAN, CSO 26/28994: "Slave Dealing and Child Stealing": Secretary, Southern Provinces, Enugu, to Chief Secretary, 14 June 1934.
73. Ibid.
74. Ibid.
75. Ibid.
76. Pratten, *The Man-Leopard Murders*, pp. 167–68.
77. NAN, CSO 26/36005: "Traffic in Girls from Nigeria to the Gold Coast".
78. Cf. Richard L. Sklar, *Nigerian Political Parties: Power in an Emergent African Nation* (1963; Africa World Press edn, Trenton, NJ, 2004), pp. 48–49.
79. NAN, CSO 26/36005, statement by Prince Eikineh, 23 November 1939.
80. NAN, CSO 26/36005: "Traffic in Girls from Nigeria to the Gold Coast": Prince Eikineh to the president of the NYM, 8 Jan. 1940.
81. NAN, CSO 26/36005: "Traffic in Girls from Nigeria to the Gold Coast": Prince Eikineh to the president of the NYM, 28 June 1939.
82. NAN, CSO 26/36005, statement by Prince Eikineh, 23 November 1939.
83. NAN, CSO 26/36005: "Traffic in Girls from Nigeria to the Gold Coast": Commissioner of Police to Chief Secretary, 4 March 1940.
84. NAN, CSO 26/36005: "Traffic in Girls from Nigeria to the Gold Coast": Secretary, Eastern Provinces, to Chief Secretary, 18 March 1940.
85. NAN, CSO 26/36005: "Traffic in Girls from Nigeria to the Gold Coast": report by J.R. Dickinson, Inspector of Labour, Accra, 8 May 1940.
86. NAN, CSO 26/36005: "Traffic in Girls from Nigeria to the Gold Coast": E.C. Nottingham, Commissioner of Police, to Colonial Secretary, Gold Coast, 15 May 1940.
87. NAN, CSO 26/36005: "Traffic in Girls from Nigeria to the Gold Coast": "Cross River Harlots", by R.S. Mallinson, 7 Feb 1941.
88. Ibid.
89. Iliffe, *Honour in African History*, pp. 268–9.
90. NAN, CSO 26/36005: minute by J.R. Dickinson, 8 May 1940.
91. NAN, CSO 26/36005: "Traffic in Girls from Nigeria to the Gold Coast":

R.S. Mallinson, District Officer Obura, to Resident, Ogoja Province, 7 February 1941.

92. Ibid.

93. NAN, Oyo Prof.1, 4113: "Crime and its Treatment": report to the Governor by Alexander Paterson, February 1944.

94. *Daily Service*, 10 May 1957.

95. NAN, CSO 26/28994: "Slave Dealing and Child Stealing": Secretary, Southern Provinces, Enugu, to Chief Secretary, 14 June 1934.

96. Ogbu U. Kalu, "Missionaries, Colonial Government and Secret Societies in South-Eastern Igboland, 1920–1950", pp. 75–90.

97. Ibid., p. 78.

98. NAN, COMCOL 1, 2481: Amos Oshinowo Shopitan to Commissioner of the Colony, 29 Dec. 1945; *West African Pilot*, 14 July 1945.

99. Ibid.

100. NAN, CSO 1/34/51: Governor to Secretary of State ("secret"), 13 February 1946.

101. NARA II, RG84, general records of the US consulate, Lagos, 1940–63, box 1: Winthrop S. Greene to Dept of State, 6 Sept. 1947.

102. Pratten, *The Man-Leopard Murders*, pp. 189, 190–95.

103. Mike A.A. Ozekhome, "Delayed Prosecution and Extra Judicial Killings: The Deadly Implications", in Patrick Keku and Tunde Akingbade (eds), *Dangerous Days and Savage Nights: Countering the Menace of Armed Robbery in Nigeria* (1st Books Library, no place given, 2003), p. 73.

104. Ibid., p. 72.

105. Pratten, *The Man-Leopard Murders*, p. 192.

106. Tekena Tamuno and Robin Horton, "The Changing Position of Secret Societies and Cults in Modern Nigeria", *African Notes*, 5, 2 (1969), p. 37.

107. Quoted in Pratten, *The Man-Leopard Murders*, p. 192.

108. Pratten, *The Man-Leopard Murders*, p. 229.

109. NAN, CSO 26/29017: intelligence report on the Aro by T.M. Shankland, 1933.

110. Marc Matera, Misty L. Bastian and Susan Kingsley Kent, *The Women's War of 1929: Gender and Violence in Colonial Nigeria* (Palgrave Macmillan, Basingstoke, 2012).

111. Perham, *Native Administration in Nigeria*, p. 29.

3. ENTER THE POLITICIANS

1. Perham, *Native Administration in Nigeria*, p. xi of the Introduction to the second impression.

2. Bourdillon, *Memorandum on the Future Political Development of Nigeria*, p. 1.

3. Pratten, *The Man-Leopard Murders*, pp. 185–95.

4. Ibid., p. 194.
5. Chibuike Uche, "Bank of England versus the IBRD: Did the Nigerian Colony Deserve a Central Bank?", *Explorations in Economic History*, 34, 2 (1997), p. 223.
6. NAN, COMCOL9/3, CDB9/vol. 1, Colony Development Board: Commissioner of the Colony to Financial Secretary, 28 Jan. 1950.
7. Gavin Williams, "Marketing Without and With Marketing Boards: The Origins of State Marketing Boards in Nigeria", *Review of African Political Economy*, 34 (1985), pp. 4–15.
8. Awolowo, *Awo*, p. 160.
9. John P. Mackintosh, *Nigerian Government and Politics* (Geo. Allen and Unwin, London, 1966), p. 23.
10. Obafemi Awolowo, *Path to Nigerian Freedom*, p. 47
11. NARA II, RG 84, general records of the US consulate, Lagos, 1940–63, box 1: Winthrop S. Greene to Dept of State, 5 Dec. 1947.
12. UK National Archives, CO 537/5942: political summary, 8 Nov. 1950.
13. Political summary, December 1948, in Lynn (ed.), *British Documents on the End of Empire. Series B, Country Volumes, Volume 7*, I, pp. 171–3.
14. UK National Archives, CO 537/7232: political intelligence notes, 17–31 July, dated 4 August 1951.
15. http://www.reformedogboni.com/node/1 [accessed 5 June 2013] is the website of the Reformed Ogboni Fraternity.
16. UK National Archives, CO 537/5804: minute dated 28 Dec. 1950.
17. Philip A. Igbafe, *Benin Under British Administration: The Impact of Colonial Rule on an African Kingdom, 1897–1938* (Longman, London, 1979), pp. 386–7.
18. *Report of the Commission Appointed to Enquire into the Owegbe Cult: Including Statement by the Government of the Mid-Western Group of Provinces* (Ministry of Internal Affairs and Information, Benin City, 1966).
19. NAN, M.L.G. (W) 17887, "Reformed Ogboni Fraternity": memorandum by J.C. Pax Osifo, n.d.
20. Sklar, *Nigerian Political Parties*, p. 254.
21. NAN, M.L.G.(W) 17887, "Reformed Ogboni Fraternity": Otu Edu to Chief Commissioner, Western Province, et al, 1 April 1950.
22. Igbafe, *Benin Under British Administration*, pp. 387.
23. The date given on the website of the National Association of Seadogs: http://www.nas-int.org
24. http://www.nas-int.org/history.html [accessed 31 May 2013].
25. Daniel A. Offiong, *Secret Cults in Nigerian Tertiary Institutions* (Fourth Dimension, Enugu, 2003), p. 3.
26. NARA II, RG 84, records of the US consulate, Lagos, 1940–63, box 1:

"Inspection Trip with the Governor of Nigeria", by Andrew G. Lynch, US consul, 13 Oct. 1944.

27. Lawal, *Corruption in Nigeria*.
28. Amadi, *Ethics in Nigerian Culture*, p. 88.
29. NAN, WarProf 1, WP 859, "Bribery and Corruption": circular by R.H. Gretton, Acting Secretary, Western Provinces, 9 Sept. 1946.
30. NAN, COMCOL 1, 1594: "Loss of Government Funds", circular leter by Chief Secretary A.E.T. Benson, 3 Sept. 1951.
31. Quoted in Iliffe, *Honour in African History*, p. 215.
32. Labanji Bolaji, "Anti-Corruption Drive: What Progress?", text of a speech to a learned society printed in the *Nigerian Tribune*, 5 Nov. 1975.
33. NAN, Oyo Prof.1, 4113: "Crime and its Treatment": report to the Governor by Alexander Paterson, February 1944.
34. Ibid.
35. Isaac Oláwálé Albert, "The Growth of an Urban Migrant Community: The Hausa Settlements in Ibadan, c.1830–1979", *Ife:Annals of the Institute of Cultural Studies*, 4 (1993), pp. 4–5.
36. NARA II, RG 59, Pol 15–1 Nga, 1/1/65, box 2524: record of conversation with Sir A. Bello attached to Edward J. Chesky to Dept of State, 27 July 1965.
37. Perham, *Native Administration in Nigeria*, p. 236.
38. Booth, *Writers and Politics*, pp. 49, 50.
39. Ibid., pp. 53–4.
40. John P. Meagher, "The Establishment of Military Government in Nigeria", 16 Feb. 1966, p. 24, NARA II, RG59, Nga Pol 15, 2/24/66, box 2522, enc. with Mathews to Dept of State, 5 Mar. 1966.
41. Stanislav Andreski, *The African Predicament: A Study in the Pathology of Modernisation* (London, 1968), p. 120.
42. Otonti Nduka, *Western Education and the Nigerian Cultural Background* (Oxford University Press, Ibadan, 1964), p. 99.
43. Important contributions on this subject include: Eyo O. Akak, *Bribery and Corruption in Nigeria* (no publisher given, Ibadan, no date [1952]); Bretton, *Power and Stability in Nigeria*; Ronald Wraith and Edgar Simpkins, *Corruption in Developing Countries* (Geo. Allen and Unwin, London, 1963); Andreski, *The African Predicament*; Iliffe, *Honour in African History*.
44. Andreski, *The African Predicament*, p. 16.
45. Perham, *Native Administration in Nigeria*, pp. 238–40.
46. Chima J. Korieh, *The Land Has Changed: History, Society, and Gender in Colonial Eastern Nigeria* (University of Calgary Press, 2010), p. 34.
47. http://www.populstat.info/Africa/nigeriac.htm [accessed 12 May 2015].

48. James S. Coleman, *Nigeria: Background to Nationalism* (University of California Press, Berkeley, CA, 1958), p. 59.
49. Ibid., p. 355.
50. Canon R.S.O. Stevens, "The Church in Urban Nigeria", memoir of a journey in May–June 1963, UK National Archives, FO 1110/1832.
51. Andreski, *The African Predicament*, p. 16.
52. Ibid., p. 41.
53. Bretton, *Power and Stability*, p. 164.
54. NARA II, RG 59, Pol 15–1 Nga, 2/1/63, box 3998: George Dolgin to Dept of State, 11 Dec. 1963.
55. Akak, *Bribery and Corruption in Nigeria*, foreword.
56. Ibid., p. 57.
57. Ibid.
58. Ibid, p. 55.
59. G.I.K. Tasie, "Religion and Moral Depravity in Contemporary Nigeria", *The Nigerian Journal of Theology*, 19 (2005), p. 90.
60. "Report on Corruption", *West Africa*, 14 Feb. 1953.
61. Billy Dudley, quoted in Gavin Williams, *State and Society in Nigeria* (Afrografika, Ondo State, 1980), pp. 80–81.
62. Williams, *State and Society in Nigeria*, p. 73.
63. Williams, "Marketing Without and With Marketing Boards", pp. 4–15.
64. Eme O. Awa, *Federal Government in Nigeria* (University of California Press, Berkeley, CA, 1964), p. 230.
65. National Archives of the UK, CO 1035/121: memo enc. with Cox to Hunt, 15 June 1956.
66. Informal notes by B.E. Sharwood-Smith, Sept. 1951, in Lynn (ed.), *British Documents on the End of Empire. Series B, Country Volumes, Volume 7*, I, pp. 422–3.
67. See the statement by Colonial Secretary Alan Lennox-Boyd in *Hansard*, House of Commons Debates, 24 July 1956, vol. 557, cc215–21.
68. Henry L. Bretton, *Power and Politics in Africa* (Longman, London, 1973), p. 110.
69. UK National Archives, CO554/693: "Bank Frauds in Nigeria", esp. minute by Sir J. Macpherson, 15 Aug. 1953.
70. Uche, "Bank of England versus the IBRD", p. 226–7.
71. UK National Archives, CO554/693: "National Bank of Nigeria" (top secret), esp. minute by Sir J. Macpherson, 15 Aug. 1953.
72. Sklar, *Nigerian Political Parties*, p. 458.
73. Douglas Rimmer, "Elements of the Political Economy", in Keith Panter-Brick (ed.), *Soldiers and Oil: The Political Transformation of Nigeria* (Frank Cass, London, 1978), p. 148.
74. C.C. Wrigley, quoted in ibid., pp. 148–9.

4. THE NATIONAL CAKE

1. Bretton, *Power and Stability*, p. 124.
2. Quoted in Taiwo Akinola, "He Fought Our Battle, That is why We are Grateful to Him", 4 Jan. 2011, https://haroldsmithmemorial.wordpress.com/harold-smith-fought-our-battle/ [accessed 13 May 2015].
3. Alkasum Abba, "The Rigging of Nigerian History: Response to Harold Smith", 22 April 2005. http://nigeriaworld.com/articles/2005/apr/220.html [accessed 15 May 2015].
4. Peregrino Brimah, "Debunked: The Harold Smith Census Lies", 10 December2013.http://saharareporters.com/2013/12/10/debunked-harold-smith-nigeria-census-lies [accessed 15 May 2015].
5. See e.g. the pro-Northern views of Colonial Secretary Oliver Lyttleton in a memorandum dated 17 August 1953, in Lynn (ed.), *British Documents on the End of Empire. Series B, Country Volumes, Volume 7* (volume II, the Stationery Office, London, 2001), document no. 234.
6. See e.g. the memoir by Bryan Sharwood Smith, *"But Always as Friends": Northern Nigeria and the Cameroons, 1921–1957* (Geo. Allen and Unwin, London, 1969).
7. Perham, *Native Administration*, p. 22.
8. NARA II, RG 59, Pol 15 Government, Nigeria 2/1/63, box 3998: John P. Meagher to Dept of State, 21 March 1963.
9. Ken Saro-Wiwa, *On a Darkling Plain: An Account of the Nigerian Civil War* (Saros, Epsom, 1989), p. 21.
10. Ibid.
11. Bretton, *Power and Stability*, p. 75
12. UK National Archives, DO 186/10: Viscount Head to Sir Henry Lintott, 12 Jan. 1963.
13. Ibid.
14. NARA II, RG 59, Pol 15–4, Nigeria, 1/1/64, box 2525: W.K. Scott to Dept of State, 6 Feb. 1964.
15. NARA II, RG 59, Nigeria 2, 1/1/65, box 2518: Birley A. Stokes to Dept of State, 2 Feb. 1966.
16. P.N.C. Okigbo, *Nigerian Public Finance* (Longman, London, 1965), p. 77.
17. Ibid, p. 64.
18. UK National Archives, DO186/10/fol.74: J.O. Moreton to V.C. Martin, 23 Aug. 1962.
19. NARA II, RG 59, Nigeria 2/1/63, 15–4, box 3998: John P. Meagher to Dept of State, 19 Dec. 1963.
20. NARA II, RG 59, 1963, Pol 18, Nigeria 2/1/63, box 3998: Robert P. Smith to Dept of State, 26 Nov. 1963.
21. UK National Archives, DO 186/10: Viscount Head to Sir Henry Lintott, 12 Jan. 1963.

22. NARA II, RG 59, 1963, Pol 18, Nigeria 2/1/63, box 3998: George Dolgin to Dept of State, 21 Feb. 1963.

23. NARA II, RG 59, Pol 18, Ng 2/1/63, box 3998: Patrick O'Sheel to Dept of State, 2 May 1963.

24. John P. Meagher, "The Establishment of Military Government in Nigeria", p. 26, 16 Feb. 1966, enclosed with Mathews to Dept of State, 5 March 1966: NARA II, RG59, Subject numeric files, Nigeria 1966, Pol 15, box 2522.

25. Ibid.

26. NARA II, RG 59, Pol 15–4 Nga, 1/1/64: box 2525: Birney A. Stokes to Dept of State, 26 Jan. 1966.

27. UK National Archives, FCO65/995: note of a conversation with Williams enc. with Smedley to Glass, 6 Jan. 1971.

28. Andreski, *African Predicament*, p. 109.

29. Ibid., p. 108.

30. Ibid., p. 77.

31. NARA II, RG 59, Pol 2, Nigeria, 1/1/64, box 2517: Alfred E. Wellons to Dept of State, 25 Dec. 1964.

32. NARA II, RG 59, Pol 14, Nga. 11/1/64, box 2520: Robert P. Smith to Dept of State, 11 Nov. 1964.

33. Ibid.

34. Richard A. Joseph, *Democracy and Prebendal Politics in Nigeria: The Rise and Fall of the Second Republic* (Cambridge University Press, 1987).

35. Strong Man of Pen [aka Okenwa Olisa], *Life Turns Man Upside Down* (Njoku and Sons, Onitsha, n.d.), p. 48.

36. Claude Ake, *Is Africa Democratizing?* (Malthouse Press, Lagos, 1996), pp. 7–8.

37. Akak, *Bribery and Corruption in Nigeria*, p. 114.

38. NARA II, RG 59, Nigeria 2, 1/1/65, box 2518: Birley A. Stokes to Dept of State, 2 Feb. 1966.

39. Ibid.

40. Andreski, *African Predicament*, p. 216.

41. Ibid.

42. UK National Archives, DO 186/10, fol. 37: Head to Clutterbuck, 5 May 1961; and fol. 56, same to same, 8 Nov. 1961.

43. UK National Archives, CO554/1226: papers concerning Commission of Enquiry into Bribery and Corruption in the Eastern Region, esp. Sir Clement Pleass, Governor, Eastern Region, to T.B. Williamson, 22 June 1955.

44. NARA II, RG 59, central foreign policy files 1963, E Nig, box 3391: Dolgin to Dept of State, 16 Mar. 1963.

45. Ibid.

46. Raymond Baker, *Capitalism's Achilles Heel: Dirty Money and How to Renew the Free-market System* (John Wiley & Sons, Hoboken, NJ, 2005), p. 12.
47. NARA II, RG 59, central foreign policy files 1963, Nigeria, box 3391: Dolgin to Dept of State, 16 March 1963.
48. NARA II, RG 59, Bureau of African Affairs, country files, 1951–63, box 6, Nigeria 1963: Patrick O'Sheel to David Post, 17 Jan. 1963.
49. NARA II, RG 59, Pol 2, Nga 1/1/64, box 2517: Patrick O'Sheel to Dept of State, 17 June 1964.
50. NARA II, RG 84, US Consulate and Embassy, Lagos, classified General Records 194–1963, box 6: file "fraudulent schemes".
51. NARA II, RG 59, Pol 14, Nig., 10/22/64, box 2520: George B. Sherry to Dept of State, 27 Oct. 1964.
52. Philip Asiodu, quoted in Nicholas Shaxson, *Poisoned Wells: The Dirty Politics of African Oil* (Palgrave Macmillan, New York, 2007), p. 11.
53. NARA II, RG 59, Pol 15–1, 2/1/63, box 3998: Robert P. Smith to Dept of State, 29 Oct. 1963.
54. NARA II, RG 59, Pol 15–4 Nga, 1/1/64: box 2525: Birney A. Stokes to Dept of State, 26 Jan. 1966.
55. NARA II, RG 59, Pol 15–4, Nigeria, 1/1/64, box 2525: W.K. Scott to Dept of State, 16 May 1964.
56. NARA II, RG 59, Pol 15–4 Nga, 1/1/64: box 2525: Birney A. Stokes to Dept of State, 26 Jan. 1966.
57. NARA II, RG 59, Pol 12 Nga, 4/4/64, box 2519: George B. Sherry to Dept of State, 20 Oct. 1964.
58. Bretton, *Power and Politics*, p. 128.
59. Bretton, *Power and Stability*, p. 78.
60. Philip Asiodu, quoted in Shaxson, *Poisoned Wells*, p. 11.
61. NARA II, RG 59, Pol 15–1 Nga, 9/1/65, box 2524: Robert J. Barnard to Dept of State, 22 Dec. 1965.
62. Bretton, *Power and Stability*, p. 90.
63. Ibid, p. 49.
64. Ibid, p. 67
65. NARA II, RG 59, Pol 18 Nga, 1/1/65, box 2525: Josiah W. Bennett to Dept of State, 24 June 1964.
66. Bretton, *Power and Politics*, p. 124.
67. Nicholas Shaxson, "The Tax Haven in the Heart of Britain", *New Statesman*, 24 February 2011.
68. Peter Gowan, *The Global Gamble: Washington's Faustian Bid for World Dominance* (Verso, London and New York, 1999), p. 38, note 8.
69. Ibid., p. 22.
70. Ronen Palan, Richard Murphy and Christian Chavagneux, *Tax Havens:*

How Globalization Really Works (Cornell Studies in Money, Cornell University Press, Ithaca, NY, 2010), p. 79.

71. Ronen Palan, *The Offshore World: Sovereign Markets, Virtual Places, and Nomad Millionaires* (Cornell University Press, London and Ithaca, 2003), pp. 2–3, 7.

72. Bretton, *Power and Politics*, p. 129.

73. Quoted in Wale Adebanwi, *A Paradise for Maggots: The Story of a Nigerian Anti-graft Czar* (published by the author, 2010), p. 105.

74. NARA II, RG 59, Pol 15–4, Nigeria, 1/1/64: Robert P. Smith to Dept of State, 21 May 1964.

75. Canon S.A. Banjo, quoted in NARA II, RG 59, Pol 15–4, Nigeria, 1/1/64: John P. Meagher to Dept of State, 27 Jan. 1964.

76. NARA II, RG 59, Pol 15, Government, 2/1/63, box 3998: John P. Meagher to Dept of State, 19 Feb. 1963.

77. Ibid.

78. UK National Archives, FO 1110/1832: notes enc. with Webber to Ure, 20 Nov. 1964.

79. NARA II, RG 59, Pol 5, Nga, 1/1/65, box 2518: J.M. Beckley, quoted in George B. Sherry to Dept of State, 23 Feb. 1966.

80. Acting Chief Justice H.U. Kaine, quoted in NARA II, RG59, Pol 15–5, Nga, 1/1/64, box 2525: Robert J. Barnard to Dept of State, 4 March 1966.

81. Bretton, *Power and Stability*, p. 49.

82. NARA II, RG 59, Pol 14, Nig., 10/22/64, box 2520: George B. Sherry to Dept of State, 27 Oct. 1964.

83. Ben Onyeachonam, "Corruption: A Spreading Cancer", *National Concord*, 19 Apr. 1983.

84. NARA II, RG 59, 1963, Pol 18, Nigeria 2/1/63, box 3998: Robert P. Smith to Dept of State, 26 Nov. 1963.

85. NARA II, RG 59, Pol 18, Nga, 1/1/66, box 2526: George B. Sherry to Dept of State, 26 Jan. 1966.

86. NARA II, RG 59, 1963, Pol 18, Nigeria 2/1/63, box 3998: George Dolgin to Dept of State, 21 Feb. 1963.

87. NARA II, RG 59, Pol 18, Nga, 4/1/66, box 2526: George B. Sherry to Dept of State, 9 June 1966.

88. NARA II, RG 59, Pol 18, Nigeria, 1/1/64, box 2525: George B. Sherry to Dept of State, 1 Sept. 1964 and 10 Oct. 1964, including undated clipping from *Sunday Express* (quotation).

89. NARA II, RG 59, Pol 18, Nigeria, 7/23/64, box 2525: George B. Sherry to Dept of State, 14 July 1964.

90. NARA II, RG 59, Pol 23–9, Nga, 1/1/66, box 2529: G. Mennen Williams to acting Sec. of State, 15 Jan. 1966.

91. NARA II, RG 59, Pol 2 Nga, 1/1/64, box 2517: John P. Meagher to Dept of State, 11 June 1964; Robert J. Barnard to Dept of State, 10 March 1966.
92. NARA II, RG 59, Pol 2 Nga, 1/1/64, box 2517: Robert J. Barnard to Dept of State, 10 March 1966.
93. NARA II, RG 59, Pol 15–5, Nga, 1/1/64, box 2125: Consul Enugu to Dept of State, 23 January 1965.
94. Andreski, *African Predicament*, p. 122.
95. J.I. Tseayo, *Conflict and Incorporation in Nigeria: The Integration of the Tiv* (Gaskia Corp., Zaria, 1975), pp. 220–21.

5. THE MEN IN UNIFORM

1. Andreski, *African Predicament*, p. 77.
2. Joe Harold, "Scrapbook of 50 Years in Nigeria" (privately printed), p. 135: copy in the archives of the SMA Fathers, Cork, Ireland.
3. NARA II, RG 59, Pol 2, Nga 1/1/65, box 2518: Information from Alhaji Sani Kontagora, Nigerian ambassador to Senegal, in Donald B. Easum to Dept of State, 21 March 1966.
4. Meagher, "The Establishment of Military Government in Nigeria", p. 26.
5. Ibid.
6. Ibid.
7. Quoted in Booth, *Writers and Politics in Nigeria*, p. 30.
8. NARA II, RG 59, Pol 23–9, Nga, 1/26/66, box 2529: Birney A. Stokes to Dept of State, 26 Jan. 1966.
9. NARA II, RG 59, Pol 2, Nga 1/1/65, box 2518: Information from Alhaji Sani Kontagora, Nigerian ambassador to Senegal, in Donald B. Easum to Dept of State, 21 March 1966.
10. NARA II, RG 59, Pol 23–9, Nga 6/1/67, box 2378: Mathews to Dept of State, 29 June 1967.
11. See Chapter Two, p. 28
12. NARA II, RG 59, Pol 15–2 Nga, 1/1/64: box 2524: Robert P. Smith to Dept of State, 15 Feb. 1965.
13. NARA II, RG 59, Pol 15–4 Nga, 1/1/64: box 2525: Birney A. Stokes to Dept of State, 26 Jan. 1966.
14. NARA II, RG 59, Pol 12 Nigeria, 8/17/65, box 2520: Alfred E. Wellons to Dept of State, 10 March 1966.
15. NARA II, RG 59, Pol 18 Nga, 4/1/66, box 2566: Birney A. Stokes to Dept of State, 22 April 1966.
16. Bretton, *Power and Politics*, pp. 130–31.
17. Terisa Turner, "Commercial Capitalism and the 1975 Coup", in K. Panter-Brick (ed.), *Soldiers and Oil*, p. 179.

18. NARA II, RG 59, Pol 15 Nga, 5/26/66: box 2523: Elbert Mathews to Dept of State, 17 July 1966.

19. NARA II, RG 59, subject-numeric files, Nigeria, box 646: report of a lecture by Sir Arthur Lewis at Univ. of Ibadan, 9 Dec. 1966.

20. Biobele Richards Briggs, "Problems of Recruitment in Civil Service: Case of the Nigerian Civil Service", *African Journal of Business Management*, 1, 6 (2007), p. 146.

21. NARA II, RG 59, Pol 15–4, Nga, 1/1/64, box 2525: Elbert G. Mathews to Dept of State, 1 July 1966.

22. NARA II, RG 59, Pol 15–2, Nga, 6/8/65, box 2524: Alfred E. Wellons to Dept of State, 15 Sept 1965.

23. *Report of the Commission Appointed to Enquire into the Owegbe Cult.*

24. NARA II, RG 59, Pol 18 Nigeria, 1/1/65, box 2525: Alfred E. Wellons to Dept of State, 21 May 1965.

25. NARA II, RG 59, Pol 15–4, Nga, 7/9/66, box 2525: Mathews to Dept of State, 14 July 1966.

26. NARA II, RG 59, Pol 18 Nga, 4/1/66, box 2566: Birney A. Stokes to Dept of State, 22 April 1966.

27. General Ironsi's broadcast to the nation, 24 May 1966, http://www.dawodu.com/irons2.htm [accessed 15 May 2015].

28. Bretton, *Power and Politics*, pp. 130–31.

29. RG 59, Pol 15–1 Nigeria, box 2508: Embassy Lagos to Secretary of State, 31 January 1972.

30. NARA II, RG 59, Pol 18 Nga, 12/1/66, box 2527: Birney A. Stokes to Dept of State, 30 Dec. 1966.

31. NARA II, RG 59, Pol 18 Nga, 12/1/66, box 2527: Charles Sharpe, managing director of *New Nigeria*, quoted in C.L. Olson to Dept of State, 8 Dec. 1966.

32. NARA II, RG 59, Pol 18 Nigeria, 1/1/64, box 2525: Josiah W. Bennett to Dept of State, 16 May 1964, reporting a car trip throughout the North in April and May.

33. Ibid.

34. NARA II, RG 59, Pol 14 Nigeria, 10/1/65, box 2522: Robert J. Barnard to Dept of State, 23 Oct. 1965.

35. NARA II, RG 59, Pol 2, Nigeria, 2/1/63, box 3997: Joseph N. Greene Jr to Dept of State, 14 Feb. 1963.

36. Ibid.

37. Ibid.

38. NARA II, RG 59, Pol 15, Nigeria, 12/1/66, box 2523: telegram Mathews to Dept of State, 30 Dec. 1966.

39. Ibid.

40. NARA II, RG 59, Pol 18, Nigeria, 2/16/66, box 2526: Robert J. Barnard to Dept of State, 2 March 1966.
41. NARA II, RG 59, Pol 23–9, Nigeria, 2/1/66, box 2529: telegram embassy Lagos to Dept of State, 2 March 1966.
42. NARA II, RG59, Pol 18 Nigeria 8/4/66, box 2526: Robert J. Barnard to Dept of State, 7 Sept 1966.
43. NARA II, RG 59, Pol 23–9, Nigeria, 2/1/66, box 2529: telegram embassy Lagos to Dept of State, 2 March 1966.
44. NARA II, RG 59, Pol 23–8, Nigeria, 6/6/66, box 2529: telegram embassy Lagos to Dept of State, 22 June 1966.
45. Archives of the World Bank, Washington DC, McNamara papers, folder 1771139/1: memorandum dated 1 October 1969 recording McNamara's meetings in Lagos.
46. Ibid.
47. Gen. Theophilus Danjuma, quoted in Martin J. Dent, "Corrective Government: Military Rule in Perspective", p. 108, in Panter-Brick, *Soldiers and Oil.*
48. NARA II, RG 59, Pol Aff Rel Biafra-Nigeria 1967, box 1872: memo by Robert P. Smith, 14 Feb. 1968.
49. *The Independent*, 6 April 1993: http://www.independent.co.uk/news/ uk/man-cleared-in-customs-heroin-sting-operation-to-arrest-business-man-for-drug-smuggling-relied-on-mercenary-as-paid-informer-1453561.html [accessed 11 July 2013].
50. NARA II, RG 59,Pol 12 Biafra 11/1/67, box 1871: Rusk to Embassy Lagos, 6 October 1967.
51. UK National Archives, FCO65/1679.
52. NARA II, RG 59, economic, FN10 Nigeria, box 931: Mulcahy to Dept of State, 27 March 1971.
53. Alhaji Bashar Ali, "Time for Action Against Groundnut Smugglers in the Northern States", *Daily Times*, 3 Feb. 1972.
54. NARA II, RG 59, EG Nigeria, box 647: embassy Lagos to Dept of State, 20 Dec. 1969.
55. Segun Odusanya, "Currency Racket Uncovered", *Daily Sketch*, 9 Nov. 1972.
56. NARA II, RG 59, EG Nigeria, box 647: embassy Lagos to Dept of State, 20 Dec. 1969.
57. Banji Kuroloja, "Smuggling", *Nigerian Tribune*, 25 February 1982.
58. Turner, "Commercial Capitalism", p. 171.
59. Quoted in Booth, *Writers and Politics*, p. 33.
60. *The Man Died*, quoted in Booth, *Writers and Politics*, p. 33.
61. Quoted in Joseph, *Democracy and Prebendal Politics*, p. 39.

62. NARA II, RG 59, Pol 2, Nigeria, 1/1/65: Alfred E. Wellons to Dept of State, 31 March 1966, reporting a trip by Raymond J. Wach.
63. William J. Chambliss, "Toward a Political Economy of Crime", *Theory and Society*, 2, 2 (1975), p. 158.
64. Ibid., p. 160.
65. Ibid., p. 165.
66. Joseph, *Democracy and Prebendal Politics*, p. 72.
67. Ibid., p. 56.
68. David Enweremadu, *Anti-Corruption Campaign in Nigeria (1999–2007): The Politics of a Failed Reform* (IFRA-Nigeria and the African Studies Centre, Ibadan and Leiden, 2012).
69. Prof. E.U. Essien-Udom, head of political science at University College, Ibadan, quoted in NARA II, RG 59, Nigeria 2, 5/6/66, box 2518: George B. Sherry to Dept of State, 3 Nov. 1966.
70. Douglas Rimmer, "Development in Nigeria: An Overview", in Henry Bienen and V.P. Diejomaoh (eds), *The Political Economy of Income Distribution in Nigeria* (Holmes and Meier, New York and London, 1981), p. 36.
71. Andreski, *The African Predicament*, p. 41.
72. NARA II, RG 84, records of the consulate-general, Lagos, 1940–63, box 2, 'Smuggling of Narcotics': Erwin P. Keeler to Dept of State, 4 Dec. 1952.
73. Ibid: memorandum for Mr Ross, 21 August 1952, attached to Robert W. Ross to Dept of State, 28 August 1952.
74. Ibid: Erwin P. Keeler to Dept of State, 4 Dec. 1952.
75. http://www.gilbertchagoury.com/ [accessed 1 July 2015].
76. NARA II, RG 59, subject-numeric files, 1967–69, FIN6–1, box 800, Nigeria: Mathews to Department of State, 8 August 1968.
77. NARA II, RG 59, subject-numeric files, 1967–69, FIN6–1, box 800, Nigeria: Strong (US Consul Ibadan) to Department of State, 3 April 1969.
78. NARA II, RG 59, subject-numeric files 1970–1973, POL 18 Nga, Box 2509: embassy Abidjan to Dept of State, 26 June 1970.

6. BOOM TIME

1. NARA II, RG 286, records of USAID, Africa, Near East and South Asia branch, subject files 1956–72, Nigeria IPS-1–3, box 37: embassy Lagos to Dept of State, 27 March 1971.
2. NARA II, RG 59, subject-numeric files, 1970–73, Political and Defense, Pol 2 Nigeria, box 2506: Reinhardt to Dept of State, 26 Nov. 1973.
3. Ibid.
4. NARA II, RG59, subject-numeric files, 1970–73, Pol 7 Nigeria, box 2507: O. Rudolph Aggrey to Assistant Secretary Armstrong, 22 May 1973.

5. Keetie Sluyterman, *Keeping Competitive in Turbulent Markets, 1973–2007: A History of Royal Dutch Shell* (Vol. IV, Oxford University Press, 2007), p. 345.

6. Turner, "Commercial Capitalism and the 1975 Coup", pp. 168–9.

7. NARA II, RG59, central foreign policy files, 1973–75: US Embassy Paris to Dept of State, 16 May 1973.

8. Quoted in Karin Brulliard, "Worldwide Slump Makes Nigeria's Online Scammers Work that Much Harder", *Washington Post*, 7 August 2009.

9. Speech by S.O. Asabia, deputy governor of the Central Bank, 9 August 1972, printed in *New Nigerian*, 19 Aug. 1972.

10. UK National Archives, FCO 65/1537: Sharkey to Ruddock, 12 Aug. 1974.

11. Robert Williams, *Political Corruption in Africa* (Gower Publishing Co., Aldershot etc., 1987), p. 67.

12. The atmosphere of the time is well described by Andrew H. Apter, *Pan-African Nation: Oil and the Spectacle of Culture in Nigeria* (University of Chicago Press, 2005).

13. UK National Archives, FCO65/1778: report enc. with Edgeley to Roberts, 10 Dec. 1976.

14. NARA II, RG 59, Subject-numeric files 1967–69, FN12 Nigeria, box 800: William G. Jones to Dept of State, 6 Sept. 1968.

15. Williams, *Political Corruption in Africa*, p. 67.

16. Biodun Famojuro and Remi Yesufu, "Motor Racket in Nigeria", *Sunday Sketch*, 12 July 1970.

17. Sola Alabi, "Uphill Task for Customs Men at the Borders", *National Concord*, 19 Oct. 1981.

18. UK National Archives, FCO65/1924: Thomson to Edgley, 30 Aug. 1977.

19. United Nations Economic Commission for Africa, *Foreign Exchange and Financial Leakages in Africa* (1985) http://repository.uneca.org/bitstream/handle/10855/10023/Bib-50651.pdf?sequence=1 [accessed 12 July 2015].

20. Editorial in the *Daily Star*, 23 July 1976.

21. The National Archives, USA, access to archival databases: Reinhardt to Newsom, 15 Nov. 1973 http://aad.archives.gov/aad/cratepdf?rid=10 1336&d5=1573&d1=823 [accessed 28 Feb. 2013].

22. Federal Republic of Nigeria, *Report of the Judicial Commission of Inquiry into the Shortage of Petroleum Products 11th November 1975* (Federal Ministry of Information, Lagos, 1976), pp. 10–12.

23. Daniel Ammann, *The King of Oil: The Secret Lives of Marc Rich* (St Martin's Press, New York, 2009), p. 100.

24. See the description in NARA II, RG 59, Pol 15–1, Nigeria, box 2508: Walter to Dept of State, 16 Dec. 1971.

25. UK National Archives, FCO65/995: Lucas to Bache, 5 Aug. 1971.
26. Williams, *Political Corruption in Africa*, pp. 67–8.
27. Ibid., p. 67.
28. Ibid., p. 69.
29. Ibid., p. 70.
30. Turner, "Commercial Capitalism", p. 174.
31. NARA II, RG 59, electronic telegrams: embassy Lagos to Secretary of State, 11 Jan. 1974.
32. Federal Republic of Nigeria, *Report of the Panel of Inquiry into the Purchase of British Leyland Buses by the Secretariat of Festac* (Federal Ministry of Information, Lagos, 1978), esp. pp. 15, 18.
33. UK National Archives, FCO 65/1930: Beaven to Petter, 12 April 1977.
34. UK National Archives, FCO 65/1930: "Corruption in Nigeria"
35. Apter, *The Pan-African Nation*, p. 41.
36. Ibid., p. 13.
37. Emman I. Akpaka, "Crime Trends in Modern Nigeria", *National Concord*, 30 Sept. 1983.
38. Apter, *The Pan-African Nation*, p. 33.
39. Ibid.
40. Dent, "Corrective Government", p. 121.
41. Stephen Ekpenyong, "Social Inequalities, Collusion, and Armed Robbery in Nigerian Cities", *British Journal of Criminology*, 29, 1 (1989), p. 22 (table 1).
42. Note in SMA archives, Cork.
43. NAN, COMCOL 1, 2403: "Pickpockets and Hooligans....Lagos": petition to Assistant Superintendent of Police, October 1954.
44. Emmanuel M.K. Dawha, *'Yan Daba, 'Yan Banga and 'Yan Daukar Amarya: A Study of Criminal Gangs in Northern Nigeria* (Occasional paper no. 9, Institut français pour la recherche en Afrique, Ibadan, 1996).
45. NARA II, RG 59, Nigeria Pol 14, 10/28/65: Sherry to Dept of State, 22 Dec. 1965 and Pol 15 Nigeria 2/24/66, box 2522, report by John P. Meagher enc. with Elbert G. Mathews to Dept of State, 5 March 1966.
46. NARA II, RG 286, records of USAID, Africa, Near East and South Asia subject files 1956–72, Nigeria, box 37, IPS-I-6: Dubose to Dept of State, 30 April 1970.
47. Ibid.
48. *Nigerian Tribune*, 8 Sept. 1986.
49. I.S. Omisakin, *Crime Trends and Prevention Strategies in Nigeria: A Study of Old Oyo State* (Monograph series no. 9, Nigerian Institute of Social and Economic Research, Ibadan, 1998), p. 2.
50. *Daily Sketch*, 8 Sept. 1986.
51. Presentation by O.O. Onoge, assistant commissioner of police, in Christine

Obemsulu (ed.), *Dimensions of Social Problems in Nigeria* (seminar proceedings, National Institute for Policy and Strategic Studies, Kuru, 1982), p. 2.

52. *West Africa*, 26 Feb. 1979, p. 330.

53. Otwin Marenin, "The Anini Saga: Armed Robbery and the Reproduction of Ideology in Nigeria", *Journal of Modern African Studies*, 25, 2 (1987), pp. 259–81.

54. Ekpenyong, "Social Inequalities, Collusion, and Armed Robbery in Nigerian Cities", p. 32.

55. Presentation by Dr F. Odekunle, in Obemsulu (ed.), *Dimensions of Social Problems in Nigeria*, p. 2.

56. Obi N.I. Ebbe, "The Political-Criminal Nexus: The Nigerian Case", *Trends in Organized Crime*, 4, 3 (1999), p. 36.

57. Ibid., pp. 35–40.

58. NARA II, RG 84, general records, Lagos, 1940–63, box 2: Erwin P. Keeler to Dept of State, 3 Feb. 1954.

59. UK National Archives, FCO 65/1530: Reuters report, 23 August 1974.

60. *Sunday Times* [Lagos], 10 March 1974; "The Redeemer is not Near", *Daily Sketch* [Lagos], 28 July 1974.

61. UK National Archives, FCO 65/1530: Reuters report, 23 August 1974.

62. *Avoid Indian Hemp*, leaflet c.1974, in "Nigeria: drugs, 1979–", press cuttings file in Nigerian Institute of International Affairs, Lagos.

63. The National Archives, USA, access to archival databases, Embassy Ndjamena to Dept of State, 29 Oct. 1974: http://aad.archives.gov/aad/createpdf?rid=224316&dt=2474&dl=1345 [accessed 2 July 2015].

64. Press release number 295, Federal Ministry of Information, Lagos, 22 March 1971, contained in press cuttings file in Nigerian Institute of International Affairs, Lagos.

65. "The Cost of War against Smuggling", *New Nigerian*, 31 August 1979.

66. Umoh James Umoh and Alhaji Nurudeen Adio-Saka, "The Problem of Smuggling among Pilgrims", *Daily Times*, 13 July 1972.

67. Ibid.

68. Chapter Two, p. 27.

69. Gobyega Okubanjo, "How to Curb Incidence of Crime in Our Society", *Daily Express*, 27 June 1978.

70. Ibid.

71. Afe Adogame, "The 419 Code as Business Unusual: Youth and the Unfolding of the Advance Fee Fraud Online Discourse", *ISA e-bulletin*, International Sociological Association, 7 (July 2007), p. 9.

72. Dr Opeyemi Ola, "The Army of Forgers Arrives!", *Sunday Times*, 4 August 1974.

73. Ibid.

74. Toye Olofintuyi, "Bribery: Still Here with Us", *Renaissance*, 8 March 1974.
75. UK National Archives, FCO 65/995: Lucas to Bache, 5 Aug. 1971.
76. UK National Archives, FCO 65/995: Pugh to Parsons, 23 Sept. 1971.
77. UK National Archives, FCO 65/1193: Pickard to Wilson, 28 Jan. 1972.
78. Remi Anifowose, "Corruption: a Political Perspective", in M. Ade Adejugbe (ed.), *Perspectives on Nigeria's Fledgling Fourth Republic* (Malthouse Press, Ikeja, 2002), p. 109.
79. UK National Archives, FCO 65/1529: draft paper by US embassy, 6 Dec. 1973.
80. *Daily Times*, 20 January 1977, p. 25.
81. Dent, "Corrective Government", p. 107.
82. Quoted in Tai Solarin, "Belief in Secret Cults", *Nigerian Tribune*, 16 Feb. 1976.
83. An official ban on cults was enacted on 18 August 1977 by the Lagos Federal Ministry of Establishment.
84. Philip Asiodu, quoted in Shaxson, *Poisoned Wells*, p. 16.
85. Pat Ama Tokunbo Williams, "Religion, Violence and Displacement in Nigeria", in Paul E. Lovejoy and Pat A.T. Williams (eds), *Displacement and the Politics of Violence in Nigeria* (Brill, Leiden, 1997), p. 36.
86. Philip Asiodu, quoted in Shaxson, *Poisoned Wells*, p. 16.
87. World Bank archives, McNamara papers, folder 1771140/18: memo from E. Peter Wright to McNamara, 22 Dec. 1975.
88. See John Iliffe, *Obasanjo, Nigeria and the World* (James Currey, Oxford, 2011).
89. NARA II, RG 59, subject-numeric files 1970–73, Pol 15–1 Nigeria, box 2508: embassy Lagos to Secretary of State, 31 Jan. 1972.
90. John E. Reinhardt to Kissinger, 18 Aug. 1975, in US Department of State, *Foreign Relations of the United States, 1969–1976, Volume E–6, Documents on Africa, 1973–1976* (United States Government Printing Office, Washington DC, 2009), p. 208. *US Foreign Relations on Africa, 1969–1976*, volume E-6, p. 208
91. UK National Archives, FCO 65/1778: Le Quesne to Secretary of State, 5 Jan. 1976.
92. "Why Government Can't Ban Secret Societies", *Nigerian Tribune*, 21 April 1976.
93. Yemi Folarin, "Cults' Secret Out", *Daily Express*, 8 Sept. 1977.
94. Prince Dosumu, the Akoogun Olufe, cited in the *Nigerian Tribune*, 21 April 1976.
95. Yemi Folarin, "Cults' secret out", *Daily Express*, 8 September 1977.
96. *War Against Indiscipline: First Anniversary Assessment* (National Institute for Policy and Strategic Studies, Kuru, 1985), p. 5.
97. Apter, *The Pan-African Nation*.

98. Ebenezer Obadare, "White-collar Fundamentalism: Interrogating Youth Religiosity on Nigerian University Campuses", *Journal of Modern African Studies*, 45, 4 (2007), p. 521.
99. Ibid., pp. 521, 523.
100. Amadi, *Ethics*, p. 13.
101. Ibid., p. 12.
102. National Association of Seadogs, Pyrates Confraternity: http:www.nasint.org [accessed 13 July 2015].
103. Reuben Abati, "How Nigerian Students Murdered Democracy", *The Guardian*, 11 December 2005.
104. World Bank archives, folder 1381546, Education project (01) Nigeria, Credit 0072, nr. 1: SJG Burt, Educational Projects Division, to D.S. Ballantyne, May 4, 1972.
105. Patrick Wilmot, *Nigeria: The Nightmare Scenario* (Interventions VI, Bookcraft and Farafina, Ibadan and Lagos, 2007), esp. pp. 2–25. See also the roundtable discussion published in *Vanguard*, 20–21 September 1999.
106. Interview in *Punch*, 8 August 1999.
107. Ben Oguntuase, interviewed in *Punch*, 8 August 1999.
108. Website of the Supreme Eiye Confraternity: http://www.airfords.org [accessed 10 March 2009].
109. Coventry Cathedral, "The Potential for Peace and Reconciliation in the Niger Delta", unpublished report by Stephen Davis, February 2009, p. 96.
110. See the interview with Ben Oguntuase in *Punch*, 8 Aug. 1999.
111. Offiong, *Secret Cults*, p. 54.
112. Amadi, *Ethics*, p. 8. A list of secret societies may be found at pp. 9–13.
113. Coventry Cathedral, "The Potential for Peace and Reconciliation", p. 98.
114. Cf. Chapter Nine.
115. Wole Soyinka, *Cults: A People in Denial* (Interventions III, Bookcraft and Farafina, Ibadan and Lagos, 2005), p. 78.
116. Ibid., p. 69.
117. Coventry Cathedral, "The Potential for Peace and Reconciliation", p. 97. See also the Neo Black Movement of Africa website http://www.nbmarena.com [accessed 1 May 2015].
118. Offiong, *Secret Cults*, pp. 56–9.
119. Femi Olugbile, "Cult Fever", *Vanguard*, 15 August 1999.
120. *Daily Times*, 27 January 1977.
121. "Cultists Confess at Fedpoly, Nekede", *Nigerian Tribune*, 14 September 1999.
122. "5 Million Cultists on the Loose", *Daily Times*, 18 July 1999.
123. Bayo Oguntunase, "The Problems of Cultism in Nigeria (1)", *National Concord*, 29 June 1998.

124. "5 Million Cultists on the Loose", *Daily Times*, 18 July 1999.

125. Oyedanmi, "How to Tackle Cultism Menace", *Guardian*, 6 January 2000.

126. Andreski, *African Predicament*, p. 207.

127. J. 'Bayo Adekanye, *The Retired Military as Emergent Power Factor in Nigeria* (Heinemann Educational Books, Ibadan, 1999), p. 29.

128. Dr Edwin Madunagu, quoted in Joe Igbokwe, *Igbos: 25 Years After Biafra* (Advent Communications, Lagos, 1995), p. 113.

129. Quentin Peel, "Nigeria's Debt Problems—Causes and Solutions: An Outsider's View", paper presented at International Conference on Foreign Debt and Nigeria's Economic Development, Lagos, 5–6 March 1984.

130. Sluyterman, *Keeping Competitive in Turbulent Markets, 1973–2007*, IV, p. 345.

131. Peel, "Nigeria's Debt Problems".

132. Ibid.

133. Ibid., p. 7.

134. Ibid.

135. "Johnson Matthey Bank Bailout Fraudster Jailed After 25 Years", 28 March 2011, http://www.insolvencyandlawblog.com/uk/?p=461 [accessed 22 May 2015].

136. Article by Lt-Gen. Theophilus Danjuma in the *Guardian*, 20 July 1986.

137. Ibid.

138. Williams, *Political Corruption*, p. 71.

139. Ibid. Statement by oil minister Tam David-West on 23 February 1984.

7. CRIME GOES GLOBAL

1. A reference to the notorious Four One Nine advance fee fraud.

2. Speech on 19 January 2006, reported in *Punch* [Lagos], 20 January 2006.

3. Cf. Michael Peel, *Nigeria-Related Financial Crime and its Links with Britain* (Royal Institute of International Affairs, London, 2006), p. 46.

4. http://worldpopulationreview.com/countries/nigeria-population/ [accessed 22 May 2015].

5. Keith Panter-Brick, "Introduction", p. 3, in Panter-Brick (ed.), *Soldiers and Oil*.

6. http://news.bbc.co.uk/2/shared/spl/hi/uk/05/born_abroad/countries/html/nigeria.stm [accessed 28 May 2015].

7. Tom Forrest, "The Political Economy of Civil Rule and the Economic Crisis in Nigeria (1979–84)", *Review of African Political Economy*, 13, 35 (1986), p. 20.

8. Ekpenyong, "Social Inequalities, Collusion, and Armed Robbery in Nigerian Cities", p. 28.

9. Nduka, *Western Education and the Nigerian Cultural Background*, p. 99.
10. Statement by US Embassy, Lagos, published in *Daily Times*, 10 December 1984, p. 3.
11. Ibid.
12. Quoted in the *Daily Times*, 26 November 1984.
13. Quoted in "…and its Nigerian connection", *Guardian* [Lagos], 30 Dec. 1984.
14. According to the newsletter *Drug Force*, the official publication of the Nigerian Drug Law Enforcement Agency: quoted in *Daily Champion* [Lagos], 9 May 1993.
15. Etannibi Alemika, "Organized Crime: Nigeria", paper presented at United Nations Office on Drugs and Crime (UNODC) workshop on West African organised crime, Dakar, 2–3 April 2004.
16. Mark Shaw, *Crime as Business, Business as Crime: West African Criminal Networks in Southern Africa* (South African Institute of International Affairs, Johannesburg, 2003), p. 11.
17. Statement by US Embassy, Lagos, published in *Daily Times* [Lagos], 10 December 1984, p. 3.
18. Rasheed Williams, "Nigeria, a Leading Heroin Market", *National Concord* [Lagos], 8 April 1985.
19. Penny Green, *Drugs, Trafficking and Criminal Policy: The Scapegoat Strategy* (Waterside Press, Winchester, 1998), p. 46.
20. "2,000 Nigerians in Foreign Jails for Drug Offences", *New Nigerian*, 13 May 1988.
21. The *Guardian* [Lagos] carried a series of reports on this matter in May and June 1983. See also Axel Klein, "Trapped in the Traffick: Growing Problems of Drug Consumption in Lagos", *Journal of Modern African Studies*, 32, 4 (1994), pp. 657–77.
22. Kofi Bentsum Quantson, *Travelling and Seeing: Johnny Just Come* (NAPASVIL Ventures, Accra, 2002), p. 67.
23. "2,000 Nigerians in Foreign Jails for Drug Offences", *New Nigerian*, 13 May 1988.
24. Jonas Okwara, "Three Nigerians Held Weekly in US on Drug Charges", *Guardian*, 15 July 1990.
25. Jackson Akpasubi, "US says 'No' to Nigeria", *Sunday Concord*, 30 June 1991. Eric Fottorino, *La Piste blanche: L'Afrique sous l'emprise de la drogue* (Balland, Paris, 1991), p. 19, gives the same figure of 15,433 for Nigerians arrested for drug offences between 1979 and 1989.
26. Fottorino, *La Piste blanche*, p. 19.
27. Segun Babatope, "Drug Trafficking: a Nation under Siege", *National Concord*, 3 February 1992.
28. Nnamdi Obasi, "Drug Trafficking", *Weekend Concord*, 1 June 1991.

29. Green, *Drugs, Trafficking and Criminal Policy*, p. 48.
30. "Adegoke's Ill-fated Deal with Skypower", *National Concord*, 30 April 1989.
31. Editorial, *Nigerian Tribune*, 24 March 2006.
32. "NDLEA Stinks—Bamaiyi", *Daily Times*, 18 February 1994.
33. Fottorino, *La Piste blanche*, pp. 57, 60
34. Martin T. Biegelman, *Identity Theft Handbook: Detection, Prevention and Security* (John Wiley, Hoboken, NJ, 2009).
35. Mark Jones, "Nigerian Crime Networks in the United States", *International Journal of Offender Therapy and Comparative Criminology*, 37, 1 (1993), p. 61.
36. Misha Glenny, *McMafia: Seriously Organised Crime* (Vintage Books, London, 2009), pp. 202–3.
37. Jones, "Nigerian Crime Networks in the United States", p. 64.
38. "Police Swoop on 83 Passengers", *Nigerian Herald*, 5 July 1978.
39. Michael Gillard, "African Conmen Rip Off the Greedy and Gullible", *The Observer*, 14 January 1996.
40. Edward Fokuoh Ampratwum, "Advance Fee Fraud '419' and Investor Confidence in the Economies of sub-Saharan Africa (SSA)", *Journal of Financial Crime*, 16, 1 (2009), p. 70.
41. David Simcox, "The Nigerian Crime Network: Feasting on America's Innocence and Slipshod ID System", *The Social Contract*, 3, 3 (1993), p. 168.
42. Quéré, "Clans criminels", p. 39, note 62.
43. Andrew Garfield, "Nigerian $8bn a Year Fraud Scam Claims Fresh Victims", *Independent*, 23 August 1999.
44. Simcox, "The Nigerian Crime Network", p. 168.
45. Quéré, "Clans criminels", p. 41.
46. Okolo Ben Simon, "Demystifying the Advance-fee Fraud Network", *African Security Review*, 18, 4 (2009), p. 7.
47. Daniel Jordan Smith, *A Culture of Corruption: Everyday Deception and Popular Discontent in Nigeria* (Princeton University Press, 2008), pp. 30–31.
48. Emmanuel Mayah, "Undercover bij oplichters uit Nigeria", *Trouw*, 15 September 2011.
49. Daniel Engber, "Who Made That Nigerian Scam?", *New York Times*, 3 January 2014.
50. Quéré, "Clans criminels", pp. 35–6.
51. Author's interview with Dutch police officer specialising in West Africa, Zoetermeer, 18 March 2008.
52. Williams, *Political Corruption*, p. 71.
53. Balogun Chike-Obi, "Smuggling and Petrol Shortages", *Guardian* [Lagos], 30 March 1987.
54. US Information Service Press Release, 30 June 1997.

55. Peter Fabricius, "Con Artist Takes NIS for R1,9-m Ride", *The Star*, 25 Feb-3 March 1993.

56. Author's discussion with Namibian Embassy official, Cotonou, 1 March 1994.

57. Author's interview with Dutch police officer specialising in West Africa, Zoetermeer, 18 March 2008.

58. Simcox, "The Nigerian Crime Network", p. 168.

59. https://www.youtube.com/watch?v=D_YjvC4ndzM [accessed 29 May 2015].

60. Author's interview with Dutch police officer specialising in West Africa, Zoetermeer, 18 March 2008.

61. http://en.wikipedia.org/wiki/Johannes_van_Damme [accessed 28 May 2015].

62. Adebanwi, *A Paradise for Maggots*, p. 79

63. Toyin Falola and Julius Ihonvbere, *The Rise and Fall of Nigeria's Second Republic, 1979–84* (Zed Books, London, 1985), p. 230.

64. The official televised declaration of WAI may be seen at https://www.youtube.com/watch?v=Aa0EQrAhO90 [accessed 4 March 2015].

65. M. Adekunle Owoade, "The Military and the Criminal Law in Nigeria", *Journal of African Law*, 33, 2 (1989), pp. 135–48.

66. News Agency of Nigeria, quoted in US Government, *Foreign Broadcast Information Service, Sub-Saharan Africa Report*, 16 April 1985, p. 42.

67. Ndaeyo Uko, *Romancing the Gun: The Press as Promoter of Military Rule* (Africa World Press, Trenton, NJ, 2003), p. 90.

68. Kayode Soyinka, *Diplomatic Baggage: Mossad and Nigeria: The Dikko Story* (Newswatch Books, Lagos, 1994).

69. Isaac O. Albert, "The Sociocultural Politics of Ethnic and Religious Conflicts", in Ernest E. Uwazie, Isaac O. Albert and Godfrey N. Uzoigwe (eds), *Inter-Ethnic and Religious Conflict Resolution in Nigeria* (Lexington Books, Langham MD, 1999), p. 81.

70. Cf. Shehu Othman, "Classes, Crises and Coup: The Demise of Shagari's Regime", *African Affairs*, 83, no. 333 (1984), pp. 441–61.

71. Iyorchia D. Ayu, "Towards a Revolutionary Resolution of the Mafia Problem", in Bala J. Takaya and Sonni Gwanle Tyoden (eds), *The Kaduna Mafia: A Study of the Rise, Development and Consolidation of a Nigerian Power Elite* (Jos University Press, 1987), pp. 125–46; a brief biography of Mamman Daura is at p. 135.

72. Moshood Fayemiwo, "The Muhammadu Buhari Regime (1984–1985): Important and Salient Issues Nigerians Must Know" http://nigeriaworld.com/feature/publication/fayemiwo/012415-nd.html [accessed 5 March 2015]

73. Peter Lewis, "From Prebendalism to Predation: The Political Economy

of Decline in Nigeria", *Journal of Modern African Studies*, 34, 1 (1996), p. 80.

74. UK National Archives, FCO65/1194: Bracken to Whitelegg, 20 Oct. 1972.

75. See Andreski, *African Predicament*, p. 123; US National Intelligence Estimate 64.2–70, 2 Nov. 1970, in State Department, *Foreign Relations of the United States, 1969–76*, vol. E-5, para 7; Chinua Achebe, *The Trouble with Nigeria* (1983; Heinemann Educational Books, Ibadan etc., 1984), pp. 45–6.

76. Author's interview with a senior official of the Nigerian Drug Law Enforcement Agency, Lagos, 2 November 2007.

77. Vittoria Luda di Cortemiglia, "Programme of Action against Trafficking in Minors and Young Women from Nigeria into Italy for the Purpose of Sexual Exploitation" (United Nations Interregional Crime and Justice Research Institute, undated), on which the following paragraph is based.

78. Jørgen Carling, *Migration, Human Smuggling and Trafficking from Nigeria to Europe* (IOM Migration Research series 23, International Organisation for Migration, Geneva, 2006), p. 25.

8. GODFATHERS

1. Yevgeniy Gontmakher, quoted in Karen Dawisha, *Putin's Kleptocracy: Who Owns Russia?* (Simon & Schuster, New York, 2014), p. 37.

2. Wilmot, *Nigeria*, p. 18.

3. Karl Maier, *This House Has Fallen: Midnight in Nigeria* (Public Affairs, New York, 2000), pp. 49–50.

4. Wilmot, *Nigeria*, p. 17.

5. Ibid, p. 16

6. Tunde Akingbade, *Historical Studies on Global Scam and Nigeria's 419: How to Overcome Fraudsters and Con Artists* (AuthorHouse, 2009), p. 8.

7. See the unofficial version of the Oputa Panel report released on 1 January 2005 by the National Democratic Movement (Washington, DC), vol. 4, p. 104, http://www.dawodu.com/oputa1.htm [accessed 24 November 2008]. Further information is in Richard Akinnola (ed.), *The Murder of Dele Giwa: Cover-up—Revelations* (Human Rights Publications, Lagos, 2001).

8. *The BCCI Affair: A Report to the Committee on Foreign Relations United States Senate by Senator John Kerry and Senator Hank Brown* (U.S. Government Printing Office, Washington DC, 1993), pp. 99–104. The quotation is on p. 49.

9. Peter Truell and Larry Gurwin, *False Profits: The Inside Story of BCCI, the World's Most Corrupt Financial Empire* (Houghton Mifflin, Boston, MA, 1992), p. 162.

10. Ibid.
11. Andrew Apter, "IBB=419: Nigerian Democracy and the Politics of Illusion", p. 287, in John L. Comaroff and Jean Comaroff (eds), *Civil Society and the Political Imagination in Africa: Critical Perspectives* (University of Chicago Press, Chicago and London, 1999), p. 287.
12. Quéré, "Clans criminels", pp. 35–6.
13. E.E. Osaghae, *Crippled Giant: Nigeria Since Independence* (Hurst & Co., London, 1998), pp. 278–9.
14. Adebanwi, *A Paradise for Maggots*, p. 115; Pita Ogaba Agbase, "The 'Stolen' Okigbo Panel Report: Of Malfeasance and Public Accountability in Nigeria", in Jane I. Guyer and LaRay Denzer (eds), *Vision and Policy in Nigerian Economics: The Legacy of Pius Okigbo* (Ibadan University Press, 2005), p. 59.
15. Osaghae, *Crippled Giant*, p. 204.
16. Nuhu Ribadu, quoted in Adebanwi, *A Paradise for Maggots*, p. 353.
17. Lewis, "From Prebendalism to Predation", p. 89.
18. Cudjoe Kpor et al, "Who Controls Forex?…The Forex Debate Goes On", *Guardian*, 19 February 1992.
19. Raimi Akanbi (ed.), *Redasel's Companies of Nigeria* (2nd edn, Research and Data Services, Lagos, 1996).
20. G. Oka Orewa, *We Are All Guilty: The Nigerian Crisis, vol. 1* (Spectrum Books, Ibadan, 1997), p. 29.
21. Osaghae, *Crippled Giant*, p. 205.
22. Stephen Ellis, *The Mask of Anarchy: The Destruction of Liberia and the Religious Dimension of an African Civil War* (1999; new edn., Hurst & Co. and New York University Press, London and New York, 2007), p. 160.
23. Speech printed in *Punch*, 20 January 2006.
24. Apter, "IBB=419", p. 287.
25. Lewis, "From Prebendalism to Predation", p. 97.
26. Isaac Olawale Albert, "Explaining 'Godfatherism' in Nigerian Politics", *African Sociological Review*, 9, 2 (2005), p. 84.
27. Ibid., p. 85.
28. Coventry Cathedral, "The Potential for Peace and Reconciliation", p. 100.
29. Rotimi Oyedanmi, "How to Tackle Cultism Menace", *Guardian*, 6 January 2000.
30. Gabriel Osu, "Stamping Cults from our Campuses", *Vanguard*, 30 August 1999.
31. Olugbile, "Cult Fever", *Vanguard*, 15 August 1999.
32. Kalu, "The Religious Dimension of the Legitimacy Crisis, 1993–1998", p. 667.
33. Osaghae, *Crippled Giant*, p. 280.

34. Frances Williams, "Swiss Judge Sets Precedent in Global Graft Fight", *Financial Times*, 23 November 2009.
35. Baker, *Capitalism's Achilles Heel*, pp. 57–68.
36. Kalu, "The Religious Dimension of the Legitimacy Crisis, 1993–1998", in Toyin Falola (ed.), *Nigeria in the Twentieth Century* (Carolina Academic Press, Durham, NC, 2002), p. 668.
37. Isaac Olawale Albert, "Smuggling Second-hand Cars Through the Benin-Nigeria Borders", in Georges Kobou (ed.), *Real Economies in Africa* (Codesria, Dakar, 2003), pp. 221–3.
38. Moshood Ademola Fayemiwo and Margie Marie Neal, *Aliko Mohammad Dangote: The Biography of the Richest Black Person in the World* (Strategic Book Publishing, Houston, TX, 2013).
39. Albert, "Explaining 'Godfatherism' in Nigerian Politics", p. 86.
40. Richard Dowden, "Can Buhari Fix Nigeria?", 28 May 2015 http://africanarguments.org/2015/05/28/can-buhari-fix-nigeria-by-richard-dowden/#comment-68042 [accessed 3 June 2015].
41. Ibid.
42. Ike Okonta, "Nigeria: Chronicle of a Dying State", *Current History*,104, 682 (May 2005), p. 205.
43. Christina Katsouris and Aaron Sayne, *Nigeria's Criminal Crude: International Options to Combat the Export of Stolen Oil* (Royal Institute of International Affairs, London, 2013), p. 5.
44. Eghosa Osaghae, Augustine Ikelegbe, Omobolaji Olarinmoye and Steven Okhomina, "Youth Militias, Self Determination and Resource Control Struggles in the Niger-Delta Region of Nigeria", unpublished study, 2007.
45. BBC News, "Missing Tanker found in Nigeria", 24 Sept 2004.
46. IRIN, "Nigeria: Conviction of Admirals Confirms Navy Role in Oil Theft", 6 January 2005 http://www.irinnews.org/report/52598/nigeria-conviction-of-admirals-confirms-navy-role-in-oil-theft [accessed 5 June 2015].
47. BBC News, "Blood Oil Dripping", 28 July 2007.
48. Ibid.
49. Author's discussion with senior US official responsible for Africa, Stuttgart, 3 February 2006.
50. Robin R. Sanders to Dept of State, 9 February 2009, in *AfricaFocus* bulletin, 14 December 2010.
51. Matthew Green, "Oil Groups Fear Nigeria Reforms", *Financial Times*, 20 October 2008.
52. Sluyterman, *Keeping Competitive in Turbulent Markets*, IV, p. 345.
53. William Wallis, "The Big Oil Fix", *Financial Times*, 27 May 2015.
54. Chapter Five, p. 86

55. E.g. Sebastian Junger, "Blood Oil", *Vanity Fair*, February 2007: http://www.vanityfair.com/politics/features/2007/02/junger200702 [accessed 16 July 2008].

56. Robin R. Sanders to Dept of State, 9 February 2009, in *AfricaFocus* bulletin, 14 December 2010.

57. Thomas Catan and Dino Mahtani, "The Warriors of Warri: How Oil in Nigeria is Under Siege", *Financial Times*, 7 April 2006.

58. Virginia Comolli, *Boko Haram: Nigeria's Islamist Insurgency* (Hurst & Co., London, 2015), p. 52.

59. Osaghae et al., "Youth Militias, Self Determination and Resource Control Struggles in the Niger-Delta Region of Nigeria".

60. Ibid.

61. "Norway Regrets Selling Warships to ex-Niger Delta Militant, Tompolo", *Premium Times*, 2 May 2015.

62. Dick Wittenberg, "Straffeloos olieroven in Nigeria", *NRC Handelsblad*, 22 June 2004.

63. According to a study by Global Financial Integrity on behalf of the Central Bank of Nigeria: "Export of Trade in Stolen Oil Revealed in Report", *Financial Times*, 27 May 2015, p. 5.

64. Katsouris and Sayne, *Nigeria's Criminal Crude*, p. 4.

65. BBC News, "Blood Oil Dripping", 28 July 2007.

66. Katsouris and Sayne, *Nigeria's Criminal Crude*, p. 2. A senior official of the Nigerian Drug Law Enforcement Agency doubts that cocaine is traded in the Niger Delta: see comments by Victor Cole-Showers at a conference in Washington, DC on 28 May 2009 reported at http://www.wilsoncenter.org/event/global-drug-trafficking-africas-expanding-role [accessed 22 June 2015].

67. Katsouris and Sayne, *Nigeria's Criminal Crude*, p. 6.

68. "Africa: Tracing the Oil Money", *AfricaFocus* bulletin, 16 Sept. 2014.

69. *AfricaFocus* Bulletin, 25 March 2014.

70. Katsouris and Sayne, *Nigeria's Criminal Crude*, p. 8.

71. William Wallis, "The Big Oil Fix", *Financial Times*, 27 May 2015, p. 5.

72. Lamido Sanusi, "Unanswered Questions on Nigeria's Missing Billions", *Financial Times*, 14 May 2015, p. 7.

73. BBC News, "Nigerian Leaders "Stole" $380 Billion", 20 October 2006.

74. Adebanwi, *A Paradise for Maggots*, p. 300.

75. Quoted in Albert, "The Sociocultural Politics of Ethnic and Religious Conflicts", p. 76.

76. Global Witness, *"International Thief Thief": How British Banks are Complicit in Nigerian Corruption* (London, 2010), p. 9.

77. Adebanwi, *A Paradise for Maggots*, p. 149.

78. Ibid, pp. 143–45.

NOTES   pp. [155–160]

79. BBC News, "Nigeria Pardons Goodluck Jonathan Ally, Alamieyeseigha", 13 March 2013.

80. Jon Gambrell, "Nigeria Pardons Ex-Governor who Stole Millions", 13 March 2013, http://news.yahoo.com/nigeria-pardons-ex-governor-stole-millions-085453960.html [accessed 6 June 2015].

81. *Nigerian Tribune*, 11 June 2008; *Punch*, 4 March 2008.

82. BBC News, "Nigeria Suspends Siemens Dealings", 6 December 2007.

83. Amadi, *Ethics*, p. 86.

9. THE BUSINESS OF CRIME

1. Carling, *Migration, Human Smuggling and Trafficking*, p. 21.

2. Personal communication by Professor Benjamin Soares after a visit to Guangzhou.

3. "Dongri Highlife", *Time Out Mumbai* www.timeoutmumbai.net/client_mumbai_local/mumbailocalcode=11&source=1 [6 January 2007].

4. Pauline Bax, "Vanuit het cybercafé hengelen naar geld", *NRC Handelsblad*, 2 June 2008.

5. Russell G. Smith, Michael N. Holmes and Philip Kaufmann, "Nigerian Advance Fee Fraud", *Australian Institute of Criminology, Trends & Issues*, 121 (July 1999).

6. Ted Leggett, *RainbowVice:The Drugs and Sex Industries in the New South Africa* (Zed books, London, 2002).

7. James Myburgh, "CIPRO at Epicentre of SA's Fraud Pandemic", politicsweb, 7 August 2009, http://www.politicsweb.co.za/news-and-analysis/cipro-at-epicentre-of-sas-fraud-pandemic [accessed 4 June 2015].

8. Smith, *A Culture of Corruption*.

9. Nduka, *Western Education and the Nigerian Cultural Background*, p. 99.

10. Ake, *Is Africa Democratizing?*, p. 18.

11. Soyinka, *Cults*, p.ix.

12. John Gill, "UK Looks Set to Benefit from Nigerian Student Boom", *Times Higher Education Supplement*, 11 December 2008.

13. Editorial in the *Nigerian Tribune*, 20 June 2006.

14. Soyinka, *Cults*, p. 13.

15. Ibid, p. 12.

16. Ibid.

17. Ibid.

18. Ricardo Soares de Oliveira, *Oil and Politics in the Gulf of Guinea* (Hurst & Co., London, 2007), p. 93.

19. Ibid.

20. Emmanuel Mayah, "Europe by Desert:Tears of African Migrants", p. 52, in UNESCO, *The Global Investigative Journalism Casebook* (UNESCO series on Journalism Education, Paris, 2012).

21. Joshua Oyeniyi Aransola and Suraj Olalekan Asindemade, "Understanding Cybercrime Perpetrators and the Strategies They Employ in Nigeria", *Cyberpsychology, Behavior, and Social Networking*, 14, 12 (2011), p. 762.
22. Iyke Nathan Uzorma, *Occult Grand Master Now in Christ* (private publication, Benin City, 1994), pp. 126–27 and back cover. Lakshmi is the Hindu goddess of wealth.
23. Aransola and Asindemade, "Understanding Cybercrime Perpetrators and the Strategies They Employ in Nigeria", p. 760.
24. Ibid., pp. 759–63.
25. Femi Makinde, "US Secret Service Detects 30,000 Cyber Crimes Monthly From Nigeria", *Punch*, 31 August 2005.
26. Aransola and Asindemade, "Understanding Cybercrime Perpetrators and the Strategies They Employ in Nigeria", p. 759.
27. Misha Glenny, *Dark Market: How Hackers Became the New Mafia* (2011), pp. 376–77.
28. Jennifer Williams, "'Phishing' Fraudster Jailed for £1.5 Million Student Loan Scam", *Manchester Evening News*, 15 December 2013.
29. Yvette M.M. Schoenmakers, Edo de Vries Robbé and Anton Ph. van Wijk, *Mountains of Gold: An Exploratory Research on 419 Fraud* (CrimiReeks, SWP Publishers, Amsterdam, 2009), p. 72.
30. Ibid., p. 88.
31. Ibid.
32. José Aarts, "Een Etnografische Studie over Ondergronds Bankieren in de Nigeriaanse Gemeenschap in Nederland", in Henk van de Bunt and Dina Siegel (eds), *Ondergronds Bankieren in Nederland* (Boom Juridische Uitgevers, Den Haag, 2009), pp. 59–82.
33. Peel, *Nigeria-Related Financial Crime and its Links with Britain*, pp. 33–38.
34. "Nigerian Advance-Fee Fraud in Transnational Perspective", 2009, confidential source.
35. Jones, "Nigerian Crime Networks in the United States", p. 61.
36. Jim Buchanan and Alex J. Grant, "Investigating and Prosecuting Nigerian Fraud", *United States Attorneys' Bulletin*, 49, 6 (2001), p. 40.
37. Statement at African Criminal Networks Conference, Bangkok, 16–19 May 2005.
38. Ibid.
39. Author's interview with police specialist, Amsterdam, 3 June 2003.
40. Sociale inlichtingen- en opsporingsdienst, *Beleidsdocument "Labyrint": Onderzoek Naar West-Afrikaanse Criminele Netwerken in de Sociale Zekerheid* (SIOD, Den Haag, 2005), p. 80.
41. Charlotte Corpelijn, untitled MA thesis (University of Utrecht, 2008), p. 16. See also Bovenkerk et al. (eds), *Policing Multiple Communities* (Maklu, Antwerpen etc., 2010).

42. National Police Intelligence Service (IPOL), *Nationaal Dreigingsbeeld 2012: Georganiseerde criminaliteit* (Dienst IPOL, Zoetermeer, 2012), pp. 136, 139.
43. BBC News, "Spain Holds Lottery Scam Suspects", 21 April 2004.
44. *The Times*, 21 July 2005, p. 40.
45. BBC News, "Nigerian Football Conmen Exposed", 17 July 2008.
46. Mitchell Zuckoff, "The Perfect Mark", *The New Yorker*, 15 May 2006.
47. E.g. http://www.419eater.com/
48. Daniel Engber, "Who Made That Nigerian Scam?".
49. Charlotte Corpelijn, MA thesis, p. 17.
50. Schoenmakers et al., *Mountains of Gold*, p. 86.
51. Phil Williams, "The Global Implications of West African Organized Crime", http://www.wired.com/news/culture/0/1284/53818.html [no longer available on 13 July 2015].
52. United States Department of State, *International Narcotics Control Strategy Report 2007, Volume II, Money Laundering and Financial Crimes*, p. 309. http://www.state.gov/j/inl/rls/nrcrpt/2007/vol2/html/80876.htm
53. Adebanwi, *A Paradise for Maggots*, p. 220.
54. Glenny, *McMafia*, p. 194.
55. Ibid., p. 210.
56. Jide Ogundipe, "The Banco Noroeste Fraud", paper for ICC FraudNet Conference, Singapore, 18 October 2007. https://icc-ccs.org/home/publications/viewdownload/3-publications/155-the-banco-noroeste-fraud- [accessed 5 April 2015]. This is also the main source for the following account.
57. Adebanwi, *A Paradise for Maggots*, p. 78. See Chapter Seven, p.128.
58. O.M.G. Tatafo, "Ade Bendel, Owelle of Abanga, Ibekwe and Others: Tales of Crooks Nigeria will Never Forget", 20 March 2013 http://www.omg-naija.com/2013/03/a-diary-on-ade-bendel-owelle-of-abanga-ibekwe-and-others-tales-of-crooks-nigeria-will-never-forget/#sthash.q8N2ggxH.dpbs [accessed 10 March 2015]
59. Adebanwi, *A Paradise for Maggots*, p. 79.
60. Uwe Buse, "Spam Scams: Africa's City of Cyber Gangsters", Spiegel Online International 45/2005 http://www.spiegel.de/international/spiegel/spam-scams-africa-s-city-of-cyber-gangsters-a-384317.html
61. Adebanwi, *A Paradise for Maggots*, p. 62.
62. Interview with Dutch police officer specialising in Nigerian crime, Zoetermeer, 18 March 2008; see also Ajudua's wikipedia entry http://en.wikipedia.org/wiki/Fred_Ajudua [accessed 10 June 2015].
63. BBC News, "Nigeria's EFCC Arrests Top Bankers Over 'Mega Scam'", 1 June 2015.
64. Cf. Smith, *Culture of Corruption*, p. 28.

65. United States Information Service (USIS) press release, 2 March 1998, quoted in *Punch*, 5 March 1998.

66. Henry Mintzberg, *Structure in Fives: Designing Effective Organizations* (1983; second edn, Prentice Hall, Englewood Cliffs, NJ, 1993), p. 254. The term 'adhocracy' was coined by Alvin Toffler in *Future Shock*.

67. Statement at African Criminal Networks Conference, Thailand, 16–19 May 2005.

68. Stephen Ellis, "Les prolongements du conflit israélo-arabe: le cas du Sierra Leone" *Politique Africaine*, 30 (1988), pp. 69–75.

69. Robert I. Friedman, *Red Mafiya: How the Russian Mob has Invaded America* (Little, Brown, Boston etc., 2000), pp. 57–8.

70. Emmanuel Akyeampong, "Diaspora and Drug Trafficking in West Africa: A Case Study of Ghana", *African Affairs*, 104, 416 (2005), p. 441.

71. Author's interview with Ghanaian police officer, Accra, 31 August 2008.

72. *Jane's Intelligence Review*, 1 July 2005.

73. USIS press release, 2 March 1998, quoted in *Punch*, 5 March 1998.

74. Fottorino, *La Piste blanche*, pp. 60–61; see also allegations in *Liberian Diaspora*, III, 12 (1993), p. 4, to be viewed with caution as this was a propaganda sheet for Charles Taylor.

75. "Drug: NDLEA Sends Officers' Names to Presidency", *Guardian*, 9 November 1998.

76. See interview with Gen. Bamaiyi in *Sunday Champion*, 20 June 1999.

77. John K. Cooley, *Unholy Wars: Afghanistan, America and International Terrorism* (3rd edn, Pluto Press, London and Sterling, VA, 2002), p. 143.

78. Laolu Akande, "Nigeria High on US Fraud, Drugs List", *Guardian*, 18 August 1999.

79. United Nations Office on Drugs and Crime, *Transnational Organized Crime in the West African Region* (New York, 2005), p. 21.

80. Sisca Agboh, "NDLEA Impounds N1b Worth of Cocaine", *Post Express*, 31 August 2001.

81. Laolu Akande, "Nigerian Boy, 12, Swallows 87 Condom Wraps of Heroin", *Guardian*, 13 April 2002.

82. Statement to the Senate Foreign Relations Committee Subcommittee on African Affairs, 20 July 1995, obtained from the US Information Resource Center, US Embassy, The Hague.

83. Author's interview, Lagos, 24 October 2007.

84. "237 Nigerian Drug Convicts in Arrive [sic.] Today", *Guardian*, 29 March 2003.

85. "African Community at Pratunum, Bangkok", paper presented by Royal Thai Police, African Criminal Networks conference, Bangkok, 16–19 May 2005.

86. "Nigerian Drug Barons Invade South Africa", *Guardian*, 11 April 1998.

87. The name has been suppressed for legal reasons. Information obtained from official source, Lagos, 24 October 2007.

88. Ibid.

89. Reuben Abati, "The Hanging of Amara Tochi in Singapore", *Guardian*, 28 January 2006.

90. Nigerian Drug Law Enforcement Agency (NDLEA), "An Analysis of the Drug Trafficking Issues and Trends at the Murtala Muhammed International Airport, Ikeja, Lagos (MMIA)", unpublished paper, 7pp., [September 2007].

91. Adebanwi, *A Paradise for Maggots*, p. 69.

92. Joe Brown Akubueze v The Federal Republic of Nigeria, 4 March 2003. Available via Toma Micro Publishers Ltd.: http://www.tomalegalretrieve.org/phplaw/site/index.php [accessed 23 July 2008].

93. Flemming Quist, "Drug Trafficking in West Africa 2000–2004 in an International Perspective", UNODC workshop on West African organized crime, Dakar, 2–3 April 2004.

94. ISN Security Watch, 27 February 2008: www.isn.etnz.ch [accessed 28 February 2008].

95. *This Day*, 10, 13, 15 June 2006.

96. "Gambia Makes West Africa's Biggest Ever Drugs Bust", *Afrol News*, 9 June 2010.

97. Yudhijit Bhattacharjee, "Busted Drug Sting: NSA Helped U.S. DEA Break Huge Drug Trade", *Front Page Africa*, 19 March 2015; author's discussion with Liberian intelligence chief, Monrovia, 1 August 2012.

98. Antonio L. Mazzitelli, "Transnational Organized Crime in West Africa: The Additional Challenge", *International Affairs*, 83, 6 (2007), p. 1076, note 23.

99. Author's interviews, Lagos and Abuja, October 2007; "'Blood oil' dripping from Nigeria", BBC News, 27 July 2008: http://news.bbc.co.uk/2/hi/africa/7519302.stm [accessed 25 November 2008].

100. Peter Gastrow, *Termites at work: A Report on Transnational Organized Crime and State Erosion in Kenya* (International Peace Institute, New York, 2011).

101. Intervention by UNODC official Antonio Mazzitelli, 28 May 2009, in a conference reported at http://www.wilsoncenter.org/event/global-drug-trafficking-africas-expanding-role [accessed 22 June 2015].

102. Tobi Soniyi, "Attempt on Akunyili's Life: SC Orders Nnakwe to Face Trial", *This Day*, 13 July 2013.

103. Marcia Angell, "The Body Hunters", *New York Review of Books*, LII, 15 (6 October 2005), pp. 23–5.

104. Dick Wittenberg and Sheila Kamerman, "Operatie Koolvis", *NRC Handelsblad*, 14 March 2009.

105. Police archives, Deventer, Netherlands: Operatie Koolvis zaakdossier 23: proces-verbaal.

106. Phone conversation with detective from UK Serious Organised Crime Agency, 14 November 2007.

107. Chapter Seven, pp. 134–35.

108. Franco Prina, "Trade and Exploitation of Minors and Young Nigerian Women for Prostitution in Italy", 2003, chap. 1: http://www.unicri.it/wwd/trafficking/nigeria/docs/rr_prina_eng.pdf [accessed 24 November 2008].

109. E.W. Kruisbergen, H.G. van der Bunt and E.R. Kleemans, *Georganiseerde Criminaliteit in Nederland* (Boom Lemona Uitgevers, Meppel, 2012), pp. 137–8.

110. Dina Siegel, "Nigeriaanse Madams in de Mensenhandel in Nederland", *Justitiële Verkenningen*, 33, 7 (2007), p. 45. There is also a good description in a work of fiction in Ifeoma Chinwuba, *Merchants of Flesh* (Spectrum Books, Lagos, 2003), pp. 221–5.

111. E.W. Kruisbergen, H.G. van der Bunt and E.R. Kleemans, *Georganiseerde criminaliteit in Nederland*, pp. 137–38.

112. Luda di Cortemiglia, "Programme of Action", p. 17.

113. Author's interview with Spanish Red Cross representative, Algeciras, 3 November 2009; a description of the event is in *El Faro de Ceuta*, 10 June 2009.

114. Immigration and Refugee Board of Canada, "Nigeria: Information on the Owegbe Cult: Who They Are; Where in Nigeria They are Located; and Whether they Practice Satanic or Evil Rituals", 11 October 2001, http://www.refworld.org/docid/3df4be8210.html [accessed 26 June 2015].

115. Ibid.

116. "Een nationaal onderzoek naar de handel in Nigeriaanse meisjes naar Nederland: Een analyse van de handel, de oorzaken, en de eventuele oplossingen", p. 23. This is a study into the trafficking of Nigerian girls to the Netherlands carried out by Paul Ikponwosa Oviawe, Joseph Pascal Iyare, and De Nigeriaanse Vereniging Nederland [Nigerian Democratic Movement in the Netherlands (NDMN)], commissioned by Terre des Hommes Nederland, Amsterdam, September 1999.

117. Ibid., p. 24.

118. Nationaal Rapporteur Mensenhandel, *Mensenhandel: Zevende rapportage van de Nationaal Rapporteur*, p. 396. Dutch and English versions may be found at http://www.nationaalrapporteur.nl/publicaties/Zevende/ [accessed 14 July 2015]. The B9 rule allowed victims of human traffick-

ing to stay in the country on humanitarian grounds during the time of police investigation.

119. BBC News, "Pope Benedict XVI Urges Italy to Respect Migrants", 11 Jan 2010.
120. "Nigeria 'Consistently in Top Two' for Trafficking", BBC Radio 4 news, 23 June 2015.
121. Paul Cheston, "20 Years Jail for Juju Child Sex Trafficker", *London Evening Standard*, 7 July 2011.
122. Author's discussion with detective involved in Operation Koolvis, Abuja, 1 November 2007.
123. "Een nationaal onderzoek naar de handel in Nigeriaanse meisjes naar Nederland", p. 4.
124. National Agency for the Prohibition of Trafficking in Persons (*NAPTIP*), "The Use of Voodoo (Juju) in Trafficking in Persons and its Effect on Victims of Trafficking in Criminal Justice Administration", document 01 ARVO, Koolvis file, Police archives, Deventer, Netherlands.
125. Emmanuel Mayah, "Europe by Desert", pp. 26–27.
126. "Operatie Koolvis", *NRC Handelsblad* 14 March 2009.
127. Nwando Achebe, "The Road to Italy: Nigerian Sex Workers at Home and Abroad", *Journal of Women's History*, 15, 4 (2004), p. 183, note 1.
128. Laura Gauer Bermudez, "'No Experience Necessary': The Internal Trafficking of Persons in South Africa" (unpublished paper, International Organization for Migration, 2008).
129. Caroline Moorhead, "Women and Children for Sale", *New York Review of Books*, LIV, 15 (11 October 2007), p. 15.
130. Peter O. Ebigbo, "Child Trafficking in Nigeria: The State of the Art", 2000, unpublished document.
131. BBC News, "Nigeria 'Baby Factory' Raided in Imo State", 10 May 2013.
132. Nationaal Rapporteur Mensenhandel, *Mensenhandel: Zevende Rapport*, p. 391.
133. Franco Prina, "Trade and Exploitation of Minors and Young Nigerian Women for Prostitution in Italy", 2003, chapter 5.1 of an unpaginated report: http://www.unicri.it/wwd/trafficking/nigeria/docs/rr_prina_eng.pdf
134. Email from drugs researcher, Vienna, 9 September 2013.
135. Author's conversation with senior officer from the UK's Serious Organised Crime Agency, 25 October 2014.
136. cf. Kate Meagher, "Social Capital, Social Liabilities, and Political Capital: Social Networks and Informal Manufacturing in Nigeria', *African Affairs*, 105, 421 (2006), pp. 553–82.
137. Address by US official at the African Criminal Networks conference, Bangkok, 16 May 2005.

138. Ibid.
139. "Laundering their Filthy Lucre", *Tell*, 6 September 2004.
140. Apter, *The Pan-African Nation*, p. 228.
141. Igbokwe, *Igbos*, p. 40.
142. James Cockayne, *Transnational Organized Crime: Multilateral Responses to a Rising Threat*, Coping with Crisis Working Paper (International Peace Institute, New York, March 2007), pp. 1–2.
143. Confidential source.
144. https://en.wikipedia.org/wiki/Nigerian_organized_crime
145. Email to the author, 18 June 2015.
146. Email to the author, 22 April 2015.
147. http://web.archive.org/web/20150531213202/http://www.37thnatconvention.org/ [accessed 24 June 2015].
148. http://www.thecable.ng/police-parade-11-suspected-edo-cultists-abuja [accessed 23 June 2015].

10. COSMIC POWERS

1. Statement at African Criminal Networks Conference, Thailand, 16–19 May 2005.
2. "Juju, 'Lclc Power', Used to Push Drugs in the US", *Sunday Concord*, 9 July 1989.
3. Wale Adebanwi, *Yorùbá Elites and Ethnic Politics in Nigeria: Ọbáfẹmi Awólọwọ and Corporate Agency* (Cambridge University Press, New York, 2014), p. 222.
4. Peter P. Ekeh, "Colonialism and the Two Publics in Africa: A Theoretical Statement", *Comparative Studies in Society and History*, 17, 1 (1975), pp. 91–112.
5. Kalu, "The Religious Dimension of the Legitimacy Crisis, 1993–1998", p. 670. Italics in original.
6. Ibid.
7. Ibid., p. 674.
8. Alex Osamuyi to Derek Trotter, 3 November 2005, http://www.419eater.com/html/artworld2.htm [accessed 26 June 2015].
9. Matthias Olufemi Dada Ojo, "Incorporation of Ayelala Traditional Religion into Nigerian Criminal Justice System: An Opinion Survey of Igbesa Community People in Ogun State, Nigeria", Department of Ethnology and Anthropology, University of Belgrade, *Issues in Ethnology and Anthropology*, 4, 9 (2014).
10. Obasuloyi Telewa, "A-y-e-l-a-l-a!: Changing Times for Once Powerful, Feared Ondo Deity", 12 October 2014, http://nationalmirroronline.

net/new/a-y-e-l-a-l-a-changing-times-for-once-powerful-feared-ondo-deity/ [accessed 26 June 2015].

11. Frisky Larr (Friday Agbonlahor), *Africa's Diabolical Entrapment* (AuthorHouse, Bloomington, IN, 2013), p. 88.

12. J.N. Oriji, "Warfare, the Overseas Slave Trade and Aro Expansion in the Igbo Hinterland", *Ikenga*, 7, 1–2 (1985), p. 157.

13. Estimate by Paul Lovejoy, quoted in ibid., p. 156.

14. A detailed study is A.O. Nwauwa, "Integrating Arochukwu into the Regional Chronological Structure", *History in Africa*, 18 (1991), pp. 297–310. Interesting reflections on the historiography are in A.E. Afigbo, "The Aro Phenomenon in the Historiography and Sociology of Southeastern Nigeria", in Toyin Falola (ed.), *Myth, History and Society: the collected works of Adiele Afigbo* (Africa World Press, Trenton NJ, 2006), pp. 161–74.

15. J. Anene, "The Protectorate Government of Southern Nigeria and the Aros, 1900–1902", *Journal of the Historical Society of Nigeria*, 1, 1 (1956), p. 22.

16. Afigbo, "The Eclipse of the Aro Slaving Oligarchy", pp. 3–24.

17. Ibid., p. 15.

18. Intelligence report on the Aro by T.M. Shankland, NAN, Ibadan, CSO 26/29017, p. 13.

19. Ibid.

20. Chapter Nine, pp. 166–68.

21. Afigbo, "The Eclipse of the Aro Slaving Oligarchy", p. 17.

22. Ibid.

23. Most press reports give the figure of about fifty police, although the Anambra State police commissioner later gave a figure of 200 police using fifteen vehicles: *Insider Weekly*, 23 August 2004, p. 20.

24. Stephen Ellis, "The Okija Shrine: Death and Life in Nigerian Politics", *Journal of African History*, 49, 3 (2008), pp. 445–66.

25. The figures regarding both the number of corpses and the number of people arrested vary in different reports, and were also reported differently by the police at various times.

26. "Okija", *Tell*, 6 September 2004.

27. J. Adele Bamgbose, "The Place of Deities in African Political Systems: a Case Study of Ogwugwu Shrine in Okija, Anambra State, Nigeria", *Essence: Interdisciplinary Journal of Philosophy*, 2 (2005), pp. 231–42.

28. Raymond Arazu, interviewed in *Insider Weekly*, 23 August 2004.

29. "The 'Gods' Versus the Police", *Newswatch*, 30 August 2004.

30. Ibid.

31. "Visiting the Forest of Evil", *The Source*, 30 August 2004.

32. Interview in *Tell*, 23 August 2004, p. 17.

33. "The Evil Forest", *Tell*, 16 August 2004.

34. Ibid.
35. Interviews in *Newswatch*, 23 August 2004.
36. M.G. Smith, *Report of the Inquiry into Ihiala Chieftaincy Dispute* (official document no. 18, Government Printer, Enugu, 1963: copy in NAN, CE/S6), p. 75.
37. Ibid., p. 20, para 61.
38. Quoted in *The Source*, 30 August 2004, p. 17.
39. *This Day*, 6 August 2003; Emmanuel U. Obi, "Understanding the Okija Shrine Phenomenon and the Art of Mental Poisoning: Just Before the Rush to Judgement", 25 November 2006 [www.dawodu.com/obi3.htm, accessed 22 January 2007].
40. http://home.rica.net/alphae/419coal/news1999.htm [accessed 27 June 2015].
41. *This Day online*, 19 August 2003, [www.religionnewsblogcom/8397, accessed 22 January 2007].
42. Author's interview, Awka, Anambra State, March 2002.
43. Daniel J. Smith, "The Bakassi Boys: Vigilantism, Violence, and Political Imagination in Nigeria", *Cultural Anthropology*, 19, 3 (2004), pp. 429–55.
44. Kate Meagher, "Hijacking Civil Society: The Inside Story of the Bakassi Boys Vigilante Group of South-eastern Nigeria", *Journal of Modern African Studies*, 45, 1 (2007), pp. 89–115.
45. I personally witnessed a group of Bakassi Boys pouring petrol over a middle-aged man whom they were also beating, in broad daylight, less than 100 metres from Governor Mbadinuju's office at the state capital, Awka, in March 2002.
46. "'Kalu's government is a failure'", *Tell*, 17 January 2005.
47. Ibid.
48. Ibid.
49. *Insider Weekly*, 23 August 2004.
50. Daniel J. Smith, "Corruption, culture politique et démocratie au Nigéria: réactions populaires à la croisade anti-corruption du président Obasanjo" *Politique africaine*, 106 (2007), pp. 28–45.
51. *Newswatch*, 11 October 2004.
52. *Insider Weekly*, 23 August 2004.
53. Adebanwi, *A Paradise for Maggots*, p. 218.
54. Ibid., pp. 220–21.
55. *This Day*, 6 March 2007.
56. Adebanwi, *A Paradise for Maggots*, pp. xi-xix, 215–33.
57. E.g. *Newswatch*, 6 September 2004, p. 49.
58. "The Evil Forest", *Tell*, 16 August 2004.
59. Interview with Anthony Okownkwo [sic—Okonkwo?], *Newswatch*, 23 August 2004, pp. 20–21.

60. *Newswatch*, 11 October 2004.
61. Interview, *Newswatch*, 23 August 2004, p. 25.
62. *Guardian News*, 5 August 2004.
63. "Okija", *Tell*, 6 September 2004, p. 23.
64. Interview in *Newswatch*, 23 August 2004.
65. Interview in *Tell*, 23 August 2004.
66. "Laundering their Filthy Lucre", *Tell*, 6 September 2004.
67. Ibid.
68. Quoted in *Newswatch*, 23 August 2004, p. 23.
69. Ibid.
70. Daniel J. Smith, "'The Arrow of God': Pentecostalism, Inequality, and the Supernatural in South-eastern Nigeria", *Africa* 71, 4 (2001), pp. 587–613.
71. "The Evil Forest", *Tell*, 16 August 2004.
72. Ibid.
73. Ibid.
74. Interview with Ohanaeze Ndigbo president-general Joe Irukwu, *Tell*, 23 August 2004, p. 18.
75. *Tell*, 6 September 2004, p. 25.
76. Interview with Inspector General of Police Tafa Balogun, ibid., p. 22.
77. According to Pierce, this is what Northern Nigerians mean when they refer to corruption: Steven Pierce, "Looking like a State: Colonialism and the Discourse of Corruption in Northern Nigeria", *Comparative Studies in Society and History*, 48, 4 (2006), p. 888.
78. Ibid., pp. 888–89.
79. The Overcomers' website is at http://www.overcomersworld.org/home.html [accessed 11 July 2015].
80. Alexander Ezeugo Ekewuba, interview in *Newswatch*, 6 September 2004.
81. Ibid.
82. Interview in *Newswatch*, 23 August 2004.
83. Ibid.
84. Ibid.
85. Ellis, *The Mask of Anarchy*.
86. An unfairly disparaging view is by Terence Ranger, "Scotland Yard in the Bush: Medicine Murders, Child Witches and the Construction of the Occult: A Literature Review", *Africa*, 77, 2 (2007), pp. 272–83.
87. Interview in *Tell*, 6 September 2004, p. 23.
88. The phrase is taken from Orlando Patterson, *Slavery and Social Death* (Harvard University Press, 1982).
89. *Insider Weekly*, 23 August 2004.
90. Jonathan Haynes, "Political Critique in Nigerian Video Films", *African Affairs*, 105, 421 (2006), pp. 511–33.

91. Soyinka, *Cults*, p. 30.

92. Nduka Nwosu, "Assassination, a New Culture in Igboland", *Guardian*, 2 November 2002.

93. Interview with Sheikh Ahmad Gumbi, *Punch*, 14 November 2005.

94. Cf. Ruth Marshall, *Political Spiritualities: The Pentecostal Revolution in Nigeria* (University of Chicago Press, 2009).

95. Statement at African Criminal Networks Conference, Thailand, 16–19 May 2005.

96. http://dailypost.ng/2015/06/23/how-i-manipulated-skype-to-dupe-people-internet-fraudster-tells-t-b-joshua/ [accessed 10 July 2015].

97. Author's interview with former CIA official, Washington DC, 8 November 1988.

98. Archives of the African National Congress, Fort Hare University, South Africa, Lusaka mission, part 2, Secretary General's Office, box 54, folder 10: report on developments in Mozambique during March 1987.

99. Stuart Millar and Chris McGreal, "The Mystery of £170,000, Smear Rumours and Nelson Mandela", *The Guardian* [London], 22 May 1999; see also UN press release GA/9462, on Fernandes's role with the CAR government.

100. http://www.johnhowardsanden.com/portraits-africa/africa02.htm [accessed 23 March 2015].

101. Chapter Two, p. 32.

102. Apter, *The Pan-African Nation*, p. 13.

11. NIGERIAN ORGANISED CRIME

1. Donald R. Cressey, "The Functions and Structure of Criminal Syndicates", in Patrick J. Ryan and George E. Rush (eds), *Understanding Organized Crime in Global Perspective: A Reader* (Sage Publications, Thousand Oaks, CA, etc., 1997), pp. 3–15.

2. Diego Gambetta, *The Sicilian Mafia: The Business of Private Protection* (Harvard University Press, Cambridge, MA, 1993).

3. John Dickie, *Cosa Nostra: A History of the Sicilian Mafia* (Palgrave Macmillan, London, 2005), p. 291.

4. Vadim Volkov, *Violent Entrepreneurs: The Use of Force in the Making of Russian Capitalism* (Cornell University Press, Ithaca, NY, 2002).

5. Kirill Kabanov, head of the National Anti-Corruption Committee, quoted in Charles Clover, "A Death Retold", *Financial Times*, 19 Feb. 2009.

6. Dawisha, *Putin's Kleptocracy*.

7. Passas, "Introduction", pp.xiii-xix, *Organized Crime*.

8. Yusufa Bala Usman, "The Central Role of Corruption in a Dependent Capitalist Economy: The Nigerian Experience", NISER public lecture at

the University of Lagos, 5 May 1983, published in the *Nigerian Standard*, 13 May 1983.

9. Quoted in David O. Friedrichs (ed.), *State Crime* (2 vols, Ashgate, Aldershot and Brookfield VT, 1998): *Volume 1: Defining, Delineating and Explaining State Crime*, p. 51.

10. Brague, *The Law of God*, p. 239.

11. William J. Chambliss, "State-Organized Crime—the American Society of Criminology, 1988 Presidential Address", *Criminology*, 27, 2 (1989), p. 184.

12. "Introduction", p.xvii, in Friedrichs, *State Crime, Volume 1*.

13. Stanley Cohen, "Crime and Politics: Spot the Difference", *The British Journal of Sociology*, 47, 1 (1996), pp. 1–21.

14. David Beetham, "Foreword", in Felia Allum and Renate Siebert (eds), *Organized Crime and the Challenge to Democracy* (Routledge, London and New York, 2003), p. x.

15. R.T. Naylor, *Wages of Crime: Black Markets, Illegal Finance, and the Underworld Economy* (revised edn, Cornell Univ. Press, Ithaca and London, 2004), p. 3.

16. Manuel Castells, *End of Millennium* (1998; 2nd edn, Blackwell, Oxford, 2000), p. 72, vol. III of *The Information Age*. Chapter 2 concerns what Castells calls "the rise of the Fourth World", and pp. 82–128 specifically concern Africa.

17. Tom Burgis, *The Looting Machine: Warlords, Tycoons, Smugglers and the Systematic Theft of Africa's Wealth* (William Collins, London, 2015).

18. See Smith, *A Culture of Corruption*, pp. 11–19.

19. Andreski, *African Predicament*, p. 108.

20. Cf. Jean-François Bayart, Stephen Ellis and Béatrice Hibou, *The Criminalization of the State in Africa* (James Currey, Oxford, 1999).

21. Mark Shaw, "The Political Economy of Crime and Conflict in Sub-Saharan Africa", *South African Journal of International Affairs*, 8, 2 (2001), p. 57.

22. *Olmstead v. United States*, 277 U.S. 438 (1928) http://www.fjc.gov/history/home.nsf/page/tu_olmstead_doc_15.html [accessed 26 June 2015].

23. Chapter Ten, pp. 198–206.

24. Kalu, "The Religious Dimension of the Legitimacy Crisis", p. 674.

25. Cf. Eva Joly, *Est-ce dans ce monde-là que nous voulons vivre?* (Eds. Les Arènes, Paris, 2003), p. 190.

26. Ibid., p. 208 ff.

27. Dev Kar and Joseph Spanjers, "Illicit Financial Flows from Developing Countries: 2003–2012", 16 December 2014 http://www.gfintegrity.org/report/2014-global-report-illicit-financial-flows-from-developing-countries-2003–2012/ [accessed 27 June 2015].

28. See Introduction, p. 3.
29. Smith, *A Culture of Corruption*.
30. See esp. J.-F. Bayart, "The Social Capital of the Felonious State", ch.1 of *The Criminalization of the State in Africa*.
31. A.C. Nwaogugu, "Corruption in Nigeria: Is there any Answer?", *Daily Star*, 22 Aug. 1976
32. Quoted in Ogu Enemaku, "Social Science and the Burden of Corruption", *The Guardian*, 23 January 2006, p. 65.
33. Iliffe, *Honour in African History*, p. 214.
34. Jane I. Guyer, *Marginal Gains*, p. 171.
35. A.C. Nwaogugu, "Corruption in Nigeria: Is There any Answer?", *Daily Star*, 22 August 1976
36. Perham, *Native Administration*, pp. 238–40.
37. Ibid., p. 352.
38. Ibid.
39. Achebe, *The Trouble with Nigeria*, p. 1.
40. Cf. Frederick Cooper, *Africa Since 1940:The Past of the Present* (Cambridge University Press, 2002), chapter 7.
41. Billy Dudley, quoted in Osaghae, *Crippled Giant*, p. 17.
42. Olofintuyi, "Bribery: Still Here with Us".
43. UK National Archives, FCO 65/1530: Le Quesne to Callaghan, 9 Aug. 1974.
44. Amadi, *Ethics*, pp. 88–89.
45. Soares de Oliveira, *Petroleum and Politics in the Gulf of Guinea*, p. 145.
46. Ake, *Is Africa Democratizing?*, pp. 7–8.
47. Ibid., pp. 7–8. Italics in original.
48. Ibid., p. 18.
49. John Campbell, *Nigeria: Dancing on the Brink* (Rowman and Littlefield, Lanham, MD, 2010).
50. UK National Archives, FCO 65/1531: East to Dawbarn, 9 Oct. 1974.
51. Marshall, *Political Spiritualities*.
52. Soyinka, *Cults*, p. 55. Italics in original.
53. Ted Leggett, quoted in Shaw, "The Political Economy of Crime and Conflict", p. 66.
54. Wraith and Simpkins, *Corruption in Developing Countries*, pp. 11–53.
55. Quoted in M.H. KhalilTimamy, "African Leaders and Corruption", *Review of African Political Economy*, 104–5 (2005), p. 384.
56. Saro-Wiwa, *On a Darkling Plain*, pp. 21, 24.
57. Baker, *Capitalism's Achilles Heel*.
58. Palan, *The OffshoreWorld*, pp. 10–11.
59. Joly, *Est-ce dans ce monde-là que nous voulons vivre?*, p. 193.
60. Misha Glenny, "Mobsters Get HomesickToo", *London Review of Books*, 33, 13 (30 June 2011), pp. 25–26.

BIBLIOGRAPHY

ARCHIVES

Ireland

SMA Fathers, Cork

Netherlands

Police archives, Deventer
– Operatie Koolvis files

Nigeria

National Archives of Nigeria, Ibadan [NAN].
Nigerian Institute of International Affairs, Lagos.
– Press clippings collection

United Kingdom

The National Archives of the United Kingdom, Kew
– Colonial Office files
– Dominions Office
– Foreign Office
– Foreign and Commonwealth Office

United States of America

National Archives and Records Administration (NARA II), Maryland
– RG 59, central foreign policy files
– RG 84, records of the US consulate, Lagos
– RG 286, records of USAID
Archives of the World Bank, Washington DC
– McNamara papers

BIBLIOGRAPHY

TV, RADIO, PRESS

Daily Champion, Lagos [Nigeria]
Daily Express, Lagos [Nigeria]
Daily Service, Lagos [Nigeria]
Daily Sketch, Ibadan [Nigeria]
Daily Star, Enugu [Nigeria]
Daily Times, Lagos [Nigeria]
El Faro de Ceuta, Ceuta [Spain]
Financial Times, London
Guardian, Lagos [Nigeria]
Guardian, London
Guardian News, Nigeria
Independent, London
Insider Weekly, Lagos [Nigeria]
Jane's Intelligence Review, Coulsdon [UK]
Liberian Diaspora, Monrovia [Liberia]
London Evening Standard, London
London Review of Books, London
Manchester Evening News, Manchester, 1971–2008. From 2008: Oldham
National Concord, Ikeja [Nigeria]
New Nigerian, Kaduna [Nigeria]
New Statesman, London
New York Review of Books, [New York, etc.]
New York Times, New York
New Yorker, New York
Newswatch, Ikeja [Nigeria]
Nigerian Catholic Herald, Ebute Metta [Nigeria]
Nigerian Herald, Ilorin [Nigeria]
Nigerian Tribune, Ibadan [Nigeria]
NRC Handelsblad, Rotterdam
Observer, London
Opgelicht, *TROS-TV broadcast, Nederland 1*
The Post Express, Lagos [Nigeria]
Premium Times, Abuja [Nigeria]
Punch, Ikeja [Nigeria]
Renaissance, Enugu [Nigeria] 1970–1975 (continued as *Daily Star*)
The Source, Ikeja [Nigeria]
Star, Johannesburg [South Africa]
Sunday Champion, (Sunday issue of the *Daily Champion)* Lagos [Nigeria]
Sunday Concord, Ikeja [Nigeria]
Sunday Sketch, Ibadan [Nigeria]

BIBLIOGRAPHY

Sunday Times, Lagos [Nigeria]
Tell, Ikeja [Nigeria]
This Day, Lagos [Nigeria]
Times, London
Times Higher Education Supplement, London
Trouw, Amsterdam
Vanguard, Apapa [Nigeria]
Vanity Fair, London
Washington Post, Washington, DC
Weekend Concord, Ikeja [Nigeria]
West Africa, London

WEBSITES

AfricaFocus: www.africafocus.org
African Arguments: http://africanarguments.org
Afrol News: http://www.afrol.com/
BBC News: http://news.bbc.co.uk
The Cable: http://www.thecable.ng
Daily Post: http://dailypost.ng
Dawodu: *Dedicated to Nigeria's history, socio-economic and political issues:* http://www.dawodu.com/irons2.htm
Federal Judicial Center, USA: http://www.fjc.gov
419 eater: http://www.419eater.com
Front Page Africa: http://www.frontpageafricaonline.com/
Gilbert Chagoury: http://www.gilbertchagoury.com/
Global Financial Integrity: http://www.gfintegrity.org
Harold Smith Memorial: https://haroldsmithmemorial.wordpress.com
Insolvency and Law: http://www.insolvencyandlawblog.com
IRIN: http://www.irinnews.org
ISN, international relations and security network: www.isn.etnz.ch
John Howard Sanden, American portrait painter: http://www.johnhoward-sanden.com/
National Archives, USA, access to archival databases: http://aad.archives.gov
National Association of Seadogs, Pyrates Confraternity: http://www.nas-int.org
National Mirror: http://nationalmirroronline.net
NBM of Africa (Neo Black Movement): http://www.37thnatconvention.org/
Neo Black Movement of Africa: http://www.nbmarena.com
Nigeria—the 419 coalition: http://home.rica.net/alphae/419coal
Nigeria World: http://nigeriaworld.com
OMG: http://www.omgnaija.com

BIBLIOGRAPHY

Overcomers Christian Mission, inc.: http://www.overcomersworld.org/
Oweh, Nkem, "I Go Chop Your Dollar": https://www.youtube.com/
watch?v=D_YjvC4ndzM
Politicsweb: http://www.politicsweb.co.za
Populstat: http://www.populstat.info/Africa/nigeriac.htm
Reformed Ogboni Fraternity: http://www.reformedogboni.com/node/1
Sahara Reporters: http://saharareporters.com
Spiegel Online International: http://www.spiegel.de
Supreme Eiye Confraternity: http://www.airfords.org
Time Out Mumbai: www.timeoutmumbai.net/client_mumbai_local/mum-
bailolocalcode=11&source=1
Toma Micro Publishers Ltd.: http://www.tomalegalretrieve.org/phplaw/
site/index.php
Wikipedia: https://en.wikipedia.org
Wilson Center: http://www.wilsoncenter.org
World Population Review: http://worldpopulationreview.com/countries/
nigeria-population
Yahoo News: http://news.yahoo.com

UNPUBLISHED DOCUMENTS, THESES, ETC.

African Criminal Networks Conference, Bangkok, 16–19 May 2005, docu-
ment collection.
Alemika, Etannibi, "Organized Crime: Nigeria", paper presented at United
Nations Office on Drugs and Crime (UNODC) workshop on West African
organized crime, Dakar, 2–3 April 2004.
Bermudez, Laura Gauer, "'No Experience Necessary':The Internal Trafficking
of Persons in South Africa" (unpublished paper, International Organization
for Migration, 2008).
Corpelijn, Charlotte, untitled MA thesis (University of Utrecht, 2008).
Coventry Cathedral, "The Potential for Peace and Reconciliation in the Niger
Delta", unpublished report by Stephen Davis, February 2009.
Ebigbo, Peter O., "Child Trafficking in Nigeria: The State of the Art", 2000,
unpublished document.
Findlay, G.H., Report on the reorganization of the Colony, 1927, cited by
L.C. Gwam in his catalogue to the colonial archives at the National Archives
of Nigeria, Ibadan.
Harold, Joe, "Scrapbook of 50 Years in Nigeria" (privately printed): copy in
the archives of the SMA Fathers, Cork, Ireland.
Luda di Cortemiglia, Vittoria, "Programme of Action against Trafficking in
Minors and Young Women from Nigeria into Italy for the Purpose of Sexual
Exploitation" (United Nations Interregional Crime and Justice Research
Institute, undated).
Meagher, John P., "The Establishment of Military Government in Nigeria",
16 Feb. 1966, 32pp., enclosed with Mathews to Dept of State, 5 March

BIBLIOGRAPHY

1966: NARA II, RG 59, Subject numeric files, Nigeria 1966, Pol 15, box 2522. An excellent eye-witness account of the January 1966 military coup.

"Nigerian Advance-Fee Fraud in Transnational Perspective", 2009, confidential source.

Nigerian Drug Law Enforcement Agency (NDLEA), "An Analysis of the Drug Trafficking Issues and Trends at the Murtala Muhammed International Airport, Ikeja, Lagos (MMIA)", unpublished paper, 7pp. [September 2007].

Ogundipe, Jide, "The Banco Noroeste Fraud", paper for ICC FraudNet Conference, Singapore, 18 October 2007. https://icc-ccs.org/home/publications/viewdownload/3-publications/155-the-banco-noroeste-fraud-

Oputa panel report, unofficial report at: http://www.dawodu.com/oputa1.htm

Osaghae, Eghosa, Augustine Ikelegbe, Omobolaji Olarinmoye and Steven Okhonmina, "Youth Militias, Self Determination and Resource Control Struggles in the Niger-Delta Region of Nigeria", unpublished study, 2007.

Peel, Quentin, "Nigeria's Debt Problems—Causes and Solutions: An Outsider's View", paper presented at International Conference on Foreign Debt and Nigeria's Economic Development, Lagos, 5–6 March 1984.

Prina, Franco, "Trade and Exploitation of Minors and Young Nigerian Women for Prostitution in Italy", 2003: http://www.unicri.it/wwd/trafficking/nigeria/docs/rr_prina_eng.pdf

Quéré, Stéphane, "Les clans criminels nigérians" (diplôme universitaire, Université de Paris II Panthéon-Assas, 2001).

Quist, Flemming, "Drug Trafficking in West Africa 2000–2004 in an International Perspective", UNODC workshop on West African organized crime, Dakar, 2–3 April 2004.

Royal Thai Police, "African Community at Pratunum, Bangkok", paper presented at the African Criminal Networks conference, Bangkok, 16–19 May 2005.

Sociale inlichtingen- en opsporingsdienst, *Beleidsdocument "Labyrint": Onderzoek naar West-Afrikaanse Criminele Netwerken in de Sociale Zekerheid* (SIOD, Den Haag, 2005).

Terre des Hommes Nederland, "Een nationaal onderzoek naar de handel in Nigeriaanse meisjes naar Nederland: Een analyse van de handel, de oorzaken, en de eventuele oplossingen". [A study into the trafficking of Nigerian girls to the Netherlands carried out by Paul Ikponwosa Oviawe, Joseph Pascal Iyare, and de Nigeriaanse Vereniging Nederland (Amsterdam, September 1999).

Williams, Phil, "The Global Implications of West African Organized Crime", http://www.wired.com/news/culture/0/1284/53818.html [no longer available on 13 July 2015].

BIBLIOGRAPHY

OFFICIAL REPORTS

Bourdillon, Sir Bernard, *Memorandum on the Future Political Development of Nigeria* ("confidential", Government Printer, Lagos, 1939). Copy in the National Archives of Nigeria, Ibadan, at MN/B4A.

Federal Republic of Nigeria, *Report of the Judicial Commission of Inquiry into the Shortage of Petroleum Products 11th November 1975* (Federal Ministry of Information, Lagos, 1976),

Federal Republic of Nigeria, *Report of the Panel of Inquiry into the Purchase of British LeylandBuses by the Secretariat of Festac* (Federal Ministry of Information, Lagos, 1978).

Hansard, edited verbatim report of proceedings of the United Kingdom Parliament.

Immigration and Refugee Board of Canada, "Nigeria: Information on the Owegbe Cult: Who They Are; Where in Nigeria They are Located; and Whether they Practice Satanic or Evil Rituals", 11 October 2001, http://www.refworld.org/docid/3df4be8210.html

IPOL, *Nationaal Dreigingsbeeld 2012: Georganiseerde criminaliteit* (Dienst IPOL, Zoetermeer, 2012).

Nationaal Rapporteur Mensenhandel, *Mensenhandel: Zevende rapport van de Nationaal Rapporteur*. Dutch and English versions may be found at http://www.nationaalrapporteur.nl/publicaties/Zevende/

Report of the Commission Appointed to Enquire into the Owegbe Cult: Including Statement by the Government of the Mid-Western Group of Provinces (Ministry of Internal Affairs and Information, Benin City, 1966).

Smith, M.G., *Report of the Inquiry into Ihiala Chieftaincy Dispute* (official document no. 18, Government Printer, Enugu, 1963: copy in NAN, CE/S6).

United Nations Economic Commission for Africa, *Foreign Exchange and Financial Leakages in Africa* (1985) http://repository.uneca.org/bitstream/handle/10855/10023/Bib-50651.pdf?sequence=1

United States Department of State, *International Narcotics Control Strategy Report 2007,Volume II, Money Laundering and Financial Crimes*: http://www.state.gov/j/inl/rls/nrcrpt/2007/vol2/html/80876.htm

United States Government, *Foreign Broadcast Information Service, Sub-Saharan Africa Report*, 16 April 1985.

ARTICLES, BOOKS

Aarts, José, "Een Etnografische Studie over Ondergronds Bankieren in de Nigeriaanse Gemeenschap in Nederland", in Henk van de Bunt and Dina Siegel (eds), *Ondergronds Bankieren in Nederland* (Boom Juridische Uitgevers, Den Haag, 2009), pp. 59–82.

Achebe, Chinua, *The Trouble with Nigeria* (1983; Heinemann Educational Books, Ibadan etc., 1984).

BIBLIOGRAPHY

Achebe, Nwando, "The Road to Italy: Nigerian Sex Workers at Home and Abroad", *Journal of Women's History*, 15, 4 (2004), pp. 178–85.

Adebanwi, Wale, *A Paradise for Maggots: The Story of a Nigerian Anti-graft Czar* (published by the author, 2010).

———, *Authority Stealing: Anti-corruption War and Democratic Politics in Post-Military Nigeria* (Carolina Academic Press, Durham, NC, 2012).

———, *Yorùbá Elites and Ethnic Politics in Nigeria: Ọbáfẹmi Awólọwọ and Corporate Agency* (Cambridge University Press, New York, 2014).

Adekanye, J. 'Bayo, *The Retired Military as Emergent Power Factor in Nigeria* (Heinemann Educational Books, Ibadan, 1999).

Adogame, Afe, "The 419 Code as Business Unusual: Youth and the Unfolding of the Advance Fee Fraud Online Discourse", *ISA e-bulletin*, International Sociological Association, 7 (July 2007), pp. 4–25.

Afigbo, A.E., "The Eclipse of the Aro Slaving Oligarchy of South-Eastern Nigeria, 1901–1927", *Journal of the Historical Society of Nigeria*, 6, 1 (1971), pp. 3–24.

———, *The Abolition of the Slave Trade in Southeastern Nigeria, 1885–1950* (University of Rochester Press, Rochester, NY, 2006).

———, "The Aro Phenomenon in the Historiography and Sociology of Southeastern Nigeria", in Toyin Falola (ed.), *Myth, History and Society: the Collected Works of Adiele Afigbo* (Africa World Press, Trenton NJ, 2006), pp. 161–74.

Agbase, Pita Ogaba, "The 'Stolen' Okigbo Panel Report: Of Malfeasance and Public Accountability in Nigeria", in Jane I. Guyer and LaRay Denzer (eds), *Vision and Policy in Nigerian Economics: The Legacy of Pius Okigbo* (Ibadan University Press, 2005), pp. 55–75.

Agozino, Biko, "Crime, Criminology and Post-colonial Theory: Criminological Reflections on West Africa", in James Sheptycki and Ali Wardak (eds), *Transnational and Comparative Criminology* (Glasshouse Press, London, 2005), pp. 117–34.

Akak, Eyo O., *Bribery and Corruption in Nigeria* (no publisher given, Ibadan, no date [1952]).

Akanbi, Raimi (ed.), *Redasel's Companies of Nigeria* (2nd edn, Research and Data Services, Lagos, 1996).

Ake, Claude, *Is Africa Democratizing?* (CASS Monograph no. 5, Malthouse Press, Ikeja, 1996).

Akingbade, Tunde, *Historical Studies on Global Scam and Nigeria's 419: How to Overcome Fraudsters and Con Artists* (AuthorHouse, 2009).

Akinnola, Richard (ed.), *The Murder of Dele Giwa: Cover-up—Revelations* (Human Rights Publications, Lagos, 2001).

Akyeampong, Emmanuel, "Diaspora and Drug Trafficking in West Africa: A Case Study of Ghana", *African Affairs*, 104, 416 (2005), pp. 429–47.

BIBLIOGRAPHY

Albert, Isaac Oláwálé, "The Growth of an Urban Migrant Community: The Hausa Settlements in Ibadan, c.1830–1979", *Ife: Annals of the Institute of Cultural Studies*, 4 (1993), pp. 1–15.

———, "The Sociocultural Politics of Ethnic and Religious Conflicts", in Ernest E. Uwazie, Isaac O. Albert and Godfrey N. Uzoigwe (eds), *Inter-Ethnic and Religious Conflict Resolution in Nigeria* (Lexington Books, Langham MD, 1999), pp. 69–86.

———, "Smuggling Second-hand Cars Through the Benin-Nigeria Borders", in Georges Kobou (ed.), *Real Economies in Africa* (Codesria, Dakar, 2003), pp. 217–33.

———, "Explaining 'Godfatherism' in Nigerian Politics", *African Sociological Review*, 9, 2 (2005), pp. 79–105.

Amadi, Elechi, *Ethics in Nigerian Culture* (Heinemann Educational Books, London, 1982).

Ammann, Daniel, *The King of Oil: The Secret Lives of Marc Rich* (St Martin's Press, New York, 2009).

Ampratwum, Edward Fokuoh, "Advance Fee Fraud '419' and Investor Confidence in the Economies of sub-Saharan Africa (SSA)", *Journal of Financial Crime*, 16, 1 (2009), pp. 67–79.

Andreski, Stanislav, *The African Predicament: A Study in the Pathology of Modernisation* (Michael Joseph, London, 1968).

Anene, J., "The Protectorate Government of Southern Nigeria and the Aros, 1900–1902", *Journal of the Historical Society of Nigeria*, 1, 1 (1956), pp. 20–6.

Anifowose, Remi, "Corruption: A Political Perspective", in M. Ade Adejugbe (ed.), *Perspectives on Nigeria's Fledgling Fourth Republic* (Malthouse Press, Ikeja, 2002), pp. 108–25.

Apter, Andrew H., "IBB=419: Nigerian Democracy and the Politics of Illusion", in John L. Comaroff and Jean Comaroff (eds), *Civil Society and the Political Imagination in Africa: Critical Perspectives* (University of Chicago Press, Chicago and London, 1999), pp. 267–307.

———, *Pan-African Nation: Oil and the Spectacle of Culture in Nigeria* (University of Chicago Press, 2005).

Aransola, Joshua Oyeniyi, and Suraj Olalekan Asindemade, "Understanding Cybercrime Perpetrators and the Strategies They Employ in Nigeria", *Cyberpsychology, Behavior, and Social Networking*, 14, 12 (2011), pp. 759–63.

Awa, Eme O., *Federal Government in Nigeria* (University of California Press, Berkeley, CA, 1964).

Awolowo, Obafemi, *The Path to Nigerian Freedom* (Faber & Faber, London, 1947).

———, *Awo: The Autobiography of Chief Obafemi Awolowo* (Cambridge University Press, 1960).

BIBLIOGRAPHY

Ayu, Iyorchia D., "Towards a Revolutionary Resolution of the Mafia Problem", in Bala J. Takaya and Sonni Gwanle Tyoden (eds), *The Kaduna Mafia: A Study of the Rise, Development and Consolidation of a Nigerian Power Elite* (Jos University Press, 1987), pp. 125–46.

Baker, Raymond, *Capitalism's Achilles Heel: Dirty Money and How to Renew the Free-market System* (John Wiley & Sons, Hoboken, NJ, 2005).

Bamgbose, J. Adele, "The Place of Deities in African Political Systems: a Case Study of Ogwugwu Shrine in Okija, Anambra State, Nigeria", *Essence: Interdisciplinary Journal of Philosophy*, 2 (2005), pp. 231–42.

Bayart, Jean-François, Stephen Ellis and Béatrice Hibou, *The Criminalization of the State in Africa* (James Currey, Oxford, 1999).

Beetham, David, "Foreword", in Felia Allum and Renate Siebert (eds), *Organized Crime and the Challenge to Democracy* (Routledge, London and New York, 2003).

Biegelman, Martin T., *Identity Theft Handbook: Detection, Prevention and Security* (John Wiley, Hoboken, NJ, 2009).

Booth, James, *Writers and Politics in Nigeria* (Hodder & Stoughton, London, 1981).

Bovenkerk, Frank, Marleen Easton, Lodewijk Gunther Moor, and Paul Ponsaers (eds.), *Policing Multiple Communities*. Cahiers Politiestudies nr. 15, 2010/12 (Maklu Uitgevers, Antwerpen-Apeldoorn-Portland, 2010).

Brague, Rémi, *The Law of God: The Philosophical History of an Idea* (trans. Lydia G. Cochrane, University of Chicago Press, Chicago and London, 2007).

Bretton, Henry L., *Power and Stability in Nigeria: The Politics of Decolonization* (Frederick A. Praeger, New York, 1962).

———, *Power and Politics in Africa* (Longman, London, 1973).

Briggs, Biobele Richards, "Problems of Recruitment in Civil Service: Case of the Nigerian Civil Service", *African Journal of Business Management*, 1, 6 (2007), pp. 142–153.

Buchan, James, *Frozen Desire: The Meaning of Money* (Farrar, Straus, and Giroux, New York, 1997).

Buchanan, Jim, and Alex J. Grant, "Investigating and Prosecuting Nigerian Fraud", *United States Attorneys' Bulletin*, 49, 6 (2001), pp. 39–47.

Burgis, Tom, *The Looting Machine: Warlords, Tycoons, Smugglers and the Systematic Theft of Africa's Wealth* (William Collins, London, 2015).

Callaway, Helen, and Dorothy O. Helly, "Crusader for Empire: Flora Shaw/ Lady Lugard", in Nupur Chaudhuri and Margaret Strobel (eds), *Western Women and Imperialism: Complicity and Resistance* (Indiana University Press, Bloomington and Indianapolis, 1992), pp. 79–97.

Campbell, John, *Nigeria: Dancing on the Brink* (Rowman and Littlefield, Lanham, MD, 2010).

Carling, Jørgen, *Migration, Human Smuggling and Trafficking from Nigeria to*

Europe (IOM Migration Research series 23, International Organisation for Migration, Geneva, 2006).

Castells, Manuel, *End of Millennium* (1998; 2nd edn, Blackwell, Oxford, 2000).

Chambliss, William J., "Toward a Political Economy of Crime", *Theory and Society*, 2, 2 (1975), pp. 149–70.

―――, "State-Organized Crime—the American Society of Criminology, 1988 Presidential Address", *Criminology*, 27, 2 (1989), pp. 183–208.

Chinwuba, Ifeoma, *Merchants of Flesh* (Spectrum Books, Lagos, 2003).

Cockayne, James, *Transnational Organized Crime: Multilateral Responses to a Rising Threat*, Coping with Crisis Working Paper (International Peace Institute, New York, March 2007).

Cohen, Stanley, "Crime and Politics: Spot the Difference", *The British Journal of Sociology*, 47, 1 (1996), pp. 1–21.

Coleman, James S., *Nigeria: Background to Nationalism* (University of California Press, Berkeley, CA, 1958).

Comolli, Virginia, *Boko Haram: Nigeria's Islamist Insurgency* (Hurst & Co., London, 2015).

Cooley, John K., *Unholy Wars: Afghanistan, America and International Terrorism* (3rd edn, Pluto Press, London and Sterling, VA, 2002).

Cooper, Frederick, *Africa Since 1940: The Past of the Present* (Cambridge University Press, 2002).

Cressey, Donald R., "The Functions and Structure of Criminal Syndicates", in Patrick J. Ryan and George E. Rush (eds), *Understanding Organized Crime in Global Perspective: A Reader* (Sage Publications, Thousand Oaks, CA, etc., 1997), pp. 3–15.

Crocker, W.R., *Australian Ambassador: International Relations at First Hand* (Melbourne University Press, Carlton, VA, 1971).

Crowder, Michael, "Indirect Rule: French and British Style", *Africa*, 34, 3 (1964), pp. 197–205.

Dawha, Emmanuel M.K., *'Yan Daba, 'Yan Banga and 'Yan Daukar Amarya: A Study of Criminal Gangs in Northern Nigeria* (Occasional paper, no. 9, Institut français pour la recherche en Afrique, Ibadan, 1996).

Dawisha, Karen, *Putin's Kleptocracy: Who Owns Russia?* (Simon & Schuster, New York, 2014).

Dent, Martin J., "Corrective Government: Military Rule in Perspective", in K. Panter-Brick (ed.), *Soldiers and Oil*, pp. 101–40.

Deschamps, Hubert, "Et maintenant, Lord Lugard?", *Africa*, 33, 4 (1963), pp. 293–306.

Dickie, John, *Cosa Nostra: A History of the Sicilian Mafia* (Palgrave Macmillan, London, 2005).

BIBLIOGRAPHY

Ebbe, Obi N.I., "The Political-Criminal Nexus: The Nigerian Case", *Trends in Organized Crime*, 4, 3 (1999), pp. 29–59.

Eboh, Simeon O., "Law and Order in the Society: The Nigerian Experience", *The Nigerian Journal of Theology*, 18 (2004), pp. 18–35.

Ekeh, Peter P., "Colonialism and the Two Publics in Africa: A Theoretical Statement", *Comparative Studies in Society and History*, 17, 1 (1975), pp. 91–112.

Ekpenyong, Stephen, "Social Inequalities, Collusion, and Armed Robbery in Nigerian Cities", *British Journal of Criminology*, 29, 1 (1989), pp. 21–34.

Ellis, Stephen, "Les prolongements du conflit israélo-arabe: le cas du Sierra Leone", *Politique Africaine*, 30 (1988), pp. 69–75.

————, *The Mask of Anarchy: The Destruction of Liberia and the Religious Dimension of an African Civil War* (1999; new edn, Hurst & Co. and New York University Press, London and New York, 2007).

————, "The Okija Shrine: Death and Life in Nigerian Politics", *Journal of African History*, 49, 3 (2008), pp. 445–66.

————, and Gerrie ter Haar, *Worlds of Power: Religious Thought and Political Practice in Africa* (Hurst & Co., London, 2004).

Enweremadu, David, *Anti-Corruption Campaign in Nigeria (1999–2007): The Politics of a Failed Reform* (IFRA-Nigeria and the African Studies Centre, Ibadan and Leiden, 2012).

Falola, Toyin, "Money and Informal Credit Institutions in Colonial Western Nigeria", in Jane Guyer (ed.), *Money Matters: Instability, Values and Social Payments in the Modern History of West African Communities* (James Currey, London, 1995), pp. 162–87.

————, and Julius Ihonvbere, *The Rise and Fall of Nigeria's Second Republic, 1979–84* (Zed Books, London, 1985).

Fayemiwo, Moshood Ademola, and Margie Marie Neal, *Aliko Mohammad Dangote: The Biography of the Richest Black Person in the World* (Strategic Book Publishing, Houston, TX, 2013).

Forrest, Tom, "The Political Economy of Civil Rule and the Economic Crisis in Nigeria (1979–84)", *Review of African Political Economy*, 13, 35 (1986), pp. 4–26.

Fottorino, Eric, *La Piste blanche: L'Afrique sous l'emprise de la drogue* (Balland, Paris, 1991).

Fourchard, Laurent, "Prêt sur gages et traite des femmes au Nigéria, fin 19ᵉ-années 1950", in Bénédicte Lavaud-Legendre (ed.), *Prostitution nigériane, entre rêves de migration et réalité de la traite* (Karthala, Paris, 2013), pp. 15–32.

Friedman, Robert I., *Red Mafiya: How the Russian Mob has Invaded America* (Little, Brown, Boston etc., 2000).

BIBLIOGRAPHY

Friedrichs, David O. (ed.), *State Crime* (2 vols, Ashgate, Aldershot and Brookfield VT, 1998).

Gambetta, Diego, *The Sicilian Mafia: The Business of Private Protection* (Harvard University Press, Cambridge, MA, 1993).

Gastrow, Peter, *Termites at Work: A Report on Transnational Organized Crime and State Erosion in Kenya* (International Peace Institute, New York, 2011).

Gates, Henry Louis, "Powell and The Black Elite", *The New Yorker*, 25 September 1995.

Gauchet, Marcel (trans. Oscar Burge), *The Disenchantment of the World: A Political History of Religion* (Princeton University Press, Princeton, NJ, 1999).

Glenny, Misha, *McMafia: Seriously Organised Crime* (Vintage Books, London, 2009).

———, *Dark Market: How Hackers Became the New Mafia* (Vintage Books, London, 2012).

Glickman, Harvey, "The Nigerian '419' Advance Fee Scams: Prank or Peril?", *Canadian Journal of African Studies*, 39, 3 (2005), pp. 463–76.

Global Witness, *"International Thief Thief": How British Banks are Complicit in Nigerian Corruption* (London, 2010).

Goodchild, Philip, *The Theology of Money* (SCM Press, London, 2007).

Gowan, Peter, *The Global Gamble: Washington's Faustian Bid for World Dominance* (Verso, London and New York, 1999).

Graeber, David, *Debt: The First 5,000 Years* (Melville House, Hoboken, NJ, 2011).

Green, Penny, *Drugs, Trafficking and Criminal Policy: The Scapegoat Strategy* (Waterside Press, Winchester, 1998).

Guyer, Jane I., *Marginal Gains: Monetary Transactions in Atlantic Africa* (University of Chicago Press, Chicago and London, 2004).

Hailey, Lord (William Malcolm), *An African Survey* (Oxford University Press, London, 1938).

Haynes, Jonathan, "Political Critique in Nigerian Video Films", *African Affairs*, 105, 421 (2006), pp. 511–33.

Hives, Frank, and Gascoine Lumley, *Ju-Ju and Justice in Nigeria* (1930; Penguin edn., Harmondsworth, 1940).

Horton, Robin, "Stateless Societies in the History of West Africa", in J.F. Ade Ajayi and Michael Crowder (eds), *History of West Africa* (2 vols, Harlow, 1985), I, pp. 78–119.

———, *Patterns of Thought in Africa and the West: Essays on Magic, Religion and Science* (Cambridge University Press, 1997).

Igbafe, Philip A., *Benin Under British Administration: The Impact of Colonial Rule on an African Kingdom, 1897–1938* (Longman, London, 1979).

BIBLIOGRAPHY

Igbokwe, Joe, *Igbos: 25 Years After Biafra* (Advent Communications, no place given, 1995).

Iliffe, John, *Honour in African History* (Cambridge University Press, 2005).

———, *Obasanjo, Nigeria and the World* (James Currey, Oxford, 2011).

Joly, Eva, *Est-ce dans ce monde-là que nous voulons vivre?* (Eds. Les Arènes, Paris, 2003).

Jones, Mark, "Nigerian Crime Networks in the United States", *International Journal of Offender Therapy and Comparative Criminology*, 37, 1 (1993), pp. 59–73.

Joseph, Richard A., *Democracy and Prebendal Politics in Nigeria: The Rise and Fall of the Second Republic* (Cambridge University Press, 1987).

Kalu, Ogbu U., "Missionaries, Colonial Government and Secret Societies in South-Eastern Igboland, 1920–1950", *Journal of the Historical Society of Nigeria*, 9, 1 (1977), pp. 75–90.

———, "The Religious Dimension of the Legitimacy Crisis, 1993–1998", in Toyin Falola (ed.), *Nigeria in the Twentieth Century* (Carolina Academic Press, Durham, NC, 2002), pp. 667–85.

Katsouris, Christina, and Aaron Sayne, *Nigeria's Criminal Crude: International Options to Combat the Export of Stolen Oil* (Royal Institute of International Affairs, London, 2013).

Kirk-Greene, A.H.M. (ed.), *Lugard and the Amalgamation of Nigeria: A Documentary Record* (Frank Cass, London, 1968).

———, "Introduction", in Kirk-Greene (ed.), *Lugard and the Amalgamation of Nigeria*, pp. 1–35.

Klein, Axel, "Trapped in the Traffick: Growing Problems of Drug Consumption in Lagos", *Journal of Modern African Studies*, 32, 4 (1994), pp. 657–77.

Korieh, Chima J., *The Land Has Changed: History, Society, and Gender in Colonial Eastern Nigeria* (University of Calgary Press, 2010).

Kruisbergen, E.W., H.G. van der Bunt and E.R. Kleemans, *Georganiseerde Criminaliteit in Nederland* (Boom Lemona Uitgevers, Meppel, 2012).

Larr, Frisky (Friday Agbonlahor), *Africa's Diabolical Entrapment* (AuthorHouse, Bloomington, IN, 2013).

Lawal, A.A., *Corruption in Nigeria: A Colonial Legacy* (University of Lagos, 2006), text of an inaugural lecture on 7 June 2006.

Leggett, Ted, *Rainbow Vice: The Drugs and Sex Industries in the New South Africa* (Zed Books, London, 2002).

Lewis, Peter, "From Prebendalism to Predation: The Political Economy of Decline in Nigeria", *Journal of Modern African Studies*, 34, 1 (1996), pp. 79–103.

Lugard, Lord (Frederick), *The Dual Mandate in British Tropical Africa* (1922; 5th edn, Frank Cass, London 1965).

———, "Report on the Amalgamation of Northern and Southern Nigeria", in Kirk-Greene (ed.), *Lugard and the Amalgamation of Nigeria*.

Lynn, M. (ed.), *British Documents on the End of Empire. Series B, Country Volumes, Volume 7* (The Stationery Office, London, 2001).

Mackintosh, John P., *Nigerian Government and Politics* (Geo. Allen and Unwin, London, 1966).

Maier, Karl, *This House Has Fallen: Midnight in Nigeria* (2000; Basic Books, New York, 2002).

Marenin, Otwin, "The Anini Saga: Armed Robbery and the Reproduction of Ideology in Nigeria", *Journal of Modern African Studies*, 25, 2 (1987), pp. 259–81.

Marshall, Ruth, *Political Spiritualities: The Pentecostal Revolution in Nigeria* (University of Chicago Press, 2009).

Martin, Felix, *Money: The Unauthorised Biography* (Bodley Head, London, 2013).

Matera, Marc, Misty L. Bastian and Susan Kingsley Kent, *The Women's War of 1929: Gender and Violence in Colonial Nigeria* (Palgrave Macmillan, Basingstoke, 2012).

Mayah, Emmanuel, "Europe by Desert: Tears of African Migrants", in UNESCO, *The Global Investigative Journalism Casebook* (UNESCO series on Journalism Education, Paris, 2012), pp. 50–66.

Mazzitelli, Antonio L., "Transnational Organized Crime in West Africa: The Additional Challenge", *International Affairs*, 83, 6 (2007), pp. 1071–90.

Meagher, Kate, "Social Capital, Social Liabilities, and Political Capital: Social Networks and Informal Manufacturing in Nigeria', *African Affairs*, 105, 421 (2006), pp. 553–82.

———, "Hijacking Civil Society: The Inside Story of the Bakassi Boys Vigilante Group of South-eastern Nigeria", *Journal of Modern African Studies*, 45, 1 (2007), pp. 89–115.

Mintzberg, Henry, *Structure in Fives: Designing Effective Organizations* (1983; second edn, Prentice Hall, Englewood Cliffs, NJ, 1993).

Naylor, R.T., *Wages of Crime: Black Markets, Illegal Finance, and the Underworld Economy* (revised edn., Cornell Univ. Press, Ithaca and London, 2004).

Nduka, Otonti, *Western Education and the Nigerian Cultural Background* (Oxford University Press, Ibadan, 1964).

Nicolson, I.F., *The Administration of Nigeria 1900–1960: Men, Methods and Myths* (Clarendon Press, Oxford, 1969).

Nkwoh, Marius, *The Sorrows of Man* (Okolue's Bookshop, Enugu, 1963).

Nwauwa, A.O., "Integrating Arochukwu into the Regional Chronological Structure", *History in Africa*, 18 (1991), pp. 297–310.

Obadare, Ebenezer, "White-collar fundamentalism: interrogating youth religiosity on Nigerian university campuses", *Journal of Modern African Studies*, 45, 4 (2007), pp. 517–37.

Obemsulu, Christine (ed.), *Dimensions of Social Problems in Nigeria* (seminar proceedings, National Institute for Policy and Strategic Studies, Kuru, 1982).

Offiong, Daniel A., *Secret Cults in Nigerian Tertiary Institutions* (Fourth Dimension, Enugu, 2003).

Ojo, Matthias Olufemi Dada, "Incorporation of Ayelala Traditional Religion into Nigerian Criminal Justice System: An Opinion Survey of Igbesa Community People in Ogun State, Nigeria", Department of Ethnology and Anthropology, University of Belgrade, *Issues in Ethnology and Anthropology*, 4, 9 (2014). Available on Internet at: http://www.anthroserbia.org/Content/PDF/Articles/5838b065d0dc4e7cbb8c2985efc7edcf.pdf [accessed 26 June 2015].

Okigbo, P.N.C., *Nigerian Public Finance* (Longman, London, 1965).

Okonkwo, C.O., *Okonkwo and Naish on Criminal Law in Nigeria* (1964; Sweet and Maxwell, London, 2nd edn, 1980).

Okonta, Ike, "Nigeria: Chronicle of a Dying State", *Current History* 104, 682 (May 2005), pp. 203–8.

Olukoju, Ayodeji, "Self-help Criminality as Resistance? Currency Counterfeiting in Colonial Nigeria", *International Review of Social History*, 45, 3 (2000), pp. 385–407.

Omisakin, I.S., *Crime Trends and Prevention Strategies in Nigeria: A Study of Old Oyo State* (Monograph series no. 9, Nigerian Institute of Social and Economic Research, Ibadan, 1998).

Onwubiko, K.B.C., *School Certificate History of West Africa*, 1973.

Orewa, G. Oka, *We Are All Guilty: The Nigerian Crisis*, vol. 1 (Spectrum Books, Ibadan, 1997).

Oriji, J.N., "Warfare, the Overseas Slave Trade and Aro Expansion in the Igbo Hinterland", *Ikenga*, 7, 1–2 (1985), pp. 156–66.

Osaghae, Eghosa, *Crippled Giant: Nigeria Since Independence* (Hurst & Co., London, 1998).

Osifodunrin, Paul, "Escapee Criminals and Crime Control in Colonial Southwestern Nigeria, 1861–1945", *IFRA Special Research Issue*, 1 (2005), pp. 57–77.

Othman, Shehu, "Classes, Crises and Coup: The Demise of Shagari's Regime", *African Affairs*, 83, 333 (1984), pp. 441–61.

Owoade, M. Adekunle, "The Military and the Criminal Law in Nigeria", *Journal of African Law*, 33, 2 (1989), pp. 135–148.

Ozekhome, Mike A.A., "Delayed Prosecution and Extra Judicial Killings: The Deadly Implications", in Patrick Keku and Tunde Akingbade (eds),

BIBLIOGRAPHY

Dangerous Days and Savage Nights: Countering the Menace of Armed Robbery in Nigeria (1ˢᵗ Books Library, no place given, 2003), pp. 55–102.

Palan, Ronen, *The Offshore World: Sovereign Markets, Virtual Places, and Nomad Millionaires* (Cornell University Press, London and Ithaca, 2003).

————, Richard Murphy and Christian Chavagneux, *Tax Havens: How Globalization Really Works* (Cornell Studies in Money, Cornell University Press, Ithaca, NY, 2010).

Panter-Brick, Keith (ed.), *Soldiers and Oil: The Political Transformation of Nigeria* (Frank Cass, London, 1978).

Passas, Nikos (ed.), *Organized Crime* (Dartmouth Publishing Co., Aldershot, 1995).

Patterson, Orlando, *Slavery and Social Death* (Harvard University Press, 1982).

Peel, J.D.Y., *Religious Encounter and the Making of the Yoruba* (Indiana University Press, Bloomington, IN, 2000).

Peel, Michael, *Nigeria-Related Financial Crime and its Links with Britain* (Royal Institute of International Affairs, London, 2006).

Perham, Margery, *Native Administration in Nigeria* (1937; 2ⁿᵈ impression, Oxford University Press, 1962).

Pierce, Steven, "Looking like a State: Colonialism and the Discourse of Corruption in Northern Nigeria", *Comparative Studies in Society and History*, 48, 4 (2006), pp. 887–914.

Pratten, David, *The Man-Leopard Murders: History and Society in Colonial Nigeria* (Edinburgh University Press, Edinburgh, 2007).

Quantson, Kofi Bentsum, *Travelling and Seeing: Johnny Just Come* (NAPASVIL Ventures, Accra, 2002).

Ranger, Terence, "Scotland Yard in the Bush: Medicine Murders, Child Witches and the Construction of the Occult: A Literature Review", *Africa*, 77, 2 (2007), pp. 272–83.

Rimmer, Douglas, "Elements of the Political Economy", in K. Panter-Brick (ed.), *Soldiers and Oil*, pp. 141–65.

————, "Development in Nigeria: An Overview", in Henry Bienen and V.P. Diejomaoh (eds), *The Political Economy of Income Distribution in Nigeria* (Holmes and Meier, New York and London, 1981), pp. 29–87.

Saro-Wiwa, Ken, *On a Darkling Plain: An Account of the Nigerian Civil War* (Saros, Epsom, 1989).

Schoenmakers, Yvette M.M., Edo de Vries Robbé and Anton Ph. van Wijk, *Mountains of Gold: An Exploratory Research on 419 Fraud* (CrimiReeks, SWP Publishers, Amsterdam, 2009).

Seaford, Richard, *Money and the Early Greek Mind: Homer, Philosophy, Tragedy* (Cambridge University Press, 2004).

BIBLIOGRAPHY

Sharwood Smith, Bryan, *"But Always as Friends"*: *Northern Nigeria and the Cameroons, 1921–1957* (Geo. Allen and Unwin, London, 1969).

Shaw, Mark, "The Political Economy of Crime and Conflict in Sub-Saharan Africa", *South African Journal of International Affairs*, 8, 2 (2001), pp. 57–69.

―――, *Crime as Business, Business as Crime: West African Criminal Networks in Southern Africa* (South African Institute of International Affairs, Johannesburg, 2003).

Shaxson, Nicholas, *Poisoned Wells: The Dirty Politics of African Oil* (Palgrave Macmillan, New York, 2007).

Siegel, Dina, "Nigeriaanse Madams in de Mensenhandel in Nederland", *Justitiële Verkenningen*, 33, 7 (2007), pp. 39–49.

Simcox, David, "The Nigerian Crime Network: Feasting on America's Innocence and Slipshod ID System", *The Social Contract*, 3, 3 (1993), pp. 168–71.

Simon, Okolo Ben, "Demystifying the Advance-fee Fraud Network", *African Security Review*, 18, 4 (2009), pp. 5–18.

Sklar, Richard L., *Nigerian Political Parties: Power in an Emergent African Nation* (1963; Africa World Press edn, Trenton, NJ, 2004).

Sluyterman, Keetie, *Keeping Competitive in Turbulent Markets, 1973–2007: A History of Royal Dutch Shell* (Vol. IV, Oxford University Press, 2007).

Smith, Daniel Jordan, "'The Arrow of God': Pentecostalism, Inequality, and the Supernatural in South-eastern Nigeria", *Africa* 71, 4 (2001), pp. 587–613.

―――, "The Bakassi Boys: Vigilantism, Violence and Political Imagination in Nigeria", *Cultural Anthropology*, 19, 3 (2004), pp. 429–55.

―――, "Corruption, culture politique et démocratie au Nigéria: réactions populaires à la croisade anti-corruption du président Obasanjo », *Politique africaine*, 106 (2007), pp. 28–45.

―――, A *Culture of Corruption: Everyday Deception and Popular Discontent in Nigeria* (Princeton University Press, 2008).

Smith, Russell G., Michael N. Holmes and Philip Kaufmann, "Nigerian Advance Fee Fraud", *Australian Institute of Criminology, Trends & Issues*, 121 (July 1999).

Soares de Oliveira, Ricardo, *Oil and Politics in the Gulf of Guinea* (Hurst & Co., London, 2007).

Soyinka, Kayode, *Diplomatic Baggage: Mossad and Nigeria: The Dikko Story* (Newswatch Books, Lagos, 1994).

Soyinka, Wole, *Cults: A People in Denial* (Interventions III, Bookcraft and Farafina, Ibadan and Lagos, 2005).

Strong Man of Pen [Okenwa Olisa], *Life Turns Man Upside Down* (Njoku and Sons, Onitsha, n.d.).

BIBLIOGRAPHY

Talbot, P. Amaury, *Tribes of the Niger Delta: Their Religions and Customs* (1932; Frank Cass, London, 1967).

Tamuno, Tekena, and Robin Horton, "The Changing Position of Secret Societies and Cults in Modern Nigeria", *African Notes*, 5, 2 (1969), pp. 36–62.

Tasie, G.I.K., "Religion and Moral Depravity in Contemporary Nigeria", *Nigerian Journal of Theology*, 19 (2005), pp. 88–98.

Timamy, M.H. Khalil, "African Leaders and Corruption", *Review of African Political Economy*, 104–5 (2005), pp. 383–93.

Truell, Peter, and Larry Gurwin, *False Profits: The Inside Story of BCCI, the World's Most Corrupt Financial Empire* (Houghton Mifflin, Boston, MA, 1992).

Tseayo, J.I., *Conflict and Incorporation in Nigeria: The Integration of the Tiv* (Gaskia Corp., Zaria, 1975).

Turner, Terisa, "Commercial Capitalism and the 1975 Coup", in Panter-Brick (ed.), *Soldiers and Oil*, pp. 166–97.

Uche, Chibuike, "Bank of England versus the IBRD: Did the Nigerian Colony Deserve a Central Bank?", *Explorations in Economic History*, 34, 2 (1997), pp. 220–41.

Uko, Ndaeyo, *Romancing the Gun: The Press as Promoter of Military Rule* (Africa World Press, Trenton, NJ, 2003).

United Nations Office on Drugs and Crime, *Transnational Organized Crime in the West African Region* (UN, New York, 2005).

United States Department of State, *Foreign Relations of the United States, 1969–76, Volume E-5, Part 1, Documents on Sub-Saharan Africa, 1969–1972* (United States Government Printing Office, Washington DC, 2006).

———, *Foreign Relations of the United States, 1969–1976, Volume E-6, Documents on Africa, 1973–1976* (United States Government Printing Office, Washington DC, 2009).

United States Senate, *The BCCI Affair: A Report to the Committee on Foreign Relations United States Senate by Senator John Kerry and Senator Hank Brown* (U.S. Government Printing Office, Washington DC, 1993).

Usman, Yusufa Bala, "The Central Role of Corruption in a Dependent Capitalist Economy: The Nigerian Experience", NISER public lecture at the University of Lagos, 5 May 1983, published in the *Nigerian Standard*, 13 May 1983.

Uzorma, Iyke Nathan, *Occult Grand Master Now in Christ* (private publication, Benin City, 1994).

Volkov, Vadim, *Violent Entrepreneurs: The Use of Force in the Making of Russian Capitalism* (Cornell University Press, Ithaca, NY, 2002).

War Against Indiscipline: First Anniversary Assessment (National Institute for Policy and Strategic Studies, Kuru, 1985).

Williams, Gavin, *State and Society in Nigeria* (Afrografika, Ondo State, 1980).

BIBLIOGRAPHY

————, "Marketing Without and With Marketing Boards: The Origins of State Marketing Boards in Nigeria", *Review of African Political Economy*, 34 (1985), pp. 4–15.

Williams, Pat Ama Tokunbo, "Religion, Violence and Displacement in Nigeria", in Paul E. Lovejoy and Pat A.T. Williams (eds), *Displacement and the Politics of Violence in Nigeria* (Brill, Leiden, 1997), pp. 33–49.

Williams, Robert, *Political Corruption in Africa* (Gower Publishing Co., Aldershot etc., 1987).

Wilmot, Patrick, *Nigeria: The Nightmare Scenario* (Interventions VI, Bookcraft and Farafina, Ibadan and Lagos, 2007).

Wraith, Ronald, and Edgar Simpkins, *Corruption in Developing Countries* (Geo. Allen and Unwin, London, 1963).

INDEX

Abacha, Sani, 92, 111, 129, 143, 145, 158, 159, 195; Abba, 144
Abakaliki, 40
Abba, Alkasum, 61
Abia State, 188, 202
Abidjan, 158, 172
Abubakar, Atiku, 154, 202, 203
Abuja, 7, 121, 168, 199
Accra, 92, 129
Achebe, Chinua, 106, 225
Action Group, 46, 47, 48, 49, 59, 62, 64, 69, 76, 77, 82
Adebanwi, Wade, 194
Adekunle, Benjamin, 103, 104
Addo, Emmanuel Boateng, 172
advance-fee fraud, 2, 3, 4, 126, 160, 161, 162, 163, 164, 165, 190; see also Four One Nine
Afghanistan, 9, 175, 179
Afigbo, A.E., 198
Afikpo Division, 35
Africa (general), 9, 10, 14, 16, 17, 19, 20, 23, 28, 29, 30, 31, 44, 45, 47, 50, 51, 54, 56, 57, 62, 70, 72, 73, 80, 95, 104, 106, 127, 129, 141, 146, 163, 165, 172, 173, 175, 177, 179, 184, 186, 194, 219, 224, 225, 229

African Continental Bank, 45, 58, 81
African National Congress, 212, 213
Agbakoba, Mrs, 166
Aghedo, Philip, 113, 114
Agip, 151
Aguiyi-Ironsi, Johnson, 81, 82, 83
Ajasco Boys, 27
Ajegunle, 102
Ajudua, Fred, 169, 188
Akak, Eyo A., 55, 56, 67
Akatarian, 184
Ake, Claude, 158
Akintola, Samuel, 64, 76, 80; Omodele, 64
Aklint, A.A., 70
Akosa, Fred, 125
Akubueze, Joe Brown, 178
Akunyili, Dora, 180
Alagbe, Moses, 186
Alamieyeseigha, Diepreye, 154, 155
Aliyu, Nuhu, 155
America, see United States; the Americas, 87, 182, 216; African-American 95; North, 93, 104, 121, 122, 123; South, Latin,

INDEX

122, 125, 171, 173, 174, 175, 179

Amin, Idi, 88

Amnesty International, 102

Amsterdam, 2, 162, 163, 164, 173, 179, 180, 181, 186; Schiphol Airport, 173, 179, 180, 181; Zuidoost, Bijlmer district, 162, 186

Anajemba, Ikechukwu, 167, 168; Amaka, 167, 168

Anambra State, 168, 188, 189, 198, 199, 201, 203, 205

Andreski, Stanislav, 66, 68, 91, 114, 219

Andropov (Yuri), 216

Angola, 213

Anini, Lawrence, 103

Annang, 40

Apapa, 100

Apter, Andrew, 141

Arcadia, 153

armed robbery, 32, 44, 86, 101, 102, 103, 113, 114, 159, 201; Robbery and Firearms tribunal, 102; Special Anti-Robbery Squad, 198

Aro, 33, 34, 35, 36, 197, 200, 201; Aro-Chuku, 35, 37

Arochukwu, *see* shrines

article 419, *see* Four One Nine

Aruba, 173

Aruosa church, 48

Asia, 6, 122, 169, 173, 174, 175, 177, 189; Central, 173; East, 180; Southeast, 44, 173, 175

Asiodu, Philip, 115

Atlanta (Georgia) 125

Atta, A.A., 87

Australia, 28, 43, 158

Awolowo, Obafemi, 15, 18, 19, 46, 47, 48, 52, 53, 59, 64, 75, 76, 106; University, 143

Ayelala, 185, 195, 196

Ayida, Alison, 106

Azikiwe, Nnandi, 8, 13, 24, 44, 45, 46, 47, 49, 52, 53, 57, 58, 62, 65, 80; Airport, 168

Babangida, Ibrahim, 133, 138–47, 158, 159, 171, 225, 226; Unlimited, 140; IBB, 137, 138, 141, 225; Maradona, 137

Bahamas, 92, 144

Bakassi Boys, 201, 203

Bako, Alhaji Audu, 100

Balagula, Marat, 171

Balewa, Tafawa, 51, 63, 65, 80

Balkans, 152

Balogun, Tafa, 199, 203, 206, 209

Bamaiyi, Musa, 173

Banco Noroeste, 166, 167, 168, 197

Bangkok, 6, 123, 175, 193; Pratunum district, 175

Banjo, Ayo, 114, 143

Barclays, 154

Bassey, Rev. R.N.Y., 29

Bavaria, 169

Bayelsa State, 154

BCCI, 132, 139, 140

Beirut, 91

Belgium, 181, 186

Bello, Ahmadu, 52, 53, 66, 80, 83, 138; University, 110, 138

Bende Division, 36

Benin (Republic), 88, 98, 144, 172, 178, 182

Benin City, 47, 48, 49, 64, 88, 105, 134, 135, 181, 182, 183, 184, 191, 196; Criminal Investigation Department, 184; Native Administration, 48; Oba of, 47,

48, 49, 191; University, 112, 113; *see also* Dahomey

Benin State, 103

Bermuda, 153

Berry, Mike, 165

Biafra, 84, 85, 86, 87, 89, 93, 95, 196, 205; Students Association, 87; War, 85, 86, 87, 89, 90, 91, 92, 93, 95, 97, 101, 102, 103, 107, 133, 134, 190, 228

Big Men, 33, 103; *amala*, 103

Black Axe, 112, 143, 191, 192, 210, 212

Black Boys, 27

Black Scorpion, 103

Boko Haram, 150, 210, 227

Bonny River, 86

Borini Prono, 68

Borno State, 210

Bornu, 10

Boro, Isaac Adaka, 86, 149

Boston, 164

Bourdillon, Bernard, 43

Boy Adam, 209

Brandeis, Louis, 220

Brazil, 105, 115, 152, 166, 170, 173, 197

bribery, 67, 68, 69, 70, 71, 72, 74, 75, 76, 80, 89, 90, 101, 105, 106, 139, 141, 148, 155, 156, 158, 166, 167, 218, 219; *awuf*, 51; dash system, 70, 74, 156, 228; Nigerian League of Bribe Scorners, 56

Brimah, Peregrino, 61

Britain, British, 8, 9, 10, 11, 12, 13, 14, 15, 19, 20, 23, 24, 25, 27, 33, 34, 35, 38, 39, 40, 41, 43, 44, 45, 46, 51, 52, 53, 56, 57, 58, 61, 62, 69, 70, 72, 74, 82, 87, 97, 101, 114, 117, 119, 122, 125, 132, 157, 161, 179,

183, 185, 196, 197, 209, 216, 219, 220, 228; British Crown, 8, 14, 73; High Commission, 63, 65, 68, 226; Resident, 13, 40, 48; Royal Navy, 8, 34

Buccaneers, 111, 113, 114

Buhari, Muhammadu, 129, 130, 132, 133, 138, 144, 147

Burkina Faso, 129, 172; *see also* Upper Volta

Burma, 9

Calabar, 24, 40, 110; College of Technology, 112; Province, 37, 40; University, 112

California, 87, 154

caliphate, *see* Sokoto

Cambridge, 50

Cameroon, 178; the Cameroons, 28, 36, 45, 47

Camorra, 170

campus cults, 109, 110, 111, 112, 113, 142, 143, 151, 191, 210, 221, 228

Canada, 28, 29, 97, 165, 169, 213

Cape Verde, 178

Cayman Islands, 73, 166

Celestial Church of Christ, 193

Celtel, 146

Central African Republic, 213

Central Bank of Nigeria, 88, 98, 100, 116, 117, 126, 140, 153, 159, 166, 167, 170

Ceuta, 184

Ceylon, 43

Chad, 99

Chagoury, O., 92; Gilbert, 92

Chambliss, William J., 218

Channel Islands, 73

Cheney, Dick, 156

Chicago, 193

chiefs, 10, 12, 14, 18, 20, 24, 28,

34, 40, 41, 47, 48, 72, 85, 190, 197; chieftaincies, 13, 84, 190, 200; Warrant Chiefs, 20, 41
child-trafficking, *see* sex business
China, 152, 157, 180
Chissano, President, 213
Christian(ity), 17, 29, 31, 32, 44, 47, 48, 56, 84, 108, 134, 161, 207, 208, 209, 227; churches, 23, 109, 208, 211, 212, 226, 227
Churchill, Winston, 24
Ciroma, Mallam Liman, 64, 67
civil war, *see* Biafra War
Clinton Foundation, 92
Cockayne, James, 190
Coker tribunal, 75
Cold War, 215, 221
Colombia, 123, 170
colonialism, 3, 4, 5, 7, 8, 9, 10, 11, 12, 13, 14, 15, 16, 17, 18, 19, 20, 21, 23, 24, 25, 26, 27, 28, 29, 30, 31, 33, 34, 35, 36, 38, 39, 40, 43, 44, 45, 46, 48, 51, 52, 53, 54, 55, 56, 57, 59, 61, 63, 65, 67, 68, 69, 70, 71, 87, 97, 102, 104, 114, 125, 134, 149, 190, 194, 196, 197, 198, 200, 207, 209, 211, 216, 219, 220, 223, 224, 225, 227, 228; decolonisation, 72, 73, 225, 228; precolonial, 32, 33, 96, 113, 207, 220, 223, 224
Commissioner of Prisons, 38, 51
Companies and Intellectual Properties Registration Office, 158
confidence tricksters, 18, 27, 104; Wayo tricksters, 26
confraternities, *see* secret societies; *see also* campus cults
Congo, 34, 103, 197

Constituent Assembly, 110
corruption, 4, 10, 11, 18, 19, 21, 50–56, 57–59, 63, 64, 65, 66, 67, 68, 70, 71, 72, 74–77, 79, 80, 81, 82, 83, 87, 89, 90, 91, 93, 95, 99, 100, 103, 104, 105, 106–14, 117, 119, 120, 129, 130, 132, 133, 139, 140, 141, 144, 145, 154, 155, 156, 171, 195, 206, 207, 210, 211, 216, 219, 220, 222, 223, 224, 225, 226, 228, 229; anti-corruption, 55, 56, 90, 91, 119, 128–33, 166
Côte d'Ivoire, 115, 158, 172
Cotonou, 144, 172, 186
Crentsil, P., 3, 25, 26, 28
Cross River, 33, 35, 37, 38, 197
cults, 40, 48, 49, 82, 90, 101, 106–14, 142, 143, 150, 151, 160, 191, 192, 193, 194–98, 209, 210, 213, 221, 228; *see also* campus cults, secret societies; Secret Cult and Similar Activities (Prohibition) Law, 151
culture, 3, 14, 21, 24, 30, 46, 55, 56, 72, 83, 84, 93, 95, 108, 121, 128, 157, 158, 159, 194, 195, 205, 206, 223, 230
cyber-crime, 160, 161, 162, 195; *see also* Internet
Cyprus, 155

Dahomey, 88, 98, 213
Dangote, Aliko, 146
Danjuma, Theophilus, 107, 114, 120
Dasuki, Ibrahim, 138, 139
Daura, Mamman, 132
Delta State, 135, 169
Denmark, 155
development, 45, 51, 55, 59, 96,

97, 101, 106, 149, 154, 158, 228

diaspora, 33, 114, 121, 134, 157, 195, 228

Dike, Kenneth, 93

Dikko, Umaru, 116, 131, 132

divination, 17, 23, 24, 26, 30

drug trade, 91, 92, 103, 104, 121–24, 131, 133, 139, 152, 157, 158, 162, 163, 171, 172, 173, 176, 177, 187, 188, 189, 190, 193, 211, 223, 227, 229; Drug Enforcement Administration, 6, 121

drugs, 104, 119, 121, 122, 124, 128, 131, 139, 142, 152, 169, 170–80, 190, 223, 230; amphetamines, 104, 180; cannabis, 92, 104; cocaine, 121, 122, 123, 131, 151, 152, 162, 170, 173, 175, 177, 178, 179, 190; diamorphine, 177; heroin, 87, 91, 92, 121, 122, 123, 124, 128, 131, 170, 171, 172, 173, 174, 175, 177, 178, 179, 180; mandrax, 172; marijuana, 100, 103, 104, 121, 122, 172; narcotics, 92, 121, 122, 171, 172, 173, 174, 178, 188, 193; pharmaceutical, 180

Dubai, 157, 189

Dutch, see Netherlands

Dutch Antilles, 173

East Africa, 179

Eastern Region, 38, 44, 57, 58, 62, 66, 67, 68, 75, 76, 77, 80, 81, 84, 85, 86, 133; House of Representatives, 66; Working Committee, 77

Economic and Financial Crimes Commission, 153, 166, 168, 169, 170

ECOWAS, 172

Ecuador, 154

Edegbe, Enadeghe Kingsley, 181

Edo State, 134, 135, 181, 182, 185, 186, 188, 192, 195, 212; Topmen Group, 181; Otu Edu, 49

education, 20, 21, 23, 24, 46, 54, 55, 74, 81, 84, 91, 110, 119, 120, 121, 134, 135, 142, 158, 159, 185; missionary, 21, 23, 24, 29, 53, 190, 224, 228

Egbe Omo Odudawa, 46

Egbutche, 47

Eikineh, Prince, 36, 37, 38

Eiye, 11, 192; Supreme Eiye Confraternity, 111

Ekeh, Peter, 194

Ekewuba, Alexander Ezeugo, 208

Ekpe, 205

Ekpoti, 35

Ekpumopolo, Government, 151 [Tompolo]

Ektor, Gilbert, 180, 181

Elf, 151

embezzlement, 3, 4, 71, 93, 108, 119, 137, 141, 206, 219, 230

emir, emirate, 9, 10 11, 12, 13, 14, 15, 19, 61, 65, 77, 213, 220

England, see Britain; Church of, 47; Bank of, 117

Enugu, 5, 6, 4, 89; State, 188

ethnicity, 46, 47, 49, 54, 63, 67, 83, 84, 85, 86, 114, 133–35, 137, 152, 154, 188, 189, 194

Europe, 2, 15, 17, 20, 23, 30, 33, 38, 41, 49, 56, 74, 92, 93, 100, 104, 121, 122, 123, 125, 126, 134, 144, 154, 165, 170, 172,

175, 179, 182, 183, 184, 185, 186, 187, 188, 207, 210, 216, 222, 223
Exchange Control decree, 99
Export Credits Guarantee Department, 97
Eyadéma, Gnassingbé, 172
Eyohomi, Lawrence, 186

Fani-Kayode, Remikulun, 76; Fani Power Youth Movement, 76
Fawehinmi, Gani, 223
Federal Military Government, 96, 99, 100, 110, 115
Federated Full Gospel Assemblies, 29
Fernandes, Deinde, 212, 213 [Baron Dudley, Garsan Fulani of Kano]
FESTAC, 108, 121
Feyide, M.O., 96
Finance Corporation, 58
First Republic, 82, 120, 166, 219
Foreign Jurisdiction Act, 14
Forestal, 140
Foster-Sutton, Sir Stafford, 58; tribunal, 58
Four One Nine, 2, 3, 25, 81, 97, 119, 124–8, 141, 153, 158, 159, 162, 163, 165–170, 193, 195, 201, 203, 204; mugu, 128, 163, 188
Fourth Republic, 145, 146, 158
France, 14, 17, 124, 172, 181, 229
Franco, General, 80
fraud, 2, 3, 4, 19, 26, 27, 28, 29, 51, 59, 69, 77, 81, 87, 92, 93, 97, 103, 105, 117, 119, 124, 125, 126, 127, 128, 138, 139, 140, 141, 142, 153, 158, 159, 160, 161, 162, 163, 164, 165,

166, 167, 168, 170, 188, 193, 195, 204, 206, 209, 212, 219, 222, 223, 227, 229, 230; see also Four One Nine
Freemasons, 211
Fulani, 53, 157; see also Hausa

Gadaffi, Colonel, 129
Gambia, 176, 179
Gambo, Mohammadu, 203
Gamji association, 111
Garden, J.W., 36
Gauchet, Marcel, 17
Gelbard, Robert S., 174
Geneva, 79
George V, King, 8
Germany, 69, 70, 128, 140, 155, 168, 169, 180; West, 70, 121
Ghana, 25, 80, 87, 120, 123, 129, 172, 174, 178, 186, 228; see also Gold Coast
gift-giving, 19, 32, 54, 56, 67, 70, 72, 93, 223, 224
Gilbertson, Gert, 1
Giwa, Dele, 139
Glencore, 153
Glo, 146
Global West Vessel Service, 151
godfathers, see patronage
Gold, Colin S., 92
Gold Coast, 25, 36, 37, 38, 45
Gowon, Yakubu, 84, 85, 90, 96, 100, 106, 107, 115
Greece, 30, 97, 148, 185
Guangzhou, 157
Guinea-Bissau, 178
Guinea-Conakry, 178, 179
Gulf War, 140
Gumbi, Sheikh Ahmad, 211

Hailey, Lord, 9

Haiti, 182
hajj, 104, 122
Halliburton, 155
Hamburg, 121
Harcourt, Lewis Vernon, 8
Harrison, Anthony, 185
Hausa, 11, 62, 117; language, 80;
    Hausaland, 9; Hausa-Fulani, 10,
    21, 86
hawala, 162
Hindu, 24; Lakshmi, 160;
    Siddheswari, 24
Hizbollah, 171
Hong Kong, 9, 73, 123, 168
Hope Waddell Institute, 24, 44
Horton, Robin, 12
Houston, 157, 195
Hull Crown Court, 161
human rights, 133, 139, 149, 218,
    223; Human Rights Violations
    Investigation Commission, 139,
    see also Oputa Panel
Hyland, Kevin, 185

Ibadan, 5, 49, 54, 56, 64, 66, 90,
    110; University, 109, 111, 143;
    University College, 49, 109
Ibekwe, Maurice, 128, 168
Ibibio, 39, 40, 205
Ibini Ukpabi, 36
Ibo, 28, 33, 84; Federal Union, 46;
    see Igbo
Ibrahim, Alhaji Waziri, 101
Idahosa, Benson, 108
Idiagbin, Tunde, 130, 132
Igbiniukpabi, 196
Igbo, 13, 27, 33, 46, 79, 80, 81,
    83, 84, 85, 86, 93, 114, 133,
    134, 156, 157, 158, 168, 188,
    189, 190, 196, 205, 206, 208;
    Igboland, 12, 19, 28, 34, 35, 41,

54, 159, 190, 196, 201, 205,
    208; State Union, 46
Ihiala, 198, 201
Ijaw, 86, 154
Ijebu, 54
Ikechukwe, John, 175
Ikoku, Alvan, 47
Ikom, 35
Ikorodu, 39
Ile-Ife, 109, 143, 161
Iliffe, John, 35
Imo State, 160, 168, 187, 188, 205
Independence, 4, 5, 9, 28, 46, 52,
    59, 61, 62–68, 70, 72, 74, 81,
    103, 109, 110, 120, 200, 211,
    220, 228
India, 9, 13, 24, 43, 56, 68, 79,
    88, 98, 121, 123, 168, 169, 180;
    Indian Ocean, 179
Indirect Rule, 4, 13, 14, 18, 19,
    20, 21, 23, 40, 43, 52, 54, 67,
    114, 194, 197, 219, 220, 225
Indonesia, 52
initiation societies, *see* secret
    societies
International Labour Organisation,
    187
International Monetary Fund, 140
Internet, 5, 158, 161, 162, 164,
    165, 195, 212; Internet Crime
    Complaint Center, 161
Investors Overseas Services, 92
invisible world, *see* spirit world
Iowa, 126
Iran, 179
Iraq, 218
Ironsi, *see* Aguiyi-Ironsi
Isango, 185, 195
Islam, 31, 32, 33, 56, 62, 109, 114,
    195, 207, 211, 220; law, 11, 20,
    220; Maliki, 11; reformists, 11,

109, 111, 112, 150, 208, 210, 211, 227; Shia, 171; Sufi, 109; Sunni, 196; *see also* Muslims
Isle of Man, 73
Isolo, 160
Israel, 56, 69, 131, 132, 171
Italy, 68, 69, 134, 135, 180, 181, 182, 183, 184, 185, 186, 188, 201, 215
Itsekiri Communal Lands Trust, 72
Ivory Coast, *see* Côte d'Ivoire
Izala, 210, 227

Jamaica, 138
Japan, 30, 163, 165, 180
jihad, 11, 13, 21
Johannesburg, 175
Jonathan, Goodluck, 151, 153, 154, 155
Johnson, Samuel, 212
Johnson Matthey Bank, 116, 117
Joshua, T.B., 212
juju, 17, 25, 39, 48, 82, 113, 160, 193, 195, 199, 200, 201, 209; *see also* Long Juju

Kaduna, 5, 13, 64, 67, 80, 83; Mafia, 114, 132, 142; State, 206
Kalo Kato, 210
Kalu, Ogbu, 194
Kalu, Orji Uzor, 202, 203; Eunice, 202
Kano, 13, 91, 100, 161, 180; Emir of, 65, 213; Native Authority, 65
Kansas, 125
Katsina, Hassan, 83
Katsina Province, 52
KBR, 155
Keeling, Willliam, 140
Klansman Confraternity, 111
kleptocracy, 66, 79, 89, 142, 153–56, 219

Kontagora, Alhaji Sani, 80
Kuti, Fela Anikulapo, 100
Kuwait, 62
Kwara State, 159

Lagos, 5, 7, 8, 10, 14, 25, 28, 29, 39, 45, 56, 58, 64, 69, 74, 79, 81, 86, 87, 89, 92, 96, 100, 101, 102, 105, 108, 110, 121, 123, 124, 125, 132, 135, 144, 146, 157, 159, 161, 163, 165, 169, 173, 177, 178, 179, 180, 189, 193, 201, 204, 212; Airport, 177, 188; Island, 34; University, 106; Youth Movement, 36; Oluwole market, 165; Tin Can Island, 173, 178
law, colonial, 15, 17, 18, 27, 30, 41, 52; enforcement, 6, 87, 88, 92, 104, 122, 124, 126, 161, 162, 173, 188, 221; Legislative Council, 45
Lebanon, 57, 68, 88, 91, 92, 98, 122, 171
Levant, 88
Leventis, C.P., 64; Group, 64
Lewis, Peter, 142
Liberia, 70, 73, 129, 141, 172, 178, 179, 184
Libya, 128, 129, 168
Lithuania, 162
Local Government Areas, 145, 188, 198, 201, 202
Lockheed, 101
London, 24, 44, 72, 73, 87, 98, 103, 119, 125, 131, 132, 140, 154, 155, 167, 189; City of, 72, 73, 116; University of, 49
Long Juju, 33, 34, 196, 197, 200; *see also* shrines
Los Angeles, 27

lottery, 1, 2, 164
Lovejoy, Paul, 196
Lugard, Lord (Frederick), 7, 8, 9,
    10, 11, 12, 13, 14, 16, 18, 43,
    225; Lady, 8; *see also* Shaw
Luxembourg, 144, 186
Lynch, (Consul), 50

Macgregor, J.K., 24, 25
Machel, Samora, 212
Macpherson, Sir John, 46, 217
Madrid, 2, 164
Mafia, 99, 111, 114, 127, 147,
    172, 188, 191, 213, 215, 226,
    229; *see also* Kaduna
magic, 24, 25, 26, 27, 32, 193, 194
Maiduguri, 210
Maitatsine, 210
Malaysia, 123
Mali, 186
Mandela, Nelson, 145, 213
Maputo, 213
Marfo, Tom, 186
Marketing Boards, 45, 57, 58, 64;
    Cocoa, 59; Licensed Buying
    Agents, 64
Martin, Lawrence, 125, 126
Marxism, 110, 129, 138
Mauritania, 178
Mayah, Emmanuel, 186
Mbadinuju, Chinwoke, 201, 202
Mbanugo, Dr, 77
McCall (Mr), 64
Mecca, 134
MEND, *see* Niger Delta
Merrill Lynch, 124
Mexico, 115
Mezvinsky, Edward, 126; Marc,
    126
Miami, 168
Mid-West Region, 64, 77, 82, 89

Middle Belt, 11, 77, 81, 84, 93
Middle East, 104, 122, 157, 189
Milosevic, 218
missionaries, 13, 20, 21, 23, 53,
    207, 208; *see also* education
Missouri, 87; St. Louis, 87
Modupe, Prince, 27, 28 [David
    Modupe, Modupe Paris]
Momoh, Joseph, 172
money-doublers, 26, 27, 104
money-laundering, 139, 144, 155,
    163, 165, 166, 168
Monrovia, 129
morality, 16, 17, 31, 32, 38, 51,
    53, 54, 56, 67, 75, 121, 189,
    205, 207, 208, 211, 223
Morocco, 70, 179, 184, 186
Morrison, Prince Bil, 28
Moscow, 173
Mossad, 131
Mozambique, 212, 213
MTN, 146
Muhammed, Murtala, 83, 106,
    107, 108, 115, 138
Mumbai, 157, 172
Münch, Klaus, 168
Murtala, *see* Muhammed
Muslims, 11, 13, 15, 16, 53, 66,
    104, 109, 122, 130, 134, 139,
    156, 207, 211
mystical power, *see* spiritual power

Namibia, 127
Naples, 170
National Agency for Food and Drug
    Administration and Control, 180
National Association of Seadogs,
    113; *see also* Pyrates
National Association of Sea Lords,
    111; *see also* Buccaneers
National Bank of Nigeria, 59, 72

National Church of Nigeria and the Cameroons, 47

National Council of Nigeria and the Cameroons, 28, 45, 46, 47, 49, 57, 62, 64, 65, 66, 75, 76, 77, 79, 81

National Investment Properties Company, 76

National Union of Nigerian Students, 110, 113

National Universities Commission, 110

nationalism, 15, 18, 27, 36, 44, 45, 46, 47, 48, 50–56, 70, 75, 102, 217, 227, 228

Native Administration, Authorities, 14, 19, 21, 23, 48, 53, 54, 65, 67

Ndrangheta, 184

Ndukwe, Edinmuo, 208

Near East, 92

Neo Black Movement, 112, 191

Netherlands, 1, 2, 3, 70, 126, 127, 128, 162, 163, 173, 180, 182, 183, 184, 185, 186

New Jersey, 179

New Mexico, 125

New York, 26, 28, 69, 91, 123, 126, 169, 174, 190, 193, 229; JFK Airport, 174

Ngige, Chris, 202, 203

Niger, 99

Niger Delta, 62, 85, 111, 149, 150, 151, 152, 179, 195; Movement for the Emancipation of, 150, 249; Volunteer Service, 86, 149

Niger River, 8, 10, 12, 47, 148, 197, 225

Niger State, 7

Nigerian Airways, 124, 132

Nigerian Drug Law Enforcement Agency, 124, 173, 174, 178

Nigerian High Commission, 131, 132

Nigerian Institute for International Affairs, 5

Nigerian National Petroleum Corporation, 96, 99, 126, 127, 131, 140, 148, 149, 151, 153, 159

Nigerian National Democratic Party, 64, 69, 76, 77, 81

Nigerian Security Organization, 133

Nigerian Telecommunications, 126

Nigerian Universities Commission, 159

Nigerian Youth Movement, 36, 44

Nigerianism, 95, 96, 108, 227, 228

Nkomati Accord, 212

Nkrumah, 80, 228

North Africa, 33, 186, 207, 216

Northern Nigeria, 9, 11, 12, 13, 21, 23, 29, 33, 36, 53, 64, 80, 101, 102, 104, 111, 114, 122, 130, 132, 138, 139, 145, 154, 157, 186, 189, 195, 196, 207, 210, 211, 220, 227, 228

Northern People's Congress, 46, 61, 62, 66, 77, 83, 84

Northern Protectorate, 7, 9

Northern Region, 57, 61, 62, 67, 69, 70, 77, 80, 83, 84, 93, 111, 115, 133, 220

Norway, 151

Nsukka, 110

Nwafor, Henry, 29

Nwude, Emmanuel Odinigwe, 167, 168

Nyasaland, 14

Nzeogwu, Major Patrick, 80, 81, 89

Nzeribe, Chuma, 201, 203

oaths, 20, 48, 52, 58, 59, 82, 150, 177, 183, 185, 186, 189, 191, 195, 196, 200, 201, 202, 203, 208, 209; *kokoma*, 191
Obasaki, Gaius, 48
Obasanjo, Olusegun, 107, 108, 110, 113, 115, 145, 146, 148, 154, 166, 202, 203
Oboribori, 35
Obubra, 35
Odozi Obodo (cult), 40
Ogbaudu, Felix, 199, 204
Ogboni society, 11, 47, 48, 108, 205; Reformed Ogboni Fraternity, 47, 48
Ogoni, 149
Ogun, 195
Ogun State, 102
oil, 62, 85–89, 95, 96, 97, 98, 99, 100, 103, 107, 109, 115, 116, 117, 119, 121, 126–27, 131, 133, 134, 137, 140, 142, 145, 146, 147–53, 158, 190, 195, 210, 211, 220, 221, 222, 226, 229; smuggle, 86, 99, 141, 147, 148, 149, 150, 151, 152, 159, 179, 210; Depot and Petroleum Marketer, 147; Independent Petroleum Marketers' Association of Nigeria, 147; Major Markets' Association of Nigeria, 147; Petroleum Industry Bill, 149; Petroleum Resources, 96, 129; Petroleum Special Trust Fund, 144
Ojike, Mbonu, 58, 68
Ojukwu, Chukwuemeka, 84, 85, 205
Okafor, Victor, 201, 203, 209
Okereke, Sylvester, 87
Okezie, J.O.J., 104

Okigbo, Pius, 140
Okija shrine, 198–206, 208, 220
Okon, Gloria, 139
Okonjo-Iweala, Ngozi, 146
Okonkor (cult), 160
Okonta, Ike, 147
Okotie-Eboh, Festus, 65, 66, 79, 225
Okpara, Michael, 80
Okudzeto, Raymond, 87
Okupe, Doyin, 155
Oloibiri, 62
Oluyole, Basorun, 33
Omo-Osagie, Humphrey, 48, 49
Ondo, 76
Onijkoji, Olajide, 161
Onitsha, 26, 55, 67, 180, 201
OPEC, 96, 106, 147
Operation Koolvis, 185
Oputa Panel, 139
oracles, 17, 20, 26, 30, 39, 167, 168, 177, 189, 196, 197, 198, 203, 220
ordeals, 10, 16, 20, 95, 199
Orizu, Nwafor, 28, 81 [Prince Orizu, Dr Abyssinia Akweke Nwafor]
Osaikhwuwuomwan, Samuel, 180, 181
Osunene, 186
Overcomers Christian Mission, 208
Owegbe society, 48, 49, 82, 184
Oweh, Nkem, 128
Owerri Province, 36, 205
Oxford, 9, 27, 50; University, 27; Jesus College, 27
Oyo, 76; Alafin of, 76

Pakistan, 122, 123, 179
Palmer (US Ambassador), 65

pan-Africanism, 44, 80, 110
Paris, 97, 129, 155, 181
patronage, 38, 75, 103, 109, 113,
    138, 139, 141, 142, 144, 147,
    148, 202, 203, 204, 205, 207,
    211, 215, 220
Patterson, Alexander, 52
Peel, John, 33
Pennsylvania, 45; University of, 45;
    Lincoln University, 45
Pentecostalism, 108, 109, 112,
    211, 212
people-trafficking, 21, 35, 36, 38,
    93, 105, 172, 180, 181, 183,
    184, 185, 186, 187, 209, 216,
    217; see also sex businesss
People's Democratic Party, 145,
    146, 154, 202
Perham, Margery, 9, 12, 41, 43,
    52, 62, 224
Peru, 178
Pope (the), 184
Port Harcourt, 8, 74, 85, 86, 87,
    99, 148, 160, 179; University of,
    111, 112
Powell, Colin, 3, 223
prostitution, see sex business
Putin, Vladimir, 137, 216
Price Waterhouse, 153, 167
Pyrates Confraternity, 49, 100,
    111, 112, 113

Rawlings, Jerry, 129
Reality Organization, 202
Red Beret, 111
Regional Government, 28, 46, 58,
    64, 65, 69, 75, 76, 81, 82, 84,
    91, 217
Reinhardt, John E., 95, 96
religion, 10, 11, 15, 16, 17, 20,
    23, 24, 29, 30, 47, 48, 53, 55,
    56, 80, 108, 109, 114, 137, 159,
    182, 193, 194, 195, 196, 197,
    198, 199, 204, 205, 206, 207,
    208, 209, 211–13, 223, 227
Ribadu, Mohammadu, 65; Nuhu,
    119, 141, 153, 166, 168, 169
Rich, Marc, 99
Richards, Sir Arthur, 45
Rimi, Abba Musa, 130
ritual killings, 32, 33, 34, 39, 101,
    200, 205
Rivers State, 85, 151, 210;
    University of Science and
    Technology, 143
Robertson, Sir James, 61
Rome, 134, 135, 181, 199
Roosevelt, Franklin D., 44
Rosicrucians, 211
Rotterdam, 117, 127
Russia, 137, 144, 148, 162, 172,
    179, 215, 216

Saddam Hussein, 218
Sahara, 185, 186, 216
Sahel, 11, 15, 53, 186
Sakaguchi, Nelson, 166, 167, 170,
    197
San Francisco, 27
Sandhurst, 9
Sankara, Thomas, 129
Santander (bank), 167
Sanusi, Lamido, 153
Sardauna, 53, 66, 138; see also Kano
Sarkin Musulmi, 139; see also
    Dasuki
Saro-Wiwa, Ken, 63, 45, 149, 228
Saudi Arabia, 104, 122, 123, 180,
    186, 189
Scotland, 24, 213; Royal Bank of,
    154
Scotland Yard, 125

Second Republic, 114–17, 119, 120, 131, 132
secret societies, 11, 12, 20, 21, 35, 36, 39, 40, 41, 46, 47, 48, 49, 50, 80, 107, 108, 109, 111, 112, 113, 143, 145, 148, 150, 151, 184, 196, 210, 212, 220, 224, 227, 228; see also campus cults
Sekondi, 37, 38
Senegal, 178
Serbia, 218
sex business, 37, 38, 44, 114, 134, 135, 180–87, 188, 145, 196; see also people-trafficking
Shagari, Shehu, 115, 116, 131, 132
Shapiro, Levi-Arie, 132
Sharia, see Islam
Shaw, Flora, 7
Shell-BP, 62, 82, 115, 148, 149, 150, 151; Petroleum Development Company, 149, 151
Shopitan, Amos Oshinowo, 39
shrines, 17, 18, 19, 20, 26, 33, 34, 35, 41, 48, 58, 82, 182, 185, 194–98, 198–213, 220; Arochukwu, 33, 34, 36, 41, 168, 196
Sicily, 191, 215, 229
Siemens, 156
Sierra Leone, 34, 36, 171, 178, 197; Fourah Bay College, 36
Singapore, 128, 177
Sklar, Richard, 49
slavery, slave trade, 8, 10, 11, 13, 16, 21, 31, 32, 33, 34, 35, 36, 37, 39, 52, 56, 70, 77, 85, 182, 185, 186, 187, 190, 196, 197, 198, 209, 216, 217, 223, 224, 227; Atlantic, 35, 36, 190, 216; abolition of, 33, 34, 56, 197, 216; see also people-trafficking

Smith, Harold, 61, 74
smuggling, 4, 86, 87, 88, 89, 98, 99, 104, 105, 123, 137, 147, 152, 159, 170, 230; arms, 152, 201; diamonds, 92, 171, drugs, see drug trade; oil, see oil smuggle; people, see people-trafficking
Sokoto, caliphate, 11, 33, 53, 207, 216; Province, 52, 69; Sardauna of, 53, 138; sultanate, 139, 207
South Africa, 103, 110, 117, 127, 145, 146, 154, 158, 172, 175, 176, 186, 212, 213, 219; National Immigration Service, 127
Southern Protectorate, 7, 11; Provinces, 36
Southern Nigeria, 12, 21, 26, 29, 33, 39, 53, 55, 67, 102, 104, 110, 111, 122, 144, 145, 154, 170, 180, 198, 207, 211, 220, 228
Soyinka, Wole, 49, 89, 110, 111, 158, 159, 210, 227
Spain, 2, 3, 80, 164, 167, 176, 177, 184, 185
Special Military Tribunal, 130
spirit world, 4, 15, 16, 17, 20, 26, 27, 30, 31, 32, 33, 73, 101, 160, 193, 198, 207, 208, 209, 213
spiritual power, 15, 16, 17, 24, 25, 26, 27, 31, 32, 103, 160, 193, 199, 201, 205, 207, 209, 210, 211, 212, 213
Springer-Beck, Frieda, 169
Stonehouse, John, 87
Sudan, 9
Supreme Military Council, 81, 83, 130, 132
Suriname, 181
Swaziland, 213

Sweden, 66, 69, 70
Switzerland, 92, 144, 153, 168
Syria, 88, 98

Taiwan, 123
Taiwo, Adewale, 161
Takoradi, 37
Taylor, Charles, 172
Texas, 157
Thailand, 121, 122, 123, 152, 171, 175, 178, 211
Tiv, 77, 81, 83
Tochi, Iwuchukwu Amara, 177
Togo, 172, 182
Trafigura, 153

Uba, Chris, 202, 203; Andy, 202
UBS, 154
Uburu market, 35, 45
Udo, Eket Inyang, 27
Uganda, 43, 88
Umegbolu, Chukwunweike, 174
Umeh, Chigbo, 179
Union Bank, 168
United Kingdom, 74, 97, 104, 120, 122, 125, 157, 161, 162, 168, 180, 181, 185; see also Britain
United Nations, 28, 178, 213; Office on Drugs and Crime (UNODC), 6
United States, 6, 23, 24, 27, 28, 29, 38, 39, 47, 50, 55, 63, 65, 69, 73, 74, 80, 81, 83, 84, 85, 87, 92, 108, 120, 122, 123, 124, 126, 144, 152, 155, 157, 161, 162, 165, 166, 168, 169, 171, 172, 173, 174, 178, 179, 189, 212, 215, 222, 229; Department of Justice, 173; Financial Action Task Force, 166; Secret Service, 161, 162
University of Nigeria, 110

Upper Volta, 129
Usman dan Fodio, 11, 21, 53, 139
USSR, Soviet Union, 100, 171, 216, 221; KGB, 216; see also Russia
Uzorma, Iyke Nathan, 160, 193

Van Damme, Johannes, 128
Victor Charlie Boys, 142, 210
Vikings, 111; Supreme Vikings Confraternity, 111
Vitol, 153
vodun, 182, 183, 186

Wada, Inua, 65
War Against Indiscipline, 130
Warri, 37, 72, 127, 179; Olu of, 72
Washington, 140, 141, 195
West Africa, 17, 24, 36, 45, 55, 64, 68, 70, 104, 119, 121, 122, 123, 124, 127, 128, 129, 152, 154, 162, 163, 166, 170, 171, 172, 174, 178, 179, 182, 186, 189, 197, 216, 223, 226, 227
Western Region, 5, 47, 48, 55, 57, 59, 61, 62, 64, 65, 69, 70, 74, 75, 76, 77, 80, 81, 91, 93, 102, 195; Regional Development Board, 59
Western Union, 181
White, Christopher, 29
Williams, David, 66
Wilmot, Patrick, 138, 142
Wilson, Harold, 73
witchcraft, 34, 40, 183, 194, 209, 210
Women's War, 41, 197
World Bank, 107, 110, 140, 146
World War Two, 38, 44, 45, 56, 57

Yahoo Boys, 160, 161, 188; Plus, 160, 193; Plus Plus, 160

INDEX

Yar'Adua, Shehu, 115, 145

Yenegoa, 155

Yoruba, 13, 33, 34, 46, 47, 49,
54, 84, 86, 130, 157, 189, 205;
Yorubaland, 10, 11, 12, 19, 30,
32, 75

Yusuf, Maitama, 116

Yusuf, Mohammed, 210

Yusufu, Mohammed, 131

Zik, *see* Azikiwe

Zungeru, 7, 13, 24